Fast Guide to

CUBASE 4

Simon Millward

PC Publishing

PC Publishing
Keeper's House
Merton
Thetford
Norfolk IP25 6QH
UK

Tel 01953 889900
email info@pc-publishing.com
web site http://www.pc-publishing.com

First published 2007
Reprinted 2008

ISBN 13: 978-1-906005-009

British Library Cataloguing in Publication Data
A catalogue record for this book is available from the British Library

Printed and bound in Great Britain by Cromwell Press, Trowbridge, Wilts

Introduction

Welcome to the *Fast Guide to Cubase 4*.

Cubase is the ultimate professional music production system for music creation and sound recording. It is renowned for its user-friendliness, flexibility and innovative design. This book aims to help you get the most from the software.

The *Fast Guide to Cubase 4* is not a retread of the manual. It supplies the essential information to get you up and running in the shortest possible time but, more importantly, explores advanced techniques and a wide range of theoretical knowledge which help you get better results. Topics covered include: recording, editing and arranging in the Project window; slicing and looping in the Sample editor; MIDI editing in the MIDI editors; and mixing and mastering in the Mixer. Other subjects include: recording techniques, EQ, compression, gating, limiting, effects, automation, surround sound, pattern-based arranging, quantizing, audio warping, tempo manipulation, synchronisation, media management and VST instruments. The book is packed full of hints, tips and tutorials and includes a comprehensive website list and glossary. 100 speed tips and a powerful macro library take your music production and programming skills to the next level.

Combining extensive Cubase know-how and theoretical knowledge from the worlds of sound recording and music technology, this book helps take your projects from conception and multi-track recording right through to mixing and mastering.

The *Fast Guide to Cubase 4* is the ideal companion for all users of the software, including musicians, producers, sound recordists and audio professionals.

Contents

Description and overview

This chapter provides an overall description of Cubase and gives a brief preview of the Project window, Transport panel and Mixer. This helps you become familiar with the main points of contact before moving on to a more detailed exploration of the program.

What is Cubase?

Cubase is a professional music creation and production system for the recording, editing and processing of MIDI data and digital audio. It belongs to a type of software sometimes referred to as a MIDI+audio sequencer and, when installed on your computer, is also known as a 'digital audio workstation' (DAW). A sequencer, in its simplest form, is a device which allows you to chain together sequences of musical notes or events. However, Cubase is infinitely more capable than this. It allows you to perform a multitude of music production tasks within a single, streamlined software environment. Cubase is at once a MIDI sequencer, a powerful multitrack digital audio recorder, a fully featured mixing console, a music for video production workstation, a post production workstation, an audio analysis tool, an audio loop creation tool and a multimedia tool.

Cubase can be interfaced with the usual range of MIDI devices, such as synthesizers, samplers and drum machines, and is also a digital audio recorder for recording vocals, acoustic musical instruments, line level signals from electronic musical instruments, electric guitar and bass, and anything else you can imagine. In addition, it allows the mixing of both audio and MIDI recordings in a virtual mixing console offering effects, EQ and automation. The program features the use of native audio processing which means that most of the audio processing is performed by the CPU (central processing unit) of the computer. Audio recording and processing can therefore be performed with less hardware. The program runs on PC and Macintosh computers.

Cubase provides simultaneous playback of hundreds of audio and MIDI tracks (depending on the overall speed and efficiency of the host computer). It incorporates a streamlined Project window which allows the management of most routine recording, editing and processing within a single-page environment. The virtual mixing console provides adaptable screen views within which all audio or MIDI tracks can be viewed and mixed in the same order as they appear in the Project window. Each audio track features 4-band parametric EQ, eight real-time send effects and eight real-time insert effects. Other features include VST plug-in architecture for VST instruments and audio effects, and MIDI plug-in architecture with four send and four insert effects per MIDI track. A comprehensive range of audio effects (with side chain capability), MIDI processors and VST instruments are supplied with the program. For mixing purposes, there is sample accurate automation for all mixer, VST Instrument and effects parameters and an audio mixdown facility. Offline audio processes include time-stretch, pitch shift, envelope, fade, noise gate, normalise, reverse and other processes. Special audio manipulation tools include groove extraction, audio looping, audio warping and audio quantize. For MIDI, there are Key, In-place, Drum, List, Logical, Score and Sysex editors, along with sophisticated quantize and groove manipulation functions. Unlimited undo/redo, off-line process history, user-configurable key commands, workspaces, universal presets and advanced media management help complete the picture.

Cubase supports all standard digital audio recording resolutions up to 32-bit float/96kHz. Support for ASIO allows the use of low-latency audio cards and hardware.

When was Cubase developed?

The Cubase family of sequencers already has a long history. Steinberg developed their first sequencer, the Pro 16, in 1984 on the Commodore 64 computer. This was followed by the Pro 24 for the Atari computer in 1986. The very first version of Cubase began life in 1989 as a radical new update to the Pro 24. It featured the (at the time) revolutionary Arrange window which allowed musicians to visualise and arrange their musical compositions in a dynamic graphical display of time on the horizontal axis against tracks on the vertical axis. All these early applications were concerned with the recording of MIDI data only. However, as the processing power of computers increased during the 1990s Steinberg was able to add audio recording capability to the program. During the same period, the code was ported to PC and Apple Macintosh computers.

In 1996, Steinberg introduced the concept of VST (Virtual Studio Technology) and Cubase became known as Cubase VST. VST aims to bring all those elements normally found within a real-world recording studio into a single virtual environment inside your computer. This design principle remains one of the cornerstones of Steinberg's software development strategy. With Cubase SX (introduced in 2002), Steinberg further refined and streamlined the Cubase concept into a package which is more powerful, more flexible and more logical than its predecessors. In 2006, the 'SX' was dropped from the name and the program became known simply as 'Cubase' (followed by a version number). This marked the arrival of a more mature and complete Cubase, including VST3 technology, improved audio routing, side chaining, advanced media management and a new collection of plug-ins.

Who can use Cubase?

Newcomers to the software and also experienced sequencer users may have to learn new skills in order to have meaningful contact with the many aspects of Cubase. The MIDI sequencer element of the package requires knowledge

Info

Steinberg, the company behind Cubase, was formed in 1984 by Karl Steinberg and Manfred Rurup. Cubase, therefore, benefits from a background of over 20 years of music software research and development.

of the normal techniques associated with MIDI recording but the audio aspects require knowledge from a wider range of music technology disciplines. Of course, anyone can use Cubase but, since the package involves the concept of a self-contained virtual recording studio, it follows that having knowledge of the skills required to operate a real-world recording studio is useful. This encompasses such things as sound engineering and music production. However, even users with limited sound recording skills are able to quickly benefit from the advantages of Cubase.

Why use Cubase?

There are many reasons why Cubase is an excellent music software choice. The seamless integration of MIDI and audio recording and real-time processing together with the possibility of recording large numbers of tracks, the inclusion of 4-band parametric EQ on every audio channel and the supply of a wide range of effects and processors are just some of the advantages encompassed by the program. The package is also very cost-effective since most of the audio processing takes place in the computer's main processor, so there is no need for additional DSP (digital signal processor) hardware. Cubase can produce excellent results using a fast PC or Mac computer and an ASIO low-latency audio card. The convenience of this compact arrangement is an obvious advantage.

How do I use Cubase?

This is the key question! Before you can use Cubase you must have some idea of how to record and manipulate MIDI data, how to record and manipulate audio signals, how you are going to get an audio signal into the computer and how you are going to feed it back out into the real world. These matters, and many other details related to Cubase, form the subject matter of this book.

The big picture

A simple graphical representation of the system helps us understand what is included in the Cubase package (see Figure 1.1). Firstly, there is the MIDI sequencer side of the program. MIDI (Musical Instrument Digital Interface) is a note-based interface, originally devised so that electronic keyboards and synthesizers could talk to each other. MIDI contains no audio. MIDI is a sequence of digital instructions related to a musical performance. The data contains information such as the pitch and velocity of the notes being played and travels through a

Figure 1.1
Simple visualisation of Cubase

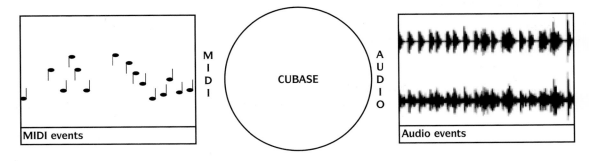

cable from one keyboard to another or from a keyboard into a computer-based sequencer like Cubase. Music recorded in this way is represented primarily as individual note events. In Cubase these events are displayed as notes on a score or as graphical blocks in a piano-roll style editor.

Secondly, there is the audio recording side of the program. This involves the recording of the actual audio signal itself. The audio is represented as waveforms of the sound signal, referred to in Cubase as audio events. The audio aspects of the program also include the virtual studio features of mixing, routing, processing and adding effects to the material.

The MIDI and audio functions of Cubase are seamlessly integrated. For example, the recording of both kinds of data can take place in the Project window, the main window of Cubase, and both kinds of data can be mixed in the same virtual mixing console, known as the Mixer. The Project window and associated Mixer form the central hub of activity for most Cubase projects. In the Project window, MIDI recordings are displayed as graphical blocks, usually containing symbols representing the notes, and audio recordings are displayed in similar graphical blocks, usually as waveforms representing the recorded signal. You can fulfil most routine recording, editing, mixing and processing tasks within the Project window and Mixer, but for editing in fine detail the system contains a wide range of specialist editors and functions (see Figure 1.2 for a basic overview).

On the MIDI side, Figure 1.2 shows the main MIDI-based editors; the Key, Score and Drum editors. These are used to edit note and controller data in fine detail and the Score editor can also produce professional quality printed scores. More distant from the central area of activities we find features like the Logical editor and the MIDI Device manager. There is also a comprehensive range of other features for the editing and processing of MIDI data including the List editor, SysEx editor, MIDI plug-in effects and sophisticated quantize functions (not shown in the diagram).

In the audio domain, the Sample editor forms the main editing environment for audio material. There are also many audio processing features such as EQ, plug-in effects and off-line audio processing. The management of audio files and events takes place in the Pool. Somewhere in between the MIDI and audio sides of Cubase we find VST Instruments (Virtual Studio Instruments) which are played using conventional MIDI data but produce their sounds using the systems audio engine. Some plug-in effects also respond to MIDI data but process audio. You can use the Mixer to mix audio, MIDI, VST Instrument, Group and other tracks. By default, the mixer channels are displayed in the same order as the corresponding tracks in the Project window. For overall project management there is the Project browser. This allows you to take a look at all events and files contained within a project.

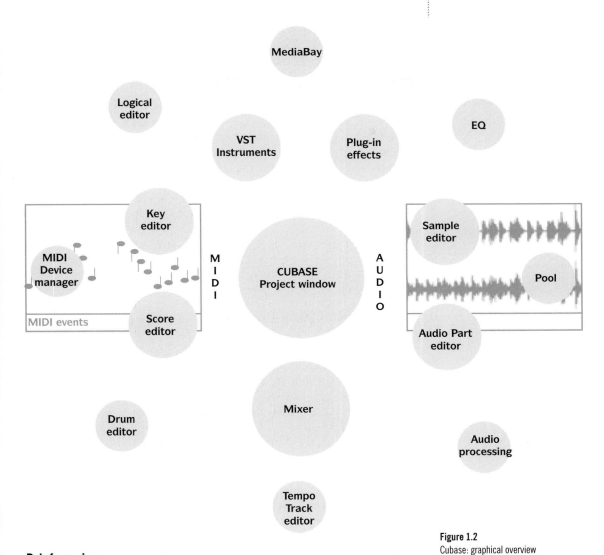

Figure 1.2
Cubase: graphical overview

Brief preview

Figure 1.2 provides a graphical overview of the main parts of Cubase which is useful for an appreciation of what the system includes. But what does Cubase actually look like on screen, where are the main areas of activity and how do you interact with the program?

You can change the appearance of Cubase to suit your own requirements but when you first launch a project you might see the Project window displayed in a similar manner to Figure 1.3, (the Project window is the upper-most window). By default, computer keys F2 and F3 open the Transport panel and Mixer. These are also shown in Figure 1.3.

The Project window is where you see a graphical representation of your audio and MIDI material in the form of rectangular blocks known as parts or events. Parts are containers which hold either audio or MIDI events. MIDI data is always

Figure 1.3
Cubase Project window, Mixer and Transport panel

contained within a part but audio data can also appear directly in the Project window as an event. Parts and events are found on tracks. There are a number of different track types including audio, MIDI, instrument, group, FX, automation, video and others. Tracks are displayed vertically in the track list and time is represented horizontally on a ruler which displays bars and beats, seconds, timecode or samples. There is a toolbar at the top of the display and an optional control area to the left of the track list, known as the Inspector. The Inspector shows additional details for the currently selected track. The Project window is the centre of activity for most Cubase operations.

The Mixer displays the tracks in the same order as they appear in the Project window but laid out as channels with volume faders, pan controls, EQ controls, effects sends and so on, similar to a conventional mixing console. Both audio and MIDI tracks are mixed in the Mixer and the mixing environment can be configured and scaled to suit your requirements and the available screen space.

The Transport panel features the normal rewind, fast-forward, stop, play, cycle and record controls and manages most playback and recording functions. The current song position is shown by a vertical line which moves across the Project window. This is known as the Project cursor.

The Cubase user interface is intuitive and direct. It features a comprehensive set of menus and icon buttons, and a large number of mouse functions, user-configurable keyboard shortcuts, and drag-and-drop editing techniques with which to control operations in the Project and other windows. These functions and a whole lot more are described in detail throughout the course of this book.

Patience, practice and understanding

This chapter gives you a foretaste of the power and elegance of Cubase. Its streamlined and easy-to-use design is the result of many years of research and development and the program represents the leading edge in native audio music software. It provides a logical and adaptable framework within which you can operate intuitively and creatively. However, despite being one of the more user-friendly music software applications, there is still a learning curve and there are still techniques with which to become familiar and concepts to understand. This requires some initial effort from the user. Achieving the best results requires patience, practice and understanding.

Setting up the system

This chapter describes the hardware you need to run Cubase, how to install the software and what kinds of overall system setups are suitable for the program.

General computer requirements

Cubase runs on PC or Apple Macintosh computers. In order to use the program comfortably you are advised to choose a computer with a very fast processor, a particularly large and fast hard drive and a large amount of RAM. The more audio tracks, effects and VST Instruments you wish to use, the more powerful your computer must be. The system should also include suitable audio hardware, preferably featuring its own dedicated ASIO driver, and a suitable MIDI interface if you intend to record MIDI data. Your computer should also feature a USB port since Cubase is protected by a special key which plugs into a USB socket.

The program has been optimised for the latest operating systems on both platforms. Windows XP is required for the PC and OSX is required for the Mac. The recording of multi-track digital audio makes special demands of a computer system so it is worth considering the details (see Appendix 1). PC users are advised to obtain a PC which has been built specifically for audio purposes. The final choice of platform (PC or Mac) is purely a matter of personal preference.

Info

For those who need more details about computer requirements please consult your user manuals and the latest computer and music technology magazines. See also Appendix 1 at the back of this book.

Installation

Before proceeding

Before proceeding with the installation of any audio hardware and software, verify that you already have one of the recommended operating systems running on the computer and that it is functioning correctly. Before installing Cubase itself, the intended audio hardware and associated driver should have already been installed on the computer.

Audio hardware and drivers

There are various ways in which Cubase can communicate with your audio hardware. This depends as much on the hardwares drivers as on the design of the hardware itself. A driver is a short software program which provides the communication link between the hardware device and the operating system (or a specific application like Cubase). The hardware is set up and initialised via the driver software. In the case of Cubase, the program communicates with the audio hardware according to what kind of driver has been installed. The main options include:

1 A dedicated ASIO (Audio Stream Input Output) driver supplied with the audio hardware. This provides direct communication between Cubase and the hardware. This is the preferred choice since it reduces the delay between user input and the computer's response. This delay is commonly known as latency. Lower latency means smoother and more accurate real-time operation of Cubase. A well-written dedicated ASIO driver should provide a latency of less than 10ms.
2 A Direct X driver supplied with the audio hardware allowing communication with Microsoft Windows Direct X. Direct X handles multimedia operations under Windows. When Cubase is installed on a PC computer system, its own ASIO Direct X driver is automatically installed. There are, therefore, two drivers involved with this option, one for the audio hardware and one for Cubase. To communicate with the audio hardware via Direct X you must choose the ASIO Direct X Full Duplex driver option for your audio device within Cubase. This option provides adequate performance but with inferior latency figures to dedicated ASIO drivers.
3 A standard Windows multimedia driver allowing communication between Windows compatible audio cards and the Windows multimedia system. This is supplied with the audio card. When Cubase is installed on a PC computer, its own ASIO Multimedia driver is automatically installed. There are, therefore, two drivers involved with this option, one for the audio hardware and one for Cubase. To communicate with the Windows multimedia compatible hardware you must choose the ASIO Multimedia driver option for your audio device within Cubase. This option provides inferior latency performance and is not recommended for professional applications.

Option 1 is strongly recommended for all Cubase systems. The best audio cards and professional audio hardware are supplied with dedicated ASIO drivers.

MIDI interface and drivers

If MIDI functionality is not included in your audio hardware, you will need to install a separate MIDI interface to record MIDI-based music. Installation of MIDI devices is usually a simple procedure involving the connection of the hardware interface to the computer, switching it on and installing the driver (usually supplied on a CD-ROM). All standard MIDI interfaces function with Cubase. See the documentation supplied with the MIDI interface for full details.

Before installing Cubase

Before installing Cubase you should:

• Preferably defragment the hard disk.
• If you have not already done so, install your audio hardware and driver(s) according to the supplied documentation (see Audio hardware and drivers, above).

- Test the functionality of the audio hardware outside of Cubase if you have other suitable software already installed (as part of the operating system, for example). This assumes that you already have your hardware's audio outputs connected to an amplifier and loudspeakers (or headphones).
- If needed, install your MIDI interface and driver according to the supplied documentation (see MIDI interface and drivers, above).

Installing Cubase

Cubase is supplied on a DVD-ROM and is easily installed onto a suitably pre-pared computer. The following steps outline what you need to do:

- Ensure that the supplied Steinberg copy protection key is not plugged into the computers USB port. This should be plugged in after the installation.
- Insert the Cubase DVD-ROM and start the installation procedure. Follow the on-screen instructions.
- After the Cubase installation you are normally invited to install the latest Syncrosoft driver. Before proceeding, re-insert the supplied Steinberg copy protection key into the computers USB port. The Syncrosoft installation installs the latest version of the Syncrosoft Licence Control Centre (LCC).
- Launch Cubase by double-clicking on the Cubase logo on the desktop or by double-clicking on the Cubase program in your list of applications.

System verification

Upon first launching Cubase you may immediately ask one important question. Where, within Cubase, do I find references to my audio hardware and MIDI interface? The answer lies in firstly knowing the type of ASIO driver supplied with the hardware and the number of audio and MIDI inputs and outputs. You can then set about finding the locations within the software where the ASIO driver and the various inputs and outputs are activated.

Verifying the ASIO driver

Cubase chooses its ASIO driver according to what hardware and driver(s) are already installed in the computer. To inspect the ASIO driver configuration select Device Setup / VST Audio System from the Devices menu. Verify which ASIO driver has been installed in the ASIO driver field (Figure 2.1). If supplied with your audio hardware, make sure that its dedicated ASIO driver is selected here. A special ASIO driver written exclusively for the hardware gives better latency performance than the other options.

Figure 2.1
Finding the ASIO driver in the Device setup window

Finding the audio inputs and outputs

When using a typical ASIO driver, the inputs and outputs of your audio hardware are shown within the software at two locations:

1 All available input/output ports are shown in Device setup / << Name of your chosen ASIO driver >> (Devices menu). By default, all ports are made visible within the system (marked by a cross in the 'Visible' column). Input/output ports that you do not need may be de-selected here by clicking in the corresponding box to de-activate the cross. The number of input/output ports depends upon the number of physical inputs and outputs on your audio hardware (Figure 2.2).

Figure 2.2
All the available inputs and outputs of your audio hardware are shown in the Device Setup window.

2 The input/output ports are connected in the input and output sections of the VST Connections window (Devices menu). This is where you assign the input and output ports to input and output busses (Figure 2.3). Busses are added using the 'Add bus' button. A buss added in the VST Connections window appears in the Mixer as a channel strip to the left and right of the other channel strips. Only those input/output ports which are actually connected become active within the system and these are marked as such in the 'State' column of the input/output port list in Device Setup.

Figure 2.3
Input and output ports are connected in the inputs and outputs sections of the VST Connections window

Finding the MIDI inputs and outputs

The available MIDI input and output ports are found in Device Setup / MIDI Port Setup (Devices menu). Here you can show/hide the available ports by clicking in the 'Visible' column (Figure 2.4). Verify that the required MIDI ports are visible. A port becomes active in the 'State' column when the corresponding port is activated on any MIDI track.

Figure 2.4
The MIDI Port Setup window showing the available MIDI ports

The MIDI ports are available in the pop-up input and output menus found in the Inspector for each MIDI track. Selecting 'All MIDI inputs' allows you to assign multiple MIDI inputs to the same track. The MIDI inputs included when you use 'All MIDI inputs' are specified in the "In 'All Inputs'" column in the MIDI Port Setup window.

Info

The MIDI input and output ports may be individually selected in the MIDI in and out menus of the MIDI track Inspector. They may also be selected in the input / output menus above the channels in the Mixer.

Overall system setup

The overall system used for Cubase may vary enormously and depends on the precise requirements of each user. By overall system we mean Cubase and all the peripheral MIDI and audio equipment which surround it (apart from the audio card/hardware already installed).

Basic system elements

The minimum overall setup needed to record and play back both MIDI and audio material involves the following elements (see Figure 2.5):

- For MIDI-based recording, you need some kind of MIDI input device such as a MIDI keyboard/synthesizer or a MIDI guitar.
- For audio recording, the bare minimum is a single microphone connected to a microphone input of the audio card/hardware, or a line-level signal connected to a line input of the audio card/hardware.
- For monitoring purposes, you normally need some kind of amplifier and speaker system (or headphones) to hear the sounds you create within Cubase. In the simplest of cases, the main stereo outputs from your audio card/hardware pass directly to the amplifier / speaker system for monitoring purposes.

Figure 2.5
Minimum setup for MIDI + audio
recording and playback.

MIDI keyboard choice

To make real-time MIDI recordings you need some kind of MIDI triggering device like a MIDI keyboard, a MIDI guitar, MIDI drum pads or a MIDI wind-blown instrument. The device should preferably be velocity sensitive and, in the case of a keyboard, have at least a five octave key span, although two octave mini-keyboards are excellent for small desktop systems where space is limited. Those keyboards which have their own sound-making circuitry should be equipped with MIDI in, out and thru sockets (now standard on regular MIDI keyboards). Some budget keyboards with no sound-making circuitry may only feature a single MIDI output, which may be all you need to trigger the other MIDI devices and VST instruments within a simple system. Other things to look out for in MIDI keyboards are high quality on-board sounds and effects, ease of programmability and keys which are comfortable to play.

Microphone matters

The microphone is the very first stage in the recording path when you are recording live vocals, musical instruments and other real-world sources so, if you are serious about your recording, it is worth investing in a well-specified model. A bad quality input signal cannot be corrected in Cubase and cannot be improved later, no matter how good the quality of your plug-ins and audio hardware.

For good all-round performance and for the recording of vocals, large diaphragm capacitor microphones usually produce the best results. These invariably require phantom power to drive the microphone. However, microphone choice depends very much on the source which is being recorded and only knowledge and experience can help make the appropriate decision.

The basic techniques for connecting a microphone to a Cubase system include the following:

1 Connection of the microphone directly to the microphone input of the audio hardware device or audio card. Many high-end audio devices feature mic inputs (or mixed mic/line inputs) with phantom power which are suitable for the direct connection of professional microphones.
2 Connection of the microphone to the audio hardware device via a separate mic pre-amp. A mic pre-amp is a unit specialised in optimising the signal from a microphone. The inputs of the mic pre-amp are suitable for the connection of professional microphones and line level or digital outputs provide the connection to the audio hardware device.
3 Connection of the microphone to an external mixing console. Professional mixing consoles provide microphone and line inputs for the connection of a variety of sources. A line level output signal from the console (e.g. a group out) is then routed to the line inputs of the audio hardware device.

For small-scale systems which do not feature a mixing console, option 2 is the preferred choice. A mic pre-amp can significantly improve the quality of the source signal and professional units often include compression, EQ, gating and valve simulation effects. However, for non-mixing console systems, option 1 also provides good results but with less flexibility. The quality of the results of option 3 depend very much upon the quality of the mixing console. There is an additional practical problem when using a microphone connected to a small-scale computer recording system: fan noise. Most computers make enough noise to interfere with a microphone recording taking place in the same room. The immediate solution is to place the microphone as great a distance away from the computer as is practical and acoustically desirable, or to use screening between the computer and the microphone. Never attempt

Info

It is difficult to recommend specific keyboard models since there are so many to choose from and many different levels of functionality. However, you are likely to find what you need among those instruments manufactured by Alesis, Emu, Evolution, Korg, Novation, Roland and Yamaha.

Info

A high-quality professional microphone can radically improve the fidelity of the input signal. Models supplied by AKG, Audio Technica, Beyer, Blue, Brauner, Calrec, Coles, Electrovoice, DPA, Microtech Gefell, Neumann, Oktava, Rode, Royer, SE, Sennheiser, Shure and Sony are highly recommended.

Info

In a computer-based recording setup, the input signal from a microphone is often further improved by using a high-quality mic pre-amp. The best mic pre-amps feature a superior signal path to many mixing consoles and often provide compression and EQ parameters. They are, therefore, desirable even if you already own a mixing console. You are likely to find what you need among the mic pre-amps supplied by Aphex, API, Art, Audient, Avalon, Crane Song, DAV Electronics, DBX, Focusrite, Joe Meek, Mackie, Manley, Neve, Presonus, SPL, SSL, TF Pro, Tube Tech and Universal Audio.

to dampen the noise of the fan by blocking the ventilation of the computer case as this could cause your computer to overheat. Of course, the ideal solution is to make all the recordings in a separate (preferably acoustically treated) room, as takes place in a professional recording studio. See Chapter 7 for more details about recording with microphones.

Recording non-microphone sources

If you are recording an electric guitarist or bassist, it is possible to route the signal directly into the line inputs of your audio card / hardware via a guitar or bass pre-amp. Many of the mic pre-amps from the manufacturers mentioned above are dual mic/line devices which can be used for both kinds of sources. This is particularly useful for the small home recording setup and for guitarists who wish to take advantage of computer based recording technology, which tends to be MIDI and keyboard centred. External electronic keyboards, synthesizers and sound modules can normally be linked to the audio card / hardware directly via line level cables or via a mixing console or pre-amplifier. See Chapter 7 for more details about recording non-microphone sources.

Monitoring

The use of professional audio monitoring equipment is essential for the best results and is a pre-requisite for all professional Cubase installations. This normally includes either active monitors or a power amplifier with passive monitors placed in an acoustically balanced room. A professional monitoring system is designed to give a clear, neutral sound so that you can make truly accurate judgements during each stage of the recording process.

Large, highly accurate monitors with a wide, flat frequency response which does not significantly colour the sound are normally chosen for professional recording studios. A pair of small near field monitors are often sufficient for home studio setups. These also serve as a second reference in larger setups where the monitoring can be switched between the main speakers and the near field speakers. The final choice of monitor is based upon its technical specifications and your own judgements about its fidelity.

The positioning of the monitors is extremely important. A good starting point is that of an equilateral triangle formed by the listening position and the two speakers. Normally, the monitors are angled slightly towards the listening position. Ideally, the distance between the two monitors should not exceed the distance from the monitors to the listener as this can affect the perception of the stereo image. It is also desirable to have the monitors placed on a non-resonant, rigid surface which does not produce any direct physical vibrations in the actual structure of the room. Also of primary importance is the use of a high quality amplifier which comfortably produces a clear, undistorted signal. The amplifier should not have to be driven to its maximum volume in order to achieve the desired listening level, so a model with sufficient headroom above the average listening level should be chosen.

Complex system considerations

Larger-scale overall setups for Cubase involve a wider range of variables. A large-scale setup is likely to include a mixing console and/or external control hardware, external sound processing equipment and effects, one or more mic pre-amps, professional studio monitors and a network of MIDI devices. These items significantly improve the functionality of Cubase. An example setup is shown in Figure 2.6.

Figure 2.6
A complex Cubase system

Do I need a mixer?

One of the first questions which might be asked when setting up a larger overall system is why do I need an external mixer when there is a virtual mixer in Cubase? The answer is that it depends upon how you want to link Cubase to the external world. Cubase's interconnectivity with the external world is limited by the installed audio hardware and the equipment in the overall system. Simple systems featuring a microphone and mic pre-amp, for example, do not really need an external mixer. In this case, Cubase's mixer might be viewed as being primarily concerned with playback and mixing.

However, an external mixing console is often more flexible for all kinds of recording, playback and routing tasks. For example, the majority of users need a way of interfacing and routing the wide range of equipment which is commonly used in the recording process. This might include one or more microphones, a lead or bass guitar, an electronic keyboard, a multi-track recorder, a CD player or any number of other musical instruments or sound sources. Any combination of these sources might be routed into Cubase via the line-outs of the external mixer. The use of an external mixer also provides direct, hands-on control of multiple faders and control knobs, which is especially convenient for recording multiple sources.

A project studio may require only a small mixer, providing enough inputs for several microphone and line signals (such as those from MIDI keyboards and modules) and enough I/O sockets to be able to interface external units and Cubase (as shown in Figure 2.6, above). For Cubase, a small, high quality external mixer with flexible routing functions is often preferable to a large console with many channels. A small mixer is fine for most recording purposes although it may not be able to handle a large-scale automated mix. In this context, the mixing facilities of Cubase become extremely useful since its virtually unlimited number of mixer channels and advanced automation facilities mean that the mix can be performed entirely within Cubase ('mixing in the box'). The use of Cubase with a small mixer therefore cuts down on the cost and space requirements of a large console.

External control surfaces

One of the limitations of computer-based multi-track audio systems is that manipulation of the controls is achieved mainly via the mouse and keyboard. This is not practical or convenient for the manipulation of some of the common audio control parameters. This is immediately apparent if you try to simultaneously move two faders in Cubase's Mixer. A mouse only allows you to move one fader at a time and a conventional computer keyboard does not feature hardware sliders. The installation of an additional hardware control surface can overcome these problems.

Hardware control surfaces include a number of hardware buttons, faders and control knobs designed for various levels of functional integration with the software. For example, the more sophisticated dedicated control surfaces include transport controls, faders, pan pots and control knobs which can be assigned to the majority of Cubases functions. They may also provide microphone and line inputs, MIDI I/O and routing capability and may therefore replace the necessity for more traditional external mixing console solutions.

Alternatively, some regular mixing consoles can double as control surfaces for Cubase (e.g. Yamaha's 01v, 02r96 and DM series consoles).

Cubase includes support for CM Motormix, Euphonix MC Mix and MC Control, JL Cooper MCS-3000 series, Mackie Control, Radikal SAC 2.x series, Roland MCR8, Steinberg Houston, Tascam US-428, Yamaha 01x, 01v, 02r96, DM1000 and DM2000, many of which feature a high level of functional integration with the program including motorised faders and other controls which reflect the current settings within Cubase. A generic remote setup option allows communication with a wide range of other control surfaces. Open the Device Setup window (Devices menu) and click on the Add device button to see the available options.

MIDI networks

Many Cubase systems include some kind of MIDI network. This is simply a collection of MIDI devices connected together using MIDI cables, usually in a 'star' network similar to that shown in Figure 2.6. Larger star networks feature a MIDI thru box (also called a MIDI splitter box) or some other central MIDI hub which enables the channelling of MIDI data to specific devices within the system. For example, the MIDI network in Figure 2.6 features a master keyboard from which the MIDI Out is sent to the MIDI In of the computer. The MIDI input data passes through Cubase and is passed back out of the computer, along with any other data which has already been recorded, to the MIDI input of the MIDI thru box. The data is then distributed to the respective outputs of the thru box and thus passed 'through' to the MIDI inputs of the master keyboard and to the other modules in the system.

Since the introduction of software-based MIDI instruments, large scale physical MIDI networks are becoming less common. Software-based instruments are commonly referred to as VST Instruments (Virtual Studio Instruments) and a number of examples are included with Cubase. VST Instruments are virtual equivalents of real-world MIDI samplers, synthesizers and drum machines. They reside in the memory of your computer and are triggered via MIDI in much the same way as their external counterparts. They do not suffer from the usual wear and tear of the physical world and they do not need any physical cabling. A vast range of VSTi products are available from Steinberg and other developers and these considerably expand the available sound palette.

CD and DVD recording

Of all the peripheral equipment surrounding Cubase, DVD and CD recorders are among the most useful. These are most often installed as DVD/CD drives within the computer itself rather than as stand-alone separate units. Using a DVD/CD recorder you can create your own Red Book audio CDs for demo or mastering purposes. DVD and CD are also invaluable for routine data back-up where the audio is stored as computer data files. DVDs are particularly appropriate for backup and archiving due to their large storage capacity.

For the creation of audio CDs, audio material may be mixed down directly as audio files onto hard disk using Cubase's Export / Audio mixdown function (this technique is often referred to as 'mixing in the box'). The audio files are

Info

An external control surface adds direct tactile controls to Cubase. This significantly helps with the practical hands-on manipulation of the parameters and puts a greater number of functions at your fingertips. There are a wide range of Cubase-compatible external control surfaces with various levels of functionality. You are likely to find what you need among those supplied by CM, Edirol, Euphonix, Gmedia, JL Cooper, Kenton, Mackie, Novation, Radikal, Roland, Steinberg, Tascam and Yamaha.

Info

Cubase features the Studio Connections protocol, developed by Steinberg and Yamaha. This provides seamless integration and total recall of the settings of various supported Yamaha hardware devices, including the Yamaha 01x, 02r96 and DM2000 mixers.

later burnt onto CD using a separate mastering / burning application, such as Steinberg Wavelab or Bias Peak. For mastering purposes the chosen application must be capable of burning Red Book audio CDs. For reliable results a good quality CD burner is required.

Summary

This chapter has explained some of the variables involved in setting up the software and overall system for Cubase. Any combination of hardware might be included, depending upon the application. Inevitably, setting up uncovers a wide range of issues from the worlds of music production, sound recording and studio design. Knowledge of these subjects not only helps you get the most out of your Cubase system, it also helps you make the right choices of audio hardware. Those readers who wish to enrich their knowledge further are advised to consult the latest music technology magazines and the recommended reading list at the back of this book.

First steps

This chapter shows you how to set up a new project, how to record MIDI and audio tracks, and explores some of the general features of the system. Most users are keen to make their first recording as soon as possible and many attempt to do this without ever having read the manual. This is certainly possible since Cubase has been designed to make the recording process as trouble-free as possible. However, it is not always certain that things will go according to plan since the recording process is controlled by many parameters. The following step-by-step guides help avoid some of the common problems which may arise during the recording process.

Recording in Cubase

Creating a new project

The Cubase environment is based upon the idea of organising all your recording, editing and processing endeavours into a project. All the data for a project is normally stored in a single directory on your system's hard disk, the location of which is chosen before you start recording. The directory for the project contains the project file itself (recognised by its .cpr file extension) and all the associated audio, edit, fade and image files. To ensure a trouble-free journey through the recording processes outlined below it is best to set up a new empty project. Proceed as follows:

1 Select New Project from the File menu and choose Empty from the dialogue which appears on screen (Figure 3.1).
2 In the Select directory dialogue which appears, choose your audio drive or an appropriate existing directory (usually the location where you intend to store all your Cubase projects) and click on the Create button to create a new directory for this

Figure 3.1
Create a new empty project

Figure 3.2
Create a directory for the new project

particular project (Figure 3.2). Choose an appropriate name, (like First recordings, for example). The directory is created on the hard disk.

3 Click on OK to leave the Select directory dialogue. An empty Cubase project with various default settings is opened on the screen (Figure 3.3). Immediately save the new project under a new name using File/Save As. The Cubase project file is saved in the directory you created in step 2. You are now ready to start work.

Figure 3.3
The resulting empty project in Cubase

Project setup

When you create a new project, Cubase gives you a working environment with various default settings. Many of these are found in the Project setup window (Figure 3.4), opened by selecting Project setup from the Project menu. The Project setup determines the settings for a number of fundamental global parameters. Whenever you start a serious project it is best to verify that the values are suitable. Most of the settings could be changed half-way through a project but the sample rate should be set once only before commencing. For the purposes of making your first recordings, as outlined below, configure your Project setup window to match the values shown in Figure 3.4.

The values in the Project setup window are saved as part of each Cubase project file. The parameters include the following:

- Start – determines the start time of the project (hours : minutes : seconds : frames). This allows you to set the start time to values other than zero and to regulate the start time when Cubase is synchronised to an external device.
- Length – determines the overall length of the project (hours : minutes : seconds : frames). Ten minutes is a good default length but this depends entirely upon the kind of project you are creating.
- Frame rate – sets the frame rate for Cubase when it is slaved to external time code.
- Display format – sets the global time line format for all ruler and position displays in Cubase.
- Display offset – allows you to set an offset for the ruler display when working with Cubase slaved to external time code (hours : minutes : seconds : frames).
- Bar offset – allows you to set a bar offset value relative to the start time chosen above. Only relevant when bars and beats are displayed in the ruler.
- Sample rate – determines the sample rate for the project. All audio playback and recording occurs at this sample rate. Here you would normally use 44.1kHz for audio-only projects and 48kHz for sound-to-picture projects. 88.2 and 96kHz help optimise audio quality and suit projects destined for high-end mastering and high-resolution formats such as DVD-Audio and SACD (see 'What bit resolution and sample rate should I use?' in Chapter 7 for more details).
- Record format – determines the bit depth for the project. Although 16-bit provides good quality, 24-bit and 32-bit float are recommended for serious projects.
- Record file type – sets the file format for all audio files recorded within the project.
- Stereo pan law – determines how the level is attenuated when audio signals are panned centre. The default setting is -3dB.

Figure 3.4
Project setup window

Info

It is not necessary to understand all the details of the parameters in the Project setup window before proceeding with your first recordings. The details are explained in other chapters. For the purposes of this chapter, configure your Project window to match the values shown in Figure 3.4. See the glossary in the back pages for an explanation of some of the jargon and terminology used here.

Your first MIDI recording

Connect the MIDI Out of your MIDI keyboard (or other MIDI device) to the MIDI In of your MIDI interface. Verify the connection by checking the MIDI activity indicator on the Transport panel while playing the MIDI keyboard (right-click on the Transport panel and select 'MIDI Activity' if no MIDI Activity indicator is visible). Connect the MIDI Out of your MIDI interface to the MIDI In of the keyboard. Activate the global MIDI Thru function in File / Preferences / MIDI.

1 Add a MIDI track and activate the record enable button

Add a new MIDI track by selecting Add track/MIDI in the Project menu. Select a track count of one and click OK. A new MIDI track is added to the track list. If preferred, you may add an Instrument track instead. An Instrument track gives you a quick connection to one of the VST Instruments available in your system (see Chapter 4 for more details). Activate the record enable button on the new MIDI track (illuminated in red = active). The record enable button is automatically activated when each track is selected, if 'Enable record on selected track' in File / Preferences / Editing is ticked (the default setting). When a track is record enabled MIDI data passes through the track, from the MIDI input to the MIDI output, allowing you to trigger the target MIDI device. Recording takes place on all record enabled tracks when you press the record button on the Transport panel.

2 Set MIDI input/output ports and MIDI channel

If it is not already visible, open the Inspector for the selected MIDI track by clicking on the Show Inspector button in the top left corner of the Project window. Set the MIDI input port to your chosen MIDI input device in the pop-up MIDI input routing menu. Set the MIDI output port to the desired MIDI output device in the pop-up MIDI output routing menu. The target device could be an external MIDI instrument such as a synthesizer, or it could be an internal VST instrument. There could be several input and output ports available, depending on the hardware and software you have installed or activated in your computer. If applicable, select a MIDI channel in the channel field of the Inspector (normally the same channel as set on the target device).

3 Set metronome

Set up an appropriate precount and guide click by activating Precount and adjusting the settings of the Metronome setup dialogue (Transport menu / Metronome setup). Try ticking 'Precount' in the Transport menu and 'Activate Audio click' in the Metronome setup dialogue. Select 'Beeps' for a standard audio beep. Alternatively, you could use a MIDI device for the click sound by ticking 'Activate MIDI click' and setting the MIDI click channel and output port to an appropriate MIDI device. Set the MIDI notes as required (C#1/37 and F#1/42 are the usual positions for a rimshot and a closed hi-hat respectively). Set a precount of 2 bars.

4 Adjust the tempo and activate click

In the Transport panel, set the tempo to Fixed mode and enter the desired value in the tempo field. Also, activate the click button and de-activate the punch in and punch out buttons (Locators section). Leave all other Transport panel settings in their default positions.

5 Start recording

To record, select the record button on the Transport panel. Cubase outputs a two bar count, (as set in the metronome), and then recording commences from bar 1. The selected track turns red to indicate that recording has been implemented. Anything played on your MIDI keyboard is recorded.

6 Stop recording

Stop recording by selecting the stop button on the Transport panel. A graphical strip known as a part remains on the track and this contains the MIDI events you have just recorded (Figure 3.13).

7 Rewind

Rewind the song position in the conventional manner using the Transport panel rewind button or, alternatively, select . on the computers numeric keypad which takes you back to the beginning of the project.

8 Now play it back

To play back the performance select the Transport panels play button.

Save your work by selecting save from the file menu or use Ctrl + S (PC) / Command + S (Mac) on the computer keyboard. The above steps should get you into MIDI recording with the minimum of fuss. Cubase has been supplied with most of the parameters already sensibly set so, in most cases, only the last few steps are necessary to actually make the recording. However, the details outlined here help you become aware of some of the other parameters involved.

Figure 3.13
Resulting MIDI part in the Project window

If you experience problems with this process verify that:

- the MIDI cables are not faulty and have been connected correctly
- the MIDI interface has been correctly installed and is active in Device Setup / MIDI Port Setup
- the relevant ports are selected in the input and output routing menus of the selected MIDI track
- the MIDI channel is appropriate in the channel field of the selected MIDI track
- any external equipment connected to the system is switched on and configured to receive MIDI information on the appropriate channel(s)

Your first audio recording

Make sure that your audio hardware is installed correctly. Open the control panel for the audio hardware and verify the settings. Make sure the first pair of audio outputs are connected to your amplifier and speaker system so that you can hear any audio output. Connect the source signal cable to the first pair of line inputs of your audio hardware. For this exercise, try recording a stereo line level source such as the stereo audio output from an electronic keyboard instrument or a CD player. Select VST Connections from the Devices menu and, in the input and output sections, verify that there is at least one input buss and one output buss assigned to the appropriate ports of your audio hardware.

1 Add an Audio track and activate the record and monitor enable buttons

Add a new Audio track by selecting Add track/Audio in the Project menu. Select stereo in the configuration menu of the pop-up Add dialogue. A new stereo Audio

Record Enable

Info

In Cubase, audio input and output routing is based upon busses. Input signals must enter the program via an input buss and output signals must exit via an output buss.

track is added to the track list. Select Tape Machine Style in File / Preferences / VST / Auto Monitoring. Activate the record enable button on the new Audio track (illuminated in red = active). The record enable button is automatically activated when each track is selected, if Enable record on selected track in File / Preferences / Editing is ticked (the default setting). This makes the channel record ready. In Tape Machine Style mode, activating the record enable button also automatically activates the monitor button when you are in Stop or Record modes. This allows you to hear the input signal and visually monitor the level on the channel's level meters. Recording takes place on all record enabled tracks when you press the record button on the Transport panel.

2 Open the Mixer and select Meter input in Global meter settings

Open the Mixer from the Devices menu or select F3 on the computer keyboard. Here you find the input buss which is connected to your audio hardware inputs (on the left) and the channel strip for the Audio track you created in step 1 (to the right). Right-click (PC) / Control + click (Mac) in blank space in the Mixer and select 'Meter input' in the Global meter settings section of the pop-up menu. In the input buss you now see the level of the incoming signal at the input of your audio hardware (before any level changes or other processing takes place within Cubase).

3 Adjust the input level while monitoring the signal in the input buss

The signal level at the input of your audio hardware is visually monitored in the meters of the input buss when the Global meter settings have been set to Meter input. At this stage, the level is adjusted using the output fader of your external mixer or directly on the output faders of the device or instrument you are recording. Some audio hardware allows adjustment of the input signal via its own control panel. The source level at the input is NOT adjusted using the input buss fader or input gain control.

Carefully adjust the source level so that no clipping occurs on the level meter of the input buss channel strip. The peak level value of the incoming signal is shown just below the channel meters. Clipping has occurred if the clip indicator under the fader is illuminated in red. The peak level should not exceed 0dBFS. Signals which exceed this level produce an unpleasant audible distortion. If you are recording at 24-bit resolution it is normal to leave a healthy amount of headroom by aiming for peaks between -10 and -6dBFS and an average signal level of around -18dBFS.

Info

As a very rough guide, when recording at 24-bit resolution, try setting input signal levels to peak at around -6dB on the input buss meters with an average level hovering around -18dB. The final decision for the precise input level is a matter of judgement and experience and is highly dependent upon the characteristics of the input signal. Overall, it is best to avoid recording signals extremely low, to minimise possible signal degradation (especially if you are recording at 16-bit resolution). Also avoid recording all your tracks too hot, not only to minimise distortion but also to help maintain a healthy gain structure when you come to do the mix.

To aurally monitor the signal make sure that the monitor enabled audio channel you created in step 1 is set to receive the signal from the appropriate input buss in the input routing menu above the channel strip (see step 5 below for details). There may be a delay between the moment the signal enters the audio hardware and the moment you hear it via Cubase. This delay is known as latency and varies according to the audio hardware and driver which is installed in your system. Audio hardware devices with special dedicated ASIO drivers give the best performance and are the preferred option.

Overall, this step ensures that the incoming signal is not producing distortion at the input of your audio hardware and is being recorded at the optimum level. This is often a once-only calibration.

4 Switch to Meter post-fader setting

Now that you know that there is no distortion at the input of your audio hardware, it is appropriate to switch the meter setting back to the default Meter post-fader position. You are now monitoring the signal after it has passed through the input gain, fader and any other processing on the input buss and it is this signal which is recorded to hard disk. If you have not changed any of the controls on the input buss then the post-fader output signal is identical to the input signal. If you are suffering from a particularly weak source signal, you may at this stage wish to adjust the input gain on the input buss. Hold Shift or Alt and adjust the input gain control as required. You may also apply insert effects or EQ on the input buss. This allows you to print effects and processing to hard disk (such as a signal with compression and EQ). Adding effects may result in an increase in signal level which is too hot to be recorded on hard disk. If this is the case reduce the level slightly using the input buss fader.

5 Select an input on the record channel

Verify that the record enabled audio channel you created in step 1 is set to receive the signal from the appropriate input buss (i.e. that to which you have connected your stereo audio source). The input buss for audio channels is chosen by clicking in the input routing menu above the channel strip (found in the Mixer or in the Inspector). You may need to extend the view of the Mixer if the input/output routing menus are not visible. The default names for the first pair of inputs for your audio hardware usually read 'S In 1'. By default, a stereo audio channel is routed to the first stereo output buss found in your system which, in turn, is connected to the first pair of outputs on the audio hardware. Note that the fader and other controls of the target record channel come *after* the signal is recorded to hard disk and are therefore used purely for monitoring and mixing purposes. The record level and record quality of the incoming audio signal is not affected by any settings you make here.

6 Adjust the metronome and tempo

Adjust the Metronome to give the desired pre-count before recording commences. It is possible to record audio with no concern for the current tempo but here it is assumed you are using the tempo of the click to keep in time. In the Transport panel, activate the click button and de-activate the punch in and punch out buttons (Locators section). Set the tempo to Fixed mode and enter the desired value in the tempo field. Leave all other Transport panel settings in their default positions.

Info

Some ASIO drivers allow the use of the Direct Monitoring option in the VST Audio System section of the Device Setup dialogue. This virtually cuts out latency altogether but does not allow the monitoring of the whole signal path which passes through Cubase.

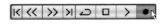

7 Start recording

To record, select the record button on the Transport panel. After the pre-count, commence the musical performance (or send the audio signal). In this exercise, recording commences at bar 1. The selected record-enabled track turns red when recording commences.

8 Stop and play back the recording

Stop recording by selecting the stop button on the Transport panel. A graphical strip remains on the track containing a waveform which represents the audio you have just recorded. This is known as an audio event. To play back the audio, rewind and press the play button (note that in Tapemachine Style mode, as chosen in step 1 above, playback automatically deactivates the monitor button so that you can hear the recorded audio).

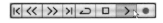

Figure 3.22
Resulting audio event in the Project window

The resulting audio event appears in a similar manner to that shown in Figure 3.22. Save your work by selecting save from the file menu or use Ctrl + S (PC) / Command + S (Mac) on the computer keyboard.

First impressions

Creating a new project and recording with Cubase reveals some of the primary features of the program. The MIDI and audio recording processes operate in a similar fashion and, once you become familiar with the parameters, recording can be accomplished with fewer steps than those outlined above. You may have also noticed that you can achieve a great deal without ever leaving the Project window. The Project window is at once a powerful multi-track recorder and a sophisticated multi-track editor in a single ergonomic environment. Its streamlined approach speeds up your production time and enhances your creativity. However, before exploring the Project window in more detail, lets look at the system in a more generalised way.

Testing the controls

Some users miss many of Cubase's peripheral features by using only the mouse in their quest for quick results. Relying on the mouse alone is not the best way of using the program. There are also a wide range of key commands which make navigating around the system faster and easier. Many of these are already assigned by default and some of the most useful are shown in Table 3.1.

Tip

In many cases, using key commands is faster and easier than using the mouse. You can at any time change the default settings or assign new key commands in the Key Commands dialogue (File / Key commands).

Table 3.1 Default key commands

Typewriter keyboard		Function
PC	**Mac**	
F2	F2	open/close Transport panel
F3	F3	open/close Mixer
F4	F4	open/close VST Connections
F8	F8	open/close video
F9	F9	select previous tool
F10	F10	select next tool
F11	F11	open/close VST instruments rack
F12	F12	open/close VST performance meter
ctrl + O	command + O	open project
ctrl + S	command + S	save project
ctrl + W	command + W	close current window
ctrl + Q	command + Q	quit program
ctrl + E	command + E	open default editor associated with the event type
ctrl + R	command + R	Score edit
ctrl + X	command + X	cut
ctrl + C	command + C	copy
ctrl + V	command + V	paste
ctrl + Z	command + Z	undo
ctrl + P	command + P	open Pool
ctrl + T	command + T	open Tempo track
alt + I	option + I	show/hide Inspector
backspace	backspace	delete selected track, part or event
return	return	open/close editor
C	C	metronome click on/off
F	F	autoscroll on/off
I	I	punch in on/off
O	O	punch out on/off
J	J	snap on/off
M	M	mute on/off
P	P	move locators to start and end points of selected part/event
R	R	record enable track
S	S	solo on/off

Learning to use Cubase is rather like learning to drive a car. In the same way as it's a good idea to become familiar with the controls of a car before taking it out on the road, it's a good idea to become familiar with the controls of Cubase before you start using it for serious projects. For example, try the following steps to get used to manipulating some of the key areas of the Project window and Mixer:

- Start a new empty project as outlined in the recording exercises above.
- Select Project / Add Track / Audio. In the dialogue which appears, enter a count of four and press OK. Four audio tracks appear in the track list.
- Press the up or down arrows on the computer keyboard to select different tracks. The selected track is highlighted.
- Press F9/F10 to select the previous/next tool in the toolbar.
- Press F11 to open/close the VST instruments rack. This is where you can load VST instruments into Cubase.
- Press F12 to show/hide the VST performance meter. This is where you can keep an eye on the CPU load and disk performance in projects which make heavy use of your computer's resources.
- Press F2 to open/close the Transport panel. Try leaving the Transport panel open and drag it to a convenient location on screen using the mouse.
- Press Alt+I to open/close the Inspector for a track (the Inspector opens to the left of the track list).
- Now press F3 to open the Mixer. The Mixer displays all tracks as channel strips in the same order in which they appear in the Project window.
- With the Mixer still open on screen, press the left/right arrows on the computer keyboard to select different channel strips.
- Press the up/down arrows on the computer keyboard to change the level of the fader of the currently selected channel strip.
- Press the M key to mute/unmute the channel.
- Press the S key to solo/unsolo the channel.
- Press the R key to record enable/record disable the channel.
- Press F3 a second time to close the Mixer.

Note that many of the key commands are on/off or open/close toggle switches for their respective functions. You can therefore handle Cubase in a very quick and logical fashion. Other immediately useful key commands include the C key for turning the guide click on and off, and the G and H keys for horizontal zoom out and zoom in.

The numeric keypad

The numeric keypad may be viewed as a kind of tape recorder remote control. Although all the controls are already available within the Transport panel (and the most important are also available in the toolbar above the Project window display), their repetition on the keypad provides a handy alternative (see Table 3.2). This is convenient for selecting the transport functions very quickly and is invaluable when the Transport panel is hidden from view.

Table 3.2 Numeric keypad shortcuts

Numeric keypad		Function
PC	Mac	
*	*	record
Enter	Enter	play
0	0	stop
–	–	rewind
+	+	fast forward
1	1	go to left locator
2	2	go to right locator
•	•	go to bar 1.1.1.0
/	/	cycle on/off

Mouse and computer keyboard ergonomics

The mouse is, above all, useful for drag-and-drop functions, changing values, using tools, selecting objects, opening menus and fine editing in the editors. It is also convenient for setting the project cursor position by clicking once in the ruler above the track display. In addition, double-clicking in the ruler starts playback from the point at which you clicked, and double-clicking a second time in the ruler stops playback. However, for the quickest and most efficient use of the program it is best not to rely exclusively on the mouse.

The best overall approach for the manipulation of the controls, tools and functions of Cubase is an intelligent combination of mouse moves and key commands. This requires a practical and ergonomic approach to the physical workspace. Arrange your equipment on your work surface so that you use your left hand for key commands on your typewriter keyboard and your right hand for mouse manipulations (or vice versa for left-handed users). This two-handed approach dramatically speeds up editing and other processes.

The menus

The menus are found under various headings at the top of the computer screen and it is well worth browsing through the menu contents to find out what is available. It is apparent from the range of menu items that Cubase is extremely versatile. Some of the most important elements include the file save and open functions; the import options; the undo and select options; project setup and media options; audio processing options; the tempo track; the MIDI editors; the quantize functions; and the score, transport and VST functions. Most of the important menu items are explored throughout the course of this book.

Cubase startup options

You can set Cubase to behave in various different ways when the program is launched by changing the selection in the 'On Startup' option in File / Preferences / General (Figure 3.23).

Figure 3.23
Changing the startup options in the general preferences dialogue.

The available options are as follows:

- Do nothing – Cubase is launched as an empty environment with no open Project window.
- Open last project – opens the last project which was worked upon in Cubase.
- Open default project – opens the Cubase default project file (named as default.cpr).
- Show open dialogue – automatically opens a Project file selection dialogue when Cubase is launched.
- Show template dialogue – opens a project template dialogue.
- Show open options dialogue – opens an options dialogue, allowing you to choose from a list of your most recent projects.

Tip

In Windows, the default project template is normally saved to C:\ Documents and Settings \ Username \ Application Data \ Steinberg \ Cubase 4 \ templates.

These options help manage how you start your Cubase sessions. If you are working on a single long-term project then 'Open last project' is the best option. If you are using Cubase as a musical notepad then you may prefer to start with the same default project at the beginning of each session, in which case you should select 'Open default project'. If you continually change between a number of simultaneous projects on the same system then try using 'Show open options dialogue'.

The Project window

This chapter provides information about the Project window, the Project window tools, track types, the Transport panel, the Inspector, event and part editing, and file handling. The Project window is the centre of activity for many of Cubase's functions and, as such, this chapter is essential reading for those not yet familiar.

The Project window

Project window basics

The Project window (Figure 4.1) features time on the horizontal axis and tracks on the vertical axis. Tracks are added to the project using the Add command in the Project menu. A number of different track types are available including audio, FX, folder, group, instrument, MIDI, marker, arranger,

Figure 4.1
The Project window.

ruler, transpose, automation and video types. Where applicable, a track can be re-named by double-clicking on its name field. Various buttons surround the track name including (for audio and MIDI tracks) the mute and solo buttons (M and S), the record and monitor buttons (circular record and speaker icons), and the read and write buttons for track automation (R and W). Tracks contain data which is shown in the central area of the Project window (arranged as graphical blocks, lines, waveforms and symbols). This central area is known as the event display.

The current time position is shown by a vertical line known as the project cursor. When in play mode, the project cursor moves along the horizontal time line which is marked by a ruler located just above the event display. By default, the ruler displays time in bars and beats but by clicking on the arrow to the right of the ruler you can also find options for displaying time in seconds, time code or samples. There can be only one active Project window at any one time. An active Project window is designated by an illuminated blue indicator in the top left corner of the toolbar. A new project may be created at any time by selecting New Project in the File menu or by pressing Ctrl (PC) / Command (Mac) + N on the computer keyboard.

The toolbar

The Project window features a toolbar above the event display which contains a number of function buttons and tools (Figure 4.2). These provide easy access to the display and editing properties of the Project window.

Info

Several projects could be opened within Cubase at the same time. However, only one can be active at any given moment (designated by an illuminated blue indicator in the top left corner of the toolbar).

Figure 4.2
The Project window toolbar

Let's firstly concentrate on the operation of the most commonly used buttons and the editing tools, as found in the default setup of the toolbar. From left to right the first five buttons include:

The show Inspector button

This shows/hides the information and editing area to the left of the event display known as the Inspector (see The Inspector (below) for more details).

The show Infoline button

This shows/hides an information line above the display which shows the details of the currently selected event.

The show Overview button

This shows/hides an overview strip above the display used for sizing and navigating within the event display.

The Open Pool button

This opens the Pool, a file display and organisation window which shows all the audio and video clips used in the active Project (see Chapter 10 for more details).

The Open Mixer button

This opens the Mixer, a virtual mixing console for the mixing of all audio, MIDI, Instrument and Group tracks and the setting up of EQ, effects and automation (see Chapter 11 for more details).

The Infoline

The Infoline (shown by clicking on the Infoline button in the toolbar) displays information about the currently selected event or part. The contents vary according to what kind of event or part is chosen. For a MIDI part the Infoline includes (from left to right) the name, start time, end time, length, offset, mute status, lock status, transpose and velocity values. Most of these are self explanatory. Offset is an amount by which the contents can be moved back and forth in time relative to the start and end of the part. Lock allows various attributes of the part, such as position and size, to be locked to avoid accidental changes to important material.

Figure 4.3
Infoline for a MIDI part

Name	Start	End	Length	Offset	Mute	Lock	Transpose	Velocity
MIDI part	43. 1. 1. 0	55. 1. 1. 0	12. 0. 0. 0	0. 0. 0. 0 -		-	~ 0	0

The infoline is particularly useful for detailed editing since all fields can be directly edited using the mouse and computer keyboard. When more than one event is selected the infoline text is shown in yellow and contains the information relevant to the first of the selected events. Editing any of the yellow values applies the changes relatively to all selected events (i.e. changing the start position from, for example, bar 17 to bar 18 moves all selected events one bar later than their current position). To apply the edits in an absolute sense hold down Ctrl while making the changes (this time, changing the start position from bar 17 to bar 18 moves all selected events to the same absolute position at bar 18).

The Infoline for an audio event is very similar but contains a greater number of data fields including the file name which is referenced by the audio event; a description field; the start, end and length; offset, snap and volume fields; fade, mute and lock fields; and transpose and fine tune. See Chapter 8 for more information about the audio event Infoline.

The Overview strip

The Overview strip (shown by clicking on the show overview button in the toolbar) shows a thumbnail view of the event display. The blue selection box outlines the horizontal bar range shown in the event display and by grabbing either end of the selection box (a double arrow appears) you can change the range. You can also grab the whole box (a hand symbol appears) and drag it to a new position within your arrangement.

Figure 4.4
Overview

Other toolbar functions

The buttons and functions visible on the toolbar may be shown/hidden using the options shown in the pop-up menu which appears when you right click (PC) / Ctrl + click (Mac) anywhere on the toolbar. Other functions include

Constrain delay compensation, Performance meter, Locators, Time display, Markers, Nudge palette and the Colour menu. Constrain delay compensation helps minimise additional latency which may be caused by the automatic delay compensation of the program while monitoring live audio or a VSTi on channels with insert effects. The Performance meter allows you to see the current load on the CPU and hard drive. The Locators option shows the left and right locator positions. The Markers option provides a numerical display of the first ten markers. The Nudge palette allows you to trim the start and end points of the current event selection or move the event back and forth in time. The colour menu provides a colour palette for changing the colour of the currently selected track or event. The order in which the buttons and functions appear on the toolbar is edited in the Setup dialogue.

The Project window tools

To choose a tool in the Project window make a selection from the tool buttons in the toolbar or click with the right mouse button (PC)/ Ctrl + click (Mac) in the event display to open a pop-up tool selection menu (a context sensitive menu known as the Quick menu). The tools are for the manipulation and editing of events and parts and they include the following:

Object selection tool (pointer tool)

The object selection tool (or pointer tool) is the default, general purpose tool for the selection, moving and copying of events and parts, and for the manipulation of data anywhere in the Project window. Its button has a small downward pointing arrow in the lower right corner. This indicates a multi-function tool. Click on the tool button a second time to reveal the other functions. There are two additional options: sizing moves contents and sizing applies time stretch. Sizing moves contents moves the contents of an event or part forward or backward in time according to whether you size the object by sliding the start or end handles, (this effectively locks the start or end of the contents to the start or end of the object). Sizing applies time stretch stretches (or compresses) the contents of an object when you re-size it. For MIDI parts the notes are re-positioned accordingly and for audio events the audio is time-stretched (or compressed).

Range selection tool

The range selection tool is for making event-independent selections of any material in the Project window. Once selected, the material can be cut, copied and pasted as required (moving range selected data automatically splits events where applicable). This is in contrast to the object selection tool which always selects whole events and parts.

Split tool

The split tool is for splicing events/parts into smaller portions. Events/parts are split at the mouse position and according to the current snap settings. Holding Alt while clicking with the split tool automatically divides the event/part into a number of smaller events at the resolution of the snap settings.

Glue tool

The glue tool is used to join together two or more events/parts. In the case of MIDI material, parts are joined to make one longer MIDI part. In the case of audio material, events/parts are grouped into one longer audio part. Holding Alt while clicking on an event glues all the following events on that track into one long event.

Erase tool

The erase tool is for deleting events by clicking on any single object or selected group of objects in the event display. Holding Alt while clicking on an event (or while clicking in blank space) deletes all the following events on that track.

Zoom tool

The zoom tool is for zooming in and out of the event display. To zoom in, select the zoom tool and click once in the event display. This zooms in to the display horizontally around the position at which you clicked. To zoom out, click with the zoom tool while holding Alt. By clicking and dragging a selection box with the zoom tool you can zoom in to specific areas of the event display. Holding Ctrl (PC) / Command (Mac) while clicking with the zoom tool steps back through the previous zoom views you have used. Holding Shift while clicking in the event display with the zoom tool gives you a view of all events in the project. By default, the zoom tool acts upon the display horizontally. For simultaneous horizontal and vertical zooming deactivate zoom tool standard mode in File / Preferences / Editing / Tools.

Mute tool

The mute tool is for muting events and parts. Click on objects individually or drag a selection box over several to implement muting. When an object is muted it is displayed in grey. Muting actions are not stored in the undo list and so cannot be undone using Ctrl/Command + Z. To undo a mute, click on the muted object a second time.

Time warp tool

The time warp tool is for dragging a bar position to a time position. This might be used to line up the start or end of a musical passage to a visual cue in a video or it might equally be used to make a musical sequence fit a specific time duration. The time warp tool operates between the left and right locators in two modes; default mode and musical events follow mode. In the default mode, all tracks are automatically switched to linear time base and do not move when you drag the warp tool in the display. In musical events follow mode, the events on all tracks which are set to musical time base mode are moved as you drag the warp tool in the display. The time warp tool is used most effectively when you set the snap mode to Events, at which time it becomes easier, for example, to drag a bar position to the start or end of an event. Inserting markers in the Marker track also helps navigate the Warp tool to the desired time position. Holding Shift while clicking in the Project window display with the Time warp tool inserts a tempo event. Holding Shift with the time warp tool in the ruler allows the deleting of tempo events. To use the time warp tool, tempo track mode must be selected in the Transport bar (time warp does not function in fixed tempo mode). For more details on the use of the time warp tool see Chapter 18.

Draw tool

The draw tool is used for drawing new empty parts by dragging the tool in the event display, adding markers in the Marker track (see below for details) and freely drawing such things as volume and pan curves on automation tracks.

Line tool

The line tool features straight line, parabola, sine, triangle and square forms which may be used to draw their respective shapes on automation tracks according to the current snap resolution.

Play/scrub tool

The play/scrub tool is a dual function tool. In its default play mode, clicking on an audio or MIDI event plays back the material from the position at which you click and continues for as long as you hold the mouse button. In scrub mode clicking and dragging over an audio or MIDI event plays back the material at the speed with which you drag, much like rocking the tape back and forth over the playback heads of a tape machine. You can change the characteristics of the scrub behaviour in File / Preferences / VST / Scrub.

Colour tool

The colour tool allows you to apply different colours to events in the display. The colour is chosen from a pop-up colour palette which appears when you click on the colour strip just below the tool button. Double-clicking on the colour strip opens the event colour dialogue where you can create your own custom colours. To change an event back to the default colour chosen for the track, click on the event with the colour tool with 'default colour' chosen from the colour palette.

Autoscroll and snap functions

Autoscroll and Suspend Autoscroll button

The Autoscroll button status is managed using the mouse or by pressing 'F' on the computer keyboard. When activated, the event display follows the project cursor. When de-activated, the event display remains static regardless of the project cursor position. An activated Suspend Autoscroll button automatically suspends autoscroll behaviour when you proceed with any kind of editing operation. The suspend status is cancelled by re-starting the transport or by clicking on the suspended autoscroll button.

The snap button

The snap button is found to the right of the autoscroll button and is activated/de-activated using the mouse or by pressing J on the computer keyboard. When activated, all tool manipulations and editing moves are sensitive to the snap settings. Snap describes the manner in which event manipulations and editing with the tools is pulled onto the nearest bar or beat (or other subdivision) of the grid. This occurs according to a chosen snap resolution.

The snap to zero crossing button

When activated, the global Snap to zero crossing button forces all editing of audio events onto the zero crossing points of the waveform. Zero crossing points are where there are the least amounts of energy in the audio signal. Editing here reduces the occurrence of audible clicks and makes for a good join when one section of audio is joined to another. This effects the re-sizing and splitting of audio events. However, when both the Snap button and the Snap to zero crossing button are activated, re-sizing or splitting audio events occurs at the nearest zero crossing point to the Snap point and not directly on the beat specified by the snap resolution, as usually happens. This may cause unforeseen side-effects when working with audio events which you expect to start or end on precise bar or beat divisions. As a general rule, the global Snap to zero crossing button is best left in its default disabled state, unless you have a specific reason for activating it.

The snap, grid and quantize menus

There are a number of menus and parameters which govern snap behaviour. Most of these are found to the right of the snap button in three menus known as the Snap type menu, the Grid type menu and the Quantize type menu (Figure 4.5).

Figure 4.5
The Snap type, Grid type and Quantize type menus

Snap type menu

The Snap type menu contains the following options:

- Grid – the snap resolution is governed by the setting of the Grid type menu to the right.
- Grid relative – the snap resolution is governed by the setting of the Grid type menu but dragged objects maintain their relative position to the nearest snap point. For example, dragging an event whose initial position is bar 1 beat 2, with Grid relative enabled and Bar selected in the Grid type menu, snaps the event to bar 2 beat 2, bar 3 beat 2, bar 4 beat 2 and so on, as you drag the event across the display. This mode is excellent for moving and copying events whose positions do not begin on precise divisions of the bar.
- Events – the start and end positions of objects become magnetic. Any events dragged near to these points are snapped onto the start or end of the nearest object.

> **Tip**
>
> Snap might be viewed as a magnetic grid which you impose upon the event display. With the snap button activated, objects moved or edited in the display are attracted to the nearest magnetic grid line.

- Shuffle – objects moved on a track are snapped tightly one against the other with no space in between. This mode may be used for changing the order of tightly grouped events by dragging and inserting objects in between each other.
- Magnetic cursor – the project cursor becomes magnetic and any objects dragged nearby are snapped to its position.
- Grid + cursor – grid and magnetic cursor modes combined.
- Events + cursor – event and magnetic cursor modes combined.
- Events + grid + cursor – event, grid and magnetic cursor modes combined.

Grid type menu

The Grid type menu changes according to which time line format has been chosen in the ruler. Click on the downward pointing arrow to the right of the ruler to change the time format. This is most commonly set to bars and beats, in which case the menu contains the following:

- Bar – tool editing and event placement snaps to the nearest 1 bar division on the ruler.
- Beat – tool editing and event placement snaps to the nearest 1 beat division on the ruler.
- Use quantize – tool editing and event placement snaps to the nearest division as chosen in the Quantize type menu (see below).

Quantize type menu

The Quantize type menu contains a list of note values which may be used to define the snap resolution. However, the quantize value is only relevant to snap behaviour when all three of the following selections are made:

- grid is selected in the Snap mode type menu (see above)
- use quantize is selected in the Grid type menu (see above)
- bars and beats is chosen as the time format on the ruler.

If any of these is not the case then the Quantize type becomes irrelevant to the snap behaviour.

Managing snap behaviour is an alternative function of the Quantize type menu, which is normally used for the main Quantize function in the MIDI menu. When used to govern the snap resolution in the Project window, quantize allows the editing and moving of events to be locked to musically meaningful positions along the time scale. This helps you complete your musical arrangement with maximum speed and accuracy. The main quantize functions (MIDI menu) automatically move recorded musical events onto the divisions of the bar chosen in the Quantize type menu. Quantize was first devised as a purely corrective function for MIDI recordings but, in Cubase, it is also used to affect the timing of audio material and govern the snap resolution for editing in general. Cubase provides two main quantize functions known as Over quantize and Iterative quantize (see the MIDI menu). Over quantize moves recorded events onto the exact divisions of the bar as chosen in the Quantize type menu, whereas Iterative quantize moves recorded events

Tip

To make adjacent events follow when you resize any event in the Project window, select shuffle in the snap mode menu before resizing. This results in gapless resizing of adjacent events since they remain tightly 'glued' together. This is particularly useful when editing speech or the gaps between the musical phrases of a solo instrument.

towards the chosen value according to a strength percentage (see Chapters 5 and 6 for more details about quantizing).

The ruler and the left and right locators

The Project window features a ruler above the event display to help you navigate within your project and to specify the timing divisions which Cubase takes into account for transport and editing operations. Click on the downward pointing arrow to the right of the ruler to change the time format (Figure 4.6). This is most commonly set to bars and beats but the time line may also be displayed in seconds, timecode and samples.

Figure 4.6
Choosing the time format in the Project window ruler.

The ruler also displays the left and right locators. These are shown as pointers at each end of a shaded area in the ruler and event display. The locators are used for defining the positions you want to start and stop recording and for setting up cycle playback and cycle recording operations (Figure 4.7). The positions of the left and right locators are set in the

Figure 4.7
The left and right locators in the ruler.

Transport panel or by clicking and dragging in the upper half of the ruler (a pencil tool appears). Moving the right locator to a position before the left locator implements skip mode where playback jumps between the start and end points of the shaded area. This is good for quickly testing alternative musical arrangements.

Info

An alternative method of setting the positions of the locators is to Ctrl / Command click in the ruler to set the left locator and Alt click in the ruler to set the right locator.

Split, divide, size and track colour functions

Vertical split point

The Project window features a vertical split point at the left edge of the event display. Pulling the split point to the left maximises the size of the event display, giving you more space to work. Pulling the split point to the right reveals more of the buttons and functions associated with the tracks.

Divide track list

Clicking on the Divide track list button divides the track list into two separate displays. This is useful when working with video tracks where the video track can be placed in the upper display while all the audio and MIDI tracks are placed in the lower display. This allows you to freely scroll within the musical arrangement while always keeping the video track visible in the upper part of the display. Similarly, the Marker track might be better placed in the upper display so that it is always visible. The divided track list is also good for using Ruler tracks set to different time displays (e.g. one set to SMPTE time in the upper display and another set to bars and beats in the lower display).

Track size

The vertical size of the tracks is scaleable. Clicking and dragging on the lower edge of a track allows you to change its vertical size. Holding Ctrl (PC) /

Command (Mac) while dragging on the lower edge sets all tracks to the same row size. Greater track size reveals more of the tracks buttons and expands the waveform or MIDI events view in the event display. By default, Cubase sizes the tracks in terms of rows but if you need to resize freely, de-activate 'Snap Track Heights' in the Track scale pop-up menu (found just above the vertical zoom control).

Track colours

Clicking on the small colour palette above the track list toggles between standard and colour-coded track displays. When colour is activated, the tracks show their default colours in the Project window, Mixer and Inspector. This helps clarify the screen display and allows you to change the default track colour from the pop-up colour palette which appears when you click in each track's colour box in the track list. Colour may be applied to all tracks.

Zoom and sizing functions in the Project window

There are a wide range of functions available for zooming in and out of the event display. This section outlines a number of techniques designed to help you manage the zoom status and general look of the display more easily.

Using the zoom tool

Info

If you prefer the traditional, no nonsense way of zooming in and out, use the horizontal and vertical zoom sliders found in the lower right corner of the Project window.

Among the simplest ways to zoom in is to select the zoom tool and click in the event display. This zooms in to the display around the position at which you clicked. Holding Alt while clicking with the zoom tool zooms back out again. Standard horizontal or combined vertical/horizontal zooming takes place according to the zoom tool mode chosen in File / Preferences / Editing. Clicking and dragging a selection box with the zoom tool allows you to zoom in to specific areas of the event display. To zoom back out again hold Ctrl (PC) / Command (Mac) while clicking in the event display with the zoom tool. This steps you back to the previous zoom view you have used.

Zoom in the ruler

Tip

To achieve a full horizontal and vertical view of all events in the project, select the Zoom tool, hold Shift and click once in the event display.

Clicking in the ruler and moving the mouse position up or down while keeping the mouse button pressed allows you to zoom in and out horizontally in the event display. Drag down to zoom in and drag up to zoom out. Note that the project cursor is automatically moved to the position of the mouse, and for the function to work correctly, Zoom while locating in time scale must be activated File / Preferences / Transport.

Zoom default key commands

There are a number of default key commands which provide quick and convenient zoom control. Press H to zoom in horizontally and G to zoom out horizontally. Press Alt + H to zoom in vertically and Alt + G to zoom out vertically. Shift + F gives you a full horizontal zoom up to the end of the events currently present in the display.

Zoom with the overview strip

The overview strip provides a graphical way of zooming and navigating within your project. The strip is shown by clicking on the Show overview button in the toolbar. The overview features a blue selection box which can be dragged to new positions and re-sized. The selection box outlines the horizontal bar range shown in the event display and by grabbing either end of the selection box (a double arrow appears) you can change the horizontal zoom. (See also The Overview Strip, above).

Zoom presets menu

The Zoom presets menu (Figure 4.8) is revealed when you click on the small downward pointing arrow to the right of the horizontal scroll bar. The menu features a number of presets for full horizontal zoom, zooming to the section inside the left and right locators and, if they are present, you can zoom in to cycle marker positions (see The Marker track below for more details about cycle markers). You can also store your own horizontal zoom presets. To achieve this, set up your desired horizontal zoom, open the Zoom presets menu, select Add and type in a suitable name in the dialogue which appears. Try setting up presets in terms of time. Horizontal zoom factors of 1sec, 10secs and 1min can prove quite useful. To help still further key commands may be assigned to the first five presets in File / Key Commands (try Alt + 1-5).

Track scale menu

The Track scale menu (Figure 4.9) is revealed when you click on the small downward pointing arrow below the vertical scroll bar. The menu features a number of presets for scaling the vertical zoom in terms of rows. Various preset row values are available and you can also use 'Zoom tracks N rows' and 'Zoom N tracks' to achieve the vertical scale of your choice.

The Quick menu

The Quick menu is a context sensitive pop-up menu opened by clicking with the right mouse button on the area of interest. The contents of the menu vary according to where you click and include only options which are relevant to the chosen area. For example, clicking in the event display opens a menu containing the Project window tools and a wide range of general editing options (Figure 4.10). This menu also varies according to whether there is an event selected and what kind of event this is. When a MIDI part is selected the Quick menu includes more MIDI related items such as the MIDI functions and advanced quantize. When an audio event is selected it contains more audio related items such as the audio processing and audio plug-in options.

   Clicking with the right mouse button in the Track list opens a Quick menu with functions relevant to tracks such as the Add functions and Show/Hide automation options (Figure 4.11). Additional functions are added to the menu if you right click directly on a track.

Figure 4.8
The Zoom presets menu.

Info

Most of the zoom techniques described in this section can also be used in the other editing windows of Cubase (where zooming is applicable).

Figure 4.9
The Track scale menu.

Figure 4.10
The Quick menu in the event display.

Figure 4.11
The Quick menu in the track list

The Transport panel

The Transport panel is a user-configurable strip for the control of standard transport operations such as record, play, stop, rewind, and various record, playback and cycle modes. It is opened by selecting Transport panel in the Transport menu or by pressing F2 on the computer keyboard (Figure 4.12). It can be dragged to any screen position and each section of the panel can be shown/hidden by right clicking anywhere on the panel and making the desired selection from the pop-up menu. All of its parameters may be updated or manipulated in some way using either the mouse or computer keyboard commands.

Figure 4.12
The Transport panel

Apart from the obvious tape recorder style controls the Transport panel also features the following:

Linear record mode selector

This determines how Cubase behaves when recording audio or MIDI events which overlap existing events in the project. There are three modes as follows:

- Normal – any audio or MIDI recording which takes place over a passage where there is existing material does NOT overwrite the previously recorded events. It produces a new event which overlaps the existing material. In the case of MIDI events, both the new and previously recorded material is heard simultaneously. In the case of audio events, only the audio event which takes playback priority is heard (normally the event which is on top in the event display).
- Merge – for audio recording, merge produces identical behaviour to normal mode (as described above). For recording MIDI over an existing

MIDI part, any new events are merged with the existing events in the part and no new MIDI part is created.

• Replace – any audio or MIDI recording which overlaps a passage where there is existing material replaces the previously recorded events in the overlapped section.

Cycle record mode selector

The cycle record mode selector determines the manner in which recordings are made when in Cycle mode. Mix and Overwrite modes are relevant mainly to MIDI recording. Keep Last and Stacked modes are relevant to both audio and MIDI recording. The modes function as follows:

• Mix (MIDI) – the current MIDI input is added to any existing recording in the same part. This is the default mode for quickly building up a rhythm part, for example, when different elements of a drum kit can be added on each lap of the cycle.

• Overwrite (MIDI) – any MIDI input replaces any existing recordings in the same part and deletes any data which occurs after the drop-in point for the current lap of the cycle.

• Keep Last (audio and MIDI) – for MIDI recordings, each completed lap of the cycle in which there is MIDI input replaces the previously recorded lap. If you do not play anything, the existing events recorded on a previous lap are kept. For audio recordings, the last lap in the cycle which is recorded up to the end of the cycle range is kept as an audio event. All previously recorded laps are kept within the audio file and may be accessed via the regions settings or other manipulations of the audio event (see Chapter 8 for more details).

• Stacked (audio and MIDI) – for MIDI recordings, a MIDI part for each lap of the cycle appears on its own lane within the vertical space of the MIDI track. The stacked MIDI parts can be directly spliced, muted or otherwise edited in the Project window, or edited in the Key editor. Edited parts may be later merged into a single composite part using Merge MIDI in Loop (MIDI menu). For audio recordings, an audio event for each lap of the cycle appears on its own lane within the vertical space of the audio track. The stacked events can be edited directly in the event display, making it easy to quickly build up a composite take while remaining in the Project window.

• Stacked 2 (no mute) – similar to the regular stacked mode outlined above except that previous takes are not automatically muted on each lap of the cycle. This is relevant mainly to MIDI recording and means that all recorded events are heard simultaneously (similar to overwrite mode except that the recordings are stored in separate events).

The left and right locator positions

These show the current positions of the left and right locators. Clicking on either of the L and R boxes moves the project cursor to the respective positions in the event display. Clicking and on any part of the locator position number or double-clicking the whole number allows you to enter a numerical value from the computer keyboard. The left and right locators can also be set by dragging the locator pointers in the ruler.

The automatic quantize button (AQ)

Used to automatically quantize a performance as it is recorded according to the quantize value set in the Quantize type menu.

The punch in and out buttons

For automatically dropping in and out of record mode at the left and right locator positions. If 'Start record at left locator' is activated in the Transport menu, Cubase always starts recording from the left locator position and when record mode is implemented the punch in button is automatically selected. However, if Cubase is rewound to a point some bars before the left locator and put into play with the punch in button manually selected, Cubase drops in to record when it reaches the left locator position. If the punch out button has also been selected, Cubase drops out of record at the right locator position. Otherwise it remains in record mode until you stop the sequencer.

Pre and post-roll parameters

The pre-roll field determines the number of bars of pre-roll which occurs when you implement playback or record. The post-roll field determines the number of bars of post-roll which occurs after dropping out of record. The latter is only relevant when you use the punch out button. To enable pre and post roll, activate 'pre/post roll' in the Transport menu or click on the pre/post roll buttons on the Transport panel.

Shuttle speed and jog wheels

The Transport panel features a useful dual dial control which helps you find specific audio material and locations within your project. This is useful for lining up the project cursor to audio cues prior to using split at cursor (Edit menu) or dropping a marker, for example. The outer dial is the shuttle speed dial which allows you to monitor the audio as you move the project cursor forwards or backwards within the material. This is a bit like standard fast forward and rewind except you can still hear the audio. The further round you drag the dial from its centre position the faster the playback speed (normal or reverse playback depending on which side of the centre position you drag the dial). The inner dial is the jog wheel. This also allows you to move the project cursor while still hearing the audio but, this time, is designed for jogging back and forth over a smaller section of material, much like a traditional jog wheel designed for lining up the playback heads of a tape machine to a specific location on tape. The jog wheel is an infinite wheel with no minimum or maximum positions so you can continuously rotate it in either direction to find the desired audio point. The centre of the dial features + and – nudge buttons. These allow you to nudge the project cursor position backwards or forwards one frame at a time (according to the current time code frame rate). These buttons are useful for fine tuning the position of the project cursor to very precise locations.

Info

When the time format is set to bars and beats the position display shows the project cursor position in bars, beats, sixteenth notes and ticks (by default, there are 120 ticks in each sixteenth note).

The position display and position slider

The position display shows the current project cursor position in two displays; the primary and secondary time displays. The primary time display is selected for the project in Project setup (Project menu) or by making a selection from the pop-up menu to the right of the primary time display or to the right of the ruler. The secondary time format is selected from the pop-up menu to the right of the secondary time display. Clicking on any part of the position display or double-clicking on it allows you to enter a numerical value from the computer keyboard. The + and – buttons allow you to move the cursor position forwards or backwards one bar, one frame, one second or one sample at a time depending on which time format has been chosen. The position slider is found just below the position display and can be used to quickly slide back and forth within the project.

Tip

To set up a click which is heard before recording commences but not during the performance, disable the click button and enable the precount button. Define the number of bars of pre-count in the Metronome setup dialogue.

The click on/off and pre-count buttons

The click button enables / disables the guide click and the pre-count button enables / disables a pre-count click for recording purposes. The number of bars for the pre-count is defined in the Metronome setup dialogue. When pre-count is activated, pre-roll is de-activated, and vice versa.

The tempo track mode and tempo/time signature displays

The tempo track mode allows the changing of the tempo behaviour between fixed and track modes. In fixed mode, the tempo follows the single tempo and time signature settings as shown in the Transport panel. In tempo track mode, the tempo follows any tempo and time signature changes as found in the Tempo track. The tempo is shown in beats per minute (BPM).

The sync button

For activating or de-activating synchronisation to an external time code generating device. When de-activated (set to INT), Cubase uses the internal timing clock of the computer for all tempo and time-based functions. When activated, Cubase may be slaved to an external clock for synchronisation with other sequencers, tape machines and drum machines.

Track types

Cubase features a number of different track types, each specialised in the handling of its own kind of data, and each displayed with a unique graphical symbol in the track list of the Project window (Figure 4.13). The main track types are described in the following sections.

Tip

Ctrl / Command click on the Click, Tempo and Sync buttons to open the Metronome, Tempo and Sync Setup windows respectively.

Figure 4.13
The different track types in the track list

Audio tracks

To create an Audio track select Add track/Audio in the Project menu. In the dialogue which appears you can choose the track count and the mono, stereo or multi-channel attributes of the track. You can also make a choice from the Track presets list by activating Browse presets. Audio tracks are for the recording and playback of audio signals. Recorded audio data is stored on hard disk and represented in the Project window within graphical blocks known as audio events. The audio data within each event is shown as a waveform. Audio events may also be grouped within other graphical blocks known as Audio parts. These are useful for grouping events together for editing purposes and the simplification of the display. Audio events and parts may be selected, moved, split and edited in a multitude of different ways using the editing tools and other functions. Audio tracks and audio recording are explained in more detail in Chapters 3, 7 and 8.

Figure 4.14
Acoustic piano and voice recorded on stereo and mono audio tracks

MIDI tracks

To create a MIDI track select Add track/MIDI in the Project menu. In the dialogue which appears you can choose the track count and, if desired, make a choice from the Track presets list by activating Browse presets. MIDI tracks are for the recording and playback of MIDI data. MIDI data is a sequence of digital instructions representing a musical performance, such as the sequence of keys pressed on your MIDI keyboard. MIDI data is represented in the Project window within graphical blocks known as MIDI parts. The MIDI data within each part is shown as notes, lines or drum symbols. MIDI parts may be selected, moved, split and edited in a multitude of different ways using the editing tools and other functions. MIDI tracks and MIDI recording are explained in more detail in Chapters 3, 5 and 6.

Figure 4.15
MIDI tracks in the Project window

Instrument tracks

Instrument tracks are a hybrid track type for the recording and playback of MIDI data which exclusively triggers a single VST Instrument. To create an Instrument track select Add track/Instrument in the Project menu. In the dialogue which appears you can choose the track count and VST Instrument and, if desired, make a choice from the presets list by activating Browse presets.

If you also activate the MIDI Input button in the Viewer section of the Browser, you can preview the presets by playing your MIDI keyboard before you actually create the Instrument track. An Instrument track provides one MIDI input and one stereo audio output, linking a MIDI-based track in the Project window to a VST instrument-based channel in the Mixer.

Figure 4.16
An Instrument track set up to trigger the supplied HalionOne sampler

Info

Similar VST Instrument tracks are created when you load a VST instrument in the VST Instrument panel (F11). These are displayed with the same colour and symbol as normal Instrument tracks but they are automatically grouped within the VST Instruments folder. These do not feature MIDI functionality and exist to provide audio output from the VST instrument and mixing controls on one or more channels in the Mixer. VST instruments activated in this way must be separately triggered from conventional MIDI tracks.

Arranger track

Description and user guide

The Arranger track is a special non-linear playback track which allows you to play different sections of your musical arrangements in any order and with any number of repeats. This could be likened to a pattern-based sequencer where various preset patterns can be chained together to form a musical composition.

There can be only one Arranger track in each Cubase project. It is managed in the Project window, the Inspector or the Arranger editor. To start using the Arranger track proceed as follows:

• Add the Arranger track to an existing project by selecting Add Track / Arranger track in the Project menu. The Arranger track appears in the Project window.
• Create some events in the new Arranger track which correspond musically with the existing arrangement by dragging across the Arranger track display with the draw tool (Figure 4.17). By default, new Arranger

Figure 4.17
Arranger parts in the event display

Figure 4.18
Drag and drop Arranger events into the current Arranger chain in the Inspector

Figure 4.19
Experimenting with Arranger events on a drum loop to create a new rhythm

events are named with the letters of the alphabet but the name may be changed on the infoline.
- Select the Arranger track and open the Inspector by clicking on the Show Inspector button on the toolbar. Alternatively, open the Arranger editor by clicking on the edit button in the Arranger track header.
- Drag and drop Arranger events from the Arranger events section of the Inspector (or Arranger editor) into the current Arranger chain (Figure 4.18). You can arrange the parts in any order you wish and adjust the number of repeats for each event in the right-hand column.
- Activate Arranger mode by clicking on the Arranger mode button in the track header of the Arranger track or in the Arranger section of the Transport panel. Playback is now governed by the order of events in the Arranger chain.

Arranger track creative techniques

The Arranger track is a great tool for remixing and loop-based dance styles. It would normally be used to re-order the sequence of events in an existing musical arrangement. For example, rather than start at the beginning of the song, you could start on the ad-lib chorus section at the end, and if the second and third bar of the solo section contains a great hook line, you could loop it twice before the start of the first verse. When working with repetitive loops, it is easy to chain your patterns together with the desired number of repeats in the Arranger chain. There are a wide range of possibilities for creatively re-arranging any existing musical structure.

The Arranger track may also be used in a more experimental way to generate new ideas. For example, try setting up an Arranger sequence within a drum loop using relatively short Arranger events of one, two and four beats in length. This is a good loop mangling technique and can help create new drum rhythms (Figure 4.19). The same technique can be used for the creative manipulation of abstract and time-stretched sound effects. Remember that Arranger events can be nested inside each other allowing you to use events of varying lengths repeatedly over the same passage (see parts E and F in Figure 4.19).

Several Arranger chains may be held in memory at the same time allowing you to develop a number of different musical arrangements within the same project. When you are happy with a new Arranger chain of events you may wish to convert it into a conventional linear arrangement. This is achieved by selecting Flatten Chain in the pop-up Arranger menu in the Inspector, or by clicking on the Flatten button in the Arranger editor. Upon selection, all relevant events are rearranged, split and repeated as necessary across the event display in a linear manner corresponding to the order of events in the current Arranger chain, and the Arranger track itself is closed. All material which is not used in the Arranger chain is deleted from the event display. Use the standard undo command if you wish to go back to the original linear version of the project.

Folder tracks

A folder track is a 'container' track for any number of other tracks, much like the folders you use to store files on your computer's hard disk. In the same way that creating a filing system on your hard disk helps organise your data, creating folder tracks in Cubase helps organise complex musical arrangements and keeps the event display uncluttered..

To create a folder track, use Add track in the Project menu and select Folder. A new folder track appears in the event display. Once the folder track is available you can drag and drop other tracks into the folder track. A green arrow appears over the folder track each time you drag another track into the appropriate position to be dropped. All track types may be dragged into a folder track, including other folder tracks. A closed folder track looks similar to that shown in Figure 4.20. The folder track can be sized and named like

Figure 4.20
A closed folder track

any other track and most basic tool editing techniques are still valid, such as splitting, erasing, muting and so on. You can open or close a folder track by clicking on the folder icon. Figure 4.21 shows the event display when the folder track in Figure 4.20 is opened.

Figure 4.21
The same folder track opened in the event display

Folder tracks are generally used for keeping different instrument categories in the same location to help clarify the display and the musical structure. Common Folder track categories include drums, percussion, strings, brass and vocals for popular music or, for an orchestra, you might choose double bass, cellos, violas, violins, woodwinds, brass and percussion. Folder tracks can free up lots of space in the event display and are therefore indispensable for projects with large track counts. They are also good for soloing and muting purposes where you might like to solo or mute whole sections of the arrangement rather than individual tracks. Or if you are working on a lead vocal part, you might like to put all the instrumental tracks into a separate folder so that you can focus on the vocal track alone.

Info

Cubase also supports input / output buss and video tracks. The input / output buss tracks are for the management of any mix automation data from the input / output busses. Video tracks are for the display of video files when you are working on sound to picture projects. These elements are covered in other chapters.

Group tracks

Info

Group tracks should not be confused with Folder tracks. Folder tracks are concerned with visual presentation and editing in the event display, whereas Group tracks are concerned with audio signal routing. For more information on Group tracks, see Chapter 11.

To create a Group track select Add track/Group in the Project menu. In the dialogue which appears you can choose the track count and the mono, stereo or multi-channel attributes of the track. Group tracks are analogous to the Group busses found on traditional mixing consoles. Essentially, Group tracks provide a logical routing buss when you wish to group a number of audio signals onto a single fader in the Mixer. For example, it is common practice to group all the audio tracks of a drum kit onto a single stereo Group track, allowing level, EQ and effects changes for the whole drum kit to be achieved more easily. Since Group tracks are primarily concerned with how you route your signals they are more relevant in the Mixer, where they appear as channel strips. In the Project window, a Group track appears in a similar fashion to other track types except that it can never contain audio events. However, its presence there allows you to automate its level and other parameters using the automation curves.

Figure 4.22
Group tracks do not contain audio events but their presence in the event display allows you to create and edit Group track automation

The Marker track and Marker window

The Marker track and Marker window are for managing guide markers inserted along the time line of your project. Markers allow you to quickly move to any position within your project and to set up cycle loops (for recording and playback purposes). To open the Marker track select Add track/Marker in the Project menu (Figure 4.23). The Marker track differs from the other track types in the sense that only one Marker track can be present for each project. Deleting the track merely removes it from view, it does not delete the data and all marker data is still present when you re-open the track. The Marker window provides a list-based overview of all markers and allows you to edit and name them as desired. There are three different types of markers: the left and right locators, cycle markers and standard markers. The Marker track and Marker window essentially deal with the same data but the Marker track allows a graphical approach whereas the Marker window provides a text-based list.

Figure 4.23
The Marker track in the event display

Adding markers

There are a number of ways to add markers as follows:

1   To add standard markers, click on the add marker button found in the track list section of the Marker track, press the insert key on the computer keyboard or click in the Marker track with the draw tool. You can also add standard markers by clicking with the object selection tool while holding Alt. Standard markers are placed at the current location of the project cursor and are automatically numbered in ascending order as they are added. Standard markers appear as vertical blue lines. They can be added on the fly (while in playback mode) or while Cubase is static. Standard markers are named in the Infoline.
2   To add cycle markers, click on the add cycle marker button found in the track list section of the Marker track. You can also assign a key command to this function in File / Key Commands. The latter functions insert the cycle markers between the left and right locators and they are automatically numbered in ascending order as they are added. Alternatively, cycle markers may be added by dragging in the Marker track with the draw tool. They appear as downward facing brackets between the left and right locator positions and may be colour coded. Cycle markers are named in the Infoline.

Editing markers

Markers are edited in a similar manner to other events in the event display. Marker events are selected by clicking on them with the object selection tool, they are deleted using the erase tool, and cycle marker events are split into two by clicking with the split tool on the horizontal line between the two cycle points. Markers may also be viewed and edited in the Inspector and the Project Browser.

The Marker window

The Marker window displays the Marker track data in list format. Any changes made in either the Marker window or the Marker track are reflected in both. Select Markers from the Project menu or Ctrl + M (PC) / Command + M (Mac) to open the Marker window (Figure 4.24).

> **Tip**
>
> You can drag the Marker track to any position in the track list. If you use the divide track list button, the Marker track automatically appears in the upper pane.

> **Tip**
>
> When the snap button is active, all marker input and editing is magnetic to the current snap resolution.

> **Info**
>
> Removing the Marker track from the track list does not remove the marker data. All data remains intact and available in other parts of the program.

Figure 4.24
The Marker window

The Marker window features a number of columns for the display of marker information. These include the following:

- ID – shows the ID number for the marker.
- Position – shows the ruler position for the marker (or the start position in the case of cycle markers).
- End – shows the end position of cycle markers.
- Length – shows the length of cycle markers.
- Description – allows you to enter a description or name for the marker or cycle marker. The left and right marker names cannot be changed.

The Marker window provides a useful overview of all the markers in the project and allows you to filter the different marker types in the show menu.

Using the markers

There are a wide range of uses for markers including marking points of interest within your music, labelling sections of your arrangement so that you can see its structure more clearly and setting up cycle loops for playback and recording purposes. For example, one classic use of markers is to mark the intro, verse, chorus, bridge, break (and so on) of a song structure. In addition, there are a number of techniques associated with markers which make navigating within your project a whole lot easier. Try the following:

- Double click between any two markers with the pointer tool to select all events in the bars between them.
- Double click between any two markers with the range selection tool to select the precise range in the bars between them.
- Double click on any standard marker to move the project cursor to the markers location.
- Double click inside any cycle marker to move the left and right locators to the start and end of the cycle range.
- Select numeric keypad numbers 3 to 9 to move the project cursor to marker numbers 3 to 9.
- In the Marker track header in the track list, open the locate pop-up menu to navigate to any one of the available markers. Open the cycle marker pop-up menu to move the left and right locators to the start and end of a chosen cycle marker range. Open the zoom pop-up menu to zoom in to a chosen cycle marker range.

Tip

By default, numeric keypad numbers 3 to 9 are the key commands for standard marker numbers 3 to 9. Also try using the markers box in the toolbar or Transport panel.

Track presets

Introduction

As well as including a wide range of presets for the on-board VST instruments and audio effects, Cubase also includes a special category of preset known as a Track preset. Presets in general are handled via the SoundFrame universal media management features which aims to centralise the handling of all audio files, MIDI files, Track presets, VST plug-in presets, video files and Cubase project files found on the hard disk(s) of the host computer. Track presets are relevant to audio, instrument and MIDI tracks (or multiple numbers of these track types) and are accessible from various locations within the Project window. They are also handled in the MediaBay, Loop browser or SoundFrame browser (Media menu). Track presets allow you to store or recall all the important channel settings for a track, including combinations of the insert effects, EQ, volume, gain, phase, VST instrument setup, MIDI Modifiers, MIDI Input Transformer, and MIDI output routing parameters, depending upon the track type.

The advantages of Track presets
The advantages of Track presets include:

- convenient addition of tracks which are already set up for specific sounds or instruments
- rapid modification of multiple settings for comparative or experimental purposes
- easy exchange of track settings between projects
- direct drag and drop from the SoundFrame browser onto the track list.

Adding a track using a Track preset
To create an Audio, MIDI or Instrument track from a Track preset, select Add track followed by the chosen track type in the Project menu. In the dialogue which appears, open the browser by clicking on the Browse presets button. The browser window includes the filter section (left) where you can filter the display according to name and category, and the viewer (right) where you can select from a list of presets (Figure 4.25). For MIDI and Instrument tracks, activating the MIDI Input button allows you to preview the presets by playing your MIDI keyboard before you actually create the track. When you are happy with your choice click on OK to add the track and close the window.

Figure 4.25
The Track preset browser for an Instrument track filtered to show only those presets in the Bass category

Applying a track preset to an existing track
Track presets may be applied to existing tracks using the Apply Track preset field in the Inspector or by right-clicking on the track to open the Quick menu and selecting Apply Track preset. This opens the Apply Track preset window

which operates in the same manner as the Track preset browser shown in Figure 4.25, above. Great care must be taken when applying Track presets to existing tracks since confirming your preset choice by clicking on the OK button sets the track permanently to the new settings. The rule here is to 'try before you apply'. In other words, always audition the presets while still remaining in the Apply presets dialogue. If you are not happy with the new settings click on the Cancel button to close the dialogue. This reverts to the original track settings as set before you opened the dialogue.

Creating your own track presets

To create your own Track preset, set up the track with the desired effects, EQ, and so on and right-click on the track in the track list to open the Quick menu. Select Create Track preset to open the Create Track preset dialogue (Figure 4.26). Click on the Tag button to open the Tag editor. The Tag editor allows you to define the Category, Character, Style and Sub Category for the preset (if required). This helps you recall presets from the Track presets browser more easily by filtering the data (as shown in Figure 4.25, above).

Figure 4.26
The Create Track preset dialogue for a MIDI track

The Inspector

The Inspector is found in the Project window to the left of the track list. It is opened and closed by clicking on the Show Inspector button in the toolbar. The Inspector contains a number of parameters and sub-sections associated with the currently selected track. It varies according to what type of track is selected. Among the two most important Inspector configurations are those for MIDI and audio tracks and these are outlined below.

The Inspector for MIDI tracks

For MIDI tracks, the Inspector features a basic settings section and seven optional sections. The tabs for the optional sections are made visible from a pop-up menu which appears when you right-click anywhere on the Inspector. Each section is opened by clicking on the corresponding tab.

Basic track settings

The basic track settings section features the MIDI track name, the mute and solo buttons, the read and write buttons for track automation, the Input Transformer button for real-time MIDI data transformation, the record and monitor buttons for record-enabling and monitor enabling, the linear/musical timebase button for switching between time (non-tempo dependent) or beat based (tempo dependent) positioning of events, the lock button for locking the attributes of events on the selected track and the lane display type button for managing lanes within the vertical space of the track. The edit channel settings button next to the name opens the channel settings window where you see a combined overview of the channel fader, insert effects, send effects and other elements within a separate window. Below the buttons there are mini-faders for controlling the MIDI volume, pan and delay time (in milliseconds). Below this there are fields for input and output routing, MIDI channel and edit instrument functions (if a VST instrument is triggered from the channel), program name (or number), MIDI drum map setup and Track preset fields.

Volume and pan are useful for quickly setting up the basic level and pan position without opening the Mixer. Delay is good for shifting the track backwards or forwards relative to the others, thus changing the feel of the music. This might include adjusting a snare or hi-hat track to be late or early, or shifting a slow strings sound earlier to anticipate the beat. The program field changes the program number / patch in the target MIDI unit / VST instrument. This is good for quickly searching for the desired patch on a synth while still remaining within the convenient environment of the Project window.

MIDI modifiers

The MIDI modifiers section features controls for the real-time manipulation of MIDI data. These include the following:

- Transpose – for transposing MIDI notes up or down (range: -127 to +127)
- Velocity shift – for adding / subtracting an amount to the velocity of MIDI notes (range: -127 to +127)
- Velocity compression – for compressing / expanding the velocity of MIDI notes according to a ratio.
- Length compression – for compressing / expanding the length of MIDI notes according to a ratio.
- Random – for adding / subtracting random numbers between a chosen minimum and maximum value. Random acts upon position, pitch, velocity or length and features two independent random fields.
- Range – for limiting / filtering MIDI notes (or notes of a chosen velocity) between a chosen minimum and maximum value. Range features a choice of velocity limit, velocity filter, note limit or note filter with two independent range fields.

Transpose can be used for trying out simple harmonies or shifting the octave for any given sound, as well as corrective transposing. Velocity shift affects the overall velocity of the MIDI data and is useful for increasing / decreasing the global intensity of a performance. Velocity shift and velocity compression might be used together to flatten out the dynamics of an over-excited track (try settings of +60 for velocity shift with 2/3 for velocity compression). Length can emphasise the staccato feel of a track by using a setting of 1/3 or 1/4. To increase a tracks legato try a value of 3/1 or more. The random section is good for humanising a MIDI performance. Try setting the first random field to position with minimum at 0 and maximum at 6, and the second random field to velocity with minimum at -20 and maximum at +20. This avoids robotic MIDI parts.

Figure 4.27
Basic track settings (Inspector for MIDI tracks)

Figure 4.28
MIDI modifiers (Inspector for MIDI tracks)

Figure 4.29
MIDI Inserts (Inspector for MIDI tracks)

Figure 4.30 (right)
MIDI Sends (Inspector for MIDI tracks)

Figure 4.31 (far right)
MIDI fader section (Inspector for MIDI tracks)

MIDI Inserts

The Inserts section features four slots for inserting MIDI effects plug-ins into the MIDI data path. This is a mirror of the MIDI Inserts section for the track as found in the extended part of the Mixer. To load a MIDI effect, click on an empty Insert slot to open the effects menu. When an effect is chosen from the menu it is immediately activated and its GUI is automatically opened. Adjust the parameters as required or choose an existing preset from the presets menu of the chosen effect. Activate playback to hear the results. MIDI insert effects transform the data in real-time. The original MIDI data remains intact unless you use Merge MIDI in loop in the MIDI menu to make the effects permanent. With Insert effects the MIDI data is routed through each activated effect in turn. MIDI Insert effect combinations may be stored as presets or recalled from Track presets using the pop-up preset management menu.

MIDI Sends

The Sends section features four slots for assigning MIDI send effects (Figure 4.30). This is a mirror of the MIDI Sends section for the track as found in the extended part of the Mixer. Each MIDI track can have its own unique set of send effects and settings. The MIDI Send effects menu is the same as that for MIDI Insert effects and choosing and setting up sends is the same as for MIDI Insert effects. Similarly, the original MIDI data remains intact unless you use Merge MIDI in loop in the MIDI menu. Each send effect takes its input from the original MIDI data and both the original data and the effect data appear at the output.

MIDI Fader

The MIDI fader section (Figure 4.31) features a mirror of the fader as found in the Mixer, with an overview strip alongside. This is convenient for changing the level and pan position of the track and for applying mute, solo, read, write, bypass inserts, disable sends, record and monitoring functions, all without needing to open the Mixer.

The Inspector for audio tracks

For audio tracks, the Inspector features a basic settings section and eight optional sections. The tabs for the optional sections are made visible from a pop-up menu which appears when you right-click anywhere in the Inspector. Each section is opened by clicking on the corresponding tab.

Basic track settings

The basic track settings section for Audio tracks features a similar group of buttons and functions as the basic track settings section for MIDI tracks (see MIDI basic track settings above). The audio basic track settings also include: an Open Device panels button for setting up graphical interfaces for audio effects and track parameters. These may be activated in the User panels sections of the Inspector or Mixer; an Auto Fades settings button for setting up a short automatic cross-fade between adjacent audio events on the track; and a Freeze Audio Channel button for freezing the pre-fader insert effects on the channel when you need to reduce the load on the CPU. There are also in and out fields for selecting the input and output ports for the track.

Figure 4.32
Basic track settings (Inspector for audio tracks)

Info

Auto fade produces glitch-free transitions between adjacent audio events by applying a short automatic crossfade. This is set globally for the project in Auto fades settings in the Project menu or it can be adjusted individually for the track in the Inspector by clicking on the auto fades settings button.

Inserts

The Inserts section features eight slots for inserting audio effects plug-ins into the audio signal path. This is a mirror of the audio Inserts section for the track as found in the extended part of the Mixer. To find out more, choose an audio track and experiment with one or more audio effects in the Inserts section. To load an audio effect, click on an empty effects slot to open the effects menu. The menu features a wide range of audio effects organised into various categories including delay, distortion, dynamics, EQ, filter, modulation and others. When an effect is chosen from the menu it is immediately activated and its GUI is automatically opened. Adjust the parameters as required or choose an existing preset from the presets browser. Activate playback to hear the results. The effects processing takes place in real-time. With Insert effects the audio signal is routed through each effect in turn. (See Chapter 12 for more details about audio effects).

Figure 4.33
Inserts section (Inspector for audio tracks)

Tip

To move the contents of any insert slot to another, drag from the source insert slot number and release over the target slot. This gives total freedom to change the order of effects. Hold Alt to copy rather than move the contents.

Equalizers

The Equalizers section features a four band parametric EQ. This is a mirror of the EQ section as found in the extended part of the Mixer. The EQ section includes four numbered modules for low, lower-mid, high-mid and high frequency bands with each module consisting of Q, frequency and gain controls. Adjustments are made by dragging the mini-faders horizontally or by double-clicking on a value. There is also an Equalizer curve section which displays the equaliser settings visually as a simple curve. Click directly in the display to change the shape of the curve using the equaliser handles which appear. To delete a handle drag it out of the display. (For more information about EQ see Chapter 11).

Sends

The Sends section (Figure 4.35) features eight slots for audio send effects each with a mini-fader for regulating the audio track signal level which is sent to the effect. The choice of send effects is determined by the number of FX channel tracks which have already been created for the project. Edit buttons for each effect allow you to open its GUI directly from the Inspector. The sends section is a mirror of the audio Sends section for the track as found in the extended part of the Mixer. The supplied effects are the same as those for the audio Insert effects (see above). To find out more, choose an audio track and experiment with one or more audio send effects. Audio send effects transform the signal in real-time. With send effects the original audio signal (dry signal) is mixed with the FX channel signal (wet signal) at the master output faders. (See Chapter 12 for more details about audio effects).

Studio Sends

Cubase features a special monitoring and signal distribution mixer known as the Control Room Mixer. This allows you to manage monitoring levels, multiple mix configurations, talkback and listen functions separately from the main mixer. The setup for the Control Room

Figure 4.34
Equalizers and Equalizer curve sections (Inspector for audio tracks)

Figure 4.35
Sends section (Inspector for audio tracks)

Mixer takes place in the VST Connections window in the Studio section. This is where you activate the Studio sends (Figure 4.36). Once activated, a Studio Send module becomes visible in the Control Room Mixer, and the corresponding Studio Send is available in the Studio Sends section of all audio-based channels. You can have up to four Studio Sends, each of which may be sent to a different destination (for example, to headphone mixes, to performance area monitoring speakers or any other suitable destination). What we see in the Inspector is a mirror of the Studio Sends section as found in the extended part of the Mixer. Each Studio Send slot features a mini-fader for level control and a pan parameter. These are all you need to set up separate mixes for each Studio Send. See Chapter 11 for more details about the Control Room Mixer and Studio Sends.

Figure 4.36
Studio Sends section (Inspector for audio tracks)

Figure 4.37
Channel section (Inspector for audio tracks)

Channel

The Channel section (Figure 4.37) is a mirror of the channel fader as found in the Mixer, with an overview strip alongside. This is convenient for changing the level and pan position of the track and for activating mute, solo, listen, read, write, edit, bypass inserts, bypass EQ, disable sends, record and monitoring functions, all without needing to open the Mixer.

Info

To set up your own presets for what sections are available in the Inspector, right click / Ctrl click anywhere in the Inspector panel and select Setup in the pop-up menu. This opens a dialogue where you can manage what tabs are visible or hidden. Each combination may be saved as a preset.

Using the tools

Arranging and editing the events in the event display is among the principal functions of the Project window and once you have recorded a number of audio events or MIDI parts you will almost certainly wish to edit them in some way. This requires a good knowledge of how to use the tools in the toolbar. Using the tools is among the most important skills in the confident handling of Cubase. See Table 4.1 for a summary of the main tool functions.

Table 4.1 Tool function table

Tool	Keys held PC	Mac	Mouse action	Result
object selection	-	-	double-click between locators	creates a new empty part
	-	-	click on event	selects event
	-	-	click in empty space and drag	opens rectangular selection box
	-	-	click on event(s) and drag	moves event(s)
	alt	alt	click on event(s) and drag	copies event(s)
	alt	alt	drag lower right corner of event	repeats event
	alt+shift	alt+shift	click on event and drag	copies event as a shared copy
range selection	-	-	click and drag	selects 'event-independent' range
split	-	-	click on event	splits event at mouse position
	alt	alt	click on event	splits event into several events
glue	-	-	click on event	joins event to the next event
	alt	alt	click on event	joins event to all those following
erase	-	-	click on event(s)	erases event(s)
	alt	alt	click on event	erases event and all those following
zoom	-	-	click in display	zooms in
	alt	alt	click in display	zooms out
mute	-	-	click on event	mutes the event
draw	-	-	click in empty space and drag	creates a new empty part
	-	-	drag within audio event	creates volume curve
play	-	-	click on event	plays event data at normal speed
scrub	-	-	drag over event	plays event data at drag speed

Common event editing operations include selecting, moving, duplicating, splitting, joining, resizing, fading, muting and erasing. If you have not yet recorded a number of events in the Project window use the events created in the recording exercises outlined in Chapter 3 as test material.

Selecting

Selecting, in itself, does not involve the direct editing of events but it is an important step before other editing operations take place. For selecting, Cubase provides the object selection and range selection tools. Any object in the event display may be selected by clicking on it with the object selection tool. Dragging a selection box around a number of events allows you to select a number of objects in one move. Holding the Shift key on the computer keyboard allows you to add to (or subtract from) an existing selection by clicking on single objects one at a time. All selections made with the object selection tool involve whole events. Conversely, the range selection tool allows event-independent selections. To use the range selection tool, drag the capture zone across the required bar and track range in the event display.

Figure 4.38
Selecting an event in the event display

Info

The range sub-menu of the Edit menu becomes active when you make a selection using the Range tool. This is useful for cut, copy and paste operations and also features special delete time, cut time and paste time options. Delete time deletes the range selection and moves all following events on the track leftwards to close the gap. Cut time is similar but also copies the deleted range to the clipboard. Paste time copies the clipboard onto a track at the start point of the range selection and moves all following events rightwards to make room for the pasted data.

Tip

Right-click in empty space in the event display to open a context sensitive pop-up menu (known as the Quick menu) containing the tools and a wide range of editing functions.

Moving

To move an event to a new position in the display, select the object selection tool, click on the event and drag it to a new position. More than one event can be moved simultaneously by clicking in empty space and dragging a selection box around several events. Clicking and dragging on any one of the selected events allows you to move all the events to a new location. Alternatively, try using the range selection tool to select an event-independent range within the display. The selection can then be moved to a new position in the same way, (events are automatically split at the appropriate positions). If the snap button is active, dragged events are magnetic to the snap resolution.

Tip

To move an event one tick at a time, select the event, place the pointer over the start tick value on the info line, and turn the wheel of your mouse.

Figure 4.39
Moving an event

Duplicating

To duplicate an event, select the object selection tool, click on the event and drag while holding Alt on the computer keyboard. A duplicate event is created which can be placed at a new location in the event display. Holding Shift + Alt while dragging the event creates a shared copy. Any subsequent audio or MIDI processing which takes place on one of the shared copies affects all the others simultaneously. Duplicating audio events always results in shared copies since the events are always referenced to the same audio clip. Shared copies can be converted to independent events by selecting convert to real copy in the edit menu.

Figure 4.40
Duplicating an event

Info

To duplicate a number of consecutive events (i.e. to repeat the events) select Repeat in the Edit menu (Ctrl/Command + K) and enter the number of repeats required in the pop-up dialogue. Alternatively, select Duplicate in the Edit menu (Ctrl/Command + D).

Splitting

To split an event, select the split tool (scissors) and click on the event at the point you wish to implement the split. If the snap button is active, the split point is magnetic to the snap resolution. The event is divided into two separate events. Holding Alt while clicking on an event, splits the event into a number of smaller parts at the resolution of the snap setting.

Figure 4.41
Splitting an event

Joining

To join one event to a following event, select the glue tool and click on the first of the events. In the case of MIDI material, the first part is joined to the second to make one longer MIDI part. In the case of audio material, the audio events are grouped together within a single audio part. Holding Alt while clicking on an event, joins all following contiguous events into one long event.

Figure 4.42
Joining events

Resizing

To resize events drag one of the small square handles which appear in the lower corners of the start and end points of the event when it is selected. A double arrow appears when you have placed the mouse in the correct position to begin resizing. For this purpose, the object selection tool is available in three modes; normal sizing, sizing moves contents and sizing applies time stretch. 'Normal sizing' resizes the object without making any changes to the data; it simply hides existing data when you reduce the size and adds blank space when you increase it. 'Sizing moves contents' moves the contents of an event forward or backward in time by locking the start or end of the contents to the start or end of the object. 'Sizing applies time stretch' stretches (or compresses) the contents of an object when you re-size it.

Normal resizing is helpful when you need to quickly top and tail an event to hear only the desired part of the audio. This applies to audio recordings where unwanted noise may have been recorded before or after the musical performance. 'Sizing moves contents' is useful when you do not want the contents at the start or end of the event to change when you drag the start and end handles. 'Sizing applies time stretch' is sometimes convenient for changing the length and tempo of drum loops to fit the current tempo of Cubase. Extreme time stretching manipulations are good for experimentation and producing sound effects.

> **Tip**
>
> Most of the tools are endowed with alternative behaviour when used in combination with the modifier keys (Shift, Ctrl, Alt, Apple command). Check out Table 4.1 for some the commonly used combinations.

Figure 4.43
Resizing an event

Fading and volume control

To fade an audio event in or out, select the event with the object selection tool and drag the blue handle in the upper left corner to create a fade in, or drag the blue handle in the upper right corner to create a fade out. The fade curve can be modified by double clicking above the curve in the display and changing the settings in the fade dialogue which appears. The middle blue handle is for modifying the volume of the event. The fade and volume handles are available for audio events only.

Figure 4.44
Creating a fade in for an event

If you need to create elaborate volume curves for audio events, Cubase features volume events. These provide a basic alternative to regular automation and have the advantage of being attached permanently to the event. To create a volume curve for an audio event proceed as follows: select the draw tool and place it within the event (a small volume curve symbol appears beside the tool). Select the event and click with the tool to insert volume handles. Drag the handles within the event to form the desired curve (see Figure 4.45). Volume events are deleted by holding the Shift key while clicking upon a volume handle.

Figure 4.45
Creating volume events within an audio event

Muting

To mute an event, select the mute tool and click on the event. You can also drag a selection box over several events to mute a number of objects simultaneously. A muted event is displayed in grey.

Figure 4.46
Muting an event

Erasing

To erase an event, select the erase tool and click once on the event. Multiple events can be deleted by selecting a group of objects and clicking once on any one of them. Holding Alt while clicking on an event deletes the event and all those which follow it on the same track.

Figure 4.47
Erasing an event

Visual clarification

The above outlines some of the tool-based event editing techniques in the Project window. More elaborate techniques in the various editors are explored in chapters 6 and 8. Figure 4.36 provides visual clarification of the basics.

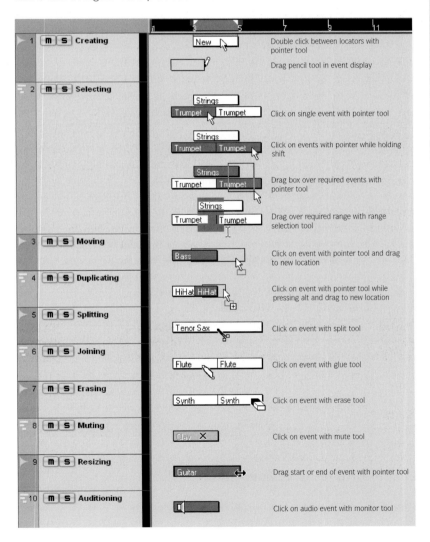

Figure 4.48
Basic event editing

Saving and opening details

Cubase supports a number of different file types for the saving and loading of data. These should be fully understood before you embark upon any serious projects. Most files are handled using the options in the File menu which include regular open and save options for native Cubase files and import and export options for file types which are not exclusive to Cubase. The type of file to be opened or saved is often recognised by its file extension and the following are the main possibilities:

Cubase project files (file extension: cpr)

Cubase project files are used to save and load all the relevant data of a Cubase project, except for the audio files themselves and various Cubase global preference settings. Cubase project files are also used to create templates. Templates are preset environments which you can prepare in advance for specific types of projects (such as 24 track audio recording, 16 track surround mixing or stereo mastering). To save a template select Save as Template in the File menu. To open a template select New project in the File menu.

Import audio files (file extensions: wav, aif, aifc, aiff, rex, rx2, sd2, mp3, mp2, mpeg, ogg, wma, w64)

Cubase can import a wide range of audio file formats. Wav is the standard audio file format used on PC computers, aif is the standard audio file format used on Mac computers and mp3 (mpeg layer 3) is a compressed audio file format designed for use with the internet. Audio files can be imported directly into the event display by selecting Import Audio file in the File menu or by dragging and dropping an audio file from the desktop. When using Import Audio File, the audio material is 'dropped' into the event display at the position of the project cursor. When dragging and dropping files the audio is dropped at the position where the mouse was released taking the current snap setting into consideration. Mp3 files are first converted into wav files before being used within Cubase.

Rex and rx2 are the file extensions for files created in Propellerheads Recycle program. Recycle is a separate program which is specialised in the processing and manipulation of audio loops. A rex file is an audio file which has been sliced up into its constituent parts thereby making it easier to manipulate in Cubase. Once imported into the program, Cubases tempo can be freely changed and the rex file automatically adjusts itself to the new tempo without affecting the pitch of the sound. You can make your own rex files if you have Recycle or alternatively they are supplied on sample CDs. Rex files cannot be created within Cubase and it is therefore an import-only format.

Export audio files (file extensions: wav, aif, mp3, wma, wav [broadcast wave])

Cubases Export option in the File menu allows the exporting of audio in the Project window between the left and right locators in most of the main audio file formats. The Export Audio Mixdown dialogue allows the exporting of audio files in mono, split stereo and stereo interleaved, and in multi-channel file formats. Bit resolutions between 8-bit and 32-bit float with sample rates between 8 and 96kHz ensure compatibility with just about any possible digital audio standard.

Import and export of standard MIDI files (file extension: mid)

A MIDI file is a special file format designed to allow the transfer of music between different makes of MIDI sequencer and between different platforms.

MIDI files come in two formats: type 0 and type 1. Type 0 files always contain only one track which plays back on many MIDI channels. Type 1 files contain the original track structure of the material and include two or more tracks on separate MIDI channels.

To export a MIDI file, select File / Export / MIDI file. After choosing a name for the file, an Export options dialogue appears. To save as a type 0 file select the type 0 box. De-select the type 0 box to save as type 1. Select the other options in the dialogue as appropriate. All settings in the Tempo track are saved in the MIDI file and all un-muted parts are included.   To import a MIDI file, select File / Import / MIDI file. Cubase recognises both MIDI file formats when importing and files may be imported into the current project at the left locator position or into a new Project.

Drum map setup files (file extension: drm)

Drum map setup files are used to load and save drum maps. A drum map defines which MIDI notes correspond with which drum sounds in the target device. Drum maps are designed and managed within the Drum Map setup window (MIDI menu / Drum Map Setup). Open the Functions menu above the map list to load or save a drum map.

Progress report

This chapter has helped you become familiar with the most important aspects of the Project window, which is of central importance to the successful handling of the program. You may have noticed that you can accomplish most routine recording, playback and editing tasks while still remaining in the Project window and that you can configure the controls to suit your own particular way of working. All this forms part of the design principle of the Project window: to provide a comfortable, personalised and streamlined software environment where you can achieve an awful lot within a small amount of screen space. Many of the skills and tools used within the Project window are transferable to other parts of the program. We have only just scratched the surface of the available possibilities within Cubase, but we are now armed with some of the essential tools with which to go on to more musically meaningful pursuits and serious recording tasks.

MIDI recording

This chapter outlines basic MIDI theory, explains how to set up a MIDI network and features some practical MIDI recording techniques for Cubase. Understanding the theory behind MIDI and setting up a logical MIDI network helps you get the most out of MIDI recording.

MIDI basics

What is MIDI?

MIDI (Musical Instrument Digital Interface) is a data communication standard, first established in 1983, for the exchange of musical information between electronic musical instruments and, subsequently, computers. It involves the serial transfer of digital information via cables terminated with 5 pin DIN connectors.

MIDI messages

MIDI is governed by a pre-defined set of rules known as the MIDI Specification. Just as the grammatical rules found in a regular language tell us how to form a sentence, the MIDI specification tells us how MIDI data should be sent and received in packets known as 'MIDI messages'. The first MIDI message to understand is that which describes the action of pressing a key on a musical keyboard. In MIDI 'talk', this is known as a 'Note on' message. A similar message needs to be sent to describe the action of releasing the key, and this is known as a 'Note off' message. Note on and note off messages contain information about the pitch of the key being pressed and the force with which it was pressed (known as the velocity). The duration of each note is governed by the length of time between the note on and note off messages. If a note off message is not sent at some stage after the note on message then the note continues to play indefinitely.

MIDI, therefore, is like a language. MIDI devices, such as synthesizers, samplers and drum machines can 'talk' to each other using MIDI messages. The sending of these messages involves two or more MIDI devices, one which is transmitting the data and the other(s) receiving it. It is important to grasp that the transmitted data consists of a series of instructions only, there is NO audio signal within the data. Note on and off messages instruct the receiving unit(s) about which note should be played, its velocity and duration. The actual sound is chosen on the receiving unit.

MIDI connections

MIDI devices normally include In, Out and Thru ports. To transmit messages from one device to another, a MIDI Out is connected to a MIDI In of a second device (using a correctly wired MIDI cable). The MIDI Thru port passes on a copy of the messages received at the MIDI In port. This is often used to daisy-chain several units together in a simple MIDI network. So, in its simplest form, hooking up a MIDI cable from the MIDI Out of your keyboard to the MIDI In of a synth module allows you to play the two devices simultaneously. The MIDI keyboard is being triggered in the normal way from its own keyboard and the synth module is being triggered by the MIDI messages it receives via the MIDI cable.

Great! But how does this help us use the MIDI side of Cubase? Well, instead of hooking up the MIDI cable from your MIDI keyboard to a synth module, plug it into the MIDI interface of your computer setup. You can now send MIDI messages into Cubase and thereby record a musical performance.

MIDI data in Cubase

MIDI-based music recorded in Cubase is displayed as individual events. These events are grouped together in the event display inside graphical blocks known as MIDI parts. They may also be viewed in more detail in the MIDI editors, as notes on a score or graphical events on a piano-roll style grid.

Changing the sound

Once the MIDI data has been recorded, it can be transmitted to any of the MIDI devices present in your system, allowing you to mix and match the available sounds long after the original recording has been made. The sounds in your MIDI devices are usually stored as presets. Presets are also known as programs or patches and are recalled by manual selection on the unit or by sending a Program Change message via MIDI.

MIDI message types

What happens to the outgoing MIDI data if you turn the pitch wheel of your keyboard while playing a note? It is tempting to think that the MIDI note data itself is modified in some way. In fact, the note data remains the same and the pitch data is sent separately as another type of MIDI message known, not surprisingly, as a Pitch bend message. Pitch bend messages instruct the receiving unit how to bend the note(s) in question. A similar thing happens if you turn the modulation wheel. This sends out another type of message known as a Control change message (Continuous Controller). Other types of messages include Aftertouch (Channel Key pressure) and Program Change.

MIDI message types fall into two main categories: Channel and System messages. Channel messages have two sub categories known as Channel Voice messages and Channel Mode messages.

Channel Messages

Channel Voice messages

All the message types described so far come under the same category within the MIDI specification and are known as Channel Voice messages. Channel

Voice messages are characterised by the fact that MIDI channel information (see below) is embedded within the message. 'Voice' means that this type of message is directed to and controls the receiving instrument's voices (or sounds). Channel Voice messages are likely to be the message types with which you most often come into contact in the routine use of Cubase. To summarise, Channel Voice messages include the following message types:

- Note off – the releasing of a key to terminate the playing of a note.
- Note on – the pressing of a key to begin the playing of a note.
- Polyphonic Key pressure (Aftertouch) – key pressure taking into consideration the pressure applied to each individual key.
- Control Change (Continuous Controller) – for the control of various non-note parameters like modulation (vibrato), breath control, volume and pan.
- Program Change – changes the sound preset in the receiving unit.
- Channel key pressure (Aftertouch) – key pressure taken as an overall pressure reading for the MIDI channel.
- Pitch Bend – instructs the receiving unit to change (bend) the pitch of any currently sounding notes (normally sent using the pitch bend wheel of the master keyboard).

Channel Mode messages
Channel mode messages are a group of reserved control change messages (between controllers 120 and 127). These reset and change the mode of operation of the receiving device. They include the following:

- Controller 120 (All sound off) – switches off sounds on all channels.
- Controller 121 (Reset all controllers) – resets all controllers to their default parameters.
- Controller 122 (Local on/off) – Local off disconnects the keyboard from the sound-making circuitry in the receiving device. Local on re-connects the keyboard to the sound-making circuitry
- Controller 123 (All notes off) – switches off all currently sounding notes. This is MIDI's panic button and is used to switch off hanging notes.
- Controller 124 (Omni mode off, all notes off) – the receiving device responds to messages on a single MIDI channel. This message also switches off all currently sounding notes. (Normally corresponds with a MIDI mode 3 status in the receiver, see below).
- Controller 125 (Omni mode on, all notes off) – the receiving device responds to messages on all MIDI channels. This message also switches off all currently sounding notes. (Normally corresponds with a MIDI mode 1 status in the receiver, see below).
- Controller 126 (Mono mode on/poly mode off, all notes off) – the receiving device responds to messages monophonically. This message also determines the number of monophonic MIDI channels used to process incoming MIDI notes. It switches off all currently sounding notes. (Normally corresponds with a MIDI mode 4 status in the receiver, see below).
- Controller 127 (Poly mode on/mono mode off, all notes off) – the

receiving device responds to messages polyphonically. This message also switches off all currently sounding notes. (Normally corresponds with a MIDI mode 3 status in the receiver, see below).

MIDI Modes

Controller messages 124 to 127 can be combined to produce four modes known as MIDI modes. These are operational modes governing how a MIDI device manages data on different channels and whether it responds poly-phonically or monophonically. The MIDI modes are as follows:

- Mode 1 (Omni On/Poly) – the receiver responds to messages on all MIDI channels polyphonically. Commonly known as Omni mode.
- Mode 2 (Omni On/Mono) – the receiver responds to messages on all MIDI channels monophonically. Rarely used mode.
- Mode 3 (Omni Off/Poly) – the receiver responds to messages on the chosen MIDI channel polyphonically. Commonly known as Poly mode.
- Mode 4 (Omni Off/Mono) – the receiver responds to messages on the chosen MIDI channel(s) monophonically. In this mode, response to incoming MIDI notes is shared between a number of monophonic channels. Commonly known as Mono mode.

The MIDI modes are slightly outdated but are still implemented in some form on most devices. Mode 1 might be used for troubleshooting and testing. Mode 2 is rarely used. Mode 4 is useful for guitar synthesizers (and similar instruments) since it allows you to assign each string to a different mono-phonic MIDI channel, thereby more closely approximating the performance behaviour of the real-world instrument. Most MIDI devices power up in MIDI Mode 3. Multi-timbral functionality (now common in many devices) is not covered by the standard MIDI modes. Multi-timbral mode is therefore assigned on the instrument itself and is normally known as 'Multi Mode'. Multi Mode operation might be viewed as a number of separate polyphonic instruments within a single device (each set to MIDI Mode 3).

System messages

System messages form the other main type of message in the MIDI specifi-cation. These include System Common, System Real Time and System Exclusive messages. System Common messages include such things as MIDI Time Code, song position pointer, song select and tune request messages. System Real Time includes timing clock (24 ppqn) and start, stop and con-tinue messages for sequencer synchronisation purposes. System Exclusive involves manufacturer-specific messages and Universal System Exclusive messages like MIDI file dump, sample dump, GM system on/off, MIDI Show Control and MIDI Machine Code. System Common and System Real Time messages are transmitted globally to all units in the MIDI network and do not use a MIDI channel for transmission or reception purposes. System Exclusive is used for transferring manufacturer and model-specific data to/from indi-vidual units and is generally only recognised by a single targeted device. This is typically used for dumping sounds and setup configurations from the MIDI device into a sequencer (like Cubase).

MIDI channels

In order to transmit MIDI messages to different targets within the same network, MIDI adopts a system of sixteen different channels. Channel Voice messages can be transmitted on any one of these channels. MIDI devices are usually set to receive polyphonically on one channel (Mode 3) or polyphonically on several channels simultaneously (multi-timbral). Messages on all sixteen MIDI channels can be transmitted simultaneously via a single MIDI cable.

To understand MIDI channels, it is helpful to think of your network of MIDI devices as a number of televisions. The signals from the TV broadcasting stations are being transmitted on a continuous basis, but you decide which one you are going to watch on screen by changing the channel on your TV. If you have several televisions you can set each one to a different channel. You can do exactly the same with your network of MIDI devices. Each unit is like a television which can be tuned to the appropriate channel. In such a system, Cubase is like a group of TV broadcasting stations. It transmits multiple channel MIDI data to the whole network. However, only those units which are tuned to the appropriate channels produce the appropriate sound. Certain MIDI devices can be set to receive on several channels simultaneously. This is known as multi-timbral or multi mode (as mentioned above) and allows a single unit to perform polyphonically on several channels at once. This means that you can trigger a number of different sounds simultaneously to hear a whole musical arrangement from a single unit (such as drums, bass, piano, strings and brass).

What MIDI is not

MIDI is NOT audio. MIDI is a sequence of digital instructions related to a musical performance whereas audio is a recording of the actual sound itself.

MIDI network details

For MIDI requirements, Cubase is normally connected to some kind of MIDI-equipped electronic keyboard and one or more external MIDI devices such as synth modules, samplers, drum machines or effects units. The VST Instruments supplied by Steinberg and third party developers may also form part of the system. The main keyboard you use to trigger the other devices is usually referred to as the master keyboard and most musical performances take place using this instrument. The overall MIDI system and how all the devices are connected together is known as the MIDI network.

A simple MIDI network

Figure 5.1 shows a very simple MIDI network. The MIDI output from the master keyboard is routed directly into the MIDI input of the computer's MIDI interface. The diagram assumes that a MIDI interface is installed inside the computer (e.g. a PCI card featuring MIDI input and output ports). The MIDI input data passes through Cubase (via the activated global MIDI Thru in the program, see below) and is routed back out, along with any other data which has already been recorded, to the MIDI input of the master keyboard. A copy of the data arriving at the MIDI In is sent out from the MIDI Thru port of the

Info

Cubase is supplied with a number of VST (Virtual Studio) Instruments and others can be installed from the vast range of VSTi products available from Steinberg and other developers. These are triggered via MIDI in much the same way as their real-world counterparts and they form a valuable extension to your MIDI network (see Chapter 18 for more details).

Figure 5.1
A simple MIDI 'daisy chain' network

master keyboard and routed to a synth module. The data arriving at the MIDI In of the synth module is passed on to a MIDI sampler in the same manner (via the MIDI Thru of the synth module). This type of configuration is known as a 'daisy-chain' network.

A daisy-chain network is easy to set up but suffers from two disadvantages:

1 Inflexibility – although it may suit very simple setups, more complex MIDI routing may require awkward re-plugging of the MIDI cables.
2 Data corruption risk – if the data passes through several units in the daisy-chain there is more risk of MIDI delays and data corruption.

A complex MIDI network

More complex MIDI networks typically feature a MIDI thru box (also called a MIDI splitter box) which enables the channelling of MIDI data to specific locations in the system. The MIDI network in Figure 5.2 shows a master keyboard whose MIDI Out is connected to the MIDI In of a computer via a MIDI thru box. The diagram assumes that a MIDI interface is installed inside the computer (e.g. a PCI sound card featuring MIDI input and output ports). The MIDI input data passes through Cubase via the activated global MIDI Thru in the program and is passed back out, along with any other data which has already been recorded, to the MIDI input of the MIDI thru box. The data is split among the outputs of the MIDI thru box and routed to the various devices in the system (including back to the master keyboard itself). This type of configuration is known as a MIDI 'star' network. In such a system, the MIDI thru box allows the connection of any input to any number of outputs and often includes MIDI data merge functionality. This allows the merging of two or more MIDI inputs into one MIDI data stream. In Figure 5.2, the master instrument's keyboard has been disconnected from its sound making circuit-

Figure 5.2
A complex MIDI 'star' network

ry (commonly known as Local off mode). In this mode, the sound making circuitry is triggered by incoming MIDI messages only. The master keyboard, therefore, triggers its sound making circuitry via Cubase. Note also that MIDI outputs are always connected to MIDI inputs and involve single cables between each output/input pair of sockets.

A MIDI star network is recommended for ensuring better MIDI timing, particularly for systems featuring more than two modules in addition to the master keyboard. It is also more flexible since, with a sufficiently well-specified MIDI thru box, any MIDI output can be routed to any MIDI input. This allows two-way handshaking operations when dumping MIDI data from an external unit into the computer and vice versa.

If you have not already done so, try making a clear, logical diagram of your own MIDI network with all the MIDI inputs and outputs clearly labelled. This helps clarify your own setup and is invaluable for troubleshooting if you run into problems. It is also helpful to include all the peripheral audio equipment and audio connections, once again clearly labelling all the inputs and outputs. (See Figure 2.6 for an example). If you have the opportunity use colour in your diagram to colour code the MIDI and audio connections.

> **Info**
>
> Making a clear, logical diagram of your own Cubase MIDI and audio connections and peripheral equipment helps clarify the structure of your system and is valuable for troubleshooting. In such a diagram, be sure to label all inputs and outputs clearly and, if possible, use colour-coding to differentiate between the MIDI and audio connection cables.

Record modes for MIDI recording

The precise manner in which MIDI recording takes place is governed by the record mode section of the Transport panel. You are advised to become familiar with the record modes before commencing any serious recording projects. These affect both the linear and cycle recording behaviour of the program. The linear record modes determine what happens when a new MIDI recording 'overlaps' an existing part on the same track. The cycle record modes determine what happens when you record multiple takes over the same range in a continuous cycle (when the Transport panel cycle button is activated). The function of each record mode is outlined in the following table:

Record modes for MIDI recording

Linear record modes		Cycle record modes	
Mode	Overlap behaviour	Mode	Cycle behaviour
Normal	pastes new part on top	Mix	mixes with previous lap data
Merge	merges data into existing part	Overwrite	overwrites to end of lap
Replace	replaces data in existing part	Keep Last	keeps last lap only
		Stacked	records laps in lanes

MIDI recording in detail

The following steps help clarify the MIDI recording process beyond the level achieved in earlier chapters. Proceed as follows:

Preparing the system

Create a new project

To create a new project, select 'New Project' from the File menu and choose 'Empty' from the dialogue which appears. In the Select directory dialogue, choose your audio drive or an appropriate existing directory and click on the Create button to create a new directory for this particular project. Choose an appropriate name. The directory is created on the hard disk. Click on OK to leave the Select directory dialogue. An empty Cubase project is opened.

Verify MIDI Thru and set MIDI filter

It is standard practice to pass MIDI data through Cubase. To achieve this, tick the MIDI Thru Active box in File / Preferences / MIDI. This ensures that all data received at the MIDI In port(s) is echoed to the MIDI Out port(s). Also make sure that SysEx is filtered in the record and thru sections of the MIDI filter in File / Preferences / MIDI / Filter. This avoids recording any unnecessary data in the recording exercises outlined below.

Set Local Off

Set your master keyboard to Local Off. Most MIDI keyboards include a parameter for Local on/off control. Local Off means that the musical keyboard is disconnected from the sound making part of the instrument. All sound is now triggered via incoming MIDI only. This avoids double notes and stops the master keyboard being triggered inappropriately when other instruments in the network are being played live via MIDI.

Add a MIDI track and set the input and output

Select Project / Add Track / MIDI to add a new MIDI track. Once created, choose an appropriate MIDI input and output port in the input and output fields of the Inspector for the track (Figure 5.3). These would normally correspond to the MIDI input and output ports of the MIDI interface you have installed in your computer. You can now play any of the external devices in the MIDI network by changing the MIDI channel in the channel field.

It is also possible to play any available VST instruments (Virtual Studio instruments) by selecting the instrument in the output menu. For a VST instrument to be available it must have already been activated in the VST instruments panel (opened from the Devices menu). Alternatively, if you intend to use a single track which triggers a VST instrument you may prefer to add an Instrument track instead of a MIDI track. An Instrument track is already set up to trigger the chosen instrument and depending on your needs may be a better option than a standard MIDI track.

Figure 5.3
Set the MIDI input, output and channel in the Inspector

Troubleshooting

If you experience difficulties with triggering your real-world or virtual instruments verify that:

• the target devices are switched on and are functioning correctly.
• the MIDI cables are of the approved type, are correctly connected between Cubase and the devices in the network, and are not faulty.
• the record enable or monitor enable button for the chosen MIDI track is active. This allows MIDI data to pass from the MIDI input to the MIDI output.
• the MIDI activity indicator in the Transport panel registers MIDI input and output activity when you play your keyboard.
• the correct output device and channel is selected in the output menu.
• the target devices are set to the correct MIDI channels.

Set the metronome, click and tempo

In Transport / Metronome Setup activate the audio click and select beeps. Activate Metronome in record and Metronome in play, and set a precount of two bars. To ensure predictable results, activate 'Precount on' and 'Start Record at Left Locator' in the Transport menu. Activate the click button on the Transport panel by pressing the 'C' key on the computer keyboard or by clicking on the button with the mouse. Start playback to test the click and verify the tempo of Cubase. In Fixed tempo mode you can adjust the tempo on the fly by double-clicking on the Transport panel tempo field and pressing the up/down arrows on the computer keyboard to increase/decrease the tempo. When you are satisfied with the tempo, press enter on the computer keyboard.

Name the track and choose a sound

Double-click on the name of the MIDI track (or Instrument track) you created above and enter an appropriate name. Select an appropriate sound for your MIDI device on the unit itself or remotely using the patch selector field in the Inspector. The patch selector sends out MIDI program change messages when you change its value (see Figure 5.4).

Info

In order for MIDI data to pass through Cubase, either the record enable or monitor enable button for the MIDI track must be active. Several MIDI tracks may be record enabled simultaneously allowing you to trigger and record several sounds at once.

Figure 5.4
Selecting a program remotely by name, using the patch selector of the supplied GM MIDI device

Figure 5.5
Installing a MIDI device in the MIDI
Device manager

Using the patch selector for remote selection of sounds by name depends on whether the chosen device is supported in the MIDI Device Manager (Devices menu / MIDI Device manager). Click on 'Install Device' in the MIDI Device Manager for a list of supported MIDI devices. To install a device, click on the required device in the list (Figure 5.5). The device is now available in the output port menu of the MIDI track and when the device is selected a pop-up presets menu becomes available in the patch selector.

The presets for VST instruments are shown in the VST presets window or program list which opens when you click in the programs / patch selector field. The program lists for most VST instruments may be converted to the VST3 presets format allowing you to store the presets for all your instruments in the same location and thus build up your own centralised library of presets for use with Cubase. This is one of the SoundFrame features of Cubase and allows you to search for sounds by name, category, character and so on.

Figure 5.6
Using the VST presets window to search
for bass sounds in the supplied Prologue
VSTi synthesizer

Set the left and right locators

Set the left and right locators in the ruler above the event display by clicking and dragging in the upper half of the ruler (a pencil tool appears). Set the left locator to bar 3.1.1.0 and the right locator to bar 7.1.1.0 (4 bars). It is assumed here that you have set you default ruler display to bars and beats. In this mode, the bar display figures refer to the time position in bars, beats, sixteenth notes and ticks.

Linear recording

Simple recording

Ordinary linear recording (meaning when you are NOT recording in cycle mode) is often better for simple recording tasks, long performances or for detailed punching in over specific segments. Linear recording behaviour depends upon the setting made in the linear recording mode menu on the Transport panel (mix, merge or replace) and the pre-roll, post-roll and punch button settings (see below). To activate recording, record enable the MIDI track and click on the record button (or press the '*' key on the numeric keypad). If you set up the program as outlined above you hear a two bar count after which recording begins on the chosen MIDI track at the left locator position.

Setting up the punch and pre-roll parameters
When punching in over an existing recording, it may be preferable to hear the music in the bars before the punch in point (rather than just a metronome precount). This allows you to play along with the music before you reach the punch in point, often resulting in a better take. To set this up in Cubase, proceed as follows:

- drag the left and right locators in the ruler to select the range in which you wish to record.
- activate the pre and post-roll buttons in the Transport panel and enter '1' (one bar) in each.
- activate the punch in and punch out buttons on the Transport panel (click on the buttons or use the 'I' and 'O' key commands on the computer keyboard).
- choose the appropriate mode in the linear record mode menu on the Transport panel. If you are punching in over a badly played section which you definitely wish to replace it might be appropriate to choose 'Replace' mode.
- activate the record enable button of the chosen MIDI track.

Figure 5.7
Setting up the Transport panel for punching in

Selecting record automatically rolls the project cursor back one bar before starting playback. When the punch in point is reached Cubase automatically drops into record mode. Recording continues up to the punch out point. After the punch out point playback continues for a further one bar. Using a post-roll as well as a pre-roll helps you hear your take in context. In 'Replace' mode, all existing MIDI data in the recorded segment is replaced by your new performance.

Cycle recording

Preparing Cubase for Cycle recording
For cycle recording, add the following steps to those outlined above for linear MIDI recording:

- Select Project / Add Track / MIDI and enter a count of 3 in the dialogue to add three new MIDI tracks.
- Name the new tracks as 'drums', 'bass' and 'piano' or choose different names as you see fit.
- Choose appropriate MIDI input / output ports and MIDI channels for the three new tracks so that each track triggers the appropriate sound from the devices in your system when you activate its monitor or record enable button. Select the sound for each MIDI device either on the unit itself or remotely using the patch selector field.

Activate the cycle button on the Transport panel. Cubase playback and recording now cycles between the left and right locators (between bars 3.1.1.0 and 7.1.1.0, as set above).

The advantages of recording in cycle mode

In cycle mode the punch in and out buttons can be largely ignored since the punch in button is auto-selected when Cubase is put into record mode and the punch out point (the position of the right locator) is never actually reached since Cubase cycles back to the left locator position. Recording is de-activated only when Cubase is stopped manually. When recording in cycle mode, Cubase automatically remains within the segment which is being recorded upon without any further effort, and any recorded material can be instantly monitored on the next lap of the cycle. Cycle recording in mix mode is particularly useful for continually adding to the material without dropping out of record and is convenient for building up a rhythm pattern.

MIDI cycle recording project 1 (Mix mode)

This project involves recording a drum part using the 'drums' MIDI track we created, above. Select 'Mix' in the cycle record mode selector. In mix mode the current MIDI recording is added to any existing data in the same part when recording in cycle mode. The idea in this project is to gradually add to the recording on each lap of the cycle without dropping out of record mode.

Start recording

Record enable the drums track. Click on the record button of the Transport panel (key command: '*' on the numeric keypad). A pre-count is heard according to what has been set in the metronome. When recording commences, the track header turns red and the project cursor starts to move. Anything played on your keyboard is now recorded into Cubase. Try recording something simple using a bass drum and snare. Cubase cycles between the left and right locators and you may add to the recording on each lap of the cycle.

Track switching

Once you are satisfied with what you recorded on the drums track, switch to the next track (the bass track) by pressing the down arrow key on the computer keyboard. Do this without dropping out of record. Record your bass part and then switch to the piano track, once again, without dropping out of record. Record your piano part and stop Cubase when all recording is complete. If necessary, you can go back and add further data to any of the tracks by switching between them using the up/down arrows of the computer keyboard (see Figure 5.8). When you are happy with your recording, don't forget to save it by selecting the save function in the File menu (Ctrl / Command + S).

MIDI cycle recording project 2 (Overwrite mode)

Delete the events recorded in project 1, above. This time, select 'Overwrite' in the cycle record mode selector. In overwrite mode, the current MIDI input replaces any existing recordings in the same part and deletes any data which occurs after the drop-in point for each subsequent lap of the cycle.

Figure 5.8
Cycle recording multiple MIDI parts in mix mode allows you to quickly build up a MIDI arrangement

Start recording

This time we are recording a single piano part. Record enable the piano track. Click on the record button of the Transport panel (key command: '*' on the numeric keypad). A pre-count is heard according to what has been set in the metronome. When recording commences, the track header turns red and the project cursor starts to move. Anything played on your keyboard (or other master instrument) is now recorded into Cubase. Try recording a fairly complex piano part.

Practice makes perfect

Your piano performance may be lacking the first time around the cycle. Do not drop out of record just start playing again on the next lap of the cycle. Your previous recording is replaced since you are in cycle record overwrite mode. All notes which come after your drop in point are replaced by the new performance. This allows you to keep practising the part until you play it 'perfectly'. When you get it right, your performance is already captured since you are still in record mode (see Figure 5.9). When you are happy with your recording, don't forget to save your work under a new name by selecting the 'save as' function in the File menu.

Figure 5.9
Cycle recording in overwrite mode allows you to capture a great musical performance

MIDI cycle recording project 3 (Stacked mode)

Delete the events recorded in the previous projects, above. This time, select 'Stacked' in the cycle record mode selector. In stacked mode, a new MIDI part is created for each lap of the cycle. The parts are automatically stacked on separate lanes within the vertical space of the MIDI track. Each of the previous takes is automatically muted as each new take commences.

Start recording

We are now recording a single piano part again. Record enable the piano track. Click on the record button of the Transport panel (key command: '*' on the numeric keypad). A pre-count is heard according to what has been set in the metronome. When recording commences, the track header turns red and the project cursor starts to move. Anything played on your keyboard (or other master instrument) is now recorded into Cubase. Try recording a complex piano part.

Relax while you play

This time you can feel really free to experiment since all your playing is automatically and conveniently captured in separate stacked parts, one for each lap of the cycle. These are also automatically numbered and arranged within the vertical space of the MIDI track (Figure 5.10). When recording is complete, editing the parts with the splice, mute and other tools allows you to assemble a 'perfect' take while still remaining in the Project window. If desired, you can merge all the wanted material into a single composite part

Figure 5.10
Cycle recording in stacked mode gives you maximum flexibility at the editing stage

using Merge MIDI in Loop (MIDI menu). When you are happy with your recording (and editing), don't forget to save your work under a new name by selecting the 'save as' function in the File menu.

Combining cycle recording techniques

The techniques from the above three projects can be combined. How to record largely depends on what kind of recording you are making. For example, using cycle recording in mix mode is probably best suited to drum and percussion parts where you may wish to build up the rhythm on each lap of the cycle. Unless you are an excellent musician this same technique may not be so useful for recording your bass and piano parts. These might benefit more from cycle record in over-write mode. This gives you the opportunity to keep on repeating your part until you get a good take. Stacked mode probably gives you the most flexibility since it effortlessly organises your recording into neat, separate segments and leaves all your options open until you decide which takes to keep at the editing stage. Remember that you can freely switch between mix, overwrite and stacked modes on the fly without dropping out of record.

Retrospective record

When Cubase is in stop or play mode, any MIDI input is still recorded by the program, as long as one MIDI track is record enabled. This helps capture the magical performance you might produce when you are practising before starting to record or when you are playing along with an existing arrange-ment without recording. Retrospective record helps you avoid the 'if only I had recorded that!' syndrome which afflicts some recording sessions. Selecting Retrospective record from the Transport menu instantly creates a MIDI part beginning at the project cursor on the current record enabled track and this contains your recently played MIDI performance. If the MIDI input took place alongside an existing arrangement the data is synchronised with the other MIDI parts as if you had recorded it in the normal way. The amount of data which can be recorded by the Retrospective record function is chosen in File / Preferences / Record.

How do I include my MIDI recordings when I use Export/Audio Mixdown?

The problem

Cubase includes a virtual mixing console where both audio and MIDI tracks can be mixed and automated. When you have completed a combined MIDI + audio project and set up an ideal mix, it is possible to bounce the result to an audio file on hard disk using the Export/Audio mixdown function in the File menu (sometimes referred to as 'mixing in the box'). There's just one catch: the MIDI tracks which trigger your external MIDI devices are NOT included in the mixdown! The Audio mixdown function includes all audio tracks and automation between the left and right locators. It also converts all Instrument tracks and all MIDI tracks which trigger VST Instruments. However, it does NOT convert regular MIDI tracks which trigger external MIDI devices. The program has no way of knowing what audio signals these external devices are producing.

Info

See Chapter 12 for more details about Export/Audio mixdown.

The solution to the problem

The solution is to record all external MIDI devices onto regular audio tracks before using Export/Audio mixdown. The details of achieving this need not be over-complicated. The essential thing to bear in mind is the manner in which the audio outputs of your MIDI devices are routed into your overall system. Most of us use an external mixing console of some kind in order to manage the audio signals from the MIDI network. If you followed the advice (above) of making a clear, logical diagram of your MIDI network and audio system with all the inputs and outputs clearly labelled, you can make good use of it here.

Assuming that the line outputs of your MIDI devices are routed into the line inputs of your external mixing console, the following is what you need to do:

1 Set up the sound of each MIDI instrument on the external mixing console. If you intend to bounce the audio from the instruments to a stereo pair in Cubase then you should take some time setting up the mix. However, for the best results you are advised to record each instrument on a separate track of Cubase as explained in the following points.
2 Connect one (or two if you are recording in stereo) of the group outs of the external mixing console to the desired physical input(s) of the audio hardware you have connected to your computer. Route the first instrument you wish to record to the chosen group output(s).
3 Put Cubase into play mode so that you can hear the MIDI sequence of the chosen MIDI device and set up an audio track for recording in the normal way. On the chosen audio track, choose the input buss into which you have routed your MIDI device. Record the audio output of the first MIDI device (via the chosen group output(s) of your external mixing console).
4 Proceed in a similar manner to record all the MIDI parts of your external units onto separate audio tracks of Cubase. If you have multiple input audio hardware then you may prefer to record all your MIDI devices in a single pass.
5 When all the MIDI parts have been recorded onto regular audio tracks, mute all the original MIDI tracks in the Project window.
6 Set up your mix in the normal way, including the new audio tracks, and adjust the left and right locators to the start and end points of the music. Use Export/Audio mixdown to create an audio file on hard disk. The mix is now complete and includes all the audio signals from your MIDI devices.

Brief summary of MIDI recording techniques

Armed with the techniques outlined in this and previous chapters, you are now ready to tackle more elaborate MIDI recording projects. The recording projects outlined above are only exercises and must, of course, be adapted to suit your own needs. Whatever technique you choose, you can now quickly build up a number of MIDI tracks to form a musical arrangement in the Project window. To help clarify the basic process for MIDI recording Figure 5.11 presents the essential steps in the form of a flowchart. This describes what you might do when recording in a linear fashion on a single MIDI track.

Figure 5.11
MIDI recording flowchart

In summary, the basic MIDI recording techniques include linear recording on a single MIDI track (or on a number of MIDI tracks simultaneously) and MIDI recording in cycle mode. When using Export/Audio mixdown to create a complete mix which includes all MIDI and audio tracks, all audio signals from external MIDI devices must first be recorded onto audio tracks.

You can achieve a lot in both the recording and editing sense while still remaining in the Project window, and you may be surprised how quickly you can build up an entire musical arrangement. However, there are times when you need to process and edit MIDI data in fine detail and this forms the subject matter of the next chapter.

Tip

Use the tools and techniques outlined in Chapter 4 to arrange and edit your MIDI parts in the Project window event display. Do not forget to save your work at regular intervals.

MIDI editing

In Chapters 3 and 5 we explored some of the main techniques associated with the recording of MIDI-based music. This helped you to record and manipulate MIDI parts in the Project window. A wide variety of editing functions can be carried out on MIDI parts while still remaining in the Project window, but for detailed editing of the MIDI data inside a part we must open it in one of the MIDI editors. This chapter covers the Key editor, Edit In-Place editor, List editor and Drum editor, as well as the quantize functions and MIDI editing functions in general.

General features of the MIDI editors

To open a MIDI editor, select a MIDI part and choose one of the editors from the MIDI menu. Each editor includes a toolbar, an infoline, a grid and a MIDI controller display. The notes (or events) are shown as graphical strips in the Key, List and Edit In-Place editors and as diamond-shaped symbols in the Drum editor. The Edit In-Place editor is similar to the Key editor but opens up in the Project window within the expanded vertical space of the chosen MIDI track. This has the advantage of allowing you to edit and line up MIDI events relative to the events on the other tracks in the Project window.

The grid is a series of horizontal and vertical guide lines which help you place notes at the correct pitch and at meaningful positions along the time line. This is particularly relevant when the snap button is activated, at which time the vertical lines of the grid become magnetic for all newly input or edited notes. To get a better idea of how the grid behaves try selecting different values in the quantize menu (when bars and beats is chosen as the display format in the ruler). The distance between the vertical grid lines is modified for each new value chosen. De-activating the snap button might be viewed as switching off the magnetic behaviour of the grid lines, at which time notes may be freely inserted or dragged to any position along the time line.

The MIDI editor toolbar

All the MIDI editors feature a toolbar which varies slightly for each editor (Figure 6.1). The common features of the toolbars include the following (left to right):

Figure 6.1
MIDI editor toolbar (Key edit)

- solo editor button – for soloing the editor.
- acoustic feedback button – for automatic playback of selected and inserted notes via MIDI.
- info button – for showing or hiding the infoline.
- tool buttons – for selecting the various editing tools (see below).
- autoscroll button – to automatically scroll the display to follow the project cursor position.
- auto select controllers button – to automatically select all controller data within the range of the selected note(s). This helps when you wish to move/copy notes and all their associated pitch bend and modulation data (for example) since now you need only select the note(s) to select all the data at once. The target controller data must be visible in the controller lanes for this to function correctly.
- show part borders button – for activating flags which show the start and end position of the part currently being edited.
- edit active part only button – restricts all editing operation to the active part only.
- part list menu – you can select more than one part (or a whole track) for editing when you open a MIDI editor. This menu provides a list of all selected parts (or all parts in the track) allowing you to quickly choose which part you wish to edit next. The display automatically scrolls to the start of each part you choose.
- insert velocity field – for selecting the default velocity for inserted notes.
- snap button – for switching on the 'magnetic' action of the grid.
- snap type and quantize menu – for choosing how quantizing affects editing and data input, and for selecting the resolution of the grid.
- length quantize menu – for changing the length of existing notes when using length quantize from the MIDI menu and for choosing a default length for inserted notes.
- step input and MIDI input buttons – to allow the input of notes one at a time according to the current quantize resolution and to allow the modification of MIDI note and velocity values via MIDI.
- velocity colours menu – for selecting the manner in which colour is used for velocity in the controller display.

Tip

When editing parts which trigger VST Instruments it is possible to open the interface for the instrument directly from within a MIDI editor by activating the 'Edit VST instrument' button on the toolbar. The 'Edit VST Instrument' button is shown by selecting it in the pop-up toolbar menu (right click/Ctrl + click on the toolbar).

Info

The List editor toolbar features special mask and filter functions and has no infoline. The Drum editor features a Drum Solo button.

Infoline

When the infoline button is activated a horizontal information line appears between the grid and the toolbar (Figure 6.2). It displays the details of the currently selected note, including the start position, end position, length, pitch, velocity, channel and note-off velocity. Position and length information is displayed according to the time line format you have chosen in the ruler. The infoline is particularly useful for detailed editing since all fields can be directly edited using the mouse and computer keyboard. When more than one event is selected the infoline text is shown in yellow and contains the information relevant to the first of the selected events. Editing any of the yellow text values applies the changes proportionally to all selected events, (i.e. changing the velocity value from, for example, '75' to '80' adds five to the velocity of all

Start	End	Length	Pitch	Velocity	Channel	Off Velocity
3.02.02.110	3.02.03.070	0.0.0.80	G4/79	90	3	64

selected events). To apply the edits in an absolute sense hold down Ctrl while making the changes (this time, changing the velocity from '75' to '80' sets the velocity of all selected events to the absolute value of '80').

Figure 6.2
MIDI editor infoline

The MIDI editor tools

To select a tool in any of the editors, click on one of the tool buttons in the toolbar or click with the right mouse button (PC) / Ctrl + click (Mac) in the grid to open the pop-up Quick menu. The tools are for the manipulation and editing of MIDI notes and Controller events and most of the tools listed here are relevant for all the MIDI editors. They include the following:

Object selection tool (pointer)

Similar to the Project window, the object selection tool (or pointer tool) is a general purpose tool for the selection, moving and copying of MIDI notes and events and for the manipulation of parameters anywhere in the MIDI editors. It is particularly useful for re-sizing in the Key editor where either the start or end of a note can be dragged to a new position (a double arrow appears when you position the pointer over the start or end points of the note). Unlike the Project window, the object selection tool for the MIDI editors is not a multi-function tool.

Draw tool

The draw tool is for inserting new events in the note grid or controller display. It may also be used for the modification of the length of an existing note by dragging the end point, and of the value of velocity and controller data in the controller display.

Erase tool

The erase tool is for deleting events by clicking on one event or a selected group of events. Pressing Alt while clicking with the erase tool deletes all following events in the Part.

Mute tool

The mute tool is for muting events. Click on events individually or drag a selection box over several to implement muting. Click on or drag over the muted events to un-mute them. A muted event is displayed in white.

Trim tool

The trim tool is for trimming the start or end points of notes. To trim the end of a note click on it at the required new end point. To trim the start of a note click on it while pressing Alt. The trim tool is particularly helpful for producing strumming effects by staggering the start points of the notes in a chord.

Split tool

The split tool is for splicing notes into two shorter notes. Notes are split at the mouse position and according to the current snap/quantize settings. Clicking on the note while pressing Alt produces multiple splits.

Glue tool

The glue tool is used to join together notes of the same pitch to create one longer note. Clicking on the note while pressing Alt joins all following contiguous at the same pitch.

Zoom tool

The zoom tool is for zooming in and out of the grid display. To zoom in, select the zoom tool and click in the event display. To zoom out, click in the event display while pressing Alt. To zoom in to a specific area of the grid drag a box around the area of interest with the zoom tool. To step back through previously used zoom views click with the zoom tool while pressing Ctrl (PC) / Command (Mac).

Paint tool

The paint tool is a multi-function tool. Click on the button a second time to reveal the other options. The paint brush allows the free drawing of events on the note grid or in the controller display. The line, parabola, sine, triangle and square tools impose their respective shapes on inserted or edited events. The position of notes and the size of the shapes imposed by the sine, triangle and square tools is regulated by the current quantize value (when the snap button is activated).

Time warp tool

Info

When the snap button is activated and bars and beats is set as the time format in the ruler, all tool editing in the Key, List and Drum editors is magnetic to the settings in the quantize and length quantize menus. The quantize setting is mirrored by the position of the vertical lines on the grid.

The time warp tool in the MIDI editors functions in a similar manner to the time warp tool in the Project window. In order to function correctly, the MIDI editor's ruler must be set to bars and beats. The time warp tool operates within the active part in two modes; 'default' mode and 'musical events follow' mode. In the default mode, the events in the MIDI editor do not move when you drag the warp tool in the display. This might be used to match the tempo to MIDI material which was not played to a strict click. When the snap button is activated on the toolbar the time warp position snaps to the start and ends of note events. This is useful for lining up beat positions to note events. In 'musical events follow' mode, all MIDI events are moved as you drag the warp tool in the display. This could be used for tempo manipulations which must take place within a given time frame.

To insert a tempo event click in the grid with the time warp tool. To delete a tempo event click on the event in the ruler while holding Shift. When you first drag or click in the grid with the warp tool, tempo events are automatically inserted at the start and end of the active part. This ensures that the tempo of material which occurs outside the active part is not changed. To use the time warp tool 'tempo track' mode must be selected in the Transport bar.

Drumstick tool

The drumstick tool is only relevant to the Drum editor. The Drum editor does not include a pencil tool in its toolbar. Instead, the drumstick tool is used for inputting events and re-sizing controller events. The drumstick tool behaves slightly differently to the pencil tool in that clicking on an event a second time removes it from the grid and dragging horizontally inputs repeated notes at the current quantize setting (if the snap button is activated).

Step input and MIDI input buttons

The six step/MIDI input buttons are concerned with the input of notes one step at a time (step input) and the entering of note and velocity data via MIDI. The buttons function in two modes according to which of the step and MIDI input buttons has been activated.

With the step button activated, when you play a note on your MIDI keyboard it is recorded onto the grid one step at a time at the resolution of the quantize menu setting and with the note length at the length quantize menu setting. The input data is also modified according to which of the note, velocity on and velocity off buttons (the rightmost three buttons) you have selected in the toolbar. With the note button activated the pitch of the input notes follows the keys you play on your keyboard. With the note button de-activated the pitch of the input notes remains at C3/60. With the velocity on button activated the velocity of the input notes follows the velocity with which you play the notes on your keyboard. With the velocity button de-activated the velocity of the input notes matches that set in the insert velocity field. The velocity off button functions in a similar manner. A 'move insert mode' button allows you to insert notes into an existing sequence by pushing existing notes to the right.

With the MIDI input button activated, when you select an existing note on the grid and play a note on your MIDI keyboard, this imposes the received MIDI values onto the selected note according to which of the note, velocity on and velocity off buttons (the rightmost three buttons) you have selected in the toolbar. When the incoming MIDI values have been registered the editor moves on to the next note automatically. This allows you to re-record note and/or velocity data for an existing sequence in step-time.

General tips for the MIDI editors

The following tips are designed to help you get started in the MIDI editors.

- Once you have selected one note event in a MIDI editor, try using the left and right arrow keys on the computer keyboard to scroll through consecutive notes. This is often easier than using the mouse. In order to be able to hear each event as it is selected, activate the acoustic feedback button (loudspeaker symbol) in the toolbar. Use the up and down arrow keys to change the pitch of a selected note.
- Adopting a two hand approach speeds up tool selection and editing. Use the left hand to select the tools with the computer typewriter keys 1 to 9 (or F9 and F10 to step through the tools) and use the right hand for all mouse manipulations (vice versa for left handed users).
- To gain an initial understanding of the function of the grid, open a MIDI editor (the Key editor, for example), make sure bars and beats is chosen as the display format in the ruler, activate the snap button and change the quantize menu to different values. For each new value selected in the quantize menu the distance between the vertical grid lines is modified. When the snap button is activated the grid becomes 'magnetic' and any inserted notes are pulled onto the nearest vertical grid line. This also

helps you get to grips with the quantize functions. Selecting Over quantize from the MIDI menu pulls all recorded notes in the part onto the nearest vertical grid lines. You can see the effect of the quantizing action on the grid. Observing the effect of quantizing in a MIDI editor provides helpful visual feedback of what actually happens when you use the quantize functions and is a helpful for getting to know what quantize is all about.

- Clicking once in the ruler moves the project cursor to the position at which you clicked. Double clicking in the ruler starts playback from the point at which you clicked. Double clicking a second time stops playback and re-positions the project cursor to the point at which you clicked. This helps you navigate within your chosen MIDI editor.
- Use the G and H keys for horizontal zoom control in the grid display. At higher vertical zoom settings the MIDI note name/number appears inside the note strip.
- Click with the right mouse button (PC)/Ctrl + click (Mac) in the grid to open the Quick menu. This allows quick tool selection and provides rapid access to the menu items relevant to MIDI editing.
- Cubase benefits from unlimited undo/redo. Use Ctrl + Z (PC)/ Command + Z (Mac) to undo an edit. Use Ctrl + Shift + Z (PC)/Command + Shift + Z (Mac) to redo an edit. To see the current edit history open the 'History' dialogue (Edit menu). Move the blue line to step back and forth within the edit history. Note that the edit history is cleared when you close the project.

Tip

Increasing the Key editor vertical zoom resolution reveals the note names inside each event on the grid.

Key editor

The Key editor (Figure 6.3) is a piano roll style editor featuring time on the horizontal axis and pitch on the vertical axis. The main display area is the grid where notes are represented as graphical strips. There is a mini piano keyboard to the left of the display, which corresponds to the pitch, and a con-

Figure 6.3
The Key editor

troller display below where velocity and various non-note events, such as Pitch Bend and Modulation, are shown. Similar to the Project window and the other MIDI editors, there is a ruler which marks the time line in the chosen format and a toolbar and infoline (as outlined above).

To open the Key editor double-click on a MIDI part or press the Return key on the computer keyboard with a MIDI part selected. Alternatively, select 'Key editor' in the MIDI menu or press Ctrl (PC)/Command (Mac) + E on the computer keyboard (default key command). You can select more than one part from the same or different tracks and all notes in all parts are shown in the Key editor. However, the notes from only one part at a time are active and all other non-active notes are displayed in grey. Use the part list to select the active part and the 'show part borders' button to highlight the active part. Select the MIDI track alone with no parts selected to open the Key editor for all MIDI parts on the track.

Controller display

The Key editor features a controller display for velocity and non-note MIDI data such as Pitch Bend, Aftertouch, Program Change, Modulation, Main Volume and Pan. Click on the plus (+) box in the lower left corner to create a new controller lane. By default, velocity is displayed when you create a new lane. To change the type of event shown, click on the menu to the left of the controller lane to open the pop-up menu. If the type of data you wish to see is not present in the menu, click on 'Setup' to open the Controller menu setup dialogue, and add the required data type to the menu using the left pointing arrow button.

Events are shown as vertical strips which are normally colour-coded according to their value (by default, blue for low values and red for high values). This is particularly useful for velocity since it gives an immediate idea of the intensity of the musical performance. The velocity colour is also applied to the note itself on the grid, which conveys the velocity status even if the controller display is hidden from view. By adding multiple controller lanes you can simultaneously display a number of different types of MIDI data. This is invaluable for getting a graphical overview of all the data for high precision editing.

Figure 6.4
The controller display allows multiple controller lanes to be shown

Key editor basic techniques

Most routine editing in the Key editor revolves around selecting, moving, copying, inserting, re-sizing and deleting notes and controller events using the tools. The draw tool is the standard tool for drawing new note events onto the grid. Notes are pulled onto the nearest vertical grid line when the snap button is activated. Their velocity is determined by the insert velocity value on the toolbar and, with single click inserts, their length is determined by the length quantize value. Clicking and dragging to the right with the pencil tool allows you to insert a note of a longer length. Clicking and dragging in the controller display with the pencil tool inserts new controller events. If there are events already in the controller display these are updated according to the new shape drawn by the pencil tool (Figure 6.5).

Figure 6.5
Inserting new notes and new controller events using the draw tool

Tip

To select all notes of the same pitch in the Key editor, hold down Ctrl/Command and click on the relevant key in the virtual keyboard to the left of the main display.

The object selection tool (pointer) would normally be used for the selection of notes on the grid and events in the controller display. The standard selection procedures as outlined in Chapter 4 also apply to the selection of events in the Key editor. The principal methods include dragging a box around a number of events or clicking on individual events. Selected notes may be moved by clicking on one of them and dragging to a new position. Holding Alt on the computer keyboard copies the notes instead (Figure 6.6).

Figure 6.6
Selecting and moving notes

The object selection tool may be used for re-sizing notes by clicking and dragging on their start or end points. A double arrow appears when the tool is placed above the appropriate position (Figure 6.7).

Figure 6.7
Re-sizing notes using the pointer tool

Deleting notes is achieved either by dragging over the notes with the erase tool or selecting the notes and pressing backspace on the computer keyboard. If your deletions are of an experimental kind, you may prefer to temporarily mute the notes using the mute tool.

Key editor close-ups

Editing a bass line

You have recorded a perfect bass line with a great feel but some notes are too long, some are too short and some overlap. The Key editor provides a solution as follows:

- Select the draw tool.
- Click and hold the draw tool near the end point of each offending note and drag the length to the desired duration.
- If the snap button is activated, the new length is snapped to the nearest vertical grid line. De-activating the snap button allows you to freely adjust the length of the note and may be a better option for this exercise.
- 'Delete overlaps' in the MIDI functions menu may also provide a partial solution to the problem.

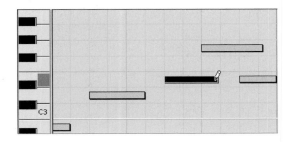

Figure 6.8
Editing the lengths of overlapping bass notes

Creating strumming effects with chords

You have successfully recorded a number of chords but would like to stagger start points of the notes to produce a strumming effect. To create the effect in the Key editor proceed as follows:

- Select the trim tool.
- Hold Alt on the computer keyboard and click on the start position of each note individually or drag across the start positions of all notes or a group of notes within the chord (a guide line is shown in the display).
- If you are seeking guitar-like strumming, a downward strum corresponds with the notes being staggered from the lower to the upper notes and an upward strum would be from the upper to the lower notes.
- Realistic strumming effects often involve staggering the notes in small groups within the chord. For example, a six-note guitar chord may sound more 'strummed' if you trim two separate groups of three notes (see Figure 6.9).

Figure 6.9
Trimming the notes within a chord to create a strumming effect

Editing note velocities

Certain high velocity notes within a sequence produce an unwanted percussive attack in the synthesizer sound you are using. To correct the problem proceed as follows:

- Select velocity in the Key editor controller display by clicking on the downward pointing arrow to the left of the Controller lane to open the pop-up controller selection menu. Normally, velocity is displayed by default when you first open the Key editor.

Figure 6.10
Changing velocity values using the draw tool

- The velocities of the recorded notes are now visible in the display as vertical strips.
- Select the draw tool and click and drag on the offending velocities to set them to appropriate new values.

Producing crescendos

If crescendos (or decrescendos) are required after the notes have been recorded then the controller display of the Key editor is one of the best places to create them. This technique is particularly useful for drum rolls and snare fills. Proceed as follows:

- Select velocity in the controller display.
- Select the paint/line tool and click and drag a line at the appropriate angle across the note velocities to which you wish to apply the crescendo.

Figure 6.11
Producing a crescendo using the parabola shape of the paint tool

- When the mouse is released a velocity ramp matching the straight line appears.
- For a more exponential crescendo try using the parabola shape tool.
- This technique can be used on other types of data. For example, processing Main Volume controller events in this way allows you to create MIDI volume fades in and out.

Producing special effects with modulation

The Modulation Controller is often used with synth patches to produce real-time modulation of some aspect of the sound, such as increasing the brightness, modifying the cut-off frequency of the filter or adding more vibrato. Using the draw tool shapes, like sine and triangle, you can create special effects by drawing shapes in the controller display. Proceed as follows:

- Select modulation in the controller display. De-activate the snap button on the toolbar.

- Select the triangle shape draw tool and click and drag to the right from the upper left corner of the controller lane (when the value field should read 127) to the lower right corner (when the value field should read 0).
- When the mouse is released a triangular-shaped sequence of modulation events appears in the display.
- Try re-activating the snap button and choosing different quantize values, length quantize values and tool shapes (sine, triangle or square). The quantize value governs the period of the shapes while the length quantize values govern the density of the events. As a preliminary experiment try setting quantize to 1/4 note and length quantize to 1/128 triplet.

Figure 6.12
Drawing modulation shapes in the controller display for special effects

Multiple controller lanes for high-precision editing and special effects
If your target synthesizer responds to Controllers 70-74, several controller lanes can be used simultaneously to set up tightly co-ordinated special effects. Proceed as follows:

- Click on the plus (+) box to the left of an existing controller lane to create a new one. Open the number of controller lanes required.
- Select the controllers you intend to use in the pop-up controller selector menus to the left of the lanes. Try starting with three controller lanes showing controllers 70, 71 and 74.
- Select a draw tool and draw the required data in the display. Try using combinations of the paintbrush, parabola, sine, triangle and square tools.

Figure 6.13
Tightly co-ordinated editing in multiple controller lanes

Edit In-Place

The Edit In-Place editor (Figure 6.14) is similar to the Key editor except that it is opened 'in-place' in the Project window. This means that you can look inside a MIDI part while still remaining in the Project window and, more importantly, you can line up individual MIDI events to events on other tracks in the event display, or vice versa (for this purpose try selecting 'Events' in the snap type menu). To open the Edit In-Place editor select a MIDI part (or MIDI / Instrument track) in the event display and select 'Edit In-Place' from the MIDI menu or press Ctrl/Command + Shift + I on the computer keyboard to toggle the editor on or off. Alternatively, try using the Edit In-Place button in the track list (if not already visible, activate it in the Track Control Settings dialogue, opened by clicking on the small downward pointing arrow at the top left of the track list).

The Edit-In Place editor opens within the vertical space of the selected track which expands to accommodate the grid. The vertical grid lines in the editor line up with the grid in the main part of the Project window. It is therefore a relatively easy task to line up MIDI events to other events along the time line. The other features of the editor include a controller display below the grid, a virtual keyboard to the left, and a toolbar above, (opened by clicking on the grey triangle found at the upper left side of the virtual keyboard).

Figure 6.14
Edit In-
Place editor

Tip

When using the Edit In-Place editor, setting the snap type menu to 'Events' allows you to snap MIDI notes to marker positions. By lining up MIDI notes to markers which were created using 'Create markers from hitpoints' (Audio menu) you can match the positions of MIDI notes to the hitpoints of an audio recording.

Edit In-Place basic techniques

To zoom in vertically in the Edit In-Place editor, place the pointer in the left part of the virtual keyboard to the left of the grid so that a hand appears. Drag the hand to the left or right to zoom in and out. Drag the hand up or down to scroll the key range shown in the editor. To zoom in and out horizontally, use the standard Cubase zoom controls (by default, key commands G and H).

Clicking on the grey triangle in the upper left corner of the Edit In-Place editor opens a toolbar. The toolbar is a reduced version of the toolbar found in the other MIDI editors. Here you have access to the acoustic feedback button, solo editor button, part list, auto select controllers, insert velocity, length quantize, velocity colours and transpose parameters.

The snap and quantize behaviour is governed from the main Project window toolbar using the snap type and quantize type menus. (The grid type menu has no function in the Edit In-Place editor). Setting the snap type menu to 'Events' is particularly helpful for lining up MIDI events to other events on other tracks in the display or vice versa.

Edit In-Place close-ups

Snapping to events

As mentioned above, activating the snap button and selecting 'Events' in the snap menu is particularly useful in the Edit In-Place editor. For example, this makes it easy to line up a MIDI note with the start of an audio event, as shown in Figure 6.15.

Moving audio events in relation to individual MIDI events is equally useful. For example, Figure 6.16 shows how you can 'punch a hole' in an audio event for the precise duration of a MIDI event. In this case, a gap is punched into an audio event (a drum loop) according to the position and length of a MIDI snare drum (D1). To achieve this the drum loop is split and the end of the resulting first event is dragged to the start of the MIDI note, while the start of the second event is dragged to the end of the MIDI note.

Figure 6.15
Lining up a MIDI crash cymbal (C#2) with the start of an audio event in the Edit In-Place editor

Figure 6.16
Punching a gap into an audio event according to the position and length of a MIDI note (D1)

Selective moving and copying

Another advantage of the Edit In-Place editor is the ability to selectively move or copy specific MIDI events within a part along with other selected events in the general event display. For example, this would allow you to copy audio events along with just the MIDI notes which trigger a cymbal in a MIDI part, as shown in Figure 6.17. All non-selected MIDI notes are not copied or moved with the selection.

Figure 6.17
Selectively copying the cymbal crashes in a MIDI part along with some audio events

The List editor

The List editor (Figure 6.18) is a list-based editor where all data is presented in a list of time-consecutive events. It differs from the other editors in that all kinds of MIDI data, score and standard MIDI file events may be viewed and edited.

The List editor is opened from the MIDI menu or you may like to assign a Key command in File / Key Commands (try Ctrl/Command + Alt + L). Similar to the Key editor, the List editor features a grid and a toolbar containing a similar set of tools. However, the most important feature of the List editor is the list itself. There are a number of columns hidden behind the grid which can be revealed by moving the split point to the right of the screen. This reveals more details about the events in the list.

Figure 6.18
The List editor

The columns contain information about each event including its type, start position, end position, length, data values 1, 2 and 3, MIDI channel and associated System Exclusive or text data in the comment column. For example, regular note events feature their pitch in the data 1 column followed by their velocity on in the data 2 column and velocity off in data 3. Controller events feature the controller name (or number) in the data 1 column followed by the value of the controller in the data 2 column. Most events have no entry in the comment column. However, the comment column for a System Exclusive event contains the System Exclusive message itself.

Features which are unique to the List editor include the Insert menu, the Mask menu, and the Filters. These are found in the toolbar.

The Insert menu

The Insert pop-up menu on the toolbar contains a list of event types. Any chosen event type may be inserted into the List by clicking with the draw tool on the grid. The event types include Note, Controller, Program Change, Aftertouch, Pitch Bend, Poly Pressure, SysEx, SMF and text.

The Mask menu and display filters

The Mask menu is used to force a display of one of the following:

1 all data of the same event type as the currently selected event
2 all data with the same event type and the same data 1 value as the currently selected event.
3 all data with the same MIDI channel as the currently selected event.

All other events are hidden from view. Alternatively, the events in the list may be filtered according to Logical editor presets.

The display filters are comprised of nine tick boxes, one for each of the main event types and for SMF and score events. The tick boxes are hidden or shown using the toolbar's 'Show filter view' button. When a box is ticked the corresponding event type is filtered out of the event list.

The Mask menu and display filters are among the most useful features of List edit. They can be used to clarify the list and to expose certain types of data for deletion or other editing.

Tip

If you select 'Increment / decrement on left-click and drag' in File / Preferences / Controls, you can change any of the values in the List editor columns simply by clicking at the appropriate location and dragging the mouse up or down.

List editor basic techniques

In the List editor, events may be edited by clicking on the column values and entering a new value with the computer keyboard (depends upon the value box setting in File / Preferences / Controls). Type a new value directly or use the up/down arrow keys to increment/decrement the value.

When the mouse pointer is moved into the grid area to the right of the list, it is automatically changed to a pencil tool. The horizontal bars in the display represent the data 2 values of events. These values may be changed graphically in the display in much the same way as in the controller display of the Key editor.

Clicking in the comment column for a System Exclusive event opens the MIDI Sysex editor. This is for editing System Exclusive data in fine detail and requires a good knowledge of SysEx theory in order to be successful. The user manual of your MIDI device normally lists the details of its SysEx messages.

The essential difference between the List and the Key editors is that the Key editor is directed towards the graphical editing of note data on the grid and controller data in the controller display, whereas the List editor is directed towards the more detailed editing of any type of event and its various values in the display list. As a general rule, the List editor is more useful for the editing of non-note events and helps when a more scientific approach is required. List edit is excellent for sorting events for analytical and troubleshooting purposes and might help you find undesirable events which are causing problems with your MIDI devices.

List editor close-ups

Editing System Exclusive messages

For the editing of System Exclusive messages proceed as follows:

• Click once in the comment column of the System Exclusive event in the list. The first part of the SysEx message is always visible in the comment column.
• The whole message is displayed in the MIDI Sysex editor which opens

Figure 6.19
Editing System Exclusive data

automatically. The data is shown in hexadecimal notation (Figure 6.19).
- Edit the data as desired and click on the OK button to keep the changes. A good knowledge of System Exclusive is required to make any meaningful changes.

Finding unwanted Program Change messages

At some time in their use of the program, most Cubase users suffer from the problem of an unwanted or incorrect program change (or some other data type) embedded somewhere among the rest of the data. This is not always easy to find for deletion or editing. With the List editor filters the task is made easier. Proceed as follows:

- Select the track or part(s) containing the unwanted Program Change message.
- Activate the Show filter view button on the toolbar. Tick the filter boxes of all those data types you do not wish to see.
- The unwanted event(s) can now be found more easily among the remaining unfiltered data displayed in the list.

Figure 6.20
Exposing Program Change events using the List editor's filters

Filter	☑ Note	☑ Controller		☑ Pitch Bend	■ Program Change		☑ Aftertouch	
L	Type	Start	End	Length	Data 1	Data 2	Channel	Comment
	Program Change	0007.04.01.000			3	0	1	
	Program Change	0010.01.01.000			54	0	1	

Inserting a Local Off Controller event

Most users set their master keyboard to Local Off for use with Cubase. This disconnects the musical keyboard from the sound-making circuitry of the instrument. Finding the Local Off control in the instrument itself is not always obvious and some instruments power up in Local On mode. To overcome these problems it is helpful to embed a Local Off message into a MIDI part which can be used within a default startup project to make sure that the master keyboard is always set to Local Off. To insert a Local Off event in List edit, proceed as follows:

• Create an empty MIDI part in the Project window, select it and open List edit.
• Select Controller in the Insert menu of the List edit toolbar.
• Select the draw tool and click once in the grid with the mouse at the beginning of the part. A new controller event with various default values is inserted into the list.
• Click once in the data 1 column of the new event and enter the number '122' using the computer's numeric keypad (Controller 122 is the Local On/Off Controller).
• Make sure that '0' is entered into the data 2 column ('0' is the off setting and '127' is the on setting for Local Control).
• Make sure that the MIDI track containing the part is transmitting to your master keyboard. When the newly created MIDI part is played, the Local Off message is sent to the keyboard and it is set to Local Off mode accordingly.

L	Type	Start	End	Length	Data 1	Data 2	Channel	Comment
	Controller	0007.03.01.000			Local Ctrl	0	1	

The Drum editor

The Drum editor is a 'drum machine' style editor featuring time on the horizontal axis and pitch in the form of drum names on the vertical axis (Figure 6.22). Like the Key editor there is a grid but, this time, notes are represented by diamond-shaped symbols. The drum names are shown as a list to the left of the display and there is a toolbar above the grid and a controller display below, similar to those found in the Key editor. To open the Drum editor, select a MIDI part and then select 'Drum editor' from the MIDI menu. As

Figure 6.21
Creating a Local Off Controller message in List edit

Figure 6.22
The Drum editor

the name implies, the Drum editor is designed for the editing of drum and percussion data. It operates in two modes depending on whether or not you have activated a drum map. Without a drum map, the editor functions in a similar way to the Key editor. When a drum map is activated, more columns appear in the display and the editor features the names and note positions of specific drum setups, such as those found in external drum machines and modules or in a standard GM drum map.

Drum maps are assigned on a track-by-track basis and each track can be assigned a different drum map. Maps are chosen from the map menu in the Drum editor or in the Inspector for the track. When a map is assigned for a track in the Project window, the data display format switches to diamond shaped symbols for all parts on the track. New maps are added to the menu using the Drum Map Setup dialogue.

Drum editor columns

When a drum map has been assigned, pulling the split point to the right reveals a number of columns which are unique to the Drum editor. These include the following:

- Selection – a blank column for triggering or selecting each instrument with the mouse.
- Pitch – defines the base note for each instrument. This is a fixed value which cannot be modified and indicates the actual pitch which gets recorded. There are 128 pitches available matching the 128 possible MIDI notes. The note in the pitch column often matches that found in the I-Note column but this may not always be the case.
- Instrument – for naming each instrument (drum) in the map.
- Quantize – for assigning an individual quantize value for each instrument which governs the resolution of any inserts or editing for the instrument on the grid.
- Mute – for muting individual instruments. Muting also occurs when you activate the 'solo instrument' button on the toolbar.
- I-Note (input note) – defines the pitch of the note you use to trigger each instrument. This is the source note you play on your master keyboard (or other controller instrument).
- O-Note (output note) – defines the pitch of the note which is transmitted from the MIDI output of Cubase when its corresponding input note is received. This is the note which is transmitted to the target MIDI device.
- Channel – for the selection of a MIDI channel for each instrument.
- Output – for the selection of a MIDI output port for each instrument. When set to 'track' the output for the instrument is transmitted via the MIDI port set for the track.

When a drum map has not been assigned, only the pitch, instrument and quantize columns are available. In this mode, you can still select the list of names and quantize values for the available maps using the Names menu (below the Map menu).

Setting up a Drum map

A Drum map is a set of 128 instrument slots each assigned to one of the 128 possible MIDI notes, and each with their corresponding name and values in the columns. Drum maps are assigned to MIDI tracks using the map menu which is found in the Drum editor or in the Inspector for the track. To set up a new map or save and load maps to/from disk, open the Drum Map Setup dialogue from the map menu (Figure 6.23).

Figure 6.23
The Drum Map Setup dialogue

Even though changes can be made to the drum map while remaining in the Drum editor, the Drum Map Setup dialogue has everything you need for drum map editing purposes. You can create an empty new map or copy a new instance of an existing map using New Map and New Copy in the Functions menu. Still in the Functions menu, Save and Load allow you to save and load maps to/from disk and Remove allows you to delete the currently selected map from the list. Edit head pairs and Init Display Notes manage how drum parts are displayed in the Score editor.

Any value in the columns is edited by clicking on it and entering a new value with the computer keyboard or making a choice from a pop-up menu. Holding Ctrl (PC)/Command (Mac) while entering a value in the quantize, channel or output columns changes all instruments to the same value for that column. The columns themselves can be moved within the display by dragging the column header to a new position with the mouse.

In summary, the basic steps for setting up a drum map are as follows:

1   Create an empty new map or copy a new instance of an existing map using New Map or New Copy in the Functions menu. The new map

appears in the list of drum maps.

2 Find the different instruments in the target drum kit by triggering the sounds via MIDI or by clicking in the selection column. Enter a suitable name for each instrument in the Instrument column.

3 Adjust the I-Note values to suit your playing style and key mapping preferences. Many musicians have become accustomed to the standard GM key positions (C1/36 for kick, D1/38 for snare and so on) but you can set up any configuration here.

4 Adjust the O-Note column values to match the target device(s). For elaborate drum programming your map may contain two or more target devices.

5 If required, adjust the MIDI channel and output port for each instrument.

Understanding the pitch, I-Note and O-Note columns

Using the Drum Map Setup window is generally straightforward but understanding the details of the pitch, I-Note and O-Note columns may require more effort. It makes things clearer to view the I-Note column as a map of where the sounds are being played on the keyboard and the O-Note column as a map of where the sounds are found in the target MIDI device. The pitch column is a series of fixed MIDI note values tagged on to each row, and it is always this pitch which actually gets recorded in Cubase. Now, imagine that you wish to set up a drum map which corresponds with the non-standard pitch values of the kick drum, snare and hi-hat sounds found in an external drum module (C0/24 for kick, D0/26 for snare and F#0/30 for hi-hat) but where you are still able to trigger these sounds from standard GM drum

Figure 6.24
Adjusting the O-Note values to match the non-standard drum note positions of a target drum module

Pitch	Instrument	Quantize	M	I-Note	O-Note	Chanr	Output
C1/36	Bass Drum	1/16		C1/36	C0/24	10	MPU-401
D1/38	Acoustic Snare	1/16		D1/38	D0/26	10	MPU-401
F#1/42	Closed Hi-Hat	1/16		F#1/42	F#0/30	10	MPU-401
A#1/46	Open Hi-Hat	1/16		A#1/46	A#0/34	10	Track

notes (C1/36 for kick, D1/38 for snare and F#/42 for hi-hat). This would mean adjusting the O-Note column values to match the non-standard note positions in the target drum module while keeping the I-note column values in standard GM positions (Figure 6.24.)

Imagine that you now wish to change the sound of the snare to one of the snares in the 'Snare Shop' preset of the HalionOne software sampler supplied with Cubase. Firstly, make sure that HalionOne is activated in the VST Instruments panel (opened from the devices menu or press F11 on the computer keyboard). Change the preset to 'Snare Shop'. To assign the snare instrument in the map to HalionOne, select HalionOne in the snare's output column. To locate your preferred snare sound adjust the O-Note value while triggering the sounds using your musical keyboard (Figure 6.25). Setting up multiple MIDI devices in this way might also mean that you need to change the MIDI channels in the channel column as well as the output ports for each of the sounds concerned.

Tip

To step through the drum sounds in a target device using the O-Note column, select the row which corresponds with the key you wish to use to trigger the sounds and double-click in the O-Note column. Use the up/down arrows on the computer keyboard to change the pitch in the O-Note column while triggering the sounds using your MIDI keyboard. Make sure the output port for the device is selected in the Output column.

Pitch	Instrument	Quantize	M	I-Note	O-Note	Chanr	Output
C1/36	Bass Drum	1/16		C1/36	B0/35	10	1 - LM4-MarkII
D1/38	Acoustic Snare	1/16		D1/38	G#3/68	10	2 - HALionOne
F#1/42	Closed Hi-Hat	1/16		F#1/42	F#0/30	10	MPU-401
A#1/46	Open Hi-Hat	1/16		A#1/46	A#0/34	10	Track

Figure 6.25
Assigning the snare instrument to the HalionOne VST Instrument

To further clarify the function of the columns, the following is a brief summary of what happens to the MIDI data when you trigger your drum sounds via a drum map:

1 The incoming MIDI note finds its corresponding pitch in the I-Note column.
2 The note is instantaneously transposed to the value found in the pitch column on the same row (it is always this pitch value which gets recorded).
3 The outgoing MIDI note is instantaneously transposed to the value found in the O-Note column on the same row. The O-Note value is the final output note sent to the target MIDI device.

Drum editor basic techniques
The Drum editor features a drumstick tool which replaces the functions of the draw tool found in the other editors. The drumstick tool is used for inserting notes onto the grid. It differs from the draw tool in that it cannot be held and dragged on the grid to adjust the length of a note as it is being inserted. Instead the length is governed by the Insert Length setting on the toolbar. However, if you click and drag the drumstick horizontally along the grid, for one sound, a series of events is inserted at the resolution set by the quantize column for that sound (if global quantize is de-activated on the toolbar), or at the resolution set by the quantize value on the toolbar (if global quantize is activated on the toolbar). If the drumstick tool is clicked over an existing event, the event is deleted.

The toolbar also features a 'solo instrument' button. This solos the currently selected instrument in the drum map. When the drum solo button is activated all instruments other than the one which is currently selected are muted in the mute column. This is excellent for soloing individual drum sounds for fine tuning in a mix.

Like the Key editor, the Drum editor features an Infoline, where existing events can be updated in terms of their position, length, pitch, velocity and channel. The Drum editor also has a controller display but it differs from the Key editor in that it shows the controller data for the currently selected instrument only. This is useful for creating velocity ramps for snare rolls, for example (see below).

Drum editor close ups

Inserting 1/16th note hi-hats
A common requirement for drum parts is the insertion of a hi-hat at regular 1/16th note intervals. To achieve this in the Drum editor, proceed as follows:

Tip

It is always the pitch column note which gets recorded in Cubase. Therefore, with a map containing O-Note data which does not match the pitch column data, the recorded notes only trigger the correct sounds when the correct drum map is active. There may be times when you no longer wish to use the drum map but wish to retain the recorded data suitably transposed to trigger the correct sounds (such as when you export your MIDI sequence as a Standard MIDI File). To achieve this, use O-Note Conversion in the MIDI menu.

- Select an Insert Velocity and an Insert Length in the toolbar.
- Activate global quantize on the toolbar and set the quantize value to '1/16 note'. This governs the resolution of any inserted events. Alternatively, de-activate global quantize and set the quantize column value for the hi-hat instrument to '1/16 note'. When global quantize is de-activated the resolution for inserted events is governed by the values found in the quantize column.

Figure 6.26
Inserting hi-hat events using the drumstick tool

- Select the drumstick tool and click and drag horizontally across the grid in the row corresponding to the closed hi-hat instrument. Drag for the desired number of bars. A series of events are inserted at the chosen resolution.

Creating crescendos for drum rolls and fills

The advantage of creating drum related crescendos in the Drum editor is that you can see the velocity data separately for each instrument in the Controller display. Proceed as follows:

- Select the instrument for which you wish to create a crescendo in the instrument list.
- Select velocity in the controller display.
- Select the line tool and click and drag a line at the appropriate angle across the appropriate note velocities.
- When the mouse is released a velocity ramp matching the line appears.
- For a more exponential crescendo try using the parabola shape of the line tool.

Figure 6.27
Using the line tool to create a crescendo in the Drum editor's controller display

Combining loop and solo

It is often helpful to replay a single drum sound repeatedly while you are adjusting its EQ and effects settings. This is particularly true of bass drum and snare sounds and could also apply to tom rolls when you are setting up pan positions. With the Drum editor this is a two stage process. Proceed as follows:

- In the Drum editor, select the events you want to hear soloed. This could be one event or the events from several bars. Click with the right mouse button (PC)/Ctrl + click (Mac) in the grid to open the Quick menu and select 'Loop selection' from the Transport section. Alternatively, select Shift + G (the default key command). Loop playback commences.

Figure 6.28
Select the events and activate 'Loop selection' from the Quick menu

Tip

As well as opening a single MIDI editor from the Project window, you can also open multiple editors on the screen and switch between them at will. Changes made in one editor are immediately reflected in the others. This is extremely useful for detailed work.

- Activate the solo editor and solo instrument buttons on the toolbar. Select the instrument you wish to hear. If you wish to hear several instruments, un-mute them in the mute column.

Figure 6.29
Solo the instrument you wish to hear

Smart moves

To help you remember the basic moves for using the MIDI editor tools, Table 6.1 summarises the main tool editing techniques. These are applicable to all the editors outlined in this chapter.

Table 6.1 Smart moves for the MIDI editors

Tool	Keys held PC	Mac	Mouse action	Result
Object selection	-	-	click on event	selects event
	-	-	click on event and drag	moves event
	alt	alt	click on event and drag	copies event
	alt	alt	click and drag in grid	inputs note of length dragged
	-	-	drag the start/end point of note	re-sizes note
	-	-	click and drag in grid	opens rectangular selection box
	shift	shift	double click on note	selects all notes on same pitch
Draw	-	-	click on note end and drag	changes length of note
	-	-	click and drag in grid	inputs note of length dragged
	-	-	click and drag in controller display	inputs/changes values of events
Drumstick	-	-	click and drag horizontally in grid	inputs multiple notes at quantize resolution
Erase	-	-	click on event	deletes event
Mute	-	-	click on event	mutes event
Trim	-	-	click on note event	trims the start of the note
	alt	alt	click on note event	trims the end of the note
Zoom	-	-	click in grid	zooms in horizontally
	alt	alt	click in grid	zooms out horizontally
Line/parabola	-	-	click and drag in controller display	changes values in straight/curved lines
Paint	-	-	click and drag in grid	paints events freely on grid

More about the MIDI menu

The MIDI menu contains a number of other important commands and a functions sub-menu. These complement the use of the main MIDI editors and help handle some of the common MIDI editing tasks with maximum speed and convenience.

Transpose

The transpose function opens a simple dialogue where you specify the amount by which you wish to transpose the currently selected part or notes. You can also specify an upper and lower barrier for the transposition which keeps the trans-posed notes within a chosen range of octaves. Transpose is good for making global transpositions of whole parts or a number of selected parts.

Merge MIDI in Loop

Merge MIDI in Loop merges all MIDI data between the left and right locators into a single new MIDI part on the currently selected track. If there is already a part on the destination track you can choose to merge this with the other data or erase it. Options are provided for including MIDI send and insert effects. Merge MIDI in Loop is the function to use when you wish to make your MIDI effects a permanent part of the data.

Freeze MIDI modifiers

Freeze MIDI modifiers makes all parameters in the MIDI Modifiers section of the Inspector a permanent part of the data.

Dissolve Part

Dissolve Part allows you to split the data in the chosen MIDI part(s) onto separate tracks according to either the channel or pitch of events. Channel is useful for split-ting the multiple MIDI channel elements of a musical arrangement which have already been merged into a single part, such as a Type 0 Standard MIDI file. Pitch is excel-lent for splitting a drum or percussion part into its constituent instruments.

The MIDI functions

The MIDI functions are found in the Functions sub-menu of the MIDI menu. The MIDI functions are a convenient set of editing commands which may be used within the MIDI editors or directly on MIDI parts in the Project window. The functions include the following:

- Legato – increases the lengths of all selected notes to the start positions of the next note. Useful for pads and strings when you need smooth chord changes and a continuous sound.
- Fixed lengths – fixes the lengths of all selected notes to the same value as that chosen in the Quantize type selector of the toolbars (Project window or the editors).
- Delete doubles – deletes all doubled notes which occur on the same pitch and at exactly the same position. Always operates on whole MIDI parts. Delete doubles is useful for 'cleaning up' after you have been recording in cycle mode.
- Delete controllers – deletes all controller, aftertouch and pitch bend data from the currently selected part. Always operates on whole MIDI parts. Delete controllers is useful when you need to strip a MIDI part back down to its notes-only state.
- Delete notes – the Delete notes function is designed to find and delete low velocity and short ghost notes which were not intended as part of the performance. The Delete notes dialogue allows you to set thresholds for length and velocity, below which offending notes are deleted.
- Restrict polyphony – allows you to match the polyphony of your MIDI

parts to the polyphony available in the target MIDI device. It functions by reducing the lengths of certain overlapping notes. This function may cause undesirable side effects and so should be used with care.

- Pedals to note length – finds all sustain pedal controller events (Controller 66) and changes the length of the notes concerned to match the on and off points of the pedal. After modifying the notes the sustain pedal events are deleted.
- Delete overlaps (mono) – adjusts the lengths of all overlapping notes which occur on the same pitch.
- Delete overlaps (poly) – adjusts the lengths of all overlapping notes in the part (regardless of pitch).
- Velocity – processes the velocity of the notes in a part according to a number of settings in a pop-up dialogue. You can add or subtract a fixed velocity, compress or expand the velocity according to a percentage, or restrict the velocity range between an upper and lower limit.
- Fixed velocity – sets all selected notes to the same velocity (as chosen in the Insert velocity field of the Key and Drum editors).
- Thin out data – reduces the density of recorded MIDI controller data. Helpful when large amounts of data are causing MIDI timing problems.
- Extract MIDI automation – converts all continuous controller data found in the MIDI part(s) into MIDI track automation data. After use, click on the left edge of the MIDI track to reveal the automation sub-tracks. To activate the automation, click on the automation read buttons (illuminated in green when active). Extract MIDI automation helps you get a clear overview of all your continuous controller data in the Project window where it can be edited more conveniently.
- Reverse – reverses the playback order of the notes in the part.
- Merge tempo from tapping – uses the distance between the notes found in the selected MIDI part to calculate a tempo map. In the MIDI merge options dialogue which appears when you use this function, you decide what timing resolution the notes in the part represent. This is most often used when you wish to create a tempo map which matches the tempo changes of an audio or MIDI performance which was created without a strictly regulated click track. To record the part which is to be used for the 'Merge tempo from tapping' function you simply 'tap' the MIDI note of your choice in time with the music (see chapter 18 for more details).

Quantize

What is quantize?

Quantize is a timing correction function applied either after a MIDI part has been recorded or at the same time as the recording is taking place (automatic quantize). It involves moving recorded events onto certain divisions of the bar according to a position-based grid. In Cubase, the resolution of these divisions is chosen in the quantize type menu on the toolbar. This imposes a grid of vertical lines across the event display which, when you activate the snap button on the toolbar, become 'magnetic' for the notes recorded nearby. Quantize was first devised as a purely corrective function but is now also used as a creative tool.

A simple corrective use of quantize might include moving all the hi-hats in a MIDI drum recording onto the nearest 1/16th note divisions of the bar. This is known as 'over quantize' or 'hard quantize'. A similar function involves moving events towards the nearest 1/16th note divisions according to a strength percentage. This is known as 'iterative quantize'. Over quantize and iterative quantize functions are found in the MIDI menu of Cubase.

Using automatic quantize when making a MIDI recording allows you to hear an immediate example of how quantize affects the MIDI data. Activate the Auto Q button on the Transport panel and select 1/4 in the Quantize type menu in the Project window toolbar. Automatic quantize uses the over quantize function to automatically quantize your performance in real-time. Try to record a hi-hat sound (for example) at 1/8 note intervals. You will find that it is impossible to do so since all notes are forced onto the 1/4 note divisions of the bar. Set the Quantize type menu to 1/8 or switch off Auto Q and you can now record your part normally.

Quantize health risks

As you heard in the latter example, heavy use of the quantize functions is not always good for your musical health. It is not always desirable to have all the notes in all parts occurring on exact divisions of the beat. Too much quantize can result in music which is robotic and lifeless, so quantize should be used with some care. Iterative quantize is often a better option than Over quantize since it retains some of the original feel of the musical performance. Of course, if your MIDI recording is performed extremely accurately it should not need any quantize at all.

Quantizing in the Project window

To quantize a MIDI part in the Project window, select it and choose a quantize value in the quantize type menu in the toolbar. Try 1/16 and select iterative quantize in the MIDI menu. Iterative Quantize tightens up parts that were loosely played but retains some of the feel of the original performance. Where strictly metronomic timing is required try Over quantize instead. Quantize your part until it sounds musically correct. If desired, you can use Iterative quantize several times in succession. This progressively tightens up the part. You can undo any quantizing action using the main undo command in the Edit menu (Ctrl/Command+Z). This takes you back to the previous quantized state if you have implemented more than one quantizing action. You can go back to your original unquantized performance using 'Undo quantize' (found in the Advanced quantize sub-menu of the MIDI menu).

If you wish to make adjustments to the quantize effect, select 'Setup' from the Quantize type menu or select 'Quantize Setup' from the MIDI menu. These open the Quantize Setup window. In Quantize Setup you can fine tune the quantize function with a range of control parameters. For example, this allows you to apply a swing factor to your performance or adjust the magnetic area within which the quantize function is sensitive. Clicking on the store button allows you to save your settings in the Quantize selector menu. Working directly out of the Quantize Setup window is a good way of becoming familiar with the quantize functions. Try ticking the Auto box to make quantize adjustments to a MIDI part 'on the fly'. For an obviously audible effect, try adjusting the swing slider to 100% with a grid setting of 1/8.

Quantizing in the MIDI Editors

In the MIDI editors, the quantize resolution is chosen in the quantize selector on the toolbar. This imposes a series of vertical lines across the display which you can actually see in the MIDI editors and, as already outlined, this is known as the grid. Try changing the quantize value in the toolbar and you will see the grid modified accordingly. Whenever you use a quantize function, the grid becomes 'magnetic' for the recorded notes in the part. Each note is pulled directly onto or towards the nearest vertical line. The MIDI editors provide excellent visual feedback of what is actually happening when you use the quantize functions. In Cubase, the quantize functions are available in two overall modes; grid quantize and groove quantize. Grid quantize mode is concerned with quantize templates based upon regular grid spacings between 1/128 and whole notes. Groove quantize mode is concerned with more complex quantizing templates which have been 'extracted' from audio and MIDI events. A groove, as the name suggests, is generally based upon the 'feel' of the music from which it is derived. But before we get into the details, let's start with the basics.

Basic quantize

Looking at the results of Over quantize and Iterative quantize graphically in the Key editor helps understand what the functions are doing to the data. Figure 6.30 shows the before-and-after case for the quantizing of an inaccurately played hi-hat to 1/16th note divisions of the bar, using Over quantize with quantize set to 1/16 on the toolbar. The first two beats of the bar are shown where each vertical line represents the 1/16th note divisions. The original part contains notes which occur at different points either side of the 1/16th note pulse. After quantization, all notes line up exactly to the grid.

Figure 6.31 shows what happens if we were to use Iterative quantize on the same hi-hat part. In this case, the corrected notes do not fall directly onto the 1/16th note divisions of the bar. Instead, they are moved slightly closer to the divisions, thus tightening things up while still retaining the original feel of the playing. This particular Iterative quantize function has a strength per-

Figure 6.30
Using Over quantize to 'hard quantize' an inaccurately played hi-hat (upper grid) to exact 1/16th note divisions of the bar (lower grid)

Figure 6.31
Using Iterative quantize to quantize an inaccurately played hi-hat (upper grid) moves the notes towards the 1/16th note divisions of the bar (lower grid)

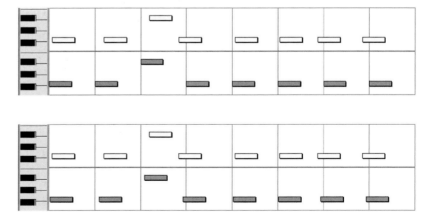

centage of 50% which means that notes are moved towards the pulse by reducing the current distance from the 1/16th note grid lines by 50%. Unlike Over quantize, Iterative quantize can be used several times in succession, on each occasion moving the notes slightly closer to the chosen quantize resolution. Iterative quantize gives us a clue as to the nature of the more creative uses of the quantize functions.

Quantize Setup in detail

The Quantize Setup window allows you to adjust the quantize parameters and create/edit presets. It functions in 'grid quantize' or 'groove quantize' modes, depending upon how the quantize data is created.

Quantize Setup (Grid mode)

To open the Quantize Setup window in standard grid quantize mode (Figure 6.32), choose 1/16 from the Quantize type menu and select Quantize Setup in the MIDI menu.

The Quantize Setup window in grid quantize mode includes the following parameters:

- Grid selector – a quantize selector menu containing a list of the possible note divisions of the bar between 1/128 and whole note values.
- Type selector – a quantize type menu with straight, triplet or dotted options.
- Swing slider – for adding a swing (shuffle) factor to the quantize function.
- Tuplet – for setting up complex quantizing functions based upon tuplet, triplet, quadruplet and more complex divisions of the bar.
- Magnetic area – determines a magnetic capture area within which notes are pulled onto or towards the grid. Notes outside the magnetic area are not affected by the quantizing action.
- Non-quantize – determines an area around each grid line within which notes will not be affected by the quantize function.
- Random quantize – adds a random number of ticks to the position of notes affected by the quantize function in order to humanise the correction effect (particularly useful for Over quantize).

Figure 6.32
The Quantize Setup window in grid quantize mode

- Iterative strength – regulates the strength of the Iterative quantize function in terms of a percentage. For example, a strength setting of 50% means that notes are moved towards the grid by reducing the note's current distance from the grid lines by 50%, each time the Iterative quantize function is used.
- Move controller – when Move controller is activated the quantize function also effects all pitch-bend, aftertouch, polyphonic pressure and continuous controller data found in the part.
- Auto – when auto is activated all changes made to the parameters are applied in real-time.
- Apply button – applies the edited quantize parameters.
- Presets section – allows the saving and loading of quantize presets and the removal of presets from the current list. These appear in the quantize type menu on the toolbar.

Adjusting any of the main parameters updates the Quantize Setup window's central display. This provides graphical feedback of the overall quantize template you have created and helps understand the function of each parameter as it is adjusted. The display shows one bar with blue lines indicating the positions of the quantize points.

Experimenting with grid quantize

Experimentation while listening to the results is one of the best ways of getting to know the quantize functions. For this purpose, it is recommended that you set up some key commands and work with the Quantize Setup window open on screen. Proceed as follows:

1   Open the Key commands window (File menu) and select MIDI in the categories list. Select the Iterative quantize command and assign the key combination 'Shift + Q'. Select the Undo quantize command and assign 'U'. Verify that Over quantize is assigned the 'Q' key (the default setting).
2   Select a MIDI part which contains notes which have not been recorded accurately (if necessary, create a special test part of badly played material)! Drum or rhythmic parts make good test material for the quantize functions.
3   While still in the Project window, open the Quick menu and select 'Loop selection'. You are now in cycle playback on the chosen MIDI part.
4   Open the Key or Drum editor and adjust the grid so that you can see the notes clearly on the screen.
5   Open the Quantize Setup window. You are now ready to start experimenting. Remember, it is important to be able to hear and see the results of your experiments.

The idea with this setup is to use the right hand with the mouse to manipulate the parameters in the Quantize Setup window and the left hand on the computer keyboard to initiate the quantize functions with the key commands.

This two-handed approach is a valuable technique which can serve you well in all your quantizing operations.

Experiment 1

Check out the differences between Over quantize and Iterative quantize and learn how to use the key commands you created in step 1 above. Proceed as follows:

- In the Quantize Setup window, select 1/16 in the grid menu and 'straight' in the type menu.
- Press Q on the computer keyboard to apply Over quantize to the part. Press U to undo the quantizing. Listen carefully to the difference. The undo command restores the part to its original state before any quantizing was applied.
- Press Shift + Q (as set up in step 1, above) to apply Iterative quantizing to the part. Try applying this several times and note how inaccurately played notes gradually move closer to the grid lines. Adjust the iterative strength parameter in the Quantize Setup window to change the intensity of the iterative quantizing effect. Listen carefully to the results. Press U to undo the quantizing.
- Try experimenting with the grid and type menu settings in the Quantize Setup dialogue and check out the effect of adding swing using the Swing slider. Swing works well with rhythmic parts and you might like to try it on 1/16th note hi-hats.

Experiment 2

Check out the effect of the quantize settings in the Quantize Setup window in real-time as you adjust the parameters. Proceed as follows:

- Activate auto in the Quantize Setup window.
- Adjust the Random quantize parameter to 10 ticks.
- Move the magnetic area slider while listening to the part. Notice how the notes bob back and forth as you increase the magnetic area and also how they gradually move closer to their nearest grid lines. The small movements are due to the random quantize setting. Each time you move the magnetic area slider the part is quantized again (from its original unquantized state) using the new slider value and other values and, each time, applying a small random value to the quantized position. This technique applies the Over quantize function. Iterative quantize cannot be applied in this way.
- Experiment with the other parameters while listening to the results in real-time.

These experiments are designed to help you explore the quantize functions in grid mode and encourage an understanding of the more creative aspects of quantizing. If, while experimenting, you stumble upon a combination of settings which gives particularly pleasing results, be sure to save it using the Store button. You can always use it at a later stage in a more serious project.

Info

Swing occurs when every second note position on the quantize grid is pushed to the right. The more the notes are pushed, the more the music swings.

Info

You can undo/redo all MIDI editing using the undo/redo functions in the Edit menu or by pressing Ctrl+Z (undo) or Ctrl+Shift+Z (redo). You can also step back through your edits using the Edit history window (select History in the Edit menu). The edit history is cleared when you close the project.

Quantize setup (Groove mode)

What is groove quantize?

In Cubase, groove quantize involves adjusting the timing and accent characteristics of musical material according to the natural 'groove' or 'feel' of a recorded musical performance (extracted from audio or MIDI recordings). While grid quantize (outlined above) processes material based upon 'regular' note values between 1/128 to whole notes, groove quantize processes material in a more 'irregular' way. This irregularity usually involves a succession of events whose timings fall at slightly different points around the beat. This is comparable to the kind of timing nuances we might find in any real-world musical performance. Cubase allows us to 'extract' such timing nuances from existing audio recordings or from MIDI parts and store the information as a groove template. Quantization using groove quantize thus allows the feel of one passage of music to be imposed upon another. You can also create a groove from scratch by adding/editing notes in a MIDI part and extracting the groove afterwards.

A groove can be quite simple, as in the case of a one bar 1/16th note shuffle groove or it can be a highly complex succession of timing events which vary over a number of bars. Groove quantize can be applied to whole arrangements or to selected elements, and different elements can be treated with different grooves.

Extracting a groove

There are two methods of creating your own groove quantize template, as follows:

1 To extract a groove from a MIDI part proceed as follows:

- Select a MIDI part in the event display. (No more than 16 bars. One, two or four bar patterns work well).
- Select 'Part to groove' in MIDI / Advanced Quantize.
- Open the Quantize type menu to reveal the newly added groove which appears last in the list with the same name as the part from which it was extracted.

2 To extract a groove from an audio event proceed as follows:

- Copy the target audio event. It is best to work on a copy to avoid damage to important material. If it is not already tightly edited, carefully edit the copy to fit a precise number of bars and beats (no more than 16 bars).
- With the newly edited event selected, use Audio / Bounce selection. Select replace in the Replace events dialogue. This creates a new audio event and corresponding audio file which is ready for processing.
- Double-click on the new event to open the Sample editor. Activate the Inspector and select the Definition section.
- In the Definition section, enter the number of bars and beats corresponding to the length of the audio event. Select the desired resolution in the Grid menu (try 1/4, 1/8 or 1/16 note). Activate the Auto adjust button to calculate the tempo of the audio. The grid lines should line up with the main peaks in the waveform.

Info

It is possible to create a groove template by selecting a tightly edited audio event and then selecting Audio / Hitpoints / Create Groove Quantize from Hitpoints. You will need to enter the tempo of the audio into a pop-up box. While this is quick, it is not always as accurate as the more detailed technique outlined here.

- Open the Hitpoints section of the Inspector and drag the Sensitivity slider to the right until one hitpoint appears for each hit in the rhythm. Audition the audio between each consecutive pair of hitpoints to verify the results.
- In the Hitpoints section, click on the Make groove button to create the groove template.
- Open the Quantize type menu to reveal the newly added groove which appears last in the list with the same name as the audio event from which it was extracted.

Info

See Chapter 8 for more detailed information about hitpoints and audio groove extraction.

Get into the groove

To explore the groove quantize functions of Cubase, open the Quantize Setup window (MIDI / Quantize setup) and switch to groove mode by choosing an existing groove quantize preset (Figure 6.33). If you cannot find an existing groove, create your own using one of the methods described above.

The Quantize Setup window in groove quantize mode includes the following parameters:

Figure 6.33
The Quantize Setup window in groove quantize mode

- Position, velocity and length sliders – these determine how much the position, velocity or length of the events in the groove template affect the target material (where 0% is no effect and 100% is maximum effect).
- Pre-quantize – allows the regular quantizing of material before it is groove quantized. This is helpful if Groove quantize produces undesirable results due to irregularities in the target part.
- Max. move in ticks – determines the maximum amount by which notes in the target are moved. Helpful for restricting the quantizing action within defined limits.
- Name and details field – gives the name of the original event/part from which the groove was extracted and details of the original tempo, time signature and event/part length. Knowing the original details can help judge whether the groove is likely to suit the target material.
- Presets menu – allows the storage and recall of quantize presets. These appear in the quantize type menu on the toolbar.
- Store, remove and Import 5.2 buttons – allows the storage of the current settings as a new preset or the deletion of the currently chosen preset. Removal involves a permanent deletion of the information and as such should be used with great care. The Import 5.2 button allows the importing of groove templates which were saved in Cubase VST 5.2 format.
- Non-quantize – determines an area around each event in the groove within which notes in the target part are not affected by the quantizing action.

- Random quantize – adds a random number of ticks to the position of notes affected by the quantize function in order to vary the correction effect.
- Iterative strength – regulates the strength of the Iterative quantize function in terms of a percentage. For example, a strength setting of 50% means that notes in the target part are moved towards the groove by reducing the note's current distance from the groove template events by 50%, each time the Iterative quantize function is used.
- Auto – when auto is activated all changes made to the parameters are applied in real-time.
- Apply quantize button – applies the edited quantize parameters using the Over quantize function.

Adjusting any of the main parameters updates the Quantize Setup window's central display. This provides graphical feedback of the overall quantize template you have created and helps understand the function of each parameter as it is adjusted. The display shows the number of bars in the groove and contains blue lines indicating the positions of the events in the groove template.

Advanced quantizing techniques

The quantizing tools of Cubase may be used purely for corrective purposes but, when used in a more creative manner, provide a powerful tool for injecting new life into your MIDI and audio recordings. The following outlines a number of advanced techniques and ideas for enhancing and experimenting with the feel of your tracks (relevant to both grid and groove modes).

Groove quantize can be used to match the timing characteristics of a MIDI part to an audio event by extracting the groove from the audio and applying the resulting groove template to the MIDI material. This is useful for making MIDI parts fit precisely alongside an existing audio arrangement. Much of the time, however, you might create a groove from an existing MIDI or audio event simply because you like the feel of the music. It is also possible to manufacture your own grooves by editing and manipulating the data in a MIDI part in the Key editor. You can then quickly create a groove template from this 'manufactured' MIDI part using 'Part to groove' (MIDI menu / Advanced). The latter technique is particularly relevant in the light of the various tips supplied below. These help understand what is going on 'inside' the groove. Quantize may be applied to both MIDI and audio material, as long as the target audio has been divided up into separate rhythmic components using Cubase's audio slicing functions.

Pushing a bass drum ahead of the beat produces a sense of urgency and delaying a snare to fall after the beat produces a lazy, 'laid back' feel. Conversely, a late bass drum produces a relaxed effect and an early snare makes things sound 'tight' and anticipated. Groove templates are best applied individually to separate bass drum and snare tracks to achieve the latter late/early effects. Experiment with your collection of grooves to hear which combinations work well together. Manipulation of the position of the

---

Tip

Not all material is suitable for groove quantizing and only certain groove templates may suit a given musical passage. You may be able to improve upon the results by experimenting with the position, velocity and length sliders and the random field in the Quantize Setup window.

Info

See Chapter 8 for more details about audio slices

snare in relation to the second and fourth beats can have a major effect on the groove of the whole song and making sure that the hi-hat part is not playing repetitions of exactly the same part throughout helps maintain the interest of the listener. To avoid exact repetitions of the same hi-hat part in Cubase, use the Random quantize field in the Quantize Setup menu to introduce a slight variation in the quantizing action (try between 3 and 5 ticks). The hi-hat itself plays a major role in the character of the groove, especially when manipulating shuffle and swing feels. Shuffles are concerned with delaying every other note in a succession of regularly spaced note events. In Cubase the amount of swing can be controlled in fine detail using the swing slider in the Quantize Setup window (Grid mode). In a similar manner to the kick and snare, moving the hi-hat ahead of the beat produces a sense of urgency and moving it late produces a looser feel. You might also be concerned with rhythmic punctuations in the arrangement such as cymbal crashes and drum rolls. Moving crashes to occur ahead of the beat can produce excitement and moving them to be late produces a sense of expectation. Some styles of music rely on specific grooves with specific relationships between the bass drum, snare and hihat. For example, many shuffle grooves rely on a bass drum and snare which are quantized tightly to the beat while the hi-hat alone is quantized to the shuffle groove. Quantize is often best applied to specific parts of the arrangement rather than to the whole kit or rhythm section. For this reason, detailed quantizing works better when the constituent parts of the rhythm section are on separate tracks (particularly the kick, snare and hi-hat).

In real-world performances, the relative timing positions of the constituent parts of a drum rhythm are often in a constant state of change but the overall characteristics of the changes remain similar. In other words, the kick might always be played ahead of the beat, the snare might fluctuate on and around the beat and the hi-hat might always be behind the beat. It is also the case that the bass drum and snare are rarely played at precisely the same moment in each bar and all the instruments are in a constant state of subtle change in terms of accent. Approximating similar behaviour with both grid and groove quantize helps humanise and enliven the material. Try experimenting with the position, velocity and length sliders (groove mode) or the swing and magnetic sliders (grid mode) along with the random field in the Quantize Setup window to simulate similar behaviour in your MIDI parts. When applied to sliced audio events, similar slider manipulations can help you to mangle drum loops beyond recognition or to find a new, original feel for the rhythm. Once processing like this has been applied successfully, an A-B comparison usually reveals just how dull the original parts were sounding.

The use of quantize does not exist in isolation from other techniques such as tempo, accent and overall musical arrangement manipulations. All these latter elements can be used to create the right feel. For example, classic tempo manipulation might involve slowing the tempo on the verses and speeding it up for the choruses. You can create still more excitement by combining an early snare with a tempo increase. The musical arrangement often benefits if the events are not too dense. Many sequencer-based musicians fall

Tip

Generally, there is no one element which is responsible for the groove. Each instrument might emphasise different beats in the bar and the groove of each element might vary. You could have late bass drums on the first and third beats of the bar combined with early snares on the second and fourth. This makes things sound tight and tense.

Tip

Maintaining lots of space in the arrangement both in a musical and in a mix sense helps give all the instruments space to breathe. This allows the groove to shine through.

into the trap of programming extremely busy drum parts which leave no space for the rhythm to breathe. Also, don't forget that the relative timing positions of different elements can be changed by simply moving whole tracks backwards or forwards in time using the track delay parameter in the Inspector. And, of course, quantize itself is not confined to the drum kit alone, it can be applied to any instrument in the arrangement.

Audio recording

Chapter 3 outlined the basic audio recording process. This chapter provides more detailed information about audio recording, routing and the general handling of audio data within Cubase.

Although this chapter is mainly concerned with the audio recording process within Cubase, it was also considered useful to include information about digital audio and recording techniques in general. Cubase does not exist in isolation from the rest of the sound recording world and it is essential to keep this in mind when using the software to record audio.

Digital audio

What is digital audio?

Audio recording in Cubase is of the digital variety. This means that the sounds you record are converted into a numerical representation of the signal using an analogue-to-digital (A/D) converter. These numbers are stored in a data retrieval system (normally your hard disk), and the sounds are reproduced by converting the numbers back into the analogue domain using a digital-to-analogue (D/A) converter. These converters are found on your audio hardware.

The quality of the audio is dependent on the general performance of the converters, the sample rate and the bit resolution. The sample rate is the number of times the analogue signal is measured (sampled) per second. The bit resolution, (also referred to as bit depth), is a measure of the accuracy of the system. The greater the number of bits the more levels of resolution are available to measure the analogue signal. Popular bit resolutions include 8, 16, 20, 24 and 32-bit float. Regular audio CDs are 16-bit with a sample rate of 44.1 kHz.

Cubase normally operates in 16, 24 or 32-bit float resolutions with a sample rate choice of 11.25 to 96kHz. Theoretically, you can achieve very high quality recordings with the system. However, there are many other factors which affect the sound quality and paramount among these is how you actually make your recordings.

Some differences between analogue and digital recording

If you were recording onto an analogue multi-track tape recorder your approach to sound recording might be very different to when using a digital system like Cubase. When recording onto analogue tape many sound engineers would record with the level meters overloading slightly on certain peaks in the signal. Although, strictly speaking, the sound is distorting, the kind of mild distortion produced is not displeasing to the ear. The extreme peaks alone are distorting and in the analogue system these are rounded off to closer to the level of the rest of the signal. This results in a natural compression effect and, some would say, adds a certain warmth to the sound.

The latter is not the case with digital audio. Digital audio systems generally use full-scale (FS) meters, as opposed to the volume unit (VU) meters often found in analogue systems. The maximum level for a digital audio system is 0dBFS. There is no additional headroom above this maximum point. Once the level goes into the red, (above 0dBFS), the distortion produced is extremely unpleasant to the ear. There is also no graduated distortion response with digital systems; it sounds bad whether you are 10dB or 0.1dB above 0dBFS. For this reason, when you record with Cubase you must ensure that no clipping occurs on the input buss.

The net result is that recording digitally sometimes results in recordings with a lower average level and less 'character' than may have been the case if you were recording the same sources onto analogue tape. The digital version needs more headroom to avoid distortion on the peaks in the signal whereas the analogue recording benefits from pushed levels and natural tape compression, as described above. Recording digitally at lower levels is sometimes problematic with 16-bit systems where there is limited dynamic range to capture the low level detail (the theoretical dynamic range of 16-bit is 96dB). However, capturing low-level detail is not an issue at higher bit depths like 24-bit and 32-bit float since these feature greatly improved dynamic range (due to less quantising errors), adding 48dB or more dynamic range at the lower end of the scale when compared to 16-bit. The theoretical dynamic range of 24-bit is 144dB. For this reason, you can safely record well below 0dBFS when using 24-bit, simultaneously obtaining greater headroom for signal peaks and better gain structure. For tracking purposes, levels might be set to produce between -10dBFS and -6dBFS on peaks with the average signal level hovering around -18dBFS.

Overall, the advantages of digital audio far outweigh the disadvantages. It suffers less from background noise and hiss, it has a better dynamic range than analogue, it can be conveniently stored on hard disk or other media, it can be easily processed in the digital domain using digital signal processing techniques, and exact copies of the original can be made with no loss of quality.

What bit resolution and sample rate should I use?

The short answer

The short answer is to use the highest bit resolution and sample rate your system can manage. For standard audio applications, 24-bit/44.1kHz is a good choice for most users. For greater fidelity assurance use 32-bit float/44.1kHz or 24-bit/96kHz.

Info

One negative aspect of digital audio is that it can seem harsh or brittle when compared to analogue tape recordings (although subjective opinions on this subject vary greatly). PSP Audioware's Vintage Warmer, Voxengo's AF TapeBus or Cubase's SoftClipper help counteract this phenomenon by emulating tape saturation and analogue warmth. However, a truly authentic emulation of tape saturation has proved particularly difficult to reproduce digitally.

Info

As a general rule, Steinberg recommend that there is no point recording at a higher bit depth than that of your audio hardwares A/D converters.

Tip

Recording at 32-bit float/44.1 can help preserve the quality of recordings which you expect to subject to plug-in processing or off-line audio processes.

The long answer

Although the short answer given above is adequate for the needs of many Cubase users, in reality the issues are slightly more complicated. Bit resolution (also known as bit depth) describes the range of values (quantising steps) available to measure the signal. There are 16,777,216 values for 24-bit and 65,536 values for 16-bit. Sample rate describes how many measurements of the signal are made per second. For example, 44.1kHz measures the signal 44,100 times per second.

The first thing to consider is the bit resolution and sample rate of the final media for which the recording is intended and then work at preferably a greater resolution within Cubase. Greater audible improvements are made by increasing the bit resolution rather than the sample rate, so it is best to concentrate on this first. The maximum possible resolution depends upon the resources of your host computer. Not all systems are capable of recording at high bit resolutions and sample rates. If you are aiming to produce a standard audio CD then the final resolution is 16-bit/44.1kHz. However, the whole recording process benefits if you do all the initial work at a higher resolution, such as 24bit/44.1kHz or even 32-bit float/44.1kHz. You only apply dithering and truncate to 16-bit at the very last stage. This results in a significant improvement in the fidelity of the final audio signal. A final 16-bit audio signal produced in this way might have an apparent bit resolution of 18 or 19 bits which equates to a 12 to 18dB increase in dynamic range. The whole idea with digital recording is to start with high resolution sources and maintain this high resolution for as long as possible until the mastering stage (until the point just before dithering and truncation to 16-bit).

The above advice suggests that if the sample rate of the destination media, such as a CD, is at 44.1kHz then we should start out recording at 44.1kHz in Cubase. This works as a rule of thumb. The objective here is to avoid the possibly detrimental effect of sample rate conversion. Working at a higher sample rate, such as 96kHz, and then converting to 44.1kHz at a later stage may result in more damage to the audio signal than if you had started out with 44.1kHz in the first place. This is especially true if you use sub-standard sample rate conversion. If you must use sample rate conversion, you are advised to use a high quality conversion plug-in such as Steinberg Wavelab's Crystal Resampler or similar to ensure optimum quality. Otherwise, play safe and set your Cubase project to the same sample rate as the final destination media (as suggested above).

It is also worth considering that you may in the future wish to release your music on one of the higher resolution audio formats such as DVD-A (Digital Versatile Disc – Audio) or SACD (Super Audio Compact Disc). DVD-A boasts a maximum resolution of 24-bit/96kHz and SACD uses an alternative high quality digital audio format known as DSD (Direct Stream Digital) which gives an equivalent performance. Working at 96kHz uses more computer resources but is likely to produce recordings with subtly improved transparency and detail. There is much debate on whether we can actually perceive the difference between 44.1 and 96kHz sample rates. 44.1 digital audio successfully produces signals up to 20kHz (the upper limit of human hearing) so, theoretically, we cannot improve matters any further by using a

96kHz sample rate, which raises the upper limit to around 48kHz (we cannot hear in this region). However, the upper threshold is not the factor which directly compromises the signal. It is rather the steep reconstruction filters in the 44.1 D/A conversion process which can be problematic. In any case, most professional mastering engineers claim they can hear the difference between 96 and 44.1kHz but most also admit that any improvement is subtle. Regardless of the debate, if your material is destined to be mastered in a professional mastering house they may well request the source files in 24-bit/96kHz format.

Info

24-bit vs 16-bit - in an ideal system, the maximum dynamic range is 144dB for 24-bit vs 96dB for 16-bit. 24-bit resolution results in less distortion during the quantisation process since there are more measurement values and thus smaller quantising steps (16,777,216 discrete steps for 24-bit vs 65,536 steps for 16-bit). However, an increase in bit depth does NOT result in an increase in level. 0dBFS remains at the same absolute level in both systems. The 48dB extra dynamic range for 24-bit is added at the lower end of the scale (the noise floor is lower due to smaller quantising errors in the digital conversion process). This means that you can leave more headroom when recording at 24-bit without fear of losing the low level detail in the signal.

Info

Avoid confusion between bit depth and sample rate. Bit depth is resolution-based and governs dynamic range. This determines the number of values available to measure the signal (quantising steps). The greater the bit depth the more measurement values available and the lower the noise floor (due to less quantising errors). Sample rate is frequency-based and governs the maximum frequency bandwidth of the system. This is the rate at which measurements of the signal are made. The faster the rate the higher the frequency which can be accurately reproduced. In Cubase, the bit depth and sample rate are set in the Project Setup window (Record Format and Sample Rate fields).

Buffer and storage considerations

Knowing the details of how digital audio is handled and stored inside your computer may help you get better results when recording and streamlining your system. Firstly, the source analogue signal is converted into digital information using the audio hardware's A/D converter. Once converted, the information is stored in a buffer (a temporary storage area). When the buffer is full, the system collects the data and stores it on your hard disk. This process happens repeatedly and very quickly. The actual speed depends upon the size of the buffer, the CPU power of the computer and the efficiency of the hard drive. The speed also contributes to the latency of the system (see below). You might like to try setting a smaller buffer size in your audio hardware driver software when you are recording. This suits recording since a smaller buffer size means less latency, and less latency means that you can monitor in real-time via Cubase with greater accuracy. However, a smaller buffer size also means that the drain on your CPU power is much greater and, in extreme cases, may cause other operational elements in the computer to slow down or fail. Therefore, when you are not recording (for example, when you are mixing), it may help to increase your buffer size slightly. This reduces your CPU overhead and allows you to use more plug-ins.

As for storage, most high performance hard drives can adequately handle the recording of digital audio. The audio files themselves are stored in the folder for the project as chosen when you first created it (by default, within a sub-directory named Audio). If you wish to verify the location of the project folder on the hard disk, open the Pool (Ctrl/Command + P) where

Figure 7.1
Keep track of the available recording time on your hard disk using the info line below the track list

the project folder is shown in the information line at the top of the window. For keeping track of how much space you have available, Cubase features a handy info line directly below the track list which shows the chosen sample rate and record format, and the remaining recording time in hours and minutes (Figure 7.1).

Latency

Latency is the delay between the input and output of a digital audio system (expressed in samples or milliseconds). All digital audio systems take a small amount of time to respond to a user input and process the data through their hardware and software. This affects real-time performance. It not only imposes a slight delay between the audio input and output signals, it also affects the delay between the moment you move a channel fader on the screen and the moment you hear the audible result, and it imposes a slight delay between the moment you press a note on your MIDI keyboard and the moment you hear the sound from a VST Instrument. If the delay is too long then it becomes difficult to play accurately in real-time performance. So where does the latency come from? Latency is actually imposed by a combination of factors in the signal chain. Paramount among these are the audio buffers of the audio hardware. The audio buffer size can usually be adjusted and is often quoted in a control panel utility supplied with your audio hardware. Typical figures include 64, 128, 256 and 512 samples. These sample values can be converted to delay times in milliseconds by dividing the quoted figure by the sample rate you are using.

For example, at a sample rate of 44.1kHz:

$$64/44.1 = 1.45ms$$
$$128/44.1 = 2.9ms$$
$$256/44.1 = 5.8ms$$

and so on. Typically, you may also expect to add another 0.5ms to this figure for each of the A/D and D/A converters, and other elements in the signal chain may also add a small amount of delay. Thus, for a quoted buffer size of 128 samples you could expect a real-world latency of around 3.5 – 4ms each, for both the recording and playback parts of the signal chain. This equates to a total latency of around 7 – 8ms when monitoring in real-time via Cubase. (This latency only affects the monitoring of a real-time performance. Any tracks which are already recorded are not subject to the same latency issues).

It is a fact that real-world machines and electronic musical instruments also suffer from similar delays, and a delay of a few milliseconds is imposed each time you move further away from your monitoring loudspeakers (around

3ms per metre). Musicians naturally compensate for the delays they hear while playing in real-time, as long as the delay remains minimal and fairly constant. However, virtuoso performers, drummers and percussionists can pick up on even the slightest irregularities when monitoring during a live performance so the effect of latency must be minimised. To provide optimum real-time performance, professional audio hardware with a dedicated ASIO driver which can achieve overall latency times of less than 10ms is highly recommended.

Audio recording techniques

Recording vocals and acoustic instruments – microphone recording techniques

The first stage in making a recording of a vocalist or live instrumentalist is deciding where they are going to perform. The acoustic environment for the performance plays a major part in giving the recorded sound its particular characteristics. In a professional recording studio this environment is often an acoustically treated performance area which is isolated from the control room and the outside world. If you are lucky enough to have a similar facility as part of your Cubase system then so much the better.

The second stage is deciding which microphone to use and where to place it in relation to the vocalist or instrumentalist. The microphone is the very first stage in the recording path when you are recording live vocals, musical instruments and other real-world sources so, if you are serious about your recording, it is worth investing in a well-specified model. For good all-round performance and for the recording of vocals, large-diaphragm capacitor (condenser) microphones are a good choice. For acoustic instruments and drum kits the choice of microphone type widens enormously from small diaphragm pencil capacitor microphones to dynamic or ribbon models. Inexperienced sound recordists may have the impression that you can place any kind of microphone anywhere in front of the source and then start recording. Unfortunately, it is not quite as simple as this, since there are a multitude of different microphone models with different pickup patterns designed for different purposes and, even if you have chosen an appropriate model, a change of even a few centimetres in microphone position can affect the sound quality. It is wise, therefore, to experiment with the microphone position and, if you have several models, the microphone type. Dont be afraid to take a little time to get the sound right at the time of the actual recording. Occasionally, this might also involve applying EQ or compression. If you are recording vocals, a pop shield reduces the explosives, (the 'p' and 'b' sounds which cause pops and low frequency rumbles), and can simultaneously help set the ideal distance the vocalist should be from the microphone.

A third consideration is the use of a microphone pre-amp before the signal reaches your mixing console or Cubase, and this is certainly highly recommended. In general, you should try to limit the number of devices through which the signal has to pass before it arrives within Cubase so, when using a mic pre-amp, you would normally pass the signal directly from there into Cubase. The best mic pre-amps feature a superior signal path to many consoles and often provide high-quality compression and EQ controls.

Info

Most latency problems are related to a combination of your computer's CPU power, RAM memory, audio hardware buffers, A/D and D/A converters and audio hardware drivers. To ensure the best real-time performance, high speed CPUs, large amounts of RAM and professional audio cards/hardware with dedicated ASIO drivers are highly recommended.

Info

See Microphone matters in Chapter 2 for more information about microphone recording techniques and connecting a microphone to a Cubase system.

Tip

You can normally safely roll off the low frequencies in a vocal recording (below 60Hz) to avoid low frequency rumbles.

Info

Using cardioid or figure-of-eight pattern microphones close to the source (close-miking) results in a phenomenon known as the proximity effect, where lower frequencies are disproportionately boosted. The proximity effect can be actively used to create a more intimate feel but, where it is not desired, EQ might be used to adjust the spectrum for a more open sound.

Recording live sounds via microphones is generally more difficult than recording line level signals like synthesizers and samplers. This is because the sound signal is in a constant state of change and is likely to feature unpredictable peaks and lows in the amplitude. The level of difficulty is increased when you are using more than one microphone simultaneously, as in the case of recording a drum kit.

A high-quality professional microphone can radically improve the fidelity of the input signal. Models supplied by AKG, Audio Technica, Beyer, Blue, Brauner, Calrec, Coles, Electrovoice, DPA, Microtech Gefell, Neumann, Oktava, Rode, Royer, SE, Sennheiser, Shure and Sony are highly recommended.

Recording electric guitars, electric basses, synthesizers and samplers

The recording of electric guitars and basses presents a whole new set of potential problems to the sound recordist. Both instruments can be recorded using DI (Direct Injection) or microphone techniques or both simultaneously. You can also use a guitar or bass pre-amp which produces a convenient line level signal as output. This can be routed to the line inputs of your external mixer or directly into your audio hardware.

When placing microphones around a guitar speaker cabinet it is common practice to use two microphones, one placed close to the speaker and the other further back to pick up more of the room sound. A bass guitar cabinet is more likely to be recorded using a single microphone designed for lower frequencies and this signal is often mixed with a DI line signal from the bass amplifier or a DI box.

One of the problems when recording electric guitar and bass is that of noise interference. This manifests itself as a background buzz or hum which varies according to the relative positions of the guitar, amplifier and speakers. This is due to electromagnetic interference between the pickups of the guitar and the amplifier and speakers (or any other electronic equipment near to the guitar). Single-coil pickups are more prone to interference than humbucking pickups. Popular solutions include minimising the interference by experimenting with the relative positions of the guitar, amplifier and speakers and using gate and noise filtering processors after the recording has been made. CRT type computer monitors also cause significant hum when used near electric guitar instruments. The preferred solution for minimising this effect in a Cubase system, is to use an LCD/TFT flat-screen monitor. Otherwise, play your guitar at some distance from the computer equipment or, if you have the facilities, use a separate room for the guitar performance. Once again, the sound signal from these instruments is often unpredictable as there can be significant changes in level from one note (or chord) to the next due to the instrument's resonant behaviour and changes in the player's technique and playing intensity.

Synthesizers and samplers are easier to record since they are generally more predictable and, if they are controlled via the MIDI sequencer of Cubase, you can re-play the parts many times over until you are satisfied that you have set the optimum record level. They also have the convenience of line outputs which are easy to handle when routed into your external mixer

Info

A mic pre-amp is highly recommended for recording vocals and live instruments. Check out the mic pre-amps supplied by Aphex, API, Art, Audient, Avalon, Crane Song, DAV Electronics, DBX, Focusrite, Joe Meek, Mackie, Manley, Neve, Presonus, SPL, SSL, TF Pro, Tube Tech and Universal Audio.

Tip

You can normally safely roll off the upper frequencies in bass guitar recordings (above 8 - 10kHz) to cut out hiss and high frequency interference. A similar technique can be employed with electric guitar depending on the precise nature of the material.

Info

For further information on how to reduce the background noise in an electric guitar recording, see 'Detect Silence' in Chapter 8.

Info

For more recording tips, see 'Ten golden rules for recording and mixing' in Chapter 12.

or directly into your audio hardware. However, synthesizer and sampler sounds can often seem lifeless and lacking in character when compared to real acoustic instruments so care needs to be taken in how you record them. The use of effects and processing is a popular method of livening things up and some sound recordists will go as far as adding noise and distortion to the signal in order to give it more character. Subtle use of Cubase's supplied AmpSimulator or SoftClipper, Voxengo's TapeBus or PSP's Vintage Warmer produce good results for this kind of processing. Effects added in this way are often intended to be an integral part of the recorded sound. If you are not sure of what the final sound should be, it is better to add the effect at the mixing stage.

The magic formula for making great sounding recordings?

Sorry! There is no magic formula for making great sounding recordings, there are only guide lines. Despite enormous technological advances in all areas of the audio and recording industries and the availability of digital audio recording tools like Cubase, it remains impossible to devise a fixed set of rules which ensure a high-quality recording. One of the problems is that each individual has a different idea of what actually sounds good. Another is that recording equipment (such as microphones and loudspeakers) and sound itself behave differently according to the acoustic environment and temperature. And, of course, when recording a live musician, no two musical performances are ever exactly the same.

So, what are the guide lines? We've already touched upon some of them in this chapter and in Chapter 2 but one of the major requirements is to learn how to use your ears. These are actually the only tools you have to judge whether or not you are making what is, in your opinion, a great sounding recording. Once you've got your ears up and running, your task is to get the best possible sounding signal recorded into Cubase. This starts at source and may encompass a wider range of elements than just the sound itself. For example, is the vocalist singing in tune? Is the guitar in tune with the synthesizer you recorded on a previous session? Is everybody playing in time? Have you minimised any noise interference at source? Have you selected the best acoustic environment in which to make your microphone recording? Is the microphone placed in the optimum position relative to the source and the acoustic space? Once you have answered these and other questions relevant to preparing your session, you can then start to judge if you are achieving the sound quality you require in Cubase. It is important to capture a good performance and to get the right sound at the time of the recording; never expect to be able to fix it in the mix. Try to get the optimum signal level recorded whilst also avoiding distortion. When recording at 24-bit resolution, signal peaks at -6dBFS with an average level around -18dBFS is a good guide line. Unpredictable sound sources, like vocals, might benefit from compression. Take your time getting things right in the early stages of the recording process and never hesitate to experiment with microphone placement before resorting to EQ.

EQ might be used for creative effects but, at the recording stage, is best used in a corrective sense to filter out any low frequency rumbles, high fre-

Tip

You cannot make judgements about sound without an accurate monitoring system in an acoustically balanced environment. One of the keys to making good recordings is accurate monitoring.

Tip

Using Cubase in cycle record mode might help you capture that once-only magical performance (see Audio recording in cycle mode below).

quency hiss or other interference which does not form part of the required signal or to flatten out the frequency response of instruments recorded using close-miking techniques. For low frequency rumbles, many microphones incorporate low frequency roll off filter switches and these might provide a better option than using EQ. When using a high or low pass filter to roll off the high or low frequencies above or below the required sound, great care must be taken to ensure that you do not shave off parts of the actual signal. You can sometimes safely reduce the top end (above around 10kHz) of such instruments as bass drums, bass guitars, bass synths, electric pianos and electric guitars.

Similarly, you can normally safely roll off the low end (below 60Hz) of such instruments as vocals, violins, hi-hats and cymbals. When using close-miking techniques, particularly on live drums, the lower frequencies are disproportionately boosted due to a phenomenon with cardioid or figure-of-eight pattern microphones known as the proximity effect. The proximity effect can be actively used to create a more intimate feel but, where it is not desired, a high-pass filter and/or low frequency shelving EQ (in the region below around 200Hz) might be used to adjust the spectrum for a more open sound. Another corrective technique includes using a narrow band parametric EQ to reduce certain over-emphasised harmonics which occasionally become apparent in bass guitar, electric guitar, organ, drum and percussion performances due to resonances in the instrument itself or in the performance space.

The use of EQ in these contexts would normally be that found on your external console or pre-amp. Bear in mind that the EQ sections of budget equipment often create more problems in the sound than they solve. Many experienced sound engineers prefer to use a minimum of EQ at the time of recording and there are some very good reasons for this. As soon as you switch in an EQ section you are routing the signal through another set of control circuits which can potentially degrade the signal. Degradation might be particularly apparent if you are using the EQ section of a budget mixing console. EQ also affects the phase of the frequency components within the signal and this can result in undesirable side effects and harshness. The guide line here is to get the sound as right as possible before it even enters your external console or mic pre-amp and, certainly, before it enters Cubase. EQ at the recording stage might be viewed as a last resort, when there is no other solution, but there are no hard and fast rules.

Last but not least, in all of the above recording techniques, monitor your sounds through high quality loudspeakers in an acoustically balanced room and avoid excessive monitoring levels.

This provides you with a very brief taste of what is involved in the wider recording process outside of the direct domain of Cubase. As you have probably realised, specific sound engineering skills are required if you intend to do a lot of audio recording using microphones. Microphone choice and placement is a big subject and it is beyond the scope of this book to cover it in detail.

Important

If you you are in doubt about any of these techniques, leave any corrective EQing to the mixing stage

Info

Readers who intend to use Cubase for vocal and live instrument recording and have no prior knowledge of sound recording are advised to seek more detailed information from specialist texts on the subject.

Audio routing in Cubase

A key element for understanding the operation of a traditional recording studio is a detailed knowledge of all the inputs and outputs of the mixing console and how all the other equipment is connected to it. In other words, you need to know where the audio signals are going to and where they are coming from, otherwise known as routing. Things are similar with Cubase. A clear understanding of how the signal travels from the source into your audio hardware, through Cubase, and finally back out again helps you grasp the details of the audio recording process. This seems like common sense but it is surprisingly easy to get confused when there are a large number of inputs and outputs in an audio system.

The input path

Figure 7.2 shows an example of the input path using a system with multiple input audio hardware. The signal is traced from its arrival at two of the physical inputs through to its destination as a stereo recording on one of Cubase's audio tracks. Looking at the signal path graphically allows you to stand back and think about what is actually taking place.

In this example, a stereo signal is connected to the line inputs of the audio hardware. It is first converted into digital form via the hardware's A/D converters. It then passes through the software audio mixer associated with the audio hardware. This is where settings which govern the operation of your audio hardware are made and, depending on the hardware in use, where the source level at the input of your audio hardware may be adjusted.

Next, the signal passes via the input section of the VST Connections window where the input ports of the audio hardware are connected to a chosen input buss. By default, at least one input buss is already present in the VST Connections window and this is normally connected to the first two audio inputs found in your audio hardware device. An input buss can be renamed in the Bus Name column and, although this is not essential, it helps clarify the source of the audio signal in other parts of the program. Intelligent labelling especially helps with multiple input/output hardware. Further input busses may be added by clicking on the Add bus button.

Now that the input buss is connected to a physical input, the input signal can be seen in the chosen input buss channel strip in the Mixer. Input busses appear to the left of all other channels in the Mixer. You can now visually monitor the level at source or the level being recorded to hard disk in the level meter of the input buss depending upon the global meter setting (Meter Input or Meter Post-fader). The input buss post-fader signal is what gets recorded to hard disk and the same signal is normally also routed to one or more audio channels for monitoring and recording purposes.

To hear the input buss post-fader signal, you must monitor enable an audio track/channel and set its input to the appropriate input buss (when monitoring via VST). The input buss is chosen in the Input Routing menu above the chosen audio channel. This opens a pop-up menu containing the available inputs, as activated in the VST Connections window. Normally, the chosen channel is also record enabled so that you can actually make your recording. Finally, when you make your recording it is represented as a waveform inside an audio event in the event display.

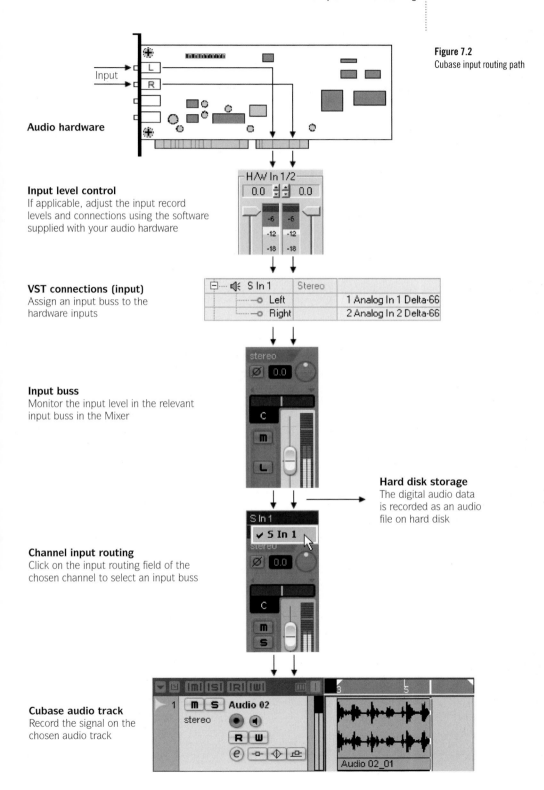

Figure 7.2
Cubase input routing path

Audio hardware

Input level control
If applicable, adjust the input record
levels and connections using the software
supplied with your audio hardware

VST connections (input)
Assign an input buss to the
hardware inputs

Input buss
Monitor the input level in the relevant
input buss in the Mixer

Hard disk storage
The digital audio data
is recorded as an audio
file on hard disk

Channel input routing
Click on the input routing field of the
chosen channel to select an input buss

Cubase audio track
Record the signal on the
chosen audio track

The output path

Once recorded to hard disk, activating playback sends the signal back through the system to the outside world. Figure 7.3 shows the output routing path for three stereo and three mono audio tracks which are routed to four outputs of a multiple I/O audio device.

In Cubase, tracks are assigned as either mono or stereo when they are first added to the project using the Add track command (Project menu). A stereo track contains two audio signals, (the left and right channels of the stereo signal), and a mono track contains a single signal. By default, the signals recorded on any audio tracks arrive at the Mixer channels in the same order as they

After arriving in the the Mixer, the audio signals are routed to various destinations according to the settings in the Output Routing menus. In this case, synths and drum loop channels are routed to the Master stereo output buss and SFX 1, 2 and 3 to a Group channel. The Group channel is, in turn, routed to a second stereo output buss. The various signals are heard on the left or right of the stereo image according to each channel's pan control setting. Overall level changes and master insert effects may be applied in the output buss channel strips which appear to the right of all other channels in the Mixer. Finally, the master buss is routed to physical outputs 1 and 2 and Bus 2 is routed to physical outputs 3 and 4 of a multiple I/O audio hardware device in the output section of the VST Connections window. By default, at least one output buss is already assigned in the VST Connections window and this is normally routed to the first two audio outputs found in your audio hardware device. Further output busses are added by clicking on the Add bus button. After being converted back into the analogue domain via the D/A converters of the audio hardware, the composite audio signal arrives back in the real world where it can be amplified and monitored as required.

Key steps for routing an input signal onto an audio track

Despite having followed the audio recording tutorial in Chapter 3 and despite having fully understood the input and output routing setup within Cubase, the audio recording process may still remain difficult to grasp and retain. This is normal since there are quite a few parameters involved. For those readers who need further clarification, the following outlines the key steps for routing an input signal onto an audio track:

• Connect the audio signal to the appropriate physical input of the audio card or audio hardware device.
• Verify that the relevant input and output ports are active and visible in Devices / Device Setup / VST Audio System / << *name of your audio hardware driver* >>
• Connect the chosen audio hardware input port to an appropriate input buss in the VST Connections window.
• Verify that there is level activity in the meters of the chosen input buss in the Mixer.
• Adjust the input level using one or more of the following: the output gain of the audio source, the output gain of the send fader on your external mixing console through which the source is routed, the input level fader

Project window

Mixer channels

Output busses

VST connections (output)

Multiple I/O hardware

Figure 7.3
Cubase output routing path

in the audio hardware's audio mixer (if available), or the input buss gain dial or fader controls.

- Add an audio track in the Project window and select the appropriate input buss by clicking on the input routing menu above the channel fader in the Mixer (or in the Inspector for the track).
- Activate the monitor button for the track. This allows you to hear and see the level of any input signal on the channel meters (assuming that you are monitoring the signal via Cubase). Activate the record enable button to make the channel ready for recording.
- Record the audio in the normal manner using the record button on the Transport panel.

Troubleshooting the recording process

If you have not yet managed to get an input signal showing in the meters or cannot hear your input signal, the following troubleshooting list may help solve the problem:

- Check that the source instrument or device which is supplying the sound signal is not faulty. Ensure that it is switched on/activated and check the audio cables for faulty connections.
- Check that there is not an impedance mismatch between the source signal and the input you have chosen on your audio card/device.
- Check that the audio card/device has been correctly installed and is operating outside of Cubase. Test the hardware for audio recording and playback functionality using a software application supplied with your operating system.
- Check that the audio card/device is connected in the VST Connections window (Device menu).
- It is easy to become confused about the left and right inputs of a stereo input device when recording mono sources and the multiple inputs of multiple I/O hardware. Make sure that the audio inputs are clearly labelled in the VST Connections window and that the correct input buss is selected on the chosen audio track.
- To hear and see the signal on the channel level meter of the chosen audio track make sure that the monitor button is activated (illuminated).

Monitoring in Cubase

The above troubleshooting steps solve the majority of problems with the setting up of the input routing of Cubase. However, you may also be encountering difficulties due to confusion about how best to monitor the signal (in both the visual and audio sense) and the manner in which Cubase behaves when you select an audio track.

Monitoring techniques
There are three basic audio monitoring techniques as follows:

Via an external mixer

If you have an external mixing console as part of your Cubase system then you may wish to monitor the signal directly from there before it arrives in the program. Most consoles allow you to do this. For this technique, choose Manual in Preferences / VST / Auto Monitoring (File menu) and do not activate the monitoring button for the chosen audio channel. However, you need to manually activate the record enable button on the channel to make your audio recording. Using an external console allows zero latency monitoring while recording, so you can work with maximum accuracy when overdubbing.

Via the audio hardware using Direct Monitoring

Some ASIO 2.0 audio hardware drivers allow the use of Direct Monitoring. This allows the routing of the audio signal in the audio hardware to be controlled from within a music software application like Cubase. Direct Monitoring is activated in VST Audio System / << name of your audio hardware driver >> section of the Device setup window by ticking the Direct Monitoring option. If the option is greyed out it is not available with your audio hardware. Direct Monitoring re-directs the input signal from its usual path within the audio hardware so that you can hear it with minimum latency. With Direct Monitoring, you can still choose a monitoring mode in Preferences / VST / Auto Monitoring (While record enabled, While record running or Tapemachine style) and you can still use the record enable and monitor buttons but you cannot monitor the whole signal path which passes through Cubase (for example, you cannot hear the EQ and effects settings for the channel). Similar to the external console option above, direct monitoring allows minimal latency monitoring while recording, which suits timing-critical overdubs.

Via Cubase

In this mode, you monitor the audio after it has passed through the input and output stages of your audio hardware and Cubase. For this technique, choose either While record enabled, While record running or Tapemachine style in Preferences / VST / Auto Monitoring. (See below for a full explanation of these options). All three cases automatically activate the monitor button so that you can hear the input signal. The advantage of monitoring via Cubase is is that you can record a dry signal while monitoring it with added reverb or other processing (a popular technique when recording vocals). The disadvantage is that the signal suffers from a slight delay (latency).

Record enable and monitor buttons

In order that there should remain no doubt as to the precise function of the record enable and monitor buttons, the following outlines the details:

- record enable button activated – activates record-ready status for the track (you can record on this track).
- record enable button de-activated – de-activates record-ready status for the track (you cannot record on this track).
- monitor button activated – activates monitoring of any incoming signal (you can hear the input signal and see its level on the meters).

Tip

By default, the record enable button is automatically activated whenever you select a track. If you wish to record several sources simultaneously, select a number of tracks by clicking on them while holding the Shift key. In this way, a number of selected tracks are automatically record enabled. Of course, the number of simultaneous sources you are actually able to record depends entirely on how many physical inputs are present in your audio hardware.

• monitor button de-activated – activates monitoring of any signal already recorded on the track (you can hear and see the level of what has already been recorded).

Monitoring modes

The monitoring modes for Cubase are chosen in Preferences / VST / Auto Monitoring (Figure 7.4). These affect the behaviour of the monitor button relative to the record, playback and record enable status of Cubase (thus affecting how you monitor an incoming audio signal when recording). The monitoring modes include the following:

• Manual – the status of the monitor button for the channel is chosen entirely manually. This means that the monitor button is never automatically activated. This mode is suitable when you are monitoring via an external mixing console and do not wish to hear the signal via Cubase.

• While record enabled – the monitor button is automatically activated whenever the track is record enabled. This means that you are always listening to the incoming audio signal until you manually deactivate the record enable or the monitor button. This is suitable for regular track laying not involving manual drop-ins and for when you need to rehearse a part before pressing the record button. In this mode, you are monitoring via Cubase.

• While record running – the monitor button is only activated when Cubase is running in record mode. This means that you are always monitoring what is already recorded on the track unless you start recording. This is useful for manual drop-ins on a previously recorded track. In this mode, you are monitoring via Cubase.

Figure 7.4
Choose your audio monitoring mode in Preferences / VST / Auto Monitoring (File menu)

- Tapemachine style – the monitor button is automatically activated whenever the record button is activated, and remains active unless Cubase is running in playback mode, i.e. you monitor the incoming signal only when Cubase is in stop mode or running in record mode. This is a good general purpose mode and is useful for manual drop-ins on a previously recorded track.

Record modes for audio recording

The precise manner in which audio recording takes place is governed by the record mode section of the Transport panel. You are advised to become familiar with the record modes before commencing any serious recording projects. These affect both the linear and cycle recording behaviour of the program. The linear record modes determine what happens when a new audio recording 'overlaps' an existing event on the same track. The cycle record modes determine what happens when you record multiple takes over the same range in a continuous cycle when the Transport panel cycle button is activated. See 'Audio recording in cycle mode' below for more details. When audio events overlap you only hear the event which takes playback priority. The function of each record mode is outlined in the following table:

Record modes for audio recording

Linear record modes		Cycle record modes	
Mode	Overlap behaviour	Mode	Cycle behaviour
Normal	pastes new event on top	Mix	creates one region/event per lap
Merge	pastes new event on top	Overwrite	creates one region/event per lap
Replace	replaces existing event	Keep Last	keeps last complete lap in display
		Stacked	records laps in lanes

Tracks, channels and playback priority

Tracks and channels

In Cubase, tracks are listed vertically in the Project window. Audio tracks might contain any number of digital audio recordings represented as graphical events along the time line of the event display. When it is created, each audio track is automatically assigned its own audio channel and you can see these in the Mixer where, by default, they appear in the same order as they are found in the Project window. The tracks and channels in Cubase are not unlike those found in traditional multi-track recording setups where the tracks on a real world multitrack recorder are routed to the channels of a separate real world mixing console. The difference with Cubase is that the multitrack recorder and mixer are not physically separate and there can be literally hundreds of audio tracks with an almost infinitely wide mixing console to accommodate them! In fact, the Mixer automatically expands/contracts as you add/delete tracks in the Project window. The assignment of tracks to channels takes place invisibly, so in the routine recording process, you do not need to be concerned

Tip

Try using 'While record enabled' as a regular track laying mode and 'While record running' as a manual drop-in mode. 'Tapemachine style' is a good general purpose mode.

Info

The record modes have a slightly different effect on record behaviour depending on whether you are recording MIDI or audio data.

Tip

For most applications it is best to activate 'Sync Project and Mixer selection' in Preferences / Editing / Project and Mixer. With this setting, all track selections in the Project window also select the corresponding channel in the Mixer and vice versa. This helps with workflow when jumping between the Project window and the Mixer.

with it. Cubase manages the available resources behind the scenes, leaving you to concentrate on the music and the recording, as you proceed with your session.

Playback priority

You can record several times on the same track over the same section but, with audio recording, the previously recorded material is never overwritten. The audio file which has been recorded on hard disk still exists, regardless of how you chop and change, cut and paste or otherwise manipulate events in the event display. The audio file is only ever deleted if you instruct Cubase expressly to do so. However, playback on the same audio track occurs according to a strict rule: an audio track can only play back one audio event at any one time. If events overlap, only one of them is heard. When working with multiple takes on the same track, use the To Front and Move to options in the Quick menu or Edit menu to choose which take you want to hear (Figure 7.5). Takes can later be merged into a single audio part and edited in fine detail in the Audio Part editor.

Figure 7.5
Use the 'To Front' option in the Quick menu to choose the take you wish to hear

Tip

To convert a stereo clip to mono, select the clip in the Pool, followed by Media / Convert files. In the Convert options pop-up, select Mono in the Channels sub-menu and 'New' in the Options sub-menu. To avoid losing the original stereo file, make a safety copy of the clip before using this technique.

Mono or stereo

The mono or stereo configuration for audio tracks is chosen when you add a new track by selecting the Add Audio track command from the Project menu. In the Add Audio track dialogue which appears, you can also choose a multitrack or surround configuration (Figure 7.6). The chosen format is fixed at the time of creation and you cannot change the status later. However, it is possible to drag a stereo event onto a mono track (for example), at which time the stereo recording is played back in mono (you hear the left and right channels merged together). Equally, you can drag a mono event onto a stereo track, at which time you hear the same mono signal in both channels. Further mono/stereo manipulations are possible using Flip Stereo in the Audio Process menu.

Figure 7.6
Choose the configuration for the new audio track in the Add Audio Track dialogue

Audio recording strategies

Basic recording

If you followed the step-by-step audio recording procedure outlined in Chapter 3 you are already familiar with audio recording in Cubase. However, in this section we are concerned with practical techniques which streamline the process. Recording in a multitrack DAW tends to involve repetitive use of the same functions. However, the precise details vary according to the task at hand.

Preliminaries

Once the input buss is set up, recording is generally handled using the record track and Inspector in the Project window or using the audio channel for the track in the Mixer. It is assumed that you have already set the record levels on the input buss and that you have assigned the input buss in the input routing menu of the Audio track upon which you intend to record. The pre-liminary settings for the recording and overdubbing scenarios outlined below are as follows:

- Select 'Tapemachine style' in Preferences / VST / Auto Monitoring.
- Select 'Enable record on selected track' in Preferences / Editing / Project and Mixer. Selecting any track now automatically activates the record enable and monitor buttons allowing you to monitor the input signal in stop or record modes.
- Activate the Snap button in the toolbar. Set the Snap type menu to 'Grid' and the Grid type menu to 'Bar'. This will help move the project cursor to convenient bar positions before commencing recording.
- Select 'Normal' in the Transport panel Linear record mode menu.
- Activate 'Use pre-roll' and 'Metronome on' in the Transport menu. De-activate all other options.
- Verify that the cycle button is de-activated and enter one or two bars in the pre-roll amount field in the Transport panel.
- Verify that 'Metronome in Record' and 'Metronome in Play' are active in the Metronome Settings window.

Scenario 1 – Recording one long take

Here we are recording one long take of the musical performance of a live musician. It is assumed that any errors in the performance would be correct-ed at a later time, so this recording is continuous until the whole performance is complete. Proceed as follows:

1 In the Transport panel, de-activate the punch in and punch out buttons. Set up the correct tempo for the musical performance in the tempo field. Here, the musician is using the metronome of Cubase to keep in time.
2 Verify that the record enable button is active on the chosen record track.
3 Define the start point for your recording by clicking in the ruler to move the cursor to the bar of your choice.
4 Press the record button or '*' on the computer's numeric keypad. The

Figure 7.7
Recording one long vocal take

project cursor rolls back the number of bars you set in the pre-roll amount field. Playback commences with a metronome click so the musician can keep in time. Cubase drops into record mode at the bar you chose in step 3.

5   Record up to the end of the performance. If you experience a false start, delete the audio event and go back to step 4 to start again.

Scenario 2 – Dropping in to repair errors in a previous take

Automatic punch in and punch out

Automatically punching in and out of recording is a common requirement with multitrack recording systems. The technique is ideal for repairing imperfect passages, such as mistakes during a musical performance or clicks in the audio file.

The punch in and punch out buttons are found on the Transport panel. They work in conjunction with the left and right locators of the ruler. The left locator marks the punch in point and the right locator marks the punch out point. To implement automatic punch in and punch out, proceed as follows:

1   Set up the left and right locators to encompass the range you wish to record. Select and record enable the target track.
2   In the Transport panel, activate the punch in and punch out buttons.
3   Press '1' on the numeric keypad to set the project cursor to the left locator position (or rewind to some point before the left locator).
4   Start playback. The musician should play along with the music before the punch in point. When the project cursor reaches the left locator position, Cubase automatically starts recording (punch in).
5   Record the new take. Cubase automatically stops recording when the project cursor reaches the right locator position (punch out).

To hear your take in context you might like to activate the post roll button with a value of one or two bars in the post roll amount field. When you reach the punch out point playback now continues afterwards for the specified number of bars and beats, allowing you to verify the join between the new take and the previous recording.

Tip

To define a precise range for the punch in, listen to the recording and insert markers on the fly using the computer keyboard Insert key to mark the start and end points. Once defined, select the Range tool and double click between the two markers to select the range between them. Finally press 'P' on the computer keyboard to move the left and right locators to the marker positions. You are now ready to punch in over the defined range.

Figure 7.8
Using automatic punch in and out to
record a guitar performance in bars 4
and 5

Manually dropping in on the fly

While automatic punch in and out is useful when you know exactly where you
want to start recording, it is also useful to be able to punch into record mode
at any moment on the currently selected (and record enabled) track. Such a
situation might occur when your vocalist or other performer decides to produce a superb performance when you are monitoring a rehearsal but not
actually recording. To drop in on the fly during playback without interrupting
the flow of the music, click on the record button on the Transport panel or
press the * key on the numeric keypad. To drop back out of record, click on
the record button a second time. Cubase continues in playback mode.

Scenario 3 – Interrupting the take

Rather than complete one long take, as outlined above, you may prefer to inter-
rupt the recording every time there is an error in the musical performance, rewind
and continue recording from some point just before the error. Proceed as follows:

1 In the Transport panel, de-activate the punch in and punch out buttons.
2 Define the start point for your recording by clicking in the ruler to move
   the cursor to the bar of your choice. Press the record button or '*' on the
   computer's numeric keypad to start recording.
3 When there is an error press the spacebar twice, the first time to stop
   recording and the second time to roll back and commence playback.
4 Audition the take to find the position of the error. Stop playback at the error.
   Press Ctrl / Command + numeric keypad (–) to move the project cursor back
   one bar. This cursor position is the drop-in point for the next step.
5 Press the record button or '*' on the computer's numeric keypad to
   engage recording. There is a pre-roll during which the musician plays
   along with the previous take. Recording recommences at the drop in
   point as set in step 4. Go to step 3.

Figure 7.9
Recording takes in smaller sections

Scenario 4 – Recording takes in lanes

In the above scenarios you can, if desired, move to a new track for each take to avoid recording events on top of each other. However, by using 'Lanes fixed' mode you can record takes on separate lanes within the same track. This allows you to see multiple events in the display with greater clarity. Proceed as follows:

1 In the Transport panel, de-activate the punch in and punch out buttons.
2 Click on the Lane display type button and select 'Lanes fixed' from the pop-up menu.
3 Press the record button or '*' on the computer's numeric keypad to start recording.
4 Make a number of recordings using the techniques outlined in the above scenarios.
5 Each take appears on a separate lane within the vertical space of the record track.

The most recent take appears in the lowest lane and playback priority is ordered from the lowest lane upwards. It is easy to see which parts of which events take playback priority since they are highlighted in green. The events may be edited directly in the event display which is convenient for assembling a composite take without ever leaving the Project window.

Figure 7.10
Selecting Lanes Fixed mode allows you to record takes onto separate lanes within the same track

Multitrack recording

For multitrack recording, it may be appropriate to open the Mixer on screen to see a number of channels simultaneously. This suits the simultaneous recording of several inputs on separate tracks. It also helps with overdubbing sessions where you may wish to change the mix of the backing tracks to suit the needs of a live performer. In these cases, open the Mixer in normal mode below the Project window (Figure 7.11).

Normal mode, (as opposed to extended mode), displays only the channel faders in the mixer and takes up less vertical space on the screen. It may also be useful to see the input and output busses. These are shown/hidden by clicking on the relevant icons in the panel to the left of the mixer channels. When recording multiple tracks, you need to record enable the appropriate number of tracks and make sure that the input routing menus are set to the appropriate input busses. The number of separate sources which can be recorded simultaneously depends on the number of active hardware inputs available on your system. Figure 7.6 shows an eight track recording taking place in Cubase. While in the Project window, you can select tracks using the

Figure 7.11
For multi-track recording, try opening the Mixer in normal mode below the Project window. This screenshot shows an eight track recording taking place in Cubase.

up/down arrow keys. While in the Mixer, you can select tracks using the left/right arrow keys. Several tracks/channels can be selected simultaneously by holding the Shift key while pressing the arrow keys. The Shift and arrow combinations provide a quick method of record enabling multiple tracks if you have activated 'Enable record on selected track' in Preferences / Editing / Project and Mixer.

Audio recording in cycle mode

Audio recording in cycle mode elevates the recording of multiple takes way beyond what you can achieve manually in linear recording mode. Cycle recording is implemented by activating the cycle button on the Transport

panel before commencing the recording. Recording takes place in a continuous cycle between the left and right locators until you click on the stop button. This is an excellent technique for capturing a magical performance since
you can leave Cubase in record mode while you perform the same segment
of music over and over again. This is particularly useful for vocalists, who
might be having difficulty with one particular section of a song or it might suit
the recording of a guitar or saxophone solo where the musician would like to
try a number of solos one after the other. You can later choose the best take
or compile the best parts of a number of takes into a final composite version.
You can even set up a cycle over the entire length of the song and perform
the whole thing several times (assuming that you have the necessary hard
disk space). Cubase makes all this very easy and benefits from an intuitive
set of tools to select and edit the takes after recording has been completed.

Audio cycle recording behaviour varies according to two main factors: the
Audio cycle record mode chosen in Preferences / Record / Audio Cycle
Record Mode and the Cycle record mode chosen in the Transport panel. All
the options record one long audio file which is automatically divided up to
match the length of each take.

Audio cycle record mode (Preferences)

The Audio cycle record mode in Preferences governs the audio aspects of the
cycle recording process. There are three options, which operate as follows:

- Create regions – regions are sections within audio clips. When Create regions
  is selected, one region is automatically created for each lap of the cycle and
  each region is automatically named with a sequential take number. When
  recording has been completed a single event appears between the left and
  right locators containing the last take. Other takes can be selected from the
  Set to Region option in the Quick menu. This is the default setting for Cycle
  record mode. See Chapter 8 for more details about regions.
- Create events – a separate audio event is created for each lap of the cycle.
  When you have finished recording, the events appear on top of each other
  between the left and right locators. You can select takes by using the To
  Front option in the Quick menu. Create events has the advantage that all the
  events are immediately available in the event display and if the material is
  not too complicated you can quickly edit the events to assemble a composite
  take while still remaining in the Project window.
- Create events and regions – creates both events and regions
  simultaneously which gives you the choice of using either regions or
  events for the manipulation of your multiple takes.

Cycle record mode (Transport panel)

Clicking on the cycle record mode selector in the Transport panel opens a
menu with a number of options which determine the manner in which recordings are made when in Cycle mode. The modes function as follows:

- Mix and Overwrite modes – in these modes the Audio cycle record
  mode, as outlined above, is taken into consideration. If Create regions is

chosen a single event (containing the last take/region) remains in the display after recording is completed. If Create events has been chosen separate events for each lap of the cycle appear in the same range on the audio track (pasted on top of each other).

- Keep Last – in this mode the Audio cycle record mode is not taken into consideration. Regions are created for each lap of the cycle but only the last complete lap in the cycle is kept as an audio event. Other takes can still be selected from the Set to Region option in the Quick menu.
- Stacked – in this mode, the Audio cycle recording mode is NOT taken into consideration. An audio event for each lap of the cycle appears on its own lane within the vertical space of the audio track. The most recent take appears in the lowest lane and playback priority is ordered from the lowest lane upwards. It is easy to see which parts of which events take playback priority since they are highlighted in green. The events may be edited directly in the event display which is convenient for assembling a composite take without ever leaving the Project window.
- Stacked 2 (No mute) – the same as stacked mode except that no muting of events takes place.

Practical audio recording projects in cycle mode

For the following cycle recording projects, set up Cubase as outlined in Preliminaries, above, but in addition activate 'Start record at left locator' in the Transport menu.

Audio cycle recording project 1 (Keep Last mode)

To record multiple takes in 'Keep Last' cycle record mode, proceed as follows:

1 Click on the cycle record mode selector in the Transport panel and select Keep Last from the pop-up menu.
2 Set the left and right locators to the appropriate range within your musical arrangement.
3 Activate the cycle button on the Transport panel (press / on the numeric keypad).
4 Select the target record track and make sure it is record enabled.
5 Press the record button or '*' on the computer's numeric keypad to start recording.
6 Record the performance as many times as you wish. On each lap of the cycle a new region is automatically created, suitably named with a sequential take number. Only the last complete take is kept as an audio event in the event display (Figure 7.12).

Figure 7.12
Recording a vocal line in Keep Last cycle record mode. Here, the fourth lap of the cycle is shown.

Keep Last mode allows you to record the musical performance repeatedly over the same range until you get a good take. When you think you have succeeded you stop recording and it is only the good take which remains in the event display. However, should you need to, you can still select any previous take using the Set to Region option in the Quick menu.

Figure 7.13
Use the Set to Region field in the Quick menu to select a previous take

Audio cycle recording project 2 (Stacked mode)

To record multiple takes in 'Stacked' cycle record mode, proceed as follows:

1 Click on the cycle record mode selector in the Transport panel and select Stacked from the pop-up menu.
2 Set the left and right locators to the appropriate segment of your musical arrangement.
3 Activate the cycle button on the Transport panel (press / on the numeric keypad).
4 Select the target record track and make sure it is record enabled. In order to be able to see the stacked lanes in the vertical space of the audio track try expanding its vertical size by clicking and dragging on the lower limit of the track in the track list.
5 Press the record button or '*' on the computer's numeric keypad to start recording.
6 Record the performance as many times as you wish. On each lap of the cycle a new event is automatically created, suitably named with a sequential take number and automatically arranged on lanes within the vertical space of the track (Figure 7.14).

Figure 7.14
Recording a vocal line in Stacked cycle record mode. Events are stacked onto separate lanes.

Stacked mode allows you to record your musical performance repeatedly over the same range and display the resulting takes as separate events within the vertical space of the record track. This means you can immediately carry out detailed editing of the events using the standard tools while still remaining in the Project window (to assemble, for example, a perfect composite take). Playback priority works from the lowest lane upwards and those parts of the events which take priority are highlighted in green.

Audio events, audio clips and audio files

The concepts of audio events, audio clips and audio files need to be fully understood to appreciate exactly how Cubase handles audio data. Luckily, you do not need to be aware of these details for routine audio recording and editing but knowledge of what is going on behind the scenes can help when you are troubleshooting or when you are involved at a deeper editing level.

Whenever you make an audio recording, there are three things which occur in Cubase as follows:

1 an audio file containing the actual audio recording is created on the hard disk.
2 an audio clip which points to this audio data is created in the Pool.
3 an audio event which points to the clip is created in the event display of the Project window.

These three elements are shown in Figure 7.15. This shows the state of affairs just after you have made an audio recording in Cubase. The details of Figure 7.15 can be explained in three steps as follows:

Info

See Chapter 10 for more details about the Pool.

Figure 7.15
An audio event points to its corresponding audio clip which, in turn, points to its corresponding audio file on hard disk

1 an audio file called X File_00 is created on the hard disk in the Audio folder of a project called ProjectX. The audio file takes its name from the name of the audio track at the time of recording.
2 an audio clip, also called X File_00, is created in the Pool and, at this stage, this audio clip provides a reference to, or points to, the whole audio file stored on hard disk. Like the audio file, the audio clip also takes its name from the name of the audio track at the time of recording.
3 an audio event is created in the event display which provides a reference to, or points to, the audio clip (at this stage it points to the whole audio clip).

Info

An audio file and its corresponding audio clip always begin with the same basic name, but the overall name may change after certain kinds of editing operations. If you change the name of the audio clip, the basic name of the audio file on disk is changed accordingly.

Figure 7.16
The relationship between the events, clip and audio files after splitting and processing an event

Let's imagine that we are only interested in the second half of the recorded audio event. We decide to split it in two and fade out the second half using the split tool and the fade out function (Audio / Process sub-menu). The result of the editing is shown in Figure 7.16. You could happily go on splitting and processing your events without too much concern about the number of audio files and clips you are creating behind the scenes. You can undo your processing in the normal way, using Ctrl/Command + Z. You can even undo it at a later date using Cubase's Offline Process History (Audio menu).

Let's take a look at the details of Figure 7.16. When you split the event, you produced two events which point to the same audio clip. The first event points to the first half of the clip and the second event points to the second half of the clip. Before you applied the processing, the clip was still pointing to the whole of the audio file. However, when you applied the processing, something unexpected happened. Rather than change the original audio file, a completely new audio file was created (X File_1) and stored in an Edits subdirectory on disk. Finally, you have two events which point to the same clip and a clip which points to two different audio files. The audio clip knows at which moment it should start pointing to the second audio file.

You may ask why Steinberg designed this part of the software like this. The main reason is that you always preserve your original recording on the hard disk in an unchanged state. This is re-assuring and means that, if things go wrong, you can always go back to it. Another reason is that when you process an audio file several times, each process is stored in a separate edit file. This allows the use of the Offline Process History to go back to a clean version of a guitar recording, one month after you applied compression, distortion and reverb to it (for example).

The following provides a summary of the above information:

- audio events are what you see in the event display and provide the means by which you visualise your audio recordings. Audio events appear at various points in time within your project and feature a start time and an end time. The placement and size of events can be edited at any time after recording has been completed. Audio events point to the whole of, or part of, an element in the Pool known as a clip. Each audio event points to a single clip – it cannot be associated with more than one.
- an audio clip is an element which points to an audio file on the hard disk. An audio clip provides an interface between the audio events in the event

display and the audio files on the hard disk. It decides which section of which audio file gets accessed by which audio event.

- an audio file is the raw audio material stored on hard disk. There are two categories of audio files; those containing the original data as captured at the time of the original recording (stored in the Audio sub-directory), and those containing edited audio data as created when audio processing is applied (stored in the Edits sub-directory).

Audio editing

This chapter describes how to edit audio material using the Audio Part editor and the Sample editor. It also covers the audio event Infoline, the audio menu options, time stretching, fades and crossfades, hitpoints, groove template creation, audio looping and audio warping.

The Audio Part editor is for the editing of audio events grouped inside an audio part. It is often more convenient to edit audio events in groups rather than as separate events. Manipulations of data in the Audio Part editor involve splicing, trimming and moving events in much the same way as takes place in the Project window. This editor also features special functions for editing events which have been recorded in Cycle Record mode, and for editing audio slices which were created in Hitpoint mode. Editing in the Audio Part editor is non-destructive. This means that the actual audio file on hard disk is not altered by any editing actions.

The Sample editor allows you to view and edit your audio data in fine detail at the sample level. Here, you are working with the actual waveform of the audio data in terms of defining regions, calculating hitpoints, cutting, copying and pasting, and performing other detailed audio processing. Editing is non-destructive in the sense that you can revert to a previous version of the file at a later date using the Offline Process History (Audio menu) and, for as long as you are working in the same continuous session, you can use the Undo command (Edit menu).

Audio event editing in the Project window

This section describes a number of event-based editing techniques in the Project window. For general tool-based audio editing see Chapter 4.

Using the Audio event Infoline

An Infoline appears above the display when you activate the info button on the toolbar in either the Project window or the Audio Part editor. This displays the details of the currently selected audio event or for the first of a multiple event selection (Figure 8.1). The Infoline is useful for directly editing various parameters associated with the audio event in both the Project window and the Audio Part editor. You can edit the values directly in the fields by double-clicking on the value and entering a new value using the computer keyboard. Alternatively, selecting 'Increment/Decrement on Left click and

File	Description	Start	End	Length	Offset	Snap	Fade In	Fade Out	Volume	Mute	Lock	Transpose	Finetune
Trumpet	Take 2	3. 1. 1. 0	5. 2. 3.105	2. 1. 2.105	0. 0. 0. 0	3. 1. 1. 0	0. 0. 0. 0	0. 0. 0. 0	0.00 dB	-	-	-1	-5

Figure 8.1
The Infoline for an audio event

drag' in File / Preferences / Editing / Controls / Value Box allows you to drag up or down in the field to change the value. In this case, the changes are sensitive to the current Snap resolution when the Snap button is activated.

When more than one event is selected the infoline text is shown in yellow and contains the information relevant to the first of the selected events. Editing any of the yellow text values applies the changes relatively to all selected events. For example, changing the start position moves the start position of all the currently selected events but maintains their relative positions. However, if you wish to apply the same absolute start position to all the selected events hold down Ctrl while making the change. In this case, the start times of all selected events snap instantly to the same position. Note that applying the same file name in the File field to a number of audio files is NOT possible since all audio files must retain a separate and unique name. However, it is possible to enter an absolute name for all descriptions in the Description field.

Other useful manipulations on the Infoline include the following:

• Edit the name of the audio file and clip associated with the audio event by entering a new name in the File field. Similarly, a description for the event may be entered in the Description field. The description appears first in the audio event followed by the name of the audio file in brackets.

Important

Changing the name in the File field of the Infoline changes the name of the clip in the Pool and the name of the actual audio file on hard disk. This is significant if you are working with a file from an audio library since you may change the name of the file on hard disk without really wanting to. Other applications in your system which accessed the same file may then have difficulty finding it. To avoid this, try activating 'Copy File to Working directory' in File / Preferences / Audio / Editing / On Import audio files / Use Settings.

• Edit the start, end and length fields to precise numerical values in (you guessed it!) the start, end and length fields. This is applicable to situations where you know the precise point at which you want the event to start or end, or the precise length. When bars and beats are shown in the ruler, these values are displayed in bars, beats, sixteenth notes and ticks (each sixteenth note contains 120 ticks).
• The offset for an audio event allows you to slide the audio back and forth in time without changing the position of the event which contains it. (The contents may also be moved by dragging in the event while pressing Ctrl + Alt). For example, if an event containing a drum kit recording begins with a snare roll but you would rather it began with the kick drum which occurs one bar later, all you need do is slide the contents to the left and line up the waveform of the kick drum to the start of the event. This is only possible if a substantial part of the associated audio clip is not visible within the event. If the audio event already plays the whole clip, the offset value cannot be adjusted.

- The Snap point value provides another way of moving an audio event to a new position in the display. This is an absolute value corresponding to a point on the ruler and does not move the position of the Snap point within the event.
- The volume field provides an alternative numerical method of changing the volume of the event, providing +24dB of boost or infinite attenuation. The volume is normally adjusted by moving the blue volume handle in the centre of the event.
- The fade in and fade out fields provide quick numerical methods of adjusting the fade in and out characteristics of the event. The fade characteristics are normally adjusted using the blue fade handles at each end of the event (as described in 'Using the tools' in Chapter 4).
- The Mute field offers a quick method of muting the currently selected event or group of selected events.
- The Lock field allows you to lock the position, size and other kinds of editing of the audio event such as volume changes, fades and audio processing. When you are happy with the audio events in a Project, possibly when it is near to completion, Lock is invaluable for protecting those audio events which you no longer wish to move or change.
- Transpose allows you to apply real-time pitch shifting to the selected audio event(s) in semitone steps in the range -24 to +24 semitones. This could be used if you change the key at a later date after having completed the recording. The pitch shifting remains reasonably transparent if the pitch change is between -3 to +3 semitones, but the quality of the result is highly dependent upon the material. If you are sure that your pitch change is permanent, you may achieve better results by using 'Freeze timestretch and transpose' in the Audio / Realtime processing sub-menu and choosing one of the MPEX3 algorithms.
- Finetune is similar to Transpose but allows pitch change in one cent steps (100th of a semitone) between -49 and +50 cents. This is useful for retuning instruments or for creating effects. For example, phasing and ADT effects may be achieved by copying an event onto a spare track and detuning it by a small amount (try between -2 and -40 cents).

Audio menu options

There are a number of very good audio editing tools in the Audio menu of Cubase. These are accessed via the Audio menu itself, via key commands or via the audio section of the Quick menu. Editing is generally directed to one or more selected audio events or parts.

Events to Part

It is often helpful to group a number of audio events into a single audio part so they can be moved around and edited as a single block. To achieve this, drag a selection box around the desired audio events and select 'Events to Part' in the Audio menu or Quick menu. This is particularly useful when events overlap or are pasted on top of each other since, once they are contained within an audio part, they can be viewed and edited with greater precision and clarity in the Audio Part editor, where the events are displayed on separate lanes.

Dissolve Part

Dissolve Part provides the opposite function to Events to Part, above. Here, the individual audio events are taken back out of the part and displayed in the event display in the normal way. This may be required when you need to make detailed changes to the musical structure in the Project window.

Bounce selection

Bounce selection creates a single new audio file and clip from the currently selected audio events or range selection and, if chosen, a single new audio event which replaces the original events or parts. All auto-fades, fades and crossfades are included in the bounce. Real-time effects are not included. For multiple selections over several tracks, the function operates on a track-by-track basis. Audio events, (and the associated audio files and clips), created with Bounce are named according to the source track name.

Bounce Selection may also be used to bounce the current range selection in the Sample editor to a new file and clip. In this case, a second instance of the Sample editor is automatically opened containing the bounced audio. When using Bounce Selection in the Project window or Audio Part editor, a dialogue appears asking if you wish to replace the currently selected material (Figure 8.2). If you click on Replace the original selected audio events or parts are replaced with a single audio event. If you click on No, the events are not replaced. In both cases, a new audio file is created on the hard disk and a new audio clip is created in the Pool. The original audio files and clips associated with the events from which the bounce was made are not deleted or modified in any way.

Figure 8.2
Bounce Selection Replace Events dialogue

Detect silence

Detect silence (Audio / Advanced sub-menu) allows you to process your audio material based upon a variable threshold for silence within the chosen audio event. This takes place in the Detect silence window which opens when you select the function. As well as finding the silence itself, the Detect Silence function is equally good at finding the wanted non-silent passages within your audio material. The following sections outline two scenarios where the Detect silence function is particularly helpful:

Scenario 1

Electric guitar recordings frequently suffer from unwanted noise and interference between the wanted parts of the performance. Detect Silence provides a way of quickly and automatically removing the unwanted noise, without resorting to noise gates or manual editing in the Sample editor. Proceed as follows:

- Select the audio event containing the electric guitar and select Detect Silence in the Audio menu. As a starting point, set the parameters to the values shown in Figure 8.3.
- Set the Open Threshold parameter to around –18dB. This governs the threshold for opening the gate to allow the wanted part of the signal through.
- Set the Close Threshold parameter to around –20dB. This governs the threshold for closing the gate to block the unwanted part of the signal (i.e. that part of the audio to be treated as silence).

Figure 8.3
Finding the unwanted noise between the wanted parts of an electric guitar performance in the Detect Silence dialogue

- Set Minimum Time Open to around 50ms. This holds the gate open for the prescribed length of time after the Open threshold level has been reached to avoid the gate opening and closing too many times during passages featuring staccato notes or other 'quick fire' material.
- Set the Minimum Time Closed to around 50ms. This holds the gate firmly shut for a prescribed length of time after the Close threshold level has been reached and is usually set to a relatively small value to avoid cutting out any wanted material.
- Set the pre and post-roll parameters to around 50ms and 70ms respectively. These add an offset before and after opening and closing the gate to make sure you do not lose any of the attack or decay in the wanted parts of the audio.
- Activate Strip Silence and de-activate Add as Regions.
- Click on the Compute button followed by the Process button.
- Close the dialogue to go back to the Project window where your original audio event has now been automatically split into a number of separate events. All those sections containing the noise are removed from the performance (Figure 8.4).

Tip

To group all events created by Detect Silence within a single audio part use 'Events to Part' (Audio menu).

Figure 8.4
A cleaner electric guitar performance in the Project window after treatment using Detect Silence

Scenario 2

Drum loop libraries on CD often feature tracks containing a series of consecutive drum and percussion loops with silence in between each loop. Detect Silence allows you to automatically detect and highlight such loops by defining them as regions. To achieve this, proceed as follows:

- Import the audio track(s) from CD using File / Import / Audio CD.
- Select the audio event containing the drum loops and then select Detect Silence in the Audio menu.
- Adjust the main parameters to similar values to the electric guitar example outlined above but use open and close thresholds of around -

Figure 8.5
Finding the relevant audio for the creation of automatic regions in the Detect Silence dialogue

30dB and activate Add as Regions and de-activate Strip Silence.
- If you want your regions to start tightly cut to the first beat of each loop, try a value of Øms for the pre-roll setting.
- Enter a generic name into the Regions Name field.
- Click on the Compute button followed by the Process button. Close the dialogue to go back to the Project window (Figure 8.5).

Info

The open and close thresholds for Detect Silence may also be managed graphically in the display by moving the green and red handles. The green handle corresponds with the open threshold and the red handle corresponds with the close threshold.

In this case, rather than stripping the silence we are automatically marking the areas of interest within the audio material. Double-click on the audio event to open the Sample editor. Activate the Show Regions button. The regions you created in the Detect Silence dialogue are now visible in the list and can be selected, played and edited as desired (Figure 8.6).

Figure 8.6
The resulting regions in the Sample editor

Time stretching

Time stretching involves changing the length of the chosen audio material without changing the pitch. The use of the term 'time stretch' is slightly mis-leading since you can both stretch and compress the length of the target audio. Time stretching is applied in two ways in Cubase: using the Time Stretch option in the Audio / Process sub-menu (outlined in Chapter 9) or using the Object selection tool in time stretch mode. The following outlines the use of the Object selection tool in time stretch mode to time stretch an audio event containing a drum loop.

The time stretch algorithms

Time stretch is available as the third function of the Object selection tool. It is implemented when you resize the audio event by dragging the start or end points. However, the actual time stretch algorithm used for the operation is chosen in File / Preferences / Editing / Audio (Figure 8.7).

Figure 8.7
Select the time stretch algorithm in the Preferences dialogue

There are two algorithms available; MPEX3 and Realtime. There are various advantages and disadvantages to each algorithm and, if you are time stretching or compressing important material, it is worth experimenting.

- MPEX3 – MPEX3 is a proprietary time stretch algorithm designed by Prosoniq for optimum audio quality. MPEX stands for "Minimum Perceived Loss Time Compression / Expansion". This gives among the best overall results, particularly if you want your sound to stay true to the character of the original. It is recommended for vocals, instrumental solos, drum loops and mixes. Set the quality menu to Preview or Mix Fast when previewing, or to one of the other settings according to the type of material you are time stretching. Poly Musical is the default high quality setting which works well with drum loops, mixes and most other material. Solo Musical is recommended for vocals and instrumental solos. If these fail to produce acceptable results, try Poly Fast or Poly Complex.
- Realtime – uses the same time stretch algorithm as that which is used in Cubase's audio warp functions. This is a good all-round alternative to MPEX3. After time stretching using Realtime, the target event is displayed with a small double-arrow in the lower right corner. The quality of the results can be modified in the Warp setting menu in the Sample editor.

Time stretching a drum loop

It is assumed here that you are inserting a drum loop into a Project which already has a fixed tempo which you do not wish to modify. To make the chosen loop fit the tempo using the Object selection tool in time stretch mode, proceed as follows:

- Import your chosen drum loop and place it in the Project window event display. Make sure that it loops for a precise number of bars (in its own original tempo). Popular lengths are one, two and four bars (Figure 8.8).

Figure 8.8
A one bar drum loop in the event display

- Make sure the Snap button is activated and the Grid type menu is set to 'Bar'. Move the drum loop audio event to its intended start position in the musical arrangement.
- Choose the MPEX3 algorithm in File / Preferences / Editing / Audio. Select Poly Musical in the quality menu.
- Select the Object selection tool in time stretch mode and drag the end point of the event to the nearest bar division in the event display. The audio is automatically time stretched according to the chosen algorithm when you release the mouse (Figure 8.9).

Figure 8.9
The one bar drum loop after time stretching

Fades and crossfades

There are many different ways in which fades and crossfades can help you achieve better results in Cubase. Simple graphical fade techniques using the fade handles of an audio event have already been described in 'Using the tools' in Chapter 4. The following sections outline some of the other techniques and the use of the various fade dialogues.

Auto fade

There are occasions when splitting events in the Project window or Audio Part editor results in digital clicks. This most often occurs when the edits are not at zero crossing points in the waveform and may be troublesome at the start or end of an event or when one event is placed immediately after another. The cure for this is found in the Auto-fade settings of Cubase. The idea with Auto-fade is to impose a short automatic fade-in, fade-out or crossfade for the events in the Project window, to disguise clicks and provide glitch-free transitions between adjacent audio events. This can be set up globally or on a track-by-track basis. Since the fades are applied in real-time, a global setting might result in unnecessary drain on your computer's CPU power. Not all tracks need Auto fades. You are therefore advised to implement auto fades only on single tracks and only when they are needed, unless you have a very powerful CPU with plenty of headroom.

The global Auto fade dialogue is opened by selecting 'Auto Fades Settings' in the Project menu. Since you are being advised here not to use a global setting, leave the parameters in the global dialogue inactive (i.e. do not tick any of the Auto fade in, Auto fade out or Auto crossfade boxes). The Auto fade dialogues for each track are opened from the track list Quick menu or by clicking on the Auto fade button in the Inspector (Figure 8.10). The track version of the dialogue is identical to the global version except that it features a 'Use Project settings' tick box. When working on a track-by-track basis, de-activate this tick box since you are setting up the parameters for this track alone.

The Auto fade dialogue allows you to set the characteristics of the fade curves by clicking on any of the preset buttons or you can set up custom shapes by dragging directly in the curve displays. The default 30ms length suits most regular auto fade and crossfade requirements. To activate the auto fade functions tick the desired Auto fade in, Auto fade out or Auto crossfade box and click on OK.

Figure 8.10
The track Auto fade dialogue

Figure 8.11
The Fade in dialogue

Fade in and Fade out dialogues

When you have set up a fade in or a fade out using the blue fade handles at the start and end of an audio event the characteristics of the fade can be modified by double-clicking above the fade line. This opens a fade in or fade out dialogue (Figure 8.11). The Fade out dialogue is simply the inverse of the Fade in dialogue shown here.

The fade in and fade out dialogues allow you to modify the characteristics of the fade curve by clicking on any of the eight preset curve buttons or you can set up custom shapes by dragging handles directly in the curve display. Spline, damped spline and linear curve characteristics are available together with a helpful length option which allows you to adjust the length of the fade from within the dialogue. A restore button allows you to reset the dialogue to the default settings. The same fade may be applied to multiple events by making a multiple selection before opening the Fade dialogue.

Fades set up using the blue handles are not applied to the audio clip itself. This means that a number of events which refer to the same audio clip can each have an independent fade curve. This differs from the fades which are applied using the Fade in and Fade out functions of the Process menu, which apply the fade to the audio clip itself (described in Chapter 9).

Info

The difference between spline and damped spline curve modes in the fade dialogues – regular spline mode radically affects the shape of the neighbouring parts of the curve as you drag the curve handle within the display and sets up a naturally balanced curve, whereas damped spline mode only has a minimal effect on the neighbouring area and sets up a curve which is more linear. Damped spline mode is therefore easier to control when dragging handles in the display. The curve modes are readily interchangeable so feel free to experiment to get the desired result.

Adjust fades to range

As an alternative to dragging the handles in the event to create fades, Cubase provides another more elegant means of achieving similar results. This involves the use of the Range selection tool as follows:

- Select the Range selection tool in either the Project window or the Audio Part editor.
- Select a range over the start of your chosen audio event corresponding with the length of fade in you want to apply. Select 'Adjust fades to Range' in the Audio menu or press 'A' on the computer keyboard to create an instant fade in (Figure 8.12).

Figure 8.12
Using the Range selection tool with 'Adjust fades to Range' to apply a fade in to an audio event

- Select a range over the end of your chosen audio event corresponding to the length of fade out you want to apply. Select 'Adjust fades to Range' in the Audio menu or press 'A' on the computer keyboard to create an instant fade out (Figure 8.13).

Figure 8.13
Using the Range selection tool with 'Adjust fades to Range' to apply a fade out to an audio event

- To automatically open the fade in or fade out dialogues (or both) select 'Adjust fades to Range' or press the 'A' key command a second time in any of the above techniques.
- Alternatively, select a range over the central area of your chosen audio event. Select 'Adjust fades to Range' in the Audio menu or press 'A' on the computer keyboard. A fade in and a fade out are simultaneously applied on either side of the selected area (Figure 8.14).

Figure 8.14
Using the Range selection tool with 'Adjust fades to Range' to simultaneously apply a fade in and a fade out to an audio event

Crossfading

Crossfades can be applied between audio events in the Project window if they are on the same track and they overlap. When they do not overlap a cross-fade might still be applied if the audio clips they are referenced to overlap. In this case, the events are resized so that the crossfade can be created. If the audio events do not overlap and the whole of the audio clip is referenced by the audio event, no crossfade can be created. Things are similar in the Audio Part editor except that the events are viewed on separate lanes, which makes it slightly easier to set up the crossfades, (see Audio Part editor basics, below).

Let's consider setting up a crossfade between two takes of an 8 bar sax-ophone melody. Take One is good until an error in bar 5. Take Two plays suc-cessfully from bar 4 to the end of the melody in bar 8. We need to create a crossfade somewhere in bar 4. To achieve this in the Project window, proceed as follows:

- Select the zoom tool and draw a selection box around the two takes, in this case over the length of the eight bars of the melody (Figure 8.15).

Figure 8.15
Zoom in to the area of interest

- Activate the Snap button, select Grid in the Snap type menu, select Use Quantize in the Grid type menu, and select 1/8 Note in the Quantize type menu. This helps you when you arrange your overlap (you may often need a smaller resolution). Find a point in bar 4 where the two takes are playing the same note in the same manner. Resize Take One so that it ends (in this case) 1/8 note after this point. Resize Take Two so that it starts 1/8 note before this point (Figure 8.16). You now have a 1/8 note overlap.

Figure 8.16
Resize each event so that they overlap

- Hold down the Ctrl key on the computer keyboard to limit horizontal movement and drag Take Two on top of Take One (Figure 8.17).

Figure 8.17
Drag one event on top of the other

- Press X on the computer keyboard. The crossfade is automatically created using the current default crossfade settings (Figure 8.18). To adjust the characteristics of the crossfade, press X a second time or double-click on the crossfade area to open the crossfade dialogue.

Figure 8.18
Press X to create a crossfade

The Crossfade dialogue

The Crossfade dialogue (Figure 8.19) is opened by double-clicking on the crossfade area. Alternatively, select the events containing the crossfade and press X on the computer keyboard. Several crossfades may be modified in the Crossfade dialogue simultaneously by selecting all the events containing the crossfades.

The Crossfade dialogue features fade out curve and fade in curve displays. You can audition the signal using the Play Fade out and Play Fade in buttons. The resulting crossfade is auditioned using the Play Crossfade button. Eight preset curves are available for each of the fade in and fade out curves with a choice of spline, damped spline or linear characteristics. The fade curves can also be edited manually by clicking and dragging directly in the curve displays.

Activating the Equal Power option ensures that the crossfade contains equal acoustical energy throughout the course of the crossfade. In other words, the perceived loudness remains constant throughout the crossfade. In this mode, the curve displays have only a single editable point which is moved horizontally in the display. Equal Power mode might have been applicable to the crossfading exercise outlined above, where you require a crossfade with no change in the perceived loudness of the signal. However, this relies on both the incoming and the outgoing signal having very similar characteristics in order to be successful. Many crossfading tasks might benefit more from

Figure 8.19
The Crossfade dialogue

Equal Gain (outlined below) or some other configuration.

Activating the Equal Gain option ensures that the summed amplitude of the two curves remains constant throughout the crossfade. This is suitable for a wide range of crossfading tasks where you want the fade in curve to automatically mirror the fade out curve for effortless, 'constant gain' crossfades.

The right panel of the dialogue features a length field where you can adjust the length of the crossfade zone, 'As Default' and 'Recall Default' buttons which allow you to specify the current settings as the default crossfade for future crossfade operations or recall the existing default, and a Preset menu where you can specify and recall your own presets.

The Audio Part editor

The Audio Part editor is opened by double-clicking on an audio part or pressing Ctrl + E (PC) / Command + E (Mac) on the computer keyboard while an audio part is selected (Figure 8.20). The editor features time on the horizontal axis and 'lanes' on the vertical axis. When events within the part overlap, each is shown on a different lane. Events can be dragged between lanes at any time. Playback priority is enforced from the bottom lane up. Lanes are particularly useful for manipulating multiple takes on the same track, as

> **Tip**
>
> To remove fades and crossfades, select the events containing the fades using the Object selection tool, or select the range containing the fades using the range selection tool, and then select 'Remove Fades' in the Audio menu.

Figure 8.20
The Audio Part editor

occurs during cycle recording, or for tidying up after you have been dropping in manually. Multiple parts can be displayed in the Audio part editor. The editor features a toolbar at the top of the window which contains a similar tool set to the Project window. However, the glue tool is not present and the scrub and play tools are on separate buttons. The operation of all other tools is similar to those found in the Project window (see 'The Project window tools' in Chapter 4 for more details). There is the usual show/hide infoline button, a solo button and the familiar scroll bars and zoom controls at the lower and right hand edges of the window. Audio events are displayed in the same manner as in the Project window.

Snap points

When the vertical zoom is set to a sufficient factor, the Audio Part editor reveals a 'Snap point' for selected events which, by default, is found at the very beginning of each audio event (Figure 8.21).

Figure 8.21
The Snap point of a selected audio event in the Audio Part editor

The Snap point is marked by an 'S' handle attached to a vertical line and this may be dragged to any point within the event. Once set at the desired position, the Snap point is used by Cubase to lock the position of the event to the current Snap resolution, whenever it is moved or quantized (assuming that the Snap button is activated). The Snap point allows you to find a musically significant moment within the event, such as the first downbeat in the bar or the precise hit point of a bass drum. This helps line up the audio material to other events and allows you to quantize audio material, especially that which has been divided into smaller sections using the audio slicing techniques of Hitpoint mode (see below).

Info

In the Project window, the Snap point of an audio event is modified using 'Snap point to cursor' (Audio menu). The Snap point is visible as a vertical blue line when it is not in its default position at the start of the event.

Audio Part editor play, scrub, audition and loop buttons

The Audio Part editor features separate play and scrub tools which are convenient for quickly auditioning the audio in any part of the display. These operate in a similar fashion to the play and scrub tools in the Project window (as described in Chapter 4).

There are also local audition and loop buttons. These provide local playback of the audio material in the Audio Part editor. When you have selected one or more events, playback takes place over the range of the selected events. Similar playback behaviour occurs when you have made a range selection using the Range selection tool. When no selection has been made, the whole audio part is played back. Pressing the loop button activates the audition button simultaneously, and loop playback continues until you press the audition button again.

All these functions provide convenient methods of auditioning material in the Audio Part editor. In addition, their use switches the signal routing to bypass any effects or EQ on the audio channel and allows you to set an exclusive auditioning level using the audition mini-fader on the toolbar. All this helps with detailed audio editing where effects and EQ might otherwise mask the result. If you wish to hear the audio through the channel in the normal way, use the standard play button of the Transport panel ('Enter' on the computer keyboard).

Editing audio events in the Audio Part editor

Editing audio events in the Audio Part editor is very similar to editing events in the Project window (see 'Using the tools' in Chapter 4 for more details). More specific editing procedures for the Audio Part editor are outlined in 'Audio Part editor basics', below, and in 'Creative audio editing techniques' later in this chapter.

Audio Part editor basics

In a similar manner to Cubase's other editors, it is a good idea to set the left and right locators around the part you are editing in the Audio Part editor. To achieve this, press 'P' on the computer keyboard. This helps keep the Project cursor visible on screen when playing back in cycle mode. Once inside the Audio Part editor, you may prefer to use the local play, cycle and audition tools rather than the main Transport functions, (as described above). When you have selected multiple parts for editing, use the part list menu on the toolbar to switch between parts. Also try activating the 'Show Part Borders' button to help navigate.

To get started with the Audio Part editor let's try creating a sound effect using a cymbal crash. This helps understand the basics and gives a preliminary idea of the creative uses of the editor. This example uses a cymbal crash of four bars in length. The objective is to split the crash into a number of segments and then re-order them in overlapped succession on different lanes within the Audio Part editor. Proceed as follows:

- Record a cymbal crash in the Project window or drag and drop an existing cymbal file onto an audio track. Edit the event so that the cymbal crash has a duration of four bars. With the cymbal event selected, open the Quick menu and select 'Events to Part' in the Audio section (Figure 8.22). This converts the audio event into an audio part.

Tip

Use the Play tool (loudspeaker icon) with the 'Edit active part only' button de-activated, to quickly switch between and audition the contents of each event / track / lane in the Audio Part editor.

Figure 8.22
Convert the audio event for the cymbal into an audio part

- Double-click on the new audio part to open the Audio Part editor. Select the Split tool in the toolbar and divide the cymbal crash into four 1 bar events (Figure 8.23).

Figure 8.23
Split the cymbal into four 1 bar events in the Audio Part editor

- Select the Object selection tool (pointer) and drag the third bar of the cymbal onto the second lane at position 1.4.1, as indicated by the tool when the event is dragged (Figure 8.24). Activate the Snap button and choose 'Beat' in the Grid type menu, to make it easier to place the events.

Figure 8.24
Drag the third bar of the cymbal onto the second lane at position 1.4.1

- Drag the second bar of the cymbal onto the third lane at position 2.3.1 (Figure 8.25)

Figure 8.25
Drag the second bar of the cymbal onto the third lane at position 2.3.1

- Finally, drag the first bar of the cymbal onto the fourth lane at position 3.2.1 and drag the fourth bar of the cymbal to position 1.1.1 on the first lane (Figure 8.26). If you found this procedure confusing just remember that all you have done is split your original cymbal into four parts and then re-assembled them in reverse order with one beat overlaps.

Figure 8.26
Drag the first bar of the cymbal to position 3.2.1 and the fourth bar of the cymbal to position 1.1.1

- Resize the event on the fourth lane so that your events span four bars. Commence playback to hear the new order of events. The result is a hybrid reverse cymbal effect. To complete the effect, select all the events (Ctrl + A / Command + A) and press 'X' on the computer keyboard. This automatically creates crossfades between the events giving smooth transitions between each part of the cymbal (Figure 8.27).

If you chose the right kind of cymbal for this exercise you should have got a pleasing result. However, some readers may be having difficulty grasping the practical use of this technique. Well, splitting and moving events around is something that occurs frequently in the Audio Part editor (such as when creating composite versions of multiple take material) and overlapping and crossfading is a popular technique for creating smooth transitions between events. The overall technique explained here could be applied to other sounds to create similar special effects and any sustained note could form the target material. The technique could also be applied to two or more different sounds or drum loops to create unique sonic transformations.

Figure 8.27
Select all the events and press 'X' on the computer keyboard to complete the effect

The Sample editor

The Sample editor is opened by double-clicking on an audio event or pressing Ctrl + E (PC) / Command + E (Mac) on the computer keyboard while an audio event is selected in the Project window (Figure 8.28). Alternatively,

double-click on an audio clip in the Pool. The Sample editor window features a toolbar and info section at the top. It also has its own Inspector to the left which is opened by activating the Show Inspector button. The contents of the toolbar may be modified by right-clicking / control clicking in the toolbar and

Figure 8.28
The Sample editor

Tip

To change the amplitude units of the vertical axis between percentage or decibels right click (PC) / Control click (Mac) in the scale to the left of the waveform display.

making a selection from the pop-up menu. Below the toolbar, there is a thumbnail view which represents the whole of the clip associated with the selected audio data. The main display area shows the waveform of the currently selected material with time on the horizontal axis and amplitude on the vertical axis. The display varies according to which tool or function is chosen.

Editing in the Sample editor is, not surprisingly, optimised for working at the sample level. Samples are the atoms of digital audio; they are the smallest particles of audio you can manipulate in Cubase. In the Sample editor, you can see these atoms strung together if you view your audio data at maximum resolution (Figure 8.29). When you make a selection in the waveform display using the Range selection tool, the start, end and length are shown in the selection display on the toolbar in the chosen time format. This allows you to edit material with surgical precision. However, this does not mean that you need to be permanently concerned with the microcosmic level of your audio material while working in the Sample editor; much of the time you can work in an intuitive fashion, using what you hear as the main basis for your editing decisions.

44.100 kHz - 16 bits - Length: 17.1.1.102   Bars+Beats   Selected: -   Edits: 0   Zoom: 1 / 20.00

Figure 8.29
A waveform at maximum resolution in the Sample editor

The Sample editor tools

The Sample editor features its own set of tools, many of which are similar in operation to those found in the Project window (see Chapter 4 for more details). These include from left to right:

Range selection tool

For manually selecting specific areas of the waveform by clicking and dragging in the main display area. Range selections are magnetic to the zero crossing points in the waveform when the 'Snap to zero crossing' button is activated. When this button is de-activated range selections are made freestyle with single sample resolution.

Zoom tool

For zooming in and out of the main display area in standard Cubase fashion. The Zoom tool is particularly useful in the Sample editor for zooming in to specific details in the waveform.

Draw tool

For detailed manual re-drawing of the waveform at high resolution. This is designed for detailed repair work such as when manually removing a digital click and is only available when the zoom resolution is lower than 1.

Play tool

For auditioning the audio material by clicking on the waveform in the display. Playback commences from the position at which you clicked and continues for as long as you hold the mouse. The playback zone is shown in blue.

Scrub tool

For auditioning the audio material by dragging over any area of the waveform. This plays back the audio at the speed with which you drag, much like rocking the tape back and forth over the playback heads of a tape machine.

Time warp tool

Similar to its function in the Project window and other editors, the time warp tool is for dragging a bar position to a time position. However, it takes on particular significance in the Sample editor for precisely lining up the tempo to audio material. This can be achieved manually by visually dragging tempo events to specific peaks in the waveform. Alternatively, tempo events can be dragged to hitpoints. This might be used to line up the beats in the bar to each beat as indicated by the hitpoints calculated for a drum loop. To use the time warp tool, hitpoint mode must be switched off. However, when you select the time warp tool any hitpoints that have already been calculated become visible. If the Snap to Zero Crossing button is activated the time warp tool snaps to the hitpoints.

Holding Shift while clicking in the Sample editor display inserts a tempo event. Holding Shift with the time warp tool in the ruler allows the deleting of tempo events. Note that to use the time warp tool, 'tempo track' mode must be selected in the Transport bar (time warp does not function in fixed tempo mode). For more details on the use of the time warp tool see Chapter 18.

Sample editor play and loop buttons

The Sample editor features its own play and loop buttons. These provide local playback of the audio material in the Sample editor. Playback occurs over the audio event or the whole clip according to the status of the Show Audio event button. If you have made a range selection playback is focused on this instead. Pressing the loop button allows playback in a continuous loop. Alternatively, try Shift + G to commence loop playback of the current range selection and Alt + spacebar to play the current range selection once.

Together with the play and scrub tools, these functions provide a convenient method of auditioning material in the Sample editor. Their use switches the signal routing to bypass any effects or EQ on the audio channel and allows you to set an exclusive auditioning level using the audition mini-fader on the toolbar. This helps with detailed editing where effects and EQ might otherwise mask the result. If you wish to hear the audio through the channel in the normal way, use the standard play button of the Transport panel ('Enter' on the computer keyboard).

Sample editor Autoscroll and Snap to zero crossing buttons

The autoscroll button has the same function as in the other windows of Cubase. When it is activated the display automatically follows the position of the Project cursor. Use the 'F' key to enable/disable autoscroll. When the Snap to zero crossing button is activated all range selection, cutting, copying and pasting, and hitpoint editing snaps to the nearest zero crossing point in the audio waveform. Zero crossing points are where there are the least amounts of energy in the audio signal. Editing here reduces the occurrence of audible clicks and makes for a good join when one section of audio is joined to another. The Snap to zero crossing button in the Project window has no effect in the Sample editor which is controlled only by its own independent Snap to zero crossing button.

Sample editor function buttons

A number of other buttons complete the functional layout of the toolbar. These include:

- the Show Inspector button – when the Show Inspector button is activated the Sample editor Inspector appears to the left of the main display. Here you define the tempo, adjust the playback algorithm, manage hitpoints, select, zoom and process the audio (see below for details).

- the Show audio event button – this enables / disables the view and flags of the audio event associated with the waveform. This button is not present if you have opened the Sample editor via an audio clip in the Pool.

- the Show regions button – this shows / hides the Regions list which appears to the right of the main display. Regions are areas within your audio material marked as sections of interest or relevance, much like you might highlight sections of interest within the text of a book. They can be created automatically when recording audio in cycle mode or they can be created manually in the Sample editor (see 'Creating and handling regions in the Sample editor', below).

The Sample editor Inspector

The Sample editor Inspector appears to the left when you activate the Show Inspector button on the toolbar. The Inspector features a number of specialised sections which help you edit the audio more conveniently. A number of the functions found here are unique to the Inspector while others are duplicates of functions found in the main menus. The details of the main display vary according to which Inspector section is currently selected. The sections include the following:

Definition – here you define the internal tempo of the audio. If you already know the tempo of the audio you can enter a value directly in the tempo field. When the tempo is unknown you can use the auto adjust button to automatically calculate the tempo of the audio. Alternatively, you can enter the duration in bars and beats and activate the manual adjust button. In manual adjust mode you can manually drag the grid in the display to match the main peaks in the waveform. Feel free to experiment in this section since you can clear the grid and start again at any time using the reset button. Once the grid is successfully matched to the audio, playback can take place at different tempi whereupon the audio material is time stretched or compressed in real-time (in Straighten Up mode). You can audition the effect of the time stretching by activating the preview button. Straighten Up mode and the time stretch algorithm is chosen in the playback section. Defining the audio like this is particularly helpful when working with loops. Loop processing and audio warping is described in more detail below.

Playback – here you choose the parameters which govern the playback of the tempo-defined audio material. The playback section allows you to specify the time stretch algorithm used when the Straighten Up button is activated. Straighten up mode locks the grid defined in the Definition section to the current tempo (or tempi) of Cubase, thereby stretching or compressing the audio in real-time. Straighten up mode includes quantize and swing parameters which affect the resolution and feel of the time stretching. To freely warp the audio activate the Free Warp button and click and drag in the display to create and edit warp tabs. The playback section also provides convenient access to the Transpose and Follow Global real-time pitch shift functions. You can freeze the real-time processing using the Flatten button. Straighten up mode and audio warping is described in more detail below.

Hitpoints – this section is for hitpoint calculation and editing. Hitpoints are used to mark the dominant peaks within the audio waveform which usually correspond with the rhythmic pulse of the material. Hitpoints are created by dragging the Sensitivity slider. The higher the setting of the slider the more hitpoints are created. The hitpoints may be edited by activating the Edit hitpoints button. The other function buttons allow you to create audio slices and groove templates or add events, regions and markers according to hitpoint positions. Hitpoint editing and hitpoints in general are described in more detail below.

Range – provides quick access to a number of common range selection and zoom functions and displays the current selection start, end and length in samples. This helps you select the area of interest within the waveform and zoom in and out (expert users may prefer to use key commands for some of these functions).

Process – provides quick access to a number of common audio processing commands such as cut, copy, paste, bounce and insert silence. From here you can also edit the current selection using the on-board processing functions and plug-ins, or select the audio process history, statistics or spectrum analyser.

Regions

Regions are areas within your audio material marked as sections of interest or relevance, much like you might highlight or underline sections of interest within the text of a book. They can be created automatically when recording audio in cycle mode or they can be created manually in the Sample editor. Click on the Show Regions button to reveal the Regions list to the right of the main display (Figure 8.30). You can create a new region at any time by selecting a range within the waveform and clicking on the Add button above the Regions list. Regions may be played, selected or removed using the corresponding buttons above the list. The start and end points of each region can be directly edited in the corresponding columns. New audio events can

Figure 8.30
Activate the Show regions button to reveal the Regions list in the Sample editor

be created from any region by Ctrl/Command dragging directly from the selected area in the waveform display or by dragging from the Regions list onto a track in the Project window.

Snap points

When the Show Audio event button is activated, a vertical line with an 'S' handle known as the Snap point is shown in the waveform display. The Snap point is usually set to a musically significant moment within the audio and, when the Snap button is activated in the Project window, is used to snap the event to the current snap resolution. The Sample editor allows you to freely drag the snap point to any position within the waveform and if you also activate the scrub tool you can hear the audio as you drag it. This helps place the Snap point with great precision. Alternatively, set the Snap point to the position of the cursor by selecting Audio / Snap point to Cursor.

Navigating in the Sample editor

Navigating and auditioning in the Sample editor

In a similar manner to Cubase's other editors, it is a good idea to set the left and right locator around the event you select for editing. As usual, the quickest way to achieve this is to press 'P' on the computer keyboard. Double-click on the event to open the Sample editor. Once inside the editor, you may prefer to use the local play, loop and audition controls for playback, rather than the main Transport controls.

Helpful key commands

At first sight, navigating within the Sample editor may seem rather confusing. The following key commands help clarify and speed up some of the basic operations:

- Zooming - use Shift + F to zoom to the whole clip associated with the event, Shift + E to zoom to the event itself, and Alt + S to zoom to the current range selection.
- Playback - use Shift + G to loop the current range selection or Alt + Spacebar to play a range selection once. Alternatively, activate File / Preferences / Transport / Playback toggle triggers local preview. This allows you to use the Spacebar to audition in the Sample editor.

The thumbnail view

The thumbnail view above the main display is particularly helpful for navigating to anywhere within the clip. This is similar to the Overview display in the Project window. The current horizontal section of the waveform you can see in the main display is marked by a corresponding blue box in the thumbnail view. You can drag the blue box to different positions within the clip and it can be resized by dragging the start or end points.

Sample editor basics

Copy and paste

One of the best ways to get to know the Sample editor is to experiment with a test audio recording. For this it is suggested that you make a recording of the spoken letters 'VST'. This avoids confusion and you can clearly see the three letters as three significant shapes in the waveform (Figure 8.33). Try pronouncing the letters in a slow, deliberate fashion in order to get a clear, usable recording. The objective is to test various editing techniques and re-order the letters using the copy and paste functions. Proceed as follows:

- Take a microphone and record the spoken letters 'VST' onto an audio track in the Project window. Double-click on the resulting audio event to open the Sample editor. The waveform should resemble that shown in Figure 8.31.

Figure 8.31
Test recording of the spoken letters 'VST'

- Reveal the audio event by activating the 'Show Audio event' button. The start, end and snap point handles are shown. Activate the 'Snap to zero crossing' button. This helps ensure click-free editing when you copy and paste in the Sample editor.

Figure 8.32
The audio event is revealed by clicking on the Show Audio event button

- Audition the audio event by clicking on the play button in the toolbar. The local play button bypasses the EQ and inserts for the channel and provides exclusive playback of the audio in the Sample editor. Adjust the playback level using the audition mini-fader on the toolbar.

- Select the Range selection tool and drag across the display area. Select the letter 'S' in your audio recording. The selection area is shaded in turquoise(see Figure 8.33).

Figure 8.33
Select and play the 'S' of your 'VST' test recording

- Press Alt + Spacebar on the computer keyboard to play the 'S' sound once. Press Shift + G on the computer keyboard to play the 'S' sound in a continuous loop.
- While still in loop playback, try adjusting the start and end positions of the range selection by dragging on the start or end points with the Range selection tool (a double arrow appears). Each time you release the mouse button, playback re-commences from the start of the range selection. This technique is particularly useful for finding and fine tuning a drum loop (Figure 8.34).

Figure 8.34
Try adjusting the start and end position of the range selection while in loop playback

Now, select 'V', (the first peak in the waveform), by dragging the mouse in the display (Figure 8.35). Copy the selection by pressing ctrl + C (PC) / Mac: command + C.

- Click once on the point just after the 'T' (the third peak in the waveform). Press Ctrl + V / Command + V on the computer keyboard to paste the 'V' just after the 'T' (Figure 8.36). When the range field on the toolbar reads zero, the contents of the clipboard are inserted into the existing waveform at the range selector position (shown by a vertical line). When the range field on the toolbar reads any value other than zero, the

Tip

Multiple Sample editors may be opened simultaneously when you are working on several clips at the same time. This is useful for copying, pasting and merging audio between different clips.

contents of the clipboard overwrite the existing waveform beginning from the start position of the range selection.

Figure 8.35
Select and copy 'V'

- Select the last two peaks in the waveform and audition the selection. The result is the required spoken letters: 'TV' (Figure 8.37).

Figure 8.36
Paste 'V' just after the 'T' at the end of the waveform

If you are happy with the edit, you could delete the first two peaks in the waveform, the original 'V' and 'S', by selecting them and pressing backspace on the computer keyboard. Alternatively, select the new 'TV' section and activate the Show Regions button. Click on the add button above the regions list and name the new region as 'TV'. If desired, Ctrl + drag the region onto the Project window to create a new audio event.

Figure 8.37
Audition 'TV'

Digital click removal in the Sample editor

Audio files occasionally suffer from digital clicks and other interference. The Sample editor allows you to manually repair the damage by zooming in to the click at high magnification and re-drawing the waveform. The following outlines the basic procedure:

- Double-click on the audio event with the unwanted click to open the Sample editor. Hopefully, the offending click is already visible in the display as a brief spike in the waveform, similar to Figure 8.38. Many kinds of interference are not so obvious and could be more difficult to find.

Figure 8.38
Open the sample editor and find the click in the waveform

- Locate the mouse in the ruler at the position of the click and drag down to zoom in (activate 'Zoom while Locating in Time Scale' in File / Preferences / Transport). Zoom in until a factor of lower than 1 is indicated on the infoline (Figure 8.39). At less than 1 the waveform is shown as a line rather than as a 'filled' form

Figure 8.39
Zoom in to the click

- The offending click is now visible in great detail in the display. If you are having difficulty finding your click look out for a small segment of the waveform which has different characteristics to the surrounding audio. One way of removing the click is to select the draw tool and manually redraw the waveform over the appropriate range (Figure 8.40). Draw the new line very carefully, attempting to match the characteristics of the surrounding waveform.

Figure 8.40
Select the Pencil tool and manually redraw the waveform

An alternative to manually redrawing is to select a short segment of the surrounding audio and to paste this over the click. The Sample editor Inspector helps with this procedure. To achieve a successful result, without changing the length of the audio clip, proceed as follows:

- Activate the Show Inspector and the Snap to zero crossing buttons on the toolbar.
- Working at high magnification, select the range of the click using the Range selection tool. In the Sample editor Inspector, select Process / Edit / Event or Range as Region. Open the Inspector Range section and make a mental note of the length of the selection in samples.
- Search for a suitable adjacent area of the waveform using the Range selection tool. Select an area whose length is the same as, or greater than, the number of samples in the region for the click (as defined in step 2).
- When you have found a suitable area, copy it using Ctrl / Command + C.
- Select the region created in step 2 and click on the Select Region button above the Regions list. This selects the range of the region in the main display.
- In the Sample editor Inspector, activate Process / Select Process / Merge Clipboard. In the Merge Clipboard dialogue which appears set the Sources mix slider to 100% copy and click on the Process button. This overwrites the click.

Creative audio editing techniques

Creating a composite recording in the Audio Part editor

The recording of a live performer sometimes requires several takes before a satisfactory result is achieved. Rather than stop Cubase after each take, it is often more convenient to record continuously in cycle mode. In cycle mode, the audio is recorded as one long audio file automatically divided into separate takes, one for each lap of the cycle. This process is outlined in 'Audio recording in cycle mode' in Chapter 7.

A multi-take recording of this kind may be conveniently edited in the Audio Part editor where the audio is automatically divided into separate regions and stacked onto separate lanes. Each lane represents the recording from one lap of the cycle and is named with a sequential take number. A 'perfect' composite recording can be assembled from the different takes by splitting, resizing and muting the material. This process is sometimes referred to as compositing or 'comping'. To create your own composite recording, proceed as follows:

- Select the raw audio event(s) recorded in cycle mode in the Project window and then select 'Audio / Events to Part' from the Quick menu. Choose 'Regions' if the 'Create Part using Regions?' dialogue appears. This creates a multi-lane audio part which is suitable for editing in the Audio Part editor. Press 'P' on the computer keyboard to set the left and right locators to the start and end of the part. Double-click on the part to open the Audio Part editor (Figure 8.41).

Figure 8.41
A multiple take recording in the Audio Part editor featuring four takes

• You may firstly wish to audition the takes to establish which versions you prefer. Only one take can be played at any one time and the lowest lane gets playback priority. Try using the Mute tool working from the lowest lane upwards to progressively mute those takes you do not wish to hear (Figure 8.42).

Figure 8.42
Use the Mute tool when auditioning the material, working from the lowest lane upwards.

• To make the task easier, it may be appropriate to colour code the different lanes and to divide all the takes into one or two bar events using the Split tool (Figure 8.43). Alternatively, try splitting the material according to the range of each musical phrase. To start with, try working with the Snap button activated and the resolution set to bars or beats. To avoid clicks at the split points, activate the 'Snap to Zero crossing' button. De-activate the button after editing is complete to avoid effecting subsequent editing tasks.

Figure 8.43
Use the Split tool to divide the takes into their constituent musical phrases or bars

• Assemble a basic composite version of the performance by muting those events you do not wish to hear. For clarity, rename the 'best' takes and the 'bad' takes in the description field of the Infoline for each event (Figure 8.44). Use Shift + G to loop around the currently selected event range.

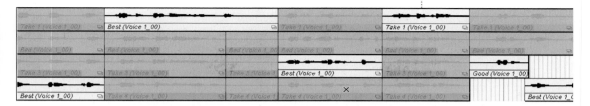

- For detailed composite take editing (especially vocal performances), you may need to audition very short sections of the material, such as when editing single words in a vocal line. In these cases, it is best to work at higher zoom factors with the Snap button de-activated (Figure 8.45).

Figure 8.44
Mute those events you do not wish to hear and, if desired, name the best performances

So far, you have been attempting to chain together all the very best parts of the material, ensuring that there are no dramatic signal level changes and no obvious extraneous noises and interference as you pass from one event to another. When all the edited events produce close to the desired composite version, you may be able to improve matters further by setting up crossfades between all adjacent events. To achieve this, delete all muted events, select the remaining events by pressing Ctrl + A on the computer keyboard, and create automatic crossfades by pressing 'X' (Figure 8.46).

Figure 8.45
Work at higher zoom factor with the Snap button de-activated for detailed editing

- If there are overlaps between the events, the crossfades have the duration of the respective overlaps. If there is no overlap between adjacent events, the events are automatically lengthened according to the default length setting in the Crossfade dialogue. If events are not adjacent, no automatic crossfade is created. The crossfade curves may be individually or globally adjusted in the Crossfade dialogue (see 'Fades and Crossfades', above). The ideal crossfade length depends very much on the effect you are trying to produce. For example, if you are aiming for seamless joins on vocal lines try a length of 30ms with a spline-shaped curve (or the default straight line) with or without Equal Gain, as shown in Figure 8.47. Special effects usually benefit from longer crossfade times.

Figure 8.46
Delete all muted events and apply crossfades for smoothing the joins between the remaining events, (the lengths of the crossfades in this screenshot have been artificially lengthened – in reality they may be much shorter)

Figure 8.47
Try these settings in the Crossfade
dialogue for seamless joins between
vocal takes

Editing miscellaneous takes in the Audio Part editor

When you have recorded different versions of the same material on several different tracks or when you have recorded a number of takes on the same track as a result of dropping in or punch recording, you may wish to edit the material in the Audio Part editor. Proceed as follows:

• Drag a selection box around the events you wish to edit. These may be on the same track or on different tracks.
• Select 'Events to Part' in the Audio menu (or use the Quick menu).
• Double-click on one of the parts to open the Audio Part editor or press Ctrl / Command + E.
• In the Audio Part editor, parts which were on different tracks in the Project window each appear in their own horizontal track in the editor. For multiple recordings which took place on the same track, each take appears in its own lane within the vertical space of its respective track (stacked).
• Use the part list menu to switch between tracks. Alternatively, use the Play tool with the 'Edit active part only' button de-activated, to switch between and audition the contents of each track/lane.
• The events may be edited using similar techniques to those outlined in 'Creating a composite recording in the Audio Part editor', above.

Creating and handling regions in the Sample editor

Regions are areas within your audio material marked as sections of interest or relevance. They provide useful 'signposts' to specific passages within your audio recordings. They are created, viewed and edited within the Sample editor but may also be created automatically when recording audio in cycle mode or when using Detect Silence. Here, we take a look at how regions are handled in the Sample editor. Let's imagine that you have made a recording of some speech from the media, some part of which you intend to use as a quotation, or as an effect in a dance track. Regions help you make your choice more easily. Proceed as follows:

• Double-click on the audio event which contains the speech to open the Sample editor. Activate the Show Regions button to open the Regions display (Figure 8.48).

Figure 8.48
Open the Sample editor and activate the Show Regions button

- Activate the local audition and loop buttons on the Sample editor toolbar. Playback commences from the start of the audio event (Figure 8.49). Listen to the audio and select an area of interest with the Range selection tool. Since you are in local playback and loop mode the cursor jumps to the range you have selected and continues to loop around the selected area.

Figure 8.49
Activate the local audition and loop buttons.

- Select a word, a phrase or a whole sentence within the audio. Fine tune the range selection by dragging the start or end points. When you are satisfied, click on the Add Region button above the Regions list and enter a name for the region. You might use the first word of each speech snippet as the region name (Figure 8.50).

Figure 8.50
Select, add and name a region

- Select the next area of interest in the audio material and add and name another region. You are still in local playback and loop mode so, each time you make a new selection, the cursor automatically loops within it. Continue in the same manner until you have marked all areas of interest. You now have a list of regions (Figure 8.51).

Figure 8.51
Select, add and name other regions to form a list of regions

• Stop playback by de-activating the Audition button. Do not deactivate the loop button. You can now audition a region in the audio clip by selecting any Region in the Regions list and clicking on the Region list Play button (Figure 8.52). Playback loops around the selected region. Audition any other region in the list by selecting it without dropping out of playback.

Figure 8.52
Audition each region by selecting it in the list and activating the Region list Play button

• The regions are shown in a time-ordered list but, of course, you can audition them in any order you like. Effectively, you can now jump to any point of interest with greater ease and, by naming each region descriptively, you have created convenient signposts which help you navigate within the audio material. When you have made a decision about which region you intend to use, fine tune its start and end points as desired and drag and drop it from the Regions list into the Project window (Figure 8.53).

Figure 8.53
Drag and drop the chosen region from the Regions list into the Project window

Creating and editing hitpoints in the Sample editor

What are hitpoints?

Hitpoints are special markers which can be assigned to an audio clip based upon the location of the main peaks in the signal. A signal peak is a point in the waveform where there is rapid amplitude gain, otherwise known as an attack transient. These points normally correspond with the main performance 'hits' in the signal and can be seen as mountain-like peaks in the waveform display. They might correspond with each note played by a musical instrument, each word sung by a vocalist, or the main percussive hits in a drum or percussion performance. By creating markers at these points we can capture the rhythmic pulse and divide the performance into its constituent parts. In Cubase, a segment of audio found between a pair of hit-points is known as an audio slice. A common objective, especially when slicing drum and percussion loops, is to finish up with a single sound or drum hit between each consecutive pair of hitpoints.

Calculating hitpoints

To calculate hitpoints select Audio / Hitpoints / Calculate Hitpoints or open the Hitpoints section in the Sample editor Inspector and drag the sensitivity slider to the right. The remainder of this section describes hitpoint calculation using the Hitpoints section of the Sample editor Inspector.

Hitpoints are calculated for the current range selection, or the whole clip if no range selection has been made. Thereafter, these hitpoints remain attached to the clip. Hitpoints are shown or hidden by toggling the Hitpoints section open or closed. Hitpoints may be re-calculated at any time by clicking on the Hitpoint section's Remove All button and resetting the sensitivity slider. Alternatively, use the commands in the Audio / Hitpoints sub-menu. You may wish to re-calculate when you have made a new range selection or are not satisfied with your hitpoint editing. The number of displayed hitpoints depends upon the sensitivity slider position and the setting in the Use menu. The sensitivity slider displays more hitpoints the more you move it to the right. When the Use menu is set to 'All', all the calculated hitpoints are active and visible. When the Use menu is set to one of the note values (1/4, 1/8, 1/16, 1/32 or metric bias) only those hitpoints which are near to the chosen note resolution are taken into account. Hitpoints may also be entered manually by activating the Edit hitpoints button and clicking in the display while holding Alt.

Figure 8.54
The Sample editor Inspector's Hitpoints section

Editing hitpoints

Hitpoint editing is only possible when the Edit hitpoints button is active. Editing is used in combination with the hitpoint sensitivity slider, in order to finish up with the desired number of hitpoints at the appropriate positions in the waveform. When the Edit hitpoints button is active, the pointer assumes a number of different functions according to where you place it in the display. These are as follows:

- Play – when moved between two hitpoints the pointer changes to a speaker symbol allowing you to audition the audio between the two points. This is used to verify the accuracy and suitability of the calculated hitpoints.
- Insert - moving the pointer to the central area of the display while holding Alt (at which time a pencil symbol is shown) allows you to manually insert a hitpoint.
- Move – locating the pointer on a hitpoint's handle in the upper part of the display (at which time the hitpoint is highlighted in green) allows you to drag the hitpoint to a new location.
- Disable – locating the pointer on a hitpoint's handle in the upper part of the display while holding Alt allows you to disable the hitpoint (the hitpoint is highlighted in green and a disable cross appears). Disabling is

useful when your chosen sensitivity setting has given you correctly positioned hitpoints throughout most of the waveform except for a small number of erroneous hitpoints. Disabling the offending hitpoints provides a quick and convenient solution (see Figure 8.55). If required, disabled hitpoints can be re-enabled by clicking on the hitpoint's handle a second time. (Note: you cannot disable a manually inserted hitpoint).

Figure 8.55
Disabling erroneous hitpoints in Edit hitpoints mode

- Lock – clicking once on the hitpoint handle locks the hitpoint (at which time it is shown in dark blue). Locking a hitpoint ensures that it is not affected by further manipulations of the hitpoint sensitivity slider. This is useful when you wish to choose a specific selection of hitpoints which are at the correct positions in the waveform and then remove the rest by lowering the sensitivity slider. Any locked hitpoints remain in the display regardless of how much you reduce the level of the sensitivity slider (see Figure 8.56).

Figure 8.56
Lock the best hitpoints and then remove all other hitpoints by lowering the hitpoint sensitivity slider

- Delete - to delete a hitpoint, drag it out of the Sample editor.

Creating a groove template from hitpoints

As outlined above, hitpoints mark those points in the audio waveform where there is rapid amplitude gain (attack transients). In the case of drum and percussion loops, these points correspond with the rhythmic pulse of the material. Since, by calculating the hitpoints, we have effectively created a rhythmic template of the performance, why not extract this data for use in other parts of Cubase? This is indeed what you can do using the Sample editor Inspector's Definition and Hitpoints sections. To create your own groove quantize template proceed as follows:

- Copy the target audio event. It is best to work on a copy to avoid damage to important material. If it is not already tightly edited, carefully edit the copy to fit a precise number of bars and beats.
- With the newly edited event selected, use Audio / Bounce selection. Select replace in the Replace events dialogue. This creates a new audio event and corresponding audio file which is ready for processing.
- Double-click on the new event to open the Sample editor. Activate the Inspector and select the Definition section.

- In the Definition section, enter the number of bars and beats corresponding to the length of the audio event. Select the desired resolution in the Grid menu (try 1/4, 1/8 or 1/16 note). Activate the Auto adjust button to calculate the tempo of the audio. The grid lines should line up with the main peaks in the waveform.
- Open the Hitpoints section of the Inspector and drag the Sensitivity slider to the right until one hitpoint appears for each hit in the rhythm (Figure 8.57). Audition the audio between each consecutive pair of hitpoints to verify the results. You may need to edit the results but you can usually rely upon the accuracy of the positions of the automatically generated hitpoints.

Figure 8.57
Adjust the hitpoint sensitivity slider to match the hitpoints to the main hits in

- In the Hitpoints section, click on the Make groove button to create the groove template (Figure 8.58).
- Open the Quantize type menu to reveal the newly added groove which appears last in the list with the same name as the audio event from which it was extracted (Figure 8.59).

Figure 8.58
Click on the Make Groove button to create the groove template

Figure 8.59
The new groove quantize preset appears in the Quantize type menu

Working with loops

Loop selection

When working with audio loops, one of the most convenient functions is 'Loop selection' found in the main Transport menu or in the Sample editor Inspector's Range / Select sub-menu. This is best activated using the default key command: Shift + G. When used in the Project window or the Audio Part editor, Loop selection automatically sets the left and right locators to the currently selected audio event(s) or range selection and commences playback in cycle mode, starting at the left locator position. When used in the Sample editor, Loop selection engages loop playback over the current range selection.

Info

It is possible to create a groove template by selecting a tightly edited audio event and then selecting Audio / Hitpoints / Create Groove Quantize from Hitpoints. You will need to enter the original tempo of the audio into a pop-up box. While this is quick, it is not as accurate as the more detailed technique outlined here.

Editing a loop in the Sample editor

This section outlines how to edit the length of a drum or percussion record-ing in the Sample editor to create a loop. Proceed as follows:

- Double-click on the audio event which contains the drum or percussion material to open the Sample editor. Use the Range selection tool to mark the approximate range of the prospective loop.
- De-activate the autoscroll button. Activate the local audition and loop buttons (or press Shift + G). Playback loops around the selected area.
- Select the Region button and add the selection to the region list. This serves as a backup of your rough loop if you should lose your selection at a later point in this process.
- Tune the length of the loop by dragging the start or end points of the selected region. The Range selection tool changes into a double arrow whenever you place it over the start or end points of the selection. Each time you set a new position for either the start or end, playback recommences from the start of the loop. This helps you set the start to the exact downbeat and fine tune the length to a precise number of bars.
- Activate the Snap to zero crossing button to avoid clicks. Alternatively, to fine tune the loop double-click in the start or end fields of the Inspector's Range section and use the up / down arrow keys on the computer keyboard to change the values one sample at a time.
- Once you are happy with the loop, mark it as a new region using the Add Region button and name it appropriately.
- To create a new event for the loop, select the new region in the Region list and drag it onto the Project window event display. Alternatively, press Ctrl / Command and drag from the range selection in the waveform display.

Tip

If you are working at high magnification and have lost the start point of your loop proceed as follows: stop playback, ensure that the autoscroll button is activated, and then press L on the computer keyboard. The Project cursor moves to the start point of the current selection. At this point in time, de-activate the autoscroll button and press Shift + G to recommence loop playback. You can now continue to fine tune the start point of your loop at high magnification.

Loop tempo matching using the Beat Calculator

The Beat Calculator (Figure 8.60) is particularly useful when working with loops. It is opened from the Project menu and can be used for matching the tempo of Cubase to that of an audio loop.

To match the tempo of Cubase to an audio loop, proceed as follows:

Figure 8.60
The Beat Calculator

- If you have not already done so, make sure that your target audio loop has been edited to fit a precise number of beats or bars.
- Alternatively import a ready-made audio loop into the Project window.
- Select the event and open the Beat Calculator from the Project menu.
- To make the tempo fit the length of your chosen event you need to know its duration in beats. Enter the beat length into the Beat Calculator and click on 'At Tempo Track Start' to change the tempo of Cubase to that of the loop.

- Play the loop alongside the metronome click to verify that it matches the newly calculated tempo.

Audio slicing a loop in the Sample editor

As outlined elsewhere, hitpoints allow you to find the main rhythmic components in your audio material. In Cubase, each section marked by a pair of hitpoints is known as an audio slice. Audio events can be automatically divided up into audio slices using the Slice and Close button in the Hitpoints section of the Sample editor Inspector or by selecting Audio / Hitpoints / Create audio slices from hitpoints. In the case of drum loops, each audio slice usually contains a single sound or hit on each beat or fraction of a beat in the loop. The events contained within the resulting sliced part automatically follow any changes in tempo without changing the pitch of the sound and without the side-effects of time stretching. This results in more natural sounding loops when you adjust them away from their original tempi and allows you to freely use tempo changes throughout the project. To create audio slices from a drum loop, proceed as follows:

- Select the audio event which contains the target loop and double-click on it to open the Sample editor. Find and select the loop using the Range selection tool. Activate the local audition and loop buttons in the toolbar or use Shift + G to commence loop playback. Fine tune the length of the loop by adjusting the start and end points. Make sure that the start point corresponds with the downbeat of the first beat of the loop and adjust the end point so that the loop plays back over the required number of beats (Figure 8.61). Ignore this first step if you are using a library drum loop which is already tightly edited and whose corresponding clip fills the whole event. In this case you need not make a range selection.

Figure 8.61
Adjust the loop so that it plays for the required number of beats

- Open the Definition section of the Sample editor Inspector. Select the desired resolution in the Grid menu (try 1/4, 1/8 or 1/16 note). Activate the Auto adjust button.
- Open the Hitpoints section of the Sample editor Inspector and drag the sensitivity slider to the right until one hitpoint appears for each hit in the rhythm (Figure 8.62).

Figure 8.62
Adjust the hitpoint sensitivity slider to match the hitpoints to the main hits in the rhythm

Tip

For click-free slices try manually dragging hitpoints to the nearest zero crossing point with the snap to zero crossing point button activated. For this technique it is best to work at high magnification factors.

- Audition the audio between each pair of hitpoints to verify the results (Figure 8.64). The audio slice turns blue as it is played. Attempt to produce audio slices where one sound or hit is present in each slice. For greater accuracy when using a range selection, you may need to re-adjust the range start point to the position of the first hitpoint. If this is the case, you should re-activate the Auto adjust button in the Definition section to re-adjust the grid. You may get better results by using a greater number of hitpoints than expected, thereby dividing up the audio into smaller slices. The more accurate the audio slices, the more accurate will be the handling of the result when played back at different tempos. You cannot always rely upon the accuracy of the automatically generated hitpoints.

Figure 8.63
Audition each audio slice by clicking between each pair of hitpoints with the Hitpoint edit tool

- When you are satisfied with the settings, click on the Slice and Close button in the Hitpoints section to create the audio slices (Figure 8.64).

Figure 8.64
Click on the Slice and Close button to create the audio slices

- As soon as you click on the Slice and Close button, the Sample editor is automatically closed and the original audio event in the Project window is replaced by an audio part which contains the new audio slices (Figure 8.65). The timing of the slices in the new audio part are automatically adjusted to match the current tempo of the project. When you change the tempo the sliced part follows.

Figure 8.65
A new audio part containing the audio slices is created in the Project window

For detailed audio slice editing, double-click on the sliced part to open the Audio Part editor. Activate cycle playback to audition the part. Without stopping playback you can double-click on any problem slice to re-open the Sample editor. De-activate autoscroll in the Sample editor. This helps you focus on the selected problem slice and you can now drag the hitpoint at the start of the slice to a new position to change its timing or ensure a clean attack. After any editing, and while still in playback, click on the Slice and

Close button again to re-calculate the slices. You can re-calculate the audio slices in this manner as many times as you wish. The new settings are immediately taken into account in the sliced part. All this can be achieved without dropping out of playback, allowing you to quickly verify the results. For fine tuning and avoiding clicks try activating the snap to zero crossing button. Placing your hitpoints at zero crossing points may help optimise the timing precision and the crispness of the attack segments of your slices.

Processing audio slices in the Audio Part editor

If you change the tempo of Cubase by a relatively small amount, the timing changes of sliced data within audio parts remain fairly transparent. However, more radical tempo changes result in gaps in the audio as the sliced events are moved further apart. This problem may be solved in the Audio Part editor. The Audio Part editor is also good for creative manipulations of audio slices, such as quantizing or deleting, exchanging or modifying individual sounds within the loop.

Closing the gap

Reducing the tempo by more than a few beats-per-minute results in gaps between each of the audio slices. Figure 8.66 shows the audio slices for a drum loop where the project has been set to the original tempo of the loop, at 120bpm.

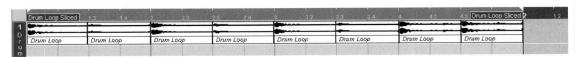

When the tempo is reduced to 110bpm gaps appear between the audio slices which interfere with the successful playback of the loop (Figure 8.67).

Figure 8.66
Audio slices for a drum loop set to its original tempo of 120bpm

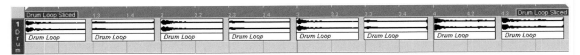

To cure the problem, select the part in the Project window (or press Ctrl + A to select all the events in the Audio Part editor) and select 'Close Gaps' in the Audio menu. This applies time stretch to each individual slice and closes all the gaps (Figure 8.68).

Figure 8.67
Gaps between the slices when the tempo is reduced

The Close Gaps function should be used only when you are sure that there will be no more tempo changes. If at a later date you decide that you wish to change the tempo again, you must revert to the original unstretched audio material.

Increasing the tempo by more than a few beats-per-minute compresses the sliced events more tightly together resulting in overlaps and some-

Figure 8.68
Close the gaps using the 'Close Gaps' function

times occasional clicks. To cure the clicks try setting up auto fades in the Auto fades dialogue for the track. Activate the fade in and fade out options and try a 5ms to 10ms fade time.

Changing the feel of the audio slices using quantize

It is sometimes appropriate to change the timing of the audio slices using the quantize functions. This can result in a loop with a tighter feel or a completely new groove. The results depend very much upon how you have sliced the audio. For audio slices which have been divided into 1/8 note segments try the following:

- Double-click on the audio part containing the audio slices to open the Audio Part editor. Select all the slices by pressing Ctrl + A on the computer keyboard.
- Open the Quantize setup dialogue from the Quantize type menu. Set 1/8 notes in Grid and Straight in Type with a swing factor of between 50% and 100%.
- Click on the Apply Quantize button. Watch as the events in the Audio Part editor are moved according to the quantize template and listen to the results. If you create something you like, try using the 'Close Gaps' function to produce a smoother effect.

This technique is sometimes effective if you need to mangle and transform your loops beyond recognition but is highly dependent upon the nature of the target material. The results can be subtle or very radical.

Matching the feel of an audio bass line to a MIDI kick drum

When an audio event is divided into its rhythmic components it becomes possible to process its timing according to the feel of other events or parts. For example, you could impose the timing characteristics of a MIDI kick drum onto an audio bass line, resulting in tightly synchronised kick and bass. To achieve this proceed as follows:

- Select all audio events on the bass instrument track.
- Press Ctrl + E to open multiple Sample editors for all audio clips associated with the selected events.
- Working on each clip in turn in the Sample editor Inspector hitpoints section, use the sensitivity slider to calculate hitpoints at each and every bass note and then select Create events. The objective is to split events into separate shorter events each containing a single bass note. Close the Sample editor window each time processing is complete for each clip.
- Select the MIDI kick drum track and activate the In Place editor for the track using the In Place editor button in the track header.
- Activate the Snap button and select 'Events' in the project window snap type menu.
- Manually drag the relevant bass note events to their nearest kick drum notes in the Project window. With the In Place editor open and 'Events' selected in the snap type menu, the bass events are now sensitive to the positions of the MIDI kick drum notes.

- Work though the whole arrangement to line up the relevant bass note events to their nearest MIDI kick drum notes.

Audio Warping in the Sample editor

Why do we need audio warping?

Most audio material of a musical nature has some kind of inherent rhythm and the speed of this rhythm can be defined as a tempo, expressed in beats-per-minute. You can record your audio to match the current tempo of the project but what happens if you later decide to change this tempo? Or what happens if you decide to use a tempo ramp which gradually increases or decreases? In these cases, the rhythmic pulse of the audio would no longer be synchronised with the tempo of Cubase. The solution to the problem is a combination of defining the internal tempo of the audio, matching this to a grid and then applying time stretching to the audio events so that they follow tempo changes. In Cubase, the latter mode of audio playback is known as Straighten up mode. This means that changing the tempo of the project is still a possibility, even after recording all the audio. Moreover, it means that you can import audio from anywhere and by defining its tempo and activating Straighten up mode you can quickly integrate the material at the current tempo of the project. In essence, real-time audio warping and Straighten up mode offer you a fuss-free way of locking audio to tempo. This liberates your creativity since you can now freely try out tempo changes and use lots of different audio loops of different internal tempos within the same project, without worrying about how you are going to make everything fit together.

Using the audio warping functions

To prepare your audio for real-time audio warping, proceed as follows:

1 Define the tempo of your audio

- Copy the target audio event. It is best to work on a copy to avoid damage to important material. If it is not already tightly edited, carefully edit the copy to fit a precise number of bars and beats. You can do this either directly in the Project window or in the Sample editor.
- With the newly edited event selected, use Audio / Bounce selection. Select replace in the Replace events dialogue. This creates a new audio event and corresponding audio file which is ready for processing. Note that the Sample rate, Record format and Record file type set in the Project Setup dialogue govern the format of the bounced audio file.
- Double-click on the new event to open the Sample editor. Activate the Inspector and select the Definition section (Figure 8.69).
- In the Definition section, enter the number of bars and beats corresponding to the length of the audio event. Select the desired resolution in the Grid menu (try 1/4, 1/8 or 1/16 note). Activate the Auto adjust button to calculate the tempo of the audio. The grid lines should line up with the main peaks in the waveform.
- If the audio event contains a drum loop of a known tempo from a sample library, you could try entering the tempo value directly in the tempo field (Figure 8.70).

Info

Cubase recognises the tempo definition and time signature information contained within Acid format WAV files. These files are therefore immediately ready for audio warping operations when they are imported into the program.

Info

Audio tempo definition, musical mode, warp tabs, the warp samples tool, audio quantize and real-time pitch shifting form the main 'audio warp' features of Cubase. Most of the details are outlined in this section ('Audio warping in the Sample editor'). Real-time pitch shifting is set up in the Infoline for an audio event (for more details, see 'Using the Audio event Infoline' at the beginning of this chapter).

Figure 8.69
Select the Definition section in the Sample editor Inspector

Figure 8.70
If you already know the tempo, enter it directly in the audio tempo field

2 Activate Straighten up mode

- When the tempo of the audio has been successfully defined using the above steps, select the Inspector Playback section and activate the Straighten up button (Figure 8.71).

Figure 8.71
Activate Straighten up mode

- Select the time-stretch algorithm which most closely corresponds to the type of audio you have processed (Figure 8.72).
- In the Project window, the audio event you set to Straighten up mode is now shown with a small musical note and double-arrow in the lower right corner. If you now impose a tempo ramp between the start and end of the event, the audio follows the tempo precisely by time-stretching the audio in real-time (Figure 8.73).

Figure 8.72
Select a time-stretch algorithm

Figure 8.73
An audio event in Straighten up mode in the Project window follows the tempo curve in the Tempo editor. Note the small double-arrow Straighten up mode symbol at the lower right corner of the audio event

Free warp and warp tabs

Free warping involves stretching or compressing the audio between chosen 'anchor points' in the waveform. These anchor points are known as 'warp tabs' and they appear as markers in the ruler and waveform display. Warp tabs may be created manually by activating the Free warp button in the Playback section of the Sample editor Inspector and clicking in the display, or they may be generated at the hitpoint positions using Audio / Realtime processing / Create Warp tabs from hitpoints. Once attached, you can apply audio quantizing or you can stretch or compress specific sections of the audio. This can help when you need to fit the audio more tightly to the bar and beat divisions. When you stretch or compress the audio in this way, fixed warp tabs are inserted at the start and end of the audio event. Your audio becomes rather like a curtain attached simultaneously at both ends of a cur-

Info

While it is not always essential for some operations it helps to define the audio tempo before calculating hitpoints or using warp tabs.

tain rail. You can stretch or compress the curtain in between for lesser or greater folds in the fabric! Free warping requires considerable skill in order to achieve acceptable results. To grasp the basics, try the following procedure:

• Double-click on the audio event which contains the target audio to open the Sample editor. Specify the number of bars and click on the auto adjust button to define the tempo of the audio (Figure 8.74). See 'Define the tempo of your audio', above.

Figure 8.74
Define the audio tempo. Here a four bar selection gives a tempo of 100.85bpm

• Enter the calculated tempo of the audio in the tempo field of the Transport bar in fixed tempo mode.
• In the Hitpoints section of the Sample editor Inspector, adjust the hitpoint sensitivity slider and edit the hitpoints until you have one hitpoint on each quarter note (Figure 8.75).

Figure 8.75
The resulting hitpoints placed on the transient peaks of the kick drum and snare (the first bar is shown)

• Select Audio / Realtime processing / Create warp tabs from hitpoints. Warp tabs are generated automatically at the positions of the hitpoints. Select the Playback section of the Sample editor Inspector and activate the Free warp button to reveal the warp tabs (Figure 8.76). The number next to each tab indicates the time-stretch status of each segment where less than 1.0 means time compression, more than 1.0 means time stretch, and exactly 1.0 means no audio warping is implemented.

Figure 8.76
Warp tabs created from hitpoints. The warp tabs and their values are shown in the ruler

- One of the main uses of audio warping is its ability to straighten up the audio using time-stretching so that it fits the meter time more tightly. At this stage there are two options. You can use the Quantize audio function to automatically stretch or compress the audio so that each warp tab lines up exactly to the beat, or you can drag the warp tabs manually to the desired positions. Figure 8.77 shows the same audio as above after using Quantize audio (Audio / Realtime processing / Quantize audio). The main hits in the audio now line up with the meter time. Quantize audio uses the current quantize type menu setting. Thus, your audio may be quantized to straight meter time or to a groove template.

Figure 8.77
The Quantize audio function lines up the warp tabs to the current quantize grid. This tightens up the feel of the audio using time stretch or compression

Figure 8.78 shows the same audio as above, but this time the warp tabs have been dragged manually so that the main hits in the audio fall slightly ahead of the beat. New warp tabs are inserted by clicking in free space in the Sample editor display when the Inspector's Playback section is selected. Warp tabs are dragged to a new position using the Free warp tool in the display which snaps to the tab when moved nearby. When the Snap to zero crossing button is active, dragged tabs snap to the nearest beat or time division in the ruler.

Figure 8.78
Dragging warp tabs manually to make the hits in the music fall ahead of the beat

Tip

To undo Free Warp audio warping, select Audio / Realtime processing / Unstretch audio or click on the reset button in the Sample editor Inspector Playback section. To make audio warping a permanent part of the audio, select Audio / Realtime processing / Freeze timestretch and transpose, or click on the Flatten timestretch button in the Sample editor Inspector Playback section.

Tip

To delete a Warp tab, press Shift and click on the tab handle in the ruler (an eraser is shown). To show / hide Warp tabs click on the Free warp button in the Sample editor Inspector Playback section.

Info

You can undo / redo all audio editing using the undo / redo functions in the Edit menu or by pressing Ctrl + Z (undo) or Ctrl + Shift + Z (redo). You can also step back through your edits using the Edit history window (select 'History' in the Edit menu). The edit history is cleared when you close the project.

Audio processing

This chapter describes the audio processing functions found in the Process sub-menu of the Audio menu. The audio processing functions are for 'offline' processing only. Off-line processing is that which does not occur in real-time and implies some kind of 'permanent' change to the stored audio files.

The audio processing functions act upon audio data on the hard disk but due to the manner in which Cubase has been designed, two types of undo functions are available. Firstly, the normal undo/redo commands in the Edit menu are available while your project is running. Secondly, after you close the project, almost all audio editing can be modified or removed at a later date using the Offline Process History dialogue (Audio menu). This means that you can use offline audio processing with an unprecedented amount of freedom since you can always go back to the original versions of your audio files.

The processing options

Figure 9.1 shows the audio processing options in the Process menu. You can also process your audio in a similar manner using the audio plug-in effects in the Plug-ins menu (these are usually used for real-time processing and are described in Chapter 12). The basic operation of the majority of the audio processing functions is fairly easy but it is not quite so obvious how and why you might use them. The 'how and why' forms the subject matter of this chapter.

What gets affected

The processing functions may be applied to audio events, audio clips or range selections. With audio clips, the processing is applied to the whole clip. With audio events, only that part of the associated audio clip which is referenced by the event gets processed. With range selections, only that part of the associated audio clip which is referenced by the range gets processed. With multiple event selections, all audio events have the same process applied in equal amounts. For example, if you select two consecutive events and apply fade out processing, the fade does not occur over the whole length of the two events but within each single event.

Envelope
Fade In
Fade Out
Gain
Merge Clipboard
Noise Gate
Normalize
Phase Reverse
Pitch Shift
Remove DC Offset
Resample
Reverse
Silence
Stereo Flip
Time Stretch

Figure 9.1
The functions in the Process menu

Common buttons in the audio processing dialogues

Most of the audio processing functions feature a dialogue window which opens when they are selected. Each window has a number of common buttons and menus available. These include, in all windows, the Preview, Process and Cancel buttons and, in the envelope and fade dialogues, the presets menu and Store and Remove buttons. The Preview button allows you to hear the result of the processing before it is actually applied. When in Preview mode, the audio is played back in a continuous loop and you can hear the effect of any changes you make to the parameters in the dialogue on the next lap of the cycle. Some parameter changes re-start the audio instantaneously. All this is very useful for experimenting. The Process button processes the target audio when you are satisfied with the settings you have made. The Cancel button allows you to leave the dialogue without applying any processing. The presets menu and buttons allow you to store (or remove) your own presets. Some dialogues have More and Less buttons for showing or hiding a number of additional parameters.

The Process functions

Envelope

The Envelope function (Figure 9.2) applies an amplitude envelope to the selected audio. Spline, damped spline or linear curves are available or you can create your own shapes by clicking and dragging on the curve, whereupon a new breakpoint is added. The breakpoint handles may be dragged to any position within the display and are deleted by dragging them outside of the window. There are always at least three breakpoints in the display; one at the start, one at the end and one somewhere in between. The uppermost limit of the display represents unity gain so that a straight line drawn at the top of the display results in no change in amplitude in the target audio.

The Envelope function is good for applying multiple breakpoint envelopes to audio files in a number of creative and corrective applications. For example, unwanted breaths or syllables which are too loud within a vocal performance can be tamed by carefully reducing the level at the offending points in the waveform. For such correction, select each offending part of the waveform in the Sample editor and apply your chosen envelope to each in turn. If you are deleting unwanted breathing and lip noise between vocal lines or within speech, a 'bowl' shaped envelope produces more natural results than applying silence (Figure 9.2).

Figure 9.2
A 'bowl' shaped envelope for reducing lip noise and interference between words and phrases in vocal takes

Fade in and Fade out

The Fade in and Fade out dialogues provide an alternative method of applying fades when you do not wish to use the usual blue fade handles within the audio events. The advantage of using the blue handles is that a number of audio events which refer to the same audio clip can each have an independent fade curve. Conversely, fades set up from the Process menu are applied directly to the audio clip. This is advantageous when you require global fade settings which are applied to all events which refer to the same section of an audio clip.

Figure 9.3
Fade in dialogue

The Fade in and Fade out functions open similar dialogue windows, except that one has the inverse fade characteristics of the other (Figure 9.3). The fade dialogues allow you to set the characteristics of the fade curves by clicking on any of the eight preset curve buttons or you can set up custom shapes by dragging handles directly in the curve display. The curve of the Fade in dialogue always starts in the lower left corner of the display and finishes in the upper right corner (the inverse is true for the Fade out dialogue). Spline, damped spline and linear curve characteristics are available and you can save and recall your own presets.

The Fade functions are sometimes useful for applying very short fades (5-10ms) at the beginning or end of an audio file to mask sharp transients or digital clicks. This would normally be achieved at a high zoom factor in the Sample editor and results in an audio file which starts and ends more smoothly. Fades out and in are also helpful when used together with the Silence function (outlined below) since fades to and from digital silence are often better than brutally cutting to silence in one move.

Gain

The Gain function (Figure 9.4) allows you to add gain or attenuate the amplitude level of the target audio between -50dB and +20dB. The parameters include a main gain slider and pre and post crossfade sliders. As you move the slider, the percentage increase in level is shown as well as the amount of increase/decrease in dBs.

When in preview mode, any audio clipping is indicated in the text line below the main gain slider. This is excellent for warning you of marginal clipping which may otherwise go unnoticed. The pre and post crossfade sliders allow you to apply the gain change gradually either at the start or end of the target audio. A Pre-Crossfade setting indicates that the gain change should start gradually from the onset of the target audio selection and should only reach its full effect at the time specified in the Pre-Crossfade field. A Post- Crossfade setting indicates that the gain change should gradually be removed, starting at the time specified in the Post-Crossfade field before the end of the audio selection.

The Gain function is a powerful level management tool which might be applied to recordings with problematic level changes, such as a vocalist who

> **Info**
>
> The difference between spline and damped spline curve modes – regular spline mode radically affects the shape of the neighbouring parts of the curve as you drag the curve handle within the display and sets up a naturally balanced curve, whereas damped spline mode only has a minimal effect on the neighbouring area and sets up a curve which is more linear. Damped spline mode is therefore easier to control when dragging handles in the display. The curve modes are readily interchangeable, so feel free to experiment to get the desired result.

Figure 9.4
Gain dialogue

Tip

When using the Process functions for editing in fine detail in the Sample editor, always work with the Snap to zero crossing button activated. This avoids clicks and glitches between the processed and unprocessed parts of the audio clip.

is occasionally singing either too close or too far away from the microphone or for cutting down sudden extreme peaks or resonances in the audio material. It is also a useful alternative for manually reducing background noise and interference in vocal and lead guitar parts. For detailed editing, it is a good idea to work with the Gain function in the Sample editor (with the Snap to Zero crossing button activated).

Merge Clipboard

Merge Clipboard (Figure 9.5) allows you to merge the contents of the clipboard with the currently selected range when working in the Sample editor. Merge Clipboard is only available if you have used Cut or Copy in the Sample editor (i.e. when the clipboard contains audio data) and no merge operation is possible unless you have made a range selection. The merge operation begins at the start point of the range selection and continues to the end of the selection or until the end of the clipboard contents, whichever comes first.

Figure 9.5
Merge Clipboard dialogue

The Merge Clipboard dialogue features a percentage slider where you can select the percentage level of the original audio (the current selection) and the copied audio (the audio data in the clipboard), and pre and post fade options for the merging operation. The pre and post options allow you to merge the clipboard gradually either at the start or end of the target audio. A Pre-Crossfade setting indicates that the clipboard should be merged gradually from the onset of the target audio selection and should only reach its full effect at the time specified in the Pre-Crossfade field. A Post-Crossfade setting indicates that merged audio should gradually be removed, starting at the time specified in the Post-Crossfade field before the end of the audio selection.

Tip

To merge the attack of one drum sound with the decay of another, try setting the Merge Clipboard percentage slider to '100% copy' and adjust the pre crossfade to between 50 and 100 ms. Activate the pre-crossfade tick box. This mixes the attack of the original with the decay of the copied sound currently in the clipboard.

Merging audio is good for creating special effects and hybrid instrument, drum and percussion sounds. For example, by merging the audio from a number of different snare drums you can create your own hybrid snare sound. In this context, it is worth experimenting with the pre and post crossfade options of the Merge Clipboard dialogue in combination with the percentage slider, where you might effectively retain the attack of the original instrument and merge the decay of the clipboard. The same technique could be applied to create your own hybrid bass drum sound. This is particularly applicable to working with audio slices in hitpoint mode where it is easier to copy and merge between different slices. When copying and merging between different audio clips try working with two or more Sample editor windows open simultaneously.

Noise Gate

A noise gate is an automatic amplitude level control device which radically attenuates the level of the target signal whenever it falls below a certain threshold. This is commonly used to filter out unwanted background noise and interference in the inactive parts of musical performances. Noise gates are very often implemented as real-time devices but the Noise Gate function in the Process menu allows you to process your audio in a more permanent and detailed fashion. The Noise Gate dialogue (Figure 9.6) features the common parameters associated with noise gating.

Figure 9.6
Noise Gate dialogue

The Threshold parameter sets the level at which the gate begins to close. When the input signal falls below the threshold, the target signal is attenuated (cut). The Attack determines the speed with which the noise gate opens to allow the signal through when the level rises above the threshold. The Minimum Opening Time sets a fixed time for which the gate is held open once the threshold has been exceeded. This allows you to impose a time for which the gate is sure to stay open in material featuring radical level changes and avoids chattering effects (rapid opening and closing of the gate). The Release Time determines how fast the signal is attenuated when it falls below the threshold. The Dry/Wet mix slider determines the mix between the original signal and the gated signal. The Pre and Post Crossfade options allow you to impose the gating action gradually either at the start or end of the target audio. A Pre-Crossfade setting indicates that the gating action should occur gradually from the onset of the target audio selection and should only reach its full effect at the time specified in the Pre-Crossfade field. A Post-Crossfade setting indicates that the gating effect should gradually be removed, starting at the time specified in the Post-Crossfade field before the end of the audio selection.

The Noise Gate function is a useful alternative to the supplied Gate and VST Dynamics plug-ins. For the gating of background noise, try setting the Attack, Minimum Opening and Release times to 1ms, 100ms and 100ms respectively and then find the best threshold level for your target material. Fine tune the parameters to suit the sound and the gating effect you require. For creative effects, Noise Gate is good for extremely tight gating where you only allow the extreme peaks to pass through. Try settings of 1ms, 140ms and 70ms for Attack, Minimum Opening and Release and set the threshold quite high (around -13dB). Fade this effect in or out using the Pre and Post Crossfade parameters. This works particularly well with drum loops and rhythm material. Figure 9.6 shows the settings used for an eight second drum loop where a tight gating effect is gradually imposed over the first 2.5 secs, remains at its maximum for around 4 secs and is then gradually reduced over the remaining 1.5 secs.

Normalize

Normalisation allows you to increase (or sometimes decrease) the overall amplitude of an audio file according to a specified maximum level. The process functions by finding the current maximum peak in the chosen audio and

Figure 9.7
Normalize dialogue

If you wish to know the current maximum peak amplitude and the average loudness of an audio clip, select the clip in the Pool and then select Statistics from the Audio menu. The resulting Statistics window shows the maximum peak amplitude (Peak Amplitude), which indicates the single highest peak found in the selection, and the average RMS power (Average), which indicates the average loudness of the signal.

Using normalisation individually on each of a collection of songs intended to be included together on a CD release is never a good idea. If you must use normalisation, it is best applied as a single process for all songs at once. This avoids unnatural and sometimes exaggerated changes in the perceived loudness between one song and the next.

establishing how many dBs it is below the new maximum level you have chosen. The whole signal is then boosted by this number of dBs.

The Normalize dialogue (Figure 9.7) features just one main slider: the maximum level parameter. This is where you choose the new required maximum level for the selected audio material. The processing can also be applied gradually at the start or end of the selection using the Pre and Post Crossfade options. A Pre-Crossfade setting indicates that normalisation occurs gradually from the onset of the target audio selection and only reaches its full effect at the time specified in the Pre-Crossfade field. A Post-Crossfade setting indicates that normalisation should gradually be removed, starting at the time specified in the Post-Crossfade field before the end of the audio selection.

The maximum level possible is 0dB but it is advisable to normalise to slightly below the theoretical maximum, especially for pre-mastering applications (try -0.3dB). Normalisation is sometimes used to boost the level of audio files which were recorded at too low a level. While this can help make up for a poorly recorded signal you should be aware that the noise floor is also boosted by the same number of dBs, thus emphasising any hiss or background noise. Normalisation should therefore not be used as a routine 'quick fix' for poor recording techniques. The best remedy for sounds recorded at too low a level is to record them again at a higher level.

Normalisation might also be used to boost the signal to its absolute maximum before transferring mixed material to CD. This is common for rock, pop and dance material. However, if you are intending to boost the loudness of the target audio, normalisation is not the best option. Normalisation does *not* boost signals according to their perceived loudness but according to the highest amplitude peak in the selected material. This means that normalising finished tracks to the same maximum level does not necessarily result in tracks which have the same perceived loudness. Perceived loudness is mainly governed by the average signal level of the material and not the extreme peaks. Loudness maximisers, multi-band compressors and other kinds of processing are often a better choice for finished tracks.

Normalize should preferably not be used several times on the same audio file since this can result in degradation of the signal. Also bear in mind that normalisation should not be necessary at all if your audio has already been recorded or mixed at an optimum level.

Phase Reverse

The Phase Reverse function inverts the phase of the selection. This turns the waveform upside down since all positive elements in the signal (those above the zero amplitude line) become negative, and all negative elements in the signal (those below the zero amplitude line) become positive. This is clearly seen if you use Phase Reverse on a small test selection at a high zoom factor in the Sample editor.

Many mixing consoles, including Cubase's own mixer, feature a phase reversal button on each channel which produces a similar result. One reason for reversing the phase of a signal is when it forms the left or right channel of a stereo image which has been recorded out of phase. With one of the signals out of phase the stereo image lacks clarity and there may also be a loss of bass frequencies. The situation becomes even worse if you try to mix the two out of phase channels into a mono signal. This can result in some of the frequencies disappearing altogether.

Figure 9.8
Phase Reverse dialogue

If you suspect that a stereo file is out of phase try applying Phase Reverse to one of the channels and then compare the result to the original. When applied to a mono selection, Phase Reverse has no configurable parameters and so does not feature a dialogue window. When applied to a stereo selection Phase Reverse features a dialogue window and phase reversal can be applied to both channels, or to the left or right channel using the 'Phase Reverse on' menu (Figure 9.8).

Pitch shift

The Pitch Shift function allows the detailed modification of the pitch of the target audio with or without changing its length. It features two pages: a regular Transpose page and an Envelope page, opened by clicking on the corresponding tabs at the top of the dialogue. The Pitch Shift function is used for corrective pitch manipulation, the creation of basic harmonies and the creation of sound effects.

Transpose page

The Transpose page (Figure 9.9) features a virtual keyboard and three parameter sections; Pitch Shift Settings, Pitch Shift Base and Pitch Shift Mode.

Figure 9.9
The Transpose Page of the Pitch Shift dialogue

The virtual keyboard display

The virtual keyboard offers a visual overview of the pitch shift settings. A red marker shows the position of the base pitch which provides a reference point from which to implement pitch shift operations. A blue marker indicates the amount of pitch shift relative to the base pitch. When the Multi Shift box is ticked there may be a number of blue markers in the display forming a chord for creating harmonies. The position of the blue marker(s) may be modified by clicking directly on the virtual keyboard, at which time guide tones are heard at the respective pitches so that you can hear the musical interval. If you wish to hear the blue marker pitch again, click on the Listen Key button. The position of the red marker (the base pitch) may be modified by clicking directly on the virtual keyboard while pressing Alt.

Pitch Shift Settings

This section allows you to set a pitch shift amount using a course value of between −16 and +16 semitones and a fine tuning value between −200 and +200 cents. There is also an amplitude slider for regulating the amplitude of the resulting pitch shifted audio. Activating Multi Shift mode allows you to specify a number of simultaneous pitch shifted notes by clicking on the virtual keyboard. A different amplitude may be set for each note in the chord. To include the base note in the result, click on the red marker in the virtual keyboard so that it turns blue. Clicking on the Listen Chord button allows you to hear the resulting harmony in the form of a chord.

Pitch Shift Base

This changes the position of the base pitch (the red marker) using note and octave values.

Pitch Shift Mode

This section displays the name of the pitch shift algorithm (MPEX3), six quality modes, and formant and time correction options.

- MPEX3 algorithm - MPEX3 is a proprietary pitch shift and time stretch algorithm designed by Prosoniq. The quality menu is only available when time correction is activated. Set the quality menu to Preview or Mix Fast when previewing, or to one of the other settings according to the type of material you are time stretching. Poly Musical is the default high quality setting which works well with drum loops, mixes and most other material. Solo Musical is recommended for vocals and instrumental solos. If these fail to produce acceptable results, try Poly Fast or Poly Complex.
- Formant mode – when activated, formant mode optimises the processing for vocal material and helps avoid some of the worst side effects of pitch shifting. For processing most other kinds of audio material, formant mode should be de-activated.
- Time correction – when time correction is activated, pitch shifting does not affect the length of the resulting audio. When time correction is deactivated, pitch shifting changes the length of the audio, resulting in an effect similar to changing the playback speed of a tape recorder.

Envelope page

The Envelope page (Figure 9.10) features a waveform display with a user configurable tuning curve and two parameter sections: Pitch Shift Settings and Pitch Shift Mode.

Figure 9.10
The Envelope page of the Pitch Shift dialogue

Waveform display

The waveform display features the waveform of the target audio and a user configurable tuning envelope. The horizontal centre line in the display represents zero pitch shift. The shape of the curve is changed by clicking directly in the waveform display, at which time a handle appears at the corresponding point along the curve. The handle is dragged to a new position to change the shape of the curve. When the curve rises above the centre line the pitch rises and when the curve falls below the centre line the pitch descends. To delete a handle drag it outside of the display. The currently selected handle is shown in red. Spline, damped spline and linear curve shapes are available.

Pitch Shift Settings

The Pitch Shift Settings feature Range, Transpose and Fine Tune parameters. Range determines the pitch range, represented vertically in the display, between −16 and +16 semitones. Transpose allows you to transpose the currently selected handle numerically as opposed to graphically in one semitone steps. Fine Tune provides numerical transposition of the currently selected handle in one cent steps.

Pitch Shift Mode

This section is identical to that found in the regular Transpose page (see 'Pitch Shift Mode' in the Transpose section, above, for a full explanation).

> **Tip**
>
> To create an effect of the audio slowing down like reducing the playback speed on a tape recorder, use the Pitch shift function in Envelope mode. Use a damped spline curve and set the range to 16 semitones. Click at the centre point of the curve to enter a new handle and then drag the existing right-most handle to the lower right corner. De-activate Time correction and click on the Process button to create the effect.

Pitch Shift summary

Using Pitch Shift in Envelope mode is excellent for manually re-tuning a melody which a vocalist has sung out of tune, and other kinds of corrective pitch manipulation. It is also good for the creation of sound effects when the time correction function is de-activated. In this context, try increasing the pitch range of the display and use spline-shaped curves for smooth pitch and speed changes.

Pitch shifting may produce undesirable side-effects, the most common of which is a 'chipmunk' effect when vocals or speech are pitch shifted upwards. Equally, when shifted downwards the human voice can take on an 'alien' character and may become unintelligible. The MPEX3 Solo Musical setting with Formant mode activated are usually the best settings for the human voice. However, some undesirable side-effects are inevitable if you are pitch shifting vocal sounds by more than 3-4 semitones.

The values you finally choose for any pitch shifting depends upon the audio characteristics of the material being processed and the desired effect. For example, if you are producing sound effects, you may be searching for the very audio artefacts which somebody who is transposing a vocal recording is attempting to avoid.

Remove DC Offset

A DC Offset occurs when there is too much direct current (DC) in the signal. In extreme cases, a DC Offset manifests itself as a waveform which is not visually centred around the zero axis in the waveform display. This is usually due to mismatches between audio equipment at the time of recording. A DC Offset is problematic since it affects where the zero crossing points in the waveform appear and interferes which certain kinds of processing.

The Remove DC Offset function eliminates the DC Offset. It is normally be applied to whole clips or whole audio files since a DC Offset is invariably present throughout an entire recording. If you wish to check a clip for DC offset, select it in the Pool and then select Statistics in the Audio menu.

Remove DC Offset has no dialogue window.

Resample

The Resample function changes the sample rate of the selected audio. Changing the sample rate affects the pitch and length. The Resample interface features two fields where you can either set a new sample rate directly or change the sample rate in terms of a percentage. The original sample rate of the selected audio is shown at the top of the dialogue. You can change the sample rate directly by double clicking in the 'New rate' field and entering a new value. Alternatively, you can change the percentage value in the 'Difference' field.

Resample allows the changing of the pitch and length over an extremely wide range providing a percentage range of between -99% and +1000%. Negative percentages speed up the sound, making the length shorter and the pitch higher. Positive percentages slow down the sound, making the length longer and the pitch lower. A value of 0% means that the audio is at its original sample rate (i.e. no change), a value of 100% is twice the sample rate, and a value of 1000% is eleven times the sample rate. -50% is half the original sample rate. Using the more extreme settings results in audio played back at ultra slow or ultra fast speeds. Resample is always worth a try for the creation of special effects and is a valuable alternative to the Pitch Shift and Time Stretch functions.

Reverse

The Reverse function simply reverses the selection. In other words, after processing, you can play the audio backwards. Great! But what could we use this for? Reversing certain kinds of audio material produces a kind of crescendo, similar to a drum roll. Favourite material for this kind of effect includes snare drum hits, (preferably with a reverb tail), and cymbals. Reversals on any kind of audio material can sometimes produce startling results which are good for sound effects, and shorter reversed segments can often find a place in a rhythmic pattern. See 'Combination Processing' below for an example of how to use the Reverse function in combination with other processing.

Figure 9.11
Resample dialogue

The Reverse function has no dialogue window.

Silence

The Silence function overwrites the current selection with complete silence. This is most often useful when working in fine detail in the Sample editor. Much of the time you might clean up audio events in the Project window by dragging the start and end points to mask the unwanted material but, for high precision silencing of multiple sections, it is easier to edit in the Sample editor. In the latter case, activate the Sample editor's Snap to Zero crossing button to avoid digital clicks.

Brutally removing all unwanted noises in a vocal recording with the Silence function alone is rarely a satisfactory solution. Sudden changes between background ambience and absolute digital silence stick out like a sore thumb and in many cases the silence actually emphasises the background noise. The Silence function is therefore best used in combination with the Fade functions (outlined above) to fade down to the silence and fade back in to the wanted material after the silence. Alternatively, use real-time noise gating or the Noise Gate function.

The Silence function has no dialogue window.

Stereo Flip

The Stereo Flip function is for various kinds of stereo processing and therefore works with stereo files only. The Stereo Flip dialogue (Figure 9.12) features a mode selection menu and Pre and Post Crossfade parameters.

Stereo Flip includes a number of modes for processing stereo material. These include the following:

Figure 9.12
Stereo flip dialogue

- Flip Left-Right – reverses the stereo image by copying the left channel to the right channel and the right channel to the left channel.
- Left to Stereo – copies the left channel to the right channel.

- Right to Stereo – copies the right channel to the left channel.
- Merge – merges the left and right channels into both channels, producing a mono result.
- Subtract – subtracts the left channel information from the right, and the right channel information from the left, thereby attenuating all audio in the centre of the stereo image.

The processing can be applied gradually at the start or end of the selection using the Pre and Post Crossfade options. A Pre-Crossfade setting indicates that the change in the stereo image occurs gradually from the onset of the target audio selection and only reaches its full effect at the time specified. A Post-Crossfade setting indicates that the stereo processing should gradually be removed, starting at the time specified in the Post-Crossfade field before the end of the audio selection.

Stereo Flip has a number of uses for the processing of stereo material. The most obvious is for the correction of a recording where the left and right sides of the stereo image were inadvertently reversed. The second, third and fourth options in the mode menu all provide ways of creating a monophonic result where both channels contain the same signal. This strengthens the centre of the stereo image. In contrast, Subtract attenuates the centre of the stereo image and is therefore useful for taking out the voice from a stereo recording, for karaoke style purposes. Using the Pre and Post Crossfade options allows you to gradually fade in or fade out the stereo manipulation, and when used with Flip Left Right mode produces stereo sweeping effects between the left and right channels.

Time Stretch

Time stretching allows the changing of the length of the chosen audio material without changing the pitch. The use of the term 'time stretch' is slightly misleading since you can both stretch and compress the length of the target audio.

Although time stretching may be applied quickly by resizing events using the time stretch function of the Object selection tool in the Project window, using the Time Stretch function in the Process menu (Figure 9.13) allows optimum use of the time stretch algorithms, the adjustment of the length in

Figure 9.13
Time Stretch dialogue

terms of tempo and gives a wider range of options. The Time Stretch function is the preferred choice when you are processing important material and want to be sure of producing the best possible result.

The Time Stretch dialogue (Figure 9.13) features a number of sections where you set various parameters which govern the time stretching operation.

Original Length and Define Bars sections

The Original Length section is where you see the details of the target audio in terms of its current length in samples and seconds. If you know the number of bars and time signature of the target selection, you can enter this in the Define Bars section. This information is used to define the tempo. This allows you to time stretch according to tempo rather than time, by changing the BPM field in the Resulting Length section.

Time Stretch Ratio and Range sections

These sections allow you to set up time stretching according to a ratio or according to a defined bar range. You may also use the current range of the left and right locators by activating 'Use Locators'. The compress / expand slider shows the amount of compression or expansion as a percentage ratio. It can be adjusted directly by moving the slider handle. When the Effect box is unticked, compress / expand values between 75 and 125% are available. This is the standard mode when you want to minimise the side-effects of time stretching. When the Effect box is ticked, compress / expand values between 10 and 1000% are available in Real-time mode and between 50 and 200% are available in MPEX3 mode. The compress / expand slider and range settings are mutually inter-dependent and modifying one always modifies the other.

Resulting Length section

The Resulting Length section shows you the length of the time stretched audio which results from the current settings in the other sections. The length is shown in samples, seconds and BPM. The values may also be directly modified, which in turn modifies the Range and Time Stretch Ratio sections.

The Algorithm section

The Algorithm section determines which time stretch algorithm is used for the operation. There are two algorithms available as follows:

- MPEX3 – MPEX3 is a proprietary time stretch algorithm designed by Prosoniq for optimum audio quality. MPEX stands for "Minimum Perceived Loss Time Compression/Expansion". This gives among the best overall results, particularly if you want your sound to stay true to the character of the original. It is recommended for vocals, instrumental solos, drum loops and mixes. Set the quality menu to Preview or Mix Fast when previewing, or to one of the other settings according to the type of material you are time stretching. Poly Musical is the default high quality setting which works well with drum loops, mixes and most other material. Solo Musical is recommended for vocals and instrumental solos. If these fail to produce acceptable results, try Poly Fast or Poly Complex.

- Realtime – uses the same time stretch algorithm as that which is used in Cubase's audio warp functions. Variations in the quality of the algorithm are chosen in the Presets menu. This is a good all-round alternative to MPEX3.

Using time stretch

Time stretch can be used to great effect for establishing new tempos for drum loops. Like pitch shifting, time stretching is also excellent for creating sound effects. When audio material is time stretched, Cubase must build the audio data required to make the file longer. Depending on the type of material being processed, this may not always sound entirely natural. A similar problem occurs when the audio material is time compressed. In general, stretching or shrinking a file by more than about 15% begins to produce undesirable audio artefacts.

When working with drum loops, the loop should already have been edited so that its duration fits a specific number of bars. The number of bars, or the tempo (if known), is entered in the Original Length or Range sections. You may then enter a new tempo for the loop in the BPM field of the Resulting Length section. Alternatively, you can set up a specific range into which you want the time stretched loop to fit by dragging a left/right locator range in the ruler and clicking the 'Use Locators' button in the Range section.

For sound effects, try using more extreme time expansion and compression percentages. This is best achieved in the Time Stretch Ratio section using the compress / expand slider with the effect box ticked. Use the Realtime algorithm in Advanced mode and set grain size to 222, overlap to 50% and variance to 100% in the Advanced Warp Settings dialogue. Good source material for this includes vocals, speech, percussion and real-world sounds such as birdsong, animal calls, running water, sea waves and atmospherics.

Combination processing

One single processing function is not always enough to bring about the desired result, especially when working in a creative context. The following describes a technique for creating a backward reverb effect.

Backward reverb (or echo) is popular for the production of surreal ambient effects, particularly with guitar and vocals. It is achieved by playing the audio backwards and adding reverb or echo effects to the reversed sound. The reverb or echo is recorded onto another track and the audio is then played in its normal direction. The result is a backward reverb or echo occurring before each part of the original audio. This produces the aforementioned surreal ambient effect. The effect is created in Cubase using the Reverse function and the supplied plug-in effects. Proceed as follows:

Figure 9.14
Select an audio event containing a drum loop or other rhythmic material

- Select the audio material you wish to process. For this exercise, it is best to work with an audio event in the Project window (Figure 9.14). Try using a drum loop or other rhythmic material.

- Select the Reverse function in the Process menu. The selected audio event now plays backwards (Figure 9.15).
- Select RoomWorks from the Audio / Plug-ins sub-menu. Here you are applying the reverb as an offline process rather than as a real-time effect (Figure 9.16).

Figure 9.15
Reverse the audio using the Reverse function

- In the RoomWorks interface, select 'FX Auxilliary Verb' in the preset menu. Click on the 'More' button and adjust the wet/dry mix to 100% and 0% respectively. Activate the Tail parameter and enter a reverb tail of 1000ms (Figure 9.17). Click on the Preview button to audition the result and when you are satisfied click on the Process button.

Figure 9.16
Select RoomWorks from the Plug-ins submenu

- Apply the Reverse function to the audio event a second time. The original audio now plays back in its normal direction but the reverb effect is reversed and placed in front of the peaks in the waveform. This produces the surreal effect described above (Figure 9.18).

Figure 9.17
Adjust the parameters in the Roomworks interface to add reverb to the selection

Figure 9.18
Reverse the audio event a second time

• At this point the start point of the drum loop is not on the first downbeat of the bar since the reversed reverb tail is now found in front of the first beat. To make it easier to place the audio event accurately in the event display, drag the Snap point to the first beat of the bar in the Sample editor (Figure 9.19).

Figure 9.19
Adjust the Snap point of the audio event in the Sample editor

• Moving the audio event in the Project window with the Snap type menu set to 'grid' and the Grid type menu set to 'bar', places the audio event accurately in the event display with the reversed reverb tail occurring before the first beat of the bar (Figure 9.20).

Figure 9.20
Move the audio event to the desired position with the Snap resolution set to 'bar'.

This kind of processing is valuable to those searching for new sound effects and, used in a subtle fashion, becomes a valuable addition to the range of effects you can produce with Cubase. Try the same procedure with any of the other reverb or delay plug-ins in your system.

Offline Process History

The Offline Process History dialogue (Figure 9.21) allows you to undo audio processing at a later date after the session is closed. This means that you can go back and remove the compression, noise gating, reverb and any other offline processing applied to an audio clip many weeks, months (or even years!) after you first applied it. This is assuming that your audio data remains intact at the same location on the hard disk.

You can always go back to the original version of your audio files. However, you may not always be able to modify, replace or remove each processing step individually. The exceptions include operations which change the length of the audio clip, such as time stretch or cut and paste editing. Such a function could only be individually modified or removed if it was the last

Figure 9.21
The Offline Process History dialogue

editing operation which took place. Functions which cannot be modified or removed are indicated by an icon with a cross in the Status column of the Offline Process History dialogue. For example, the Time Stretch operation in the list shown in Figure 9.21 cannot be individually removed unless the Pitch Shift operation which comes after it is removed first.

The Offline Process History dialogue features a list of all the offline processes which were applied to the current audio selection. You can select any of the processes in the list by clicking on it and the process may then be removed, replaced or modified using the Remove, Replace and Modify buttons (except for the cases outlined above). The Modify button is particularly useful since it opens the dialogue window for the corresponding audio process and recalls the exact settings. Modification is then a matter of tweaking the existing settings. In this context, the Offline Process History dialogue can be used as an interface for fine tuning the overall result of a complex multiple audio processing procedure.

The Pool

The Pool is designed for the management of the current project's audio and video clips and their associated files on hard disk. Each project has its own single instance of the Pool. Here, you can carry out clip-based editing and organisational tasks and keep track of which clips are currently in use and which file on hard disk is referenced by each clip. It provides a means of importing, auditioning, renaming, copying and deleting clips and files, and finding out which events in the Project window are referenced to the currently selected clip. Conversely, you can find the clip which is referenced by the currently selected event in the Project window. The Pool is also the centre of activities when you are archiving or making safety copies of whole projects. The essential thing to bear in mind when you open the Pool is that you are moving one step closer to the raw data on hard disk.

The Pool in detail

The Pool window
The Pool (Figure 10.1) is opened by selecting Open Pool Window from the Media menu, by pressing Ctrl + P (PC) / Command + P (Mac) on the computer key-

Figure 10.1
The Pool

219

Figure 10.2
The Pool View menu

board, or by pressing the Open Pool button on the Project window toolbar.

The Pool displays a list of all the audio and video clips contained within the current project. The clips are stored within the audio and video folders. There is also a trash folder which serves as a temporary storage area for clips before permanent removal from the project and from the hard disk. The audio, video and trash folders are permanent fixtures and cannot be deleted from the Pool. Any number of sub folders can be arranged within the audio, video and trash folders.

The Pool columns

The Pool's list of clips features a number of columns. Each column can be hidden or shown using the View menu (Figure 10.2). The columns display a wide range of information about the media used in the project, as follows:

- Media – shows the names of the clips in the Pool arranged in alphabetical order. The clips are stored within Audio and Video folders which may be opened and closed as required. A plus (+) sign next to a clip means that it contains regions. Click on the plus sign to reveal the regions.
- Used – shows the number of times that the clip is referenced within the project. A blank space in this column means that the clip is not currently used.
- Status – indicates the record and file status of clips and the position of the current record folder using various symbols as follows:

   * *The Record symbol* shows the position of the current record folder (by default the Audio folder). The Pool allows you to create folders inside the Audio folder, using Create Folder (Media menu), and, should you so wish, to designate the new folder as the record folder, using Set Pool Record Folder (Media menu). All new recordings thereafter are stored within the designated folder. The folder chosen as the record folder is indicated by the Record symbol in the Status column and the folder itself is marked with a red record symbol.

   * *The audio wave symbol* indicates that the clip has been processed in some way.

   * *The question mark* indicates that the clip is referenced by the project but the file associated with it could not be found on the hard disk, (in Cubase this is known as a missing file). This occurs if you have deleted, moved or renamed a file outside of Cubase or have, at some stage, changed a file common to more than one project.

   * *The X symbol* indicates that the clip is referenced to an audio file which is stored outside of the project Audio folder.
   * *The R symbol* indicates that the clip has been recorded at some time during the current session. This provides a quick means of finding recently recorded clips.

- Musical mode – shows the musical mode status of each clip. Musical mode is usually activated after having defined the number of bars and tempo for the clip in the Sample editor using the Audio tempo definition tool, but Musical mode may also be activated in the Pool by clicking on the black check box in the column. This activates musical mode only if a tempo has already been defined for the clip. Otherwise, a dialogue appears where you must enter a tempo before proceeding.

- Tempo – shows the tempo of the audio clip as defined using the Audio tempo definition tool. If no tempo has been defined, '???' is displayed in the column. (Note that a preliminary tempo is displayed for the clip as soon as you select the Audio tempo definition tool in the Sample editor. This preliminary tempo may not be the actual tempo for the audio clip and may need further editing to be accurate).
- Signature – shows the time signature of the audio clip. By default, this is set to 4/4 but it may be edited here or in the Sample editor.
- Info – displays the sample rate, bit depth, stereo / mono status and duration (in seconds) of audio clips, and the frame rate, number of frames and duration (in seconds) of video clips. For regions, the start and end time is displayed (in samples).
- Type – indicates the type of audio or video file referenced by the clip.
- Date – shows the date and time when the clip was recorded.
- Origin Time – indicates the original time position at which the clip was recorded. This is useful when you use Insert into Project (Media menu) since it inserts the clip at the same time position as when it was originally recorded. Imported audio files which were originally saved in Broadcast Wave format have a time position embedded in the file header data and this appears in the Origin Time column. This provides a method by which Broadcast Wave files recorded in other applications can be assembled in Cubase at their original time positions.
- Image – displays a waveform of the clip. Click anywhere in the waveform box to audition the clip. Playback begins from the position at which you click. This provides an alternative to using the play button on the toolbar. Note that the waveform display boxes are the same size for all clips and therefore do not reflect their durations.
- Path – shows the location on hard disk of the audio or video file referenced by the clip.
- Reel name – a parameter which may be included when you import an OMF file (Open Media Framework Interchange), intended to provide a reference to the original tape or media from which the audio file was taken.

> **Tip**
>
> Click on the title strip of the columns to sort the Pool data by name, duration, type, date, file location and so on. For example, try sorting the clips by date to find the most recently recorded files. Try also using the Optimize Width option in the View menu to clarify the column display.

The Pool toolbar

The Pool's toolbar features Info, Play and Loop buttons. These allow you to show/hide the Infoline below the clip list, audition the currently selected clip or region, or audition the currently selected clip or region in loop mode. The View menu allows you to choose which columns are displayed in the list and the All plus (+) and minus (-) boxes allow you to open or close all folders. There is an Import button for importing audio and video clips directly into the Pool and a Search button for searching for audio files on your system (see below). The toolbar also displays the path of the current project folder and the currently chosen Pool record folder.

Figure 10.3
The Pool toolbar

The Pool Infoline

The Pool Infoline is shown or hidden using the Info button on the toolbar. The Infoline displays how many audio files are present, how many are actually

```
Audio Files: 15   Used: 13   Total Size: 17.13 MB   External Files: 1
```

Figure 10.4
The Pool Infoline

used in the Project, the size of these files in Megabytes and the number of files which are located outside of the Project folder. This is excellent for getting a quick global overview of the file status and hard disk space used in the current project. For example, many experimental projects involve the auditioning of a wide range of audio files which are not all actually finally used. This may take up an unnecessarily large amount of disk space. The Infoline allows you to immediately see how many of the files are actually in use and helps you decide if you need to remove some of the unused media, or remove all of the unused media using the 'Remove Unused Media' command (Media menu).

The Pool Search function

Clicking on the Search button in the toolbar opens a search window in the lower half of the Pool. The search function behaves in much the same way as the search functions available in any standard operating system. Enter the file name or extension into the search field. The asterisk ('*') symbol may be used as a wild card. For example, to find all those wave files in your system which contain 'snare' somewhere in their name, enter *snare*.wav (see Figure 10.5).

Figure 10.5
Using the Pool's Search function to find a snare drum

Getting to know the Pool and Media menu

This section outlines the key functions of the Pool and Media menu.

Auditioning clips

You can audition any clip or region by selecting it and pressing the Play button on the toolbar. Loop playback is achieved by activating the Loop button. However, the easiest way to audition a clip is to click on the waveform image in the Image column. (Figure 10.6). Playback commences from the position at which you click.

Figure 10.6
Audition a clip by clicking on the waveform image

Importing clips

Import Medium

To import audio or video clips, click on the Import button. This opens an Import Medium dialogue where you can select a file (or a number of files) of one of the supported types from your hard disk or other storage media. Click on Open to import the chosen file(s). By default, an Import Options dialogue appears (Figure 10.7). Here, you can make a copy of the selected files in the Project's working directory and, if desired, convert the file(s) to the sample rate and/or resolution of the current Project. Making a copy of the files in the working directory is highly recommended since you can then work with them independently without fear of interfering with work in other projects or applications. The Import Medium dialogue is also opened by selecting 'Import Medium' in the Media menu.

Figure 10.7
Import Options dialogue

Import Audio CD

Cubase features an Import Audio CD function for importing audio CD tracks directly into the program without using additional CD audio grabbing applications. This scores high for many Cubase users since the use of sample and drum loop audio CDs is very popular. To help still further, the 'Import From Audio CD' dialogue allows you to audition each audio track before importing and select a name and folder for the file(s). To import from an audio CD proceed as follows:

- Insert an audio CD into the CD drive of your computer. Select Import Audio CD in the Media menu to open the 'Import From Audio CD' dialogue (Figure 10.8). If it is not already open the Pool is also opened in the background.

Figure 10.8
Open the 'Import From Audio CD' dialogue

Tip

Audio files can be auditioned before they are imported using the Play button which appears in the Import Medium dialogue.

Tip

Cubase allows the importing of audio media in the following file formats: Wave (.wav), AIFC and AIFF (.aif), REX (.rex), REX 2 (rx2), Sound Designer II (.sd2), Wave 64 (.w64), MPEG Layer 3 (.mp3), MPEG Layer 2 (.mp2), MPEG (.mpeg), Ogg Vorbis (.ogg), and Windows Media Audio (.wma). For video media, Cubase supports the following file formats: Quick Time Video (.mov and .qt), AVI Video (.avi), and MPEG video (.mpg).

- If you have more than one CD drive in your system, select the correct CD drive in the drives menu at the top of the dialogue. Audition the CD tracks by selecting a track in the track list and clicking on the play or up/down arrow buttons (Figure 10.9). The latter play a small section *from* the left marker or *to* the right marker. The markers are visible in the play progress meter and may be dragged to different positions. Use the up/down arrow keys of the computer keyboard to step through the tracks.

Figure 10.9
Audition the CD tracks using the dialogue's play button or up/down arrow buttons

- If required, choose an alternative folder for the imported audio file(s) using the Change Folder button. This would normally be left at its default setting which is the working Audio folder for the current project. Enter a name for the file(s) in the Default Name field (Figure 10.10). This is used as the generic name for importing one or more tracks from the audio CD. To select more than one track use the Shift or Ctrl modifier keys.

Figure 10.10
Enter a generic name for the chosen audio CD track(s) in the default name field

- Click on the copy button to import the audio CD track(s). A blue percentage meter registers the progress of the import operation (Figure 10.11).

Figure 10.11
Click on the copy button to import the audio CD tracks

- When the import operation is complete click on the OK button to close the Import From Audio CD dialogue. At this point the CD tracks are imported into the Pool (Figure 10.12).

Figure 10.12
The imported CD tracks in the Pool

Renaming clips

Clips are renamed by clicking once on the currently selected clip name. Enter a new name into the name field in the standard fashion (Figure 10.13). The renaming of clips should be approached with caution since re-naming a clip also re-names the referenced audio file on hard disk. This is especially haz-

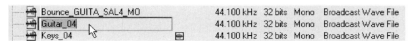

Bounce_GUITA_SAL4_MO	44.100 kHz	32 bits	Mono	Broadcast Wave File
Guitar_04	44.100 kHz	32 bits	Mono	Broadcast Wave File
Keys_04	44.100 kHz	32 bits	Mono	Broadcast Wave File

Figure 10.13
Approach renaming of clips with caution since this also renames the associated file on hard disk

ardous if you are renaming clips which reference audio files located outside of the Project's working directory (those marked with the X symbol in the Status column).

Copying clips

Clips are copied by selecting New Version in the Media menu (Figure 10.14). This makes a copy of the currently selected clip but does not create a new audio file for the clip (i.e. the clip references the same audio file as the original clip). An incremental number is added to the copy to differentiate it from the original.

Guitar_04	Minimize File
Keys_04	New Version
Keys_31	Insert into Project
Ov Head L	Select in Project
Ov Head R	Search Media...
Snare_01	

Figure 10.14
Select New Version in the Media menu to copy a clip

Dragging and dropping clips

Clips may be freely dragged from the Pool and dropped directly into the Project window. When using drag and drop, an event is created for the clip on the track at the position at which you release the mouse button. A blue marker line and position box show the current drop position before you release. To use this technique, proceed as follows:

* Place the Pool in a position where it does not obscure the Project window event display. There must be at least one audio track visible.
* Click on the chosen clip icon (to the left of the clip name) and drag. A dotted rectangle representing the clip appears.
* Drag the clip into the Project window event display.
* Release the mouse button at the appropriate position. A new event is created which is referenced to the dragged clip. The event is created at the position at which the mouse button was released and is moved to the nearest beat according to the current Snap value (if the Snap button is activated).

As well as dragging clips out of the Pool, audio and video files can be dragged directly into the Pool (or Project window) from your computer's desktop or from the file handling software of the operating system (such as Windows Explorer). This is a useful alternative to using the regular import functions.

Deleting clips

There are three ways to delete clips as follows:

* Deletion from the Pool only. This removes the clip from the Pool but does not remove the referenced file from the hard disk.
* Deletion from the Pool and from the hard disk. This removes the clip from the Pool and also permanently deletes the referenced file from the hard disk.
* Deletion from the Pool only or from the Pool and the hard disk by removing unused media. This operation is achieved using the 'Remove Unused Media' function in the Media menu.

Deleting from the Pool only

To delete a clip from the Pool only proceed as follows:

Figure 10.15 (left)
Clip is used warning dialogue

Figure 10.16 (right)
Select 'Remove from Pool' to remove the clip from the Pool only

- Select the clip in the Pool and press Backspace or Delete on the computer keyboard (or select Delete from the Edit menu).
- If the clip is used, a warning dialogue appears (Figure 10.15). Click on Remove to remove all occurrences of the clip from the event display.

- After clicking on Remove, a further dialogue appears giving a choice of removing the clip from the Pool or moving the clip into the Trash folder. Select 'Remove from Pool' to remove the clip from the Pool only (Figure 10.16). The clip is deleted from the Pool but the associated file on hard disk remains.

Deleting from the Pool and from the hard disk

To delete a clip from the Pool and from the hard disk proceed as follows:

Figure 10.17 (left)
Select 'Trash' to move the clip into the Trash folder

Figure 10.18 (right)
Select 'Empty Trash' in the Media menu and then Erase in the final Warning dialogue to permanently delete clips and their associated files on hard disk *(Caution: this operation cannot be undone!)*

- Select the clip in the Pool and press Backspace or Delete on the computer keyboard (or select Delete from the Edit menu).
- If the clip is used, a warning dialogue appears (Figure 10.15, above). Click on Remove to remove all occurrences of the clip from the event display.
- After clicking on Remove, a further dialogue appears giving a choice of removing the clip from the Pool or moving the clip into the Trash folder. Select Trash (Figure 10.17). This moves the clip into the Trash folder. The Trash folder is an intermediary storage area before the final deletion of the clip and its referenced file on hard disk. Clips may be stored there indefinitely and you can restore a clip at any time by dragging it from the Trash folder into the other media folders.
- To finally delete clips and their associated files on hard disk, select Empty Trash (Media menu). This opens a final warning dialogue giving you the choice to Erase or Remove from the Pool (Figure 10.18). Choosing Remove from the Pool removes the clips in the Trash folder from the Pool but does not erase the associated files on hard disk. Choosing Erase permanently deletes all clips currently stored in the Trash folder and also permanently deletes their associated files on hard disk! *Caution: This operation cannot be undone!*

Deleting clips in Cubase is deliberately NOT simplistically easy. This protects against accidental permanent deletion of clips and their associated files on hard disk. The Trash folder gives you the option of keeping absolutely all the files associated with a project right up until the last moment – it is a kind of 'safety buffer' between keeping and finally deleting the files on disk. Use Empty Trash only when you are 100% sure that you no longer need the files contained therein.

Removing Unused Media

To remove all unused clips from the project proceed as follows:

- Select 'Remove Unused Media' from the Media menu.
- In the dialogue which appears, select 'Remove from Pool' if you wish to remove the clips from the Pool only but retain the referenced files on hard disk. Select 'Trash' if it is your intention to remove the clips from the Pool and permanently delete the referenced files on the hard disk.
- All unused media is removed from the Pool according to the choice you have made in the previous step.

Removing all the unused clips from a project is an operation you might undertake when the Pool has become cluttered with a large number of unused clips after lengthy experimentation or the auditioning of miscellaneous material. If you are in the habit of auditioning audio material from a number of different locations outside of the current Project's working directory then you should, above all, *not* use the Trash folder when using 'Remove Unused Media'. In this case, select 'Remove from Pool' to remove the clips from the Pool only.

Finding events, clips and missing files

Find the events referring to the currently selected clip in the Pool
To find all events which refer to a clip, select the clip in question in the Pool. Select 'Select in Project' from the Media menu. This immediately selects all those events in the Project window which refer to the clip. This operation also functions with multiple selections.

Find the clip referenced by the currently selected event in the Project window
Conversely to the above example, it is also useful to find the clip referenced by any one event in the Project window. To achieve this, select the event in question in the Project window. Select 'Find Selected in Pool' from the Audio menu. If it is not already open, the Pool window is automatically opened with the corresponding clip selected.

Finding missing files
Whenever you open a Project which references files which have been moved, renamed or otherwise changed either outside of Cubase or as a result of manipulations in another Project, a 'Resolve Missing Files' dialogue appears. This allows you to locate or search for the missing files at the time of the

Figure 10.19
Use the 'Resolve Missing Files' dialogue
upon opening the Project, or at a later
stage, to find missing files

opening of the project or, if you close the dialogue, you can search for the files at a later time using 'Find Missing Files' in the Media menu. This opens the same 'Resolve Missing Files' dialogue (Figure 10.19).

The Resolve Missing Files dialogue features the following options:

- Locate – allows you to manually search and locate the file on your system. This is suitable for circumstances where you may know where the file is located and already have some idea of how it was renamed or otherwise changed.
- Folder – allows the selection of a specific folder in which to locate the missing file using the Locate button. This suits circumstances where you know the likely folder location of the missing file.
- Search – opens a search window where you can specify a file name and search location for the missing file. An asterisk (*) may be used as a wild card for generic search operations. For example, the search operation shown in Figure 10.20, searches for all wave audio files which contain "Vocal" in the first five letters of the file name. Once a file has been accepted, by clicking on the Accept button, Cubase attempts to automatically map all other missing files by searching in the same folder as the accepted file.

Figure 10.20
'Search for File' window for searching for missing files

Avoiding missing file problems

There may be occasions when you simply cannot find the missing files. Of course, the consequences of this depend very much upon the importance of the files which are missing. Unfortunately, if an important file has gone missing and remains missing despite your best efforts to find it, then there is no real way to re-create it other than to re-record from scratch. The good news is that if you follow strict procedures for recording, saving, backing up and clip and file management then you should never suffer from any missing files at all. The three essential steps to avoid missing files are as follows:

- *Always* copy any media to the working directory of the project when importing.
- *Never* permanently delete clips and their associated files for media which is located outside of the working directory of the project.
- *Never* move, rename or delete the project's audio files in another application or using the file management tools of your operating system.

Other precautionary measures include making an archive backup of the entire project either to a second hard drive or to removable media, such as CD or DVD, using external applications or saving to a new folder while remaining in Cubase using 'Save Project to New Folder' (File menu). See 'Archiving your Cubase Projects' and 'Switching to a new Project folder and making backups', below.

If you suffer from missing files as a result of a mistake or when you have intentionally permanently deleted a number of files but the clips are still located within the project, you may wish to delete them. To achieve this, select 'Remove Missing Files' from the Media menu.

The only types of missing audio files which are recoverable are edit files. If an edit file is missing and marked as 'Reconstructible' in the Status column of the Pool, then it is possible to recreate the file by selecting 'Reconstruct' in the Media menu.

Editing and processing clips

Clips may be processed directly using the Process or Plug-in options in the Audio menu. Audio processing in the Pool is best achieved using the Quick menu (Right click / Ctrl click) with the clip selected. The Quick menu gives direct access to all the available offline audio processing options in your system in the lower part of the menu display (Figure 10.21). When using audio processing at the clip level, processing is applied to the whole clip unless otherwise specified in the dialogue of the processing option itself.

Audio clips may be edited in detail by opening them in the Sample editor. To achieve this, double click on the clip icon to the left of the clip name in the Pool or select the clip and press Ctrl + E / Command + E. When the Sample editor is opened using a clip, there is no Show Event button available on the toolbar.

Figure 10.21
Use the Quick menu for rapid access to the audio processing options in your system

Minimising and freezing clips

Minimize File

Selecting 'Minimize File' in the Media menu permanently deletes all unused sections of the currently selected clip(s). This is useful when you want to minimise the amount of disk space which is taken up by a project (for example, prior to archiving). The operation involves permanent deletion of audio data on hard disk and the clearing of the entire edit history for the clip. For these reasons, the Minimize File function should be used with great caution.

Freeze Edits

'Freeze Edits' (Audio menu) allows you to make all audio processing and applied effects a permanent part of the data. If there are several clips which refer to the same audio file you must choose the new version option in the dialogue box which appears, in order to proceed with the Freeze Edits function. If the target clip is a single edit version and no other clips refer to the same audio file, the dialogue box gives you the option of replacing the original clip or creating a new one. If you are 100% sure that you will never need to revert to a previous edited version of the clip, select Replace. Using the Freeze Edits function 'Replace' option is useful when you want to reduce the amount of disk space which is taken up by a project. Like 'Minimize File' above, the operation involves permanent deletion of audio data on hard disk and the clearing of the edit history for the clip. It should therefore be approached with great caution. If in doubt, always create a new version and leave the original intact.

Archiving your Cubase projects

Archiving is usually understood to mean making a final version of a fully completed project and copying this onto removable media for long term storage. Many users archive to spare internal or external hard disks and, for maximum safety, experts recommend archiving each project to two or three physically different locations. When archiving has been successfully completed the original project can be deleted from the working hard disk, thus freeing up hard disk space for new projects.

Archiving is often a two stage process involving, firstly, optimising the size of the completed project using the 'Prepare Archive' function (Media menu) and, secondly, transferring this reduced version to removable storage media such as CD or DVD, or to a spare hard disk. You can also use 'Save Project to New Folder' (File menu) for the first stage which is a good way of creating a copy of the whole project (if you decide to use this method then follow the procedure outlined in 'Switching to a new Project folder and making backups', below). This has the advantage of leaving the original project intact. Exactly how you reduce the size of the project depends on what kind of archiving is taking place. If the archive is for a project which is totally finished then you may want to reduce the size as much as possible. Projects which may need re-working are probably best archived in their original state, unless they contain particularly large amounts of unused media.

To prepare a project for archiving proceed as follows:

- Select 'Prepare Archive' in the Media menu (Figure 10.22). 'Prepare Archive' checks for missing files, verifies that all files referenced by the clips in the Pool are contained within the working folder of the project, and gives you the option to use Freeze edits to make all audio processing a permanent part of the data.
- If there are any missing files in the project a dialogue appears giving you the option to find them (Figure 10.23). Selecting Find opens the 'Resolve Missing Files' dialogue. Selecting Cancel abandons the Prepare Archive operation. A project which contains missing files is not considered suitable for archiving purposes. If the missing files cannot be found anywhere on your system then, in order to proceed further with the Prepare Archive procedure, you must remove the missing files using the 'Remove Missing Files' function.
- When there are no missing files, the Prepare Archive process moves on to the next stage. Another dialogue appears giving you the option to make edits permanent (Figure 10.24). This allows you to make all audio processing and applied effects a permanent part of the data and operates in a similar manner to the Freeze Edits function (Audio menu). Selecting 'Permanent' freezes *all* processed clips in the project and involves permanent changes to the audio data on hard disk (see 'Minimising and Freezing', above, for more details). The Permanent button should therefore be used with caution. Selecting 'No' conducts no freeze operations on the clips in the Pool.
- After completion of the previous step, Prepare Archive ensures that all audio files referenced by the clips in the Pool are contained within the working folder of the project. Any files which are located outside of the project folder are automatically copied into the working directory. Upon completion, Cubase considers that the project is ready for archiving and a dialogue to confirm this appears (Figure 10.25).
- Copy the overall Project folder to your chosen storage medium using the file handling software of your operating system.

Who is responsible?

The above outlines just one archiving method. Bear in mind that this is not the only way of archiving your work. The above procedure should not be understood as a completely foolproof way of archiving your projects since archiving require- ments can vary enormously. The above procedure should therefore be viewed as a rough guide. This text assumes no responsibility for decisions made about whether or how you reduce the size of your audio files, whether you delete any audio files, or any other decision made with regard to the safety of your data. These decisions remain the sole responsibility of the reader.

Figure 10.22
Select 'Prepare Archive' in the Media

Figure 10.23
Missing Files warning dialogue

Figure 10.24
Prepare Archive 'Make edits permanent' dialogue

Figure 10.25
The Pool is ready for archiving

Tip

Successful archiving of your Cubase projects relies upon a thorough and complete understanding of the Pool and all the functions in the Media menu. Before embarking on serious archiving tasks, re-read this chapter thoroughly and consult the Cubase user documentation.

Switching to a new project folder and making safety backups

There are occasions when you need to save the entire project to a new location at some stage after the project has begun. These include making complete independent safety backups of a project as it progresses or saving to a
new project folder after starting your session with a generic default project.

For these purposes, use 'Save Project to New Folder' in the File menu.
This saves a complete copy of the whole project, including all audio and edit
files, to a different folder. To use 'Save Project to New Folder', proceed as
follows:

- Select 'Save Project to New Folder' in the File menu. This opens a Select
  Directory dialogue. Select a location on your hard disk and click on the
  Create button (Figure 10.26). Enter the name of your new Project folder
  in the Create New Directory dialogue.
- Click on the OK button to open the Save to Folder Options dialogue
  (Figure 10.27). Here, you can specify a new name for the project and
  choose to minimise all audio files, freeze all edited files and remove all
  unused files. These options act upon *all* the files in the project when it is
  saved. See 'Minimising and freezing' and 'Remove Unused Media',
  above, for details of what these options do. The implications of these
  functions when used with 'Save Project to New Folder' are less
  dangerous than in certain other circumstances, since you are saving
  copies of all data to a new location. The original project and all its
  associated media remain untouched in the original Project folder.

Figure 10.26
Select a location on the hard disk and
create a new directory

Figure 10.27
Specify the name and choose the save
options in the Save to Folder Options
dialogue

Tip

When working on important
projects it is a good idea to
make regular backups onto CD or
DVD. This is easily achieved using
your chosen CD/DVD writing
application. Alternatively, copy the
whole Project folder to a backup
location on a spare internal or
external hard disk. When doing so,
make sure you do not move the
Project folder instead of copying it.

- When saving is complete, the path to the original Project folder is
  automatically closed and the newly saved Project is automatically opened
  in a single active Project window. If you intend the newly saved project to
  be a safety backup you will now need to close it and re-open the original.

Importing and exporting the Pool

The Pool is usually saved as an integral part of the project but it can also be imported and exported independently. This might be useful if you need to include a number of audio files from another project in the current project or if you need to import/export the Pool from/to Steinberg's Nuendo, which recognises the same Pool file format. When a Pool file is imported, the clips contained therein are added to those currently in the Pool. For the clips contained in an imported Pool to be correctly referenced to the files on hard disk, the files themselves must be located in their original folders as indicated by the path names.

To import or export the Pool, select Import Pool or Export Pool from the Media menu. Pool files are given the extension '.npl'.

Tip

Before exporting the Pool, create a special folder using Create Folder (Media menu) and drag all the clips into it. When you later import the Pool into another Cubase or Nuendo project all the clips are neatly packaged in their own folder and are easier to find among any clips already in the current Pool.

SoundFrame and the Media browsers

SoundFrame is a universal media management system featuring the Media Bay, Loop browser and Sound browser. It also includes track presets, effects presets and synth and sampler presets. The core element of SoundFrame is the Media Bay, a special browser window where you can organise all your Cubase-related files and presets. The Media Bay is available in two other forms known as the Loop browser and the Sound browser. These three browsers provide advanced media management tools for all the audio files, MIDI files, track presets, VST plug-in effects presets, instrument presets, video files and project files in your system. However, the SoundFrame concept reaches out further than the browser windows, especially with the management of presets. Above all, it helps you to choose sounds rather than plug-ins when working with software and hardware instruments, and it helps you to organise all your effects presets into a single universal library. Recall of presets is allowed wherever you see the diamond-shaped SoundFrame symbol and, due to the tagging system, you can do such things as search for all bass sounds within your entire preset library when adding an instrument track, or show only the piano sounds for the supplied HalionOne sampler.

The Media browsers

The Media menu includes the Media Bay, Loop browser and Sound browser. These are really different versions of the the same generic browser but each is streamlined for a specific task.

Media Bay

The Media Bay is the default browser for universal media management tasks and is pre-configured to show all sections of the browser and all file types (Figure 11.1). The Media Bay features four main sections: the browser, the viewer, the scope section and the tag editor.

The browser section

The browser shows all the searchable locations in your system when you select the Full tab or it shows only the current folder selection when you select the Focus tab. When you first select a folder, the Media Bay scans its contents and displays the results in the viewer section. Folders currently being scanned are shown in red. When scanning is complete they are shown in light blue. If scanning is interrupted they are shown in orange. Folders

Figure 11.1
The Media Bay

which have not yet been scanned are shown in yellow. Activating the Deep Results button above the media list displays all relevant files in the selected folder and in all the sub-folders found therein. Activating 'Automatically check selected folders for changes' automatically re-scans a folder each time you select it. This is best left de-activated until you know you have made significant changes to the media stored on the hard disk.

The viewer

The viewer is the centre of activities in the Media Bay and includes the media list and a number of filters. The filters exist in two modes according to your selection of Details or Category mode, using the tabs above the list. In Details mode you

Figure 11.2
Detailed audio file search in the Media Bay

can select tag categories in the tag pop-up menu and then fix a search condition and criteria to the chosen tag. It is possible to activate multiple tags and conditions by clicking on the '+' symbol which appears to the right of the search criteria. The conditions include 'contains', 'omits', 'equals' and so on. For example, to search for all non-Broadcast Wave 32-bit audio files containing 'venus' in the file name, select the 'Show audio files' button above the viewer and set up three tag conditions as shown in Figure 11.2.

Category search is particularly suited to searching for sounds. For example, to search for multiple snare sound presets in the supplied HalionOne sampler activate the 'Show VST plug-in presets' button above the viewer, select Instrument, Category and Sub-category columns and activate 'HalionOne', 'Drum&Perc', and 'Snare Drum' respectively, as shown in Figure 11.3.

Of course, a detailed search based upon tags is only as good as the precision with which the files in your system are tagged in the first place. Luckily, the media supplied with Cubase is already tagged since manually tagging files can be a lengthy process. When browsing for audio files, systems which contain very large numbers of files may benefit from de-activating Deep Results in the Browser section, so that you are viewing files in the chosen folder only.

Figure 11.3
Looking for snare sounds using a Category plug-in preset search in the Media Bay

The scope section

The scope section allows you to interact with the file selected in the viewer. When an audio file is selected the waveform is displayed with play, stop, pause and cycle buttons. You can now audition the audio file from here (Figure 11.4).

Figure 11.4
Auditioning an audio file in the scope section

When a MIDI file is selected a miniature bars and beats display is shown with play and stop buttons and a MIDI output port selector. You can now play the MIDI file. When a VST instrument sound preset is selected 'MIDI input', 'Choose MIDI file' and 'Play' buttons appear. Here, you can audition the chosen sound by activating the MIDI input button and playing your MIDI keyboard or you can load a MIDI file and activate the Play button to automatically audition sounds using the chosen MIDI file. The latter is particularly useful when stepping through sounds since the MIDI file is re-triggered from the start each time you change sound, allowing you to audition effortlessly (Figure 11.5).

Figure 11.5

Auditioning Prologue chromatic percussion sounds using MIDI file playback in the scope section

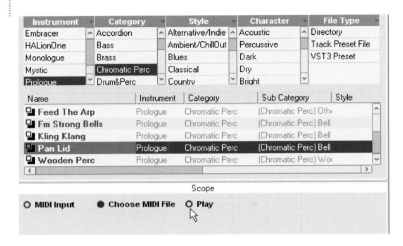

The tag editor

Media files such as audio, video, mp3 and other types have so-called 'metadata' information stored in the header of the file. This provides additional information about the file such as the length, size, bit depth and sample rate for audio files or the artist, album, bit rate and genre for mp3 files. Cubase provides additional tags which may be included in the metatata of your media files to help identify, manage, search and sort them. The tag editor is where you can edit and view the metadata of the selected file and the values of any additional tags you have attached to your media. Here you have the choice

Figure 11.6

Managed tags for a Prologue bass sound preset

to view the managed tags only, by selecting the 'Managed' tab. These include those tags you have activated for the tag editor in the Manage tags dialogue, (i.e. those you consider relevant for this file type). Or, you can view *all* the tags and metadata for the file by selecting the 'All' tab. Here you see regular attributes such as name, date created, media type, bit depth, sample rate, plug-in category, plug-in name, size and so on, as well as the additional tags provided by Cubase.

The Manage tags window

The Manage tags window is opened by clicking on the Manage tags button in the Media Bay. Here you decide which tags are displayed in the viewer columns, the viewer filter and the tag editor, for each file type. You can also create your own user tags.

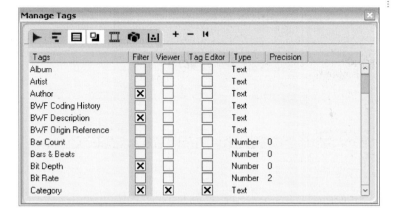

Figure 11.7
The Manage tags window

Loop browser

The Loop browser is intended for loop-based music and is pre-configured to show only audio files. The scope section features a 'play in project context' icon which allows you to audition loops at the current project tempo. Used in combination with the scope section's cycle and auto play functions, you can now automatically audition loops in context as you select them. This helps you quickly find the loops you need for the current project.

Figure 11.8
Auditioning loops at the current project tempo in the Loop browser

Sound browser

The Sound browser is pre-configured to show only track presets and VST presets. This is a good option when you are searching for soft synth and sampler sounds and for plug-in effects and track presets. It is probably among the best options when making global searches by category for instrument sounds. In the latter case, select the Category tab and activate the 'Show VST plug-in presets' button. Activate the required filters in the relevant filter columns (see Figure 11.9 for an example).

Figure 11.9
Searching for bright, chromatic, percussive bell sounds in the Sound browser

Figure 11.9
Searching for bright, chromatic, percussive bell sounds in the Sound browser

Using SoundFrame within Cubase

SoundFrame helps you get to your media quickly and accurately. Its presence is normally indicated by the diamond-shaped SoundFrame logo. The following sections outline the practical uses of SoundFrame within Cubase.

Applying Track presets

Figure 11.10
Apply Track preset field in the Inspector

The Inspector features the Apply Track preset field (Figure 11.10). Apply Track preset allows you to recall all the important channel settings for audio, MIDI, instrument or multiple tracks. These may include any combination of the insert effects, EQ, volume, gain, phase, VST instrument preset, MIDI Modifiers, MIDI Input Transformer, and MIDI output routing parameters, depending upon the track type.

Clicking on Apply Track preset opens the Apply Track preset window, a mini-browser from which you can select a Track preset, or sound if you are using an Instrument track (Figure 11.11). You can audition the preset before applying it permanently using the preview and auto-preview buttons.

Figure 11.11
Apply Track preset browser

Creating Track presets

Whenever you have set up a track for a particularly useful purpose or the combination of EQ and insert effects is particularly pleasing you can save the settings as a Track preset for future use on other tracks or in other projects. To achieve this right-click on the track in the track list and select Create Track preset in the Quick menu. This opens the Save Track preset dialogue where you can name and tag your new preset (Figure 11.12).

Loading and saving plug-in presets

Plug-in effects and VST instruments feature a Load / Save presets field. Clicking directly within the field opens a mini-browser which is fixed in position over the plug-in's GUI and is for load-only purposes. Clicking on the SoundFrame logo and selecting the load or save functions opens a separate mini-browser. When loading, the browser is set to automatically look in the correct location for those presets which are relevant to the chosen plug-in. When using the save function, a Save preset dialogue appears where you can name and tag your new preset.

Figure 11.12
To save your own Track preset select Create Track preset in the track list Quick menu

Figure 11.13
Use the Load or Save preset functions in the plug-in GUI for management of plug-in effects and VSTi sound presets

Figure 11.14
Selecting 'Extract sound from Track preset' in the Inspector for Instrument tracks

Extracting the sound from a Track preset

Instrument tracks allow you to extract the sound from a Track preset by clicking on the SoundFrame symbol below the VST instrument name in the Inspector. This is useful when you wish to use the sound only and not the other settings which were saved as part of the Track preset.

Figure 11.15
The EQ presets management menu in the Inspector

Using Inserts and EQ section presets

The Inserts and EQ sections of the Inspector or Channel settings window include functions for the loading and saving of presets or the recall of settings contained within Track presets. This is good for transferring insert and/or EQ combinations between different tracks and projects. Click on the SoundFrame symbol to the left of the Inserts or EQ bypass buttons to open the Inserts and EQ presets management menu (Figure 11.15).

Browsing Track presets when adding a new track

When adding audio, MIDI or instrument tracks you can click on the Browse presets button in the Add track dialogue to open the viewer for the Track presets relevant to the chosen track type. The browser for Instrument tracks allows you to audition the chosen Track preset before you actually create the track, by activating the MIDI input button and playing your MIDI keyboard, or by playing a MIDI file (Figure 11.16).

Figure 11.16
Auditioning Track presets via MIDI
before adding an Instrument track

Mixing and EQ

Mixing in Cubase involves similar tools to those found in a traditional recording studio. You are provided with a virtual mixing console known as the Mixer, which includes EQ controls, auxiliary sends, insert points and automation. You also have a virtual effects rack with various reverb, delay, modulation, filter, distortion and other effects supplied as standard. In Cubase, you can mix both audio and MIDI tracks in the same virtual console.

Mixing is a combination of art and science and to achieve successful results can take years of experience and training. If you are completely new to the field and have just started mixing, then you should perhaps not be surprised to find that music production is not as easy as it sounds.

The quality of the recordings we hear on commercial CD releases and every day on the radio or television is taken for granted but when you begin to attempt to achieve similar results, even with a tool like Cubase, it soon becomes obvious that there are an enormous number of parameters involved. This is not to suggest that it is impossible to achieve a good result without any prior experience of music production and mixing, but simply that it will certainly require a lot of patience, perseverance and the extensive use of, sometimes, the most under-valued tool in your arsenal, your ears! If you do not know how to listen then you do not know how to mix.

We have already touched upon various aspects of recording, routing and processing in previous chapters which helped you become familiar with recording and the virtual studio aspects of the program. This chapter proceeds to the deeper level of how you mix all your tracks together into a composite whole. It explores the Mixer and the main functions relevant to mixing and EQ. It provides specific mixing guidelines and mixing techniques to help you get a better mix and its EQ 'Hot Zone' charts help you dial in to the relevant frequencies of popular musical instruments to help you get the most out of Cubase's EQ section. Real-time audio effects are outlined in a separate chapter.

Preliminaries

In the recording studio, the mixing stage is sometimes viewed as an entirely separate activity. However, mixing cannot be completely separated from the rest of the recording process.

In popular music, the producer / engineer is often building the mix from the very first recording. As each musician adds their part, the sound image of the final mix gradually takes shape. Alternatively, in classical music, the sound image relies on the use of high quality, strategically placed microphones in, hopefully, an ideal acoustic recording environment. The mix is already largely decided at the moment of recording and any mixing which occurs is rather different from that which takes place with multi-track recordings in popular music.

In any kind of recording, mistakes made during the track laying stage are also apparent when you come to do the mix, probably more so. Each stage in the sound recording chain contributes to the final result and great care must be taken when the signal is actually recorded.

Similar considerations exist when recording MIDI tracks except that, at the time of recording, you are probably more concerned with the quality of the performance than the quality of the sound. The sound can always be changed at a later stage by changing the sound program on the MIDI device. However, even though the prime consideration might be to capture a magical performance, the chosen sound might radically affect the rest of your mix if you change it at the mixing stage. Any such changes should therefore be approached with great care.

What is mixing?

Having stated that mixing cannot be completely separated from the rest of the recording process, it remains the point at which the various elements of your recording endeavours come to fruition. The sounds you have carefully recorded are fine tuned, and reverb, EQ and other effects and processing are applied, all of which give the music that polished, finished sound. Unfortunately, it is also the point at which a collection of well recorded tracks can be destroyed by a poor mix!

But how could we define what mixing actually is? Essentially, it is the setting of all the levels of a multi-track recording in order to achieve a well-balanced stereo (or surround) result. *Balance* is the key word for mixing. The stereo image must be carefully balanced so that it is not weighted too heavily to the left or right and different instruments might be mixed more forward or back in the mix, producing a sense of depth and focus. A good mix is not too boomy at the bass end, nor too harsh in the upper frequencies. Despite careful attention at the track laying stage, some sounds may still need corrective EQ, and EQ may be used to carefully blend or highlight sounds, or for other creative purposes. The mix often includes reverb and other effects, which must be carefully mixed with the source sounds. Certain tracks also benefit from additional processing, like compression or noise gating, and the whole mix might be processed through a loudness maximiser or compressor / limiter to modify the final level and dynamics of the signal.

Ten golden rules for recording and mixing

To help create a better mix with a Cubase system, remember the following guidelines:

- Do not make a recording which sounds bad and then expect to 'fix it in the mix'. It is better to have a recording which already sounds good and then you can 'improve it in the mix'.
- When recording with a microphone, choose the best model for the application and place it carefully relative to the source and acoustic environment.
- Record at an optimum level whilst also avoiding distortion. Leave sufficient headroom for any transient peaks in the source signal.
- Be aware of the acoustic environment in which you are recording and mixing. Where necessary, use acoustic treatment to dampen undesirable reflections.
- Monitor all recordings and the mix through good quality studio monitors placed in the best position in your listening environment.
- Do not over-use EQ in your mix. Cutting frequencies is often preferable to boosting. EQ is best viewed as a way to correct, or creatively change, well-recorded sounds and balance and blend the instruments in the mix.
- Do not over-use processing and effects in your mix. This applies especially to reverb and compression. Before using any effect always have a clear objective in mind.
- Pan sounds to appropriate positions across the stereo image and attempt to achieve some depth in the sound field. In popular music, the lead vocal, bass drum and snare drum are usually panned centre with the lead vocal mixed 'forward', whereas the backing vocals are usually panned more widely and placed 'back' in the mix.
- Do not abuse your ears by monitoring at abnormally loud sound levels. Take plenty of breaks during the mixing session to maximise clarity of thought and minimise ear fatigue.
- As far as possible, know every aspect of Cubase and the peripheral equipment in your recording setup.

> **Tip**
>
> A good mix depends as much on what you take out as what you put in.

These 'rules' exist only as a guide and, where appropriate, the rules can be broken. There are not always pre-set methods of achieving the desired results and some of the most important developments in music production have occurred as a result of creative experimentation.

The Mixer

In Cubase, the Mixer takes centre stage in the mixing process and, just like a real-world mixing console, it is important to know all of its functions to get the best results.

The Mixer is laid out like a conventional console with a series of vertical modules, (or strips), each of which controls an Audio, MIDI, Group, Instrument, FX or Rewire channel (Figure 12.1). To the left and right of the central channel area there are the input and output buss strips, responsible for routing signals into and out of the program. Where applicable the channel strips are linked to their corresponding tracks in the Project window and, by default, the order of the channels follows the order of the tracks displayed in the Track list. Channels are shown when the corresponding tracks are present in the Project window or when

Figure 12.1
The Mixer

a VST instrument, FX or Rewire device is activated within the system. Group, VSTi, FX and Rewire channels are always shown to the right of the Audio, MIDI and Instrument channels. To open the Mixer, select 'Mixer' in the Device menu or press F3 on the computer keyboard.

The Mixer is displayed in normal or extended mode (click on the arrows in the Common panel to change the view). In normal mode, you have access to all the basic channel parameters including the volume, pan, mute, solo, read, write, edit channel settings, EQ and effects bypass, monitor enable and record enable controls. In extended mode, you have access to the inserts, EQ and send parameters for each channel or you can display overview, meters or surround panner. The extended view is helpful when you are adjusting the EQ for a number of channels at the same time or when you are setting up multiple sends or insert effects.

Manipulating the Mixer controls is largely mouse-based unless you have the luxury of an external control surface. The main parameters are adjusted as follows:

• Click and drag on the faders and pan controls to change their values. Hold Ctrl (PC) / Command (Mac) and click once on a fader to reset the fader to 0dB. Hold Ctrl (PC) / Command (Mac) and click once on a pan control to reset the pan to the centre position. Hold Shift to make fine fader level and pan adjustments.

- When a channel EQ is active, the EQ state button is illuminated in green. Click once on an active EQ state button to disable the EQ, at which time it is illuminated in yellow.
- When a channel Insert or Send is active, the Insert or Send state buttons are illuminated in blue. Click once on an active Insert or Send state button to disable all insert or send effects for the channel, at which time it is illuminated in yellow.
- Click on the edit button (labelled with a lower case 'e') to open the Channel Settings window where you can adjust EQ, manage effects and all other parameters for the channel.
- Click on the mute button ('M') to mute the channel, at which time the mute button is illuminated in yellow.
- Click on the solo button ('S') to solo the channel, at which time the solo button is illuminated in red and all other channels are muted.

Common panel

The left-most panel of the mixer is known as the Common panel (Figure 12.2). This is used to manage the settings of the Mixer on a global level. Changes made here affect all, or specific types, of mixer channels.

The upper-most buttons of the Common panel (those in the extended part of the Mixer) allow you to quickly change the extended view between insert, EQ, send, studio send, surround panner, large scale meters or channel overview. The Common panel is particularly useful when you wish to, for example, instantly de-activate all the mute or solo buttons after complex muting and soloing operations and helps ensure that you are reading all the available channel automation in the mix when you activate the global Read button. The channel type show / hide buttons help you view only those channel types you really need to see,

> **Info**
>
> Audio channel strips feature two level values below the fader. During playback, the upper level shows the maximum peak level meter reading after the signal has passed through all channel stages. The lower value shows the gain level of the fader. When set to 0dB no gain is applied to the channel signal. When set to any other level, gain or attenuation is applied to the channel signal.

Figure 12.2
The Common panel

clear all views in extended mixer
show all inserts

show all EQs
show all EQs with curves

show sends 1-8

show sends 1-4

show sends 5-8

show studio sends

show surround panners where applicable

show large-scale meters

show overview

all-wide and all-narrow controls

command target selectors

hide channels set to 'can hide'
'can hide' to target controls

show/hide input buss channels

show/hide audio channels

show/hide group channels

show/hide rewire channels

show/hide MIDI channels

show/hide VST instrument channels

show/hide FX channels

show/hide output buss channels

reveal all channels

store/remove view set

show/hide extended mixer

global mute on/off
global solo on/off
global listen activate/de-activate

global read automation on/off
global write automation on/off

mixer reset button

copy first selected channel settings
paste clipboard to selected channel

open VST Connections

open channel view set menu

(including showing or hiding the input and/or output busses). Clicking on the 'All targets narrow' icon allows you to see around thirty channel faders on an average 17 inch monitor. This is great for getting an overview of your mix. Also check out the 'Hide channels set to Can Hide' option which hides all those channels which have 'Can Hide' activated. The current Mixer view may be saved as a preset using the Store View Set button.

Audio channels

The number of possible Audio channels in Cubase is virtually unlimited and depends upon the processing power of the host computer. The Mixer expands automatically according to how many tracks you add. Each Audio channel strip can be mono, stereo or surround / multiple channel, depending on the configuration you choose when the track is first created. All channel formats feature a single channel fader and a single set of function buttons. The only difference with stereo and multiple channel strips is that they include dual or multiple meters (and a surround panner where applicable). Apart from these minor differences, each Audio channel strip contains the same set of parameters and these are outlined in Figure 12.3.

Figure 12.3
Audio channel control functions

phase switch
narrow/wide view selector

mute button
solo button
listen enable button

read automation button
write automation button
open channel settings window
inserts state button
EQ state button
sends state button

monitor button
record enable button

Input routing menu
Output routing menu

Input gain

channel view options pop-up
pan control

channel fader

channel level meter

fader level and peak level indicators
channel name

MIDI channels

Like regular Audio channels, the number of MIDI channels in Cubase is also virtually unlimited and depends upon the processing power of the host computer and the polyphony limitations of your peripheral MIDI devices. Once again, the Mixer expands according to how many MIDI tracks you add. MIDI channels behave in much the same way as their audio counterparts except that when you move the channel fader you are sending MIDI Volume messages and when you move the pan control you are sending MIDI Pan messages to the receiving MIDI device. The MIDI channel strips feature mute, solo, read, write, edit channel settings, bypass, record and monitor enable

edit VSTi button
input transformer
narrow/wide view selector

mute button
solo button

read automation button
write automation button
open channel settings window
inserts state button

sends state button

monitor button
record enable button

MIDI input port menu
MIDI output port menu
MIDI output channel selector

channel view options pop-up

channel fader (default level = 100)

MIDI volume / velocity level meter

fader level and peak level indicators

channel name

Figure 12.4
MIDI channel control functions

buttons which behave similarly. It is important to bear in mind that when you move the controls on a MIDI channel strip you affect MIDI data only, you are *not* directly controlling the audio itself. As mentioned elsewhere in this book, MIDI is *not* audio, it is a set of digital instructions (see Chapter 5 for full details about MIDI theory). MIDI channels control external MIDI devices, on-board VST Instruments or Rewire devices. Each MIDI channel strip contains the same set of parameters and these are outlined in Figure 12.4.

Instrument channels

Instrument channels control the audio output of VST instruments assigned to Instrument tracks and feature the same function set as audio channels except for the addition of an edit VST instrument button. Instrument tracks are a hybrid track type for the recording and playback of MIDI data which exclusively triggers a single VST Instrument. An Instrument track provides one MIDI input and one stereo audio output, linking a MIDI-based track in the Project window to a VST instrument-based channel in the Mixer.

FX channels

FX channels are specialised 'container' channels for the send effects within a project. Each FX channel might be viewed as an effects device, as found in the effects rack of a traditional recording studio. An FX channel is similar to a regular audio channel but is designed to process signals routed from the auxiliary sends of other audio-based channels. An FX channel contains at least one effect assigned as an insert, chosen at the time the FX channel is added to the project. Signals routed to the FX channel from the auxiliary sends of other channels are processed with the assigned effect. For more elaborate send processing, several effects may be assigned in series in the insert slots of the FX channel.

Traditionally, effects used as send effects have their wet / dry mix set to fully wet (100% wet). In this configuration, the FX channel produces only the

Tip

Hold Shift while moving a channel fader or pan control to make fine adjustments.

wet signal, while the channel from which the send signal is being routed produces only the dry signal. The fader of the FX channel acts as the return level for the effect. You can also pan and EQ the FX channel as desired and the channel parameters may be automated.

Group, VST Instrument and Rewire channels

Group, VST Instrument and Rewire channels are the other channel types which may be present in the Mixer. Group channels are added using the usual Add track function but VST Instrument and Rewire channels are present when the relevant device is active within the system. All these channel types handle audio signals.

Group channels are buss channels (mono, stereo or multiple) to which any number of regular audio-based channels may be routed. The function buttons and general operation of Group channels are similar to regular audio channels, with the exception of the record enable and monitor buttons which are not present. Other audio-based channels are routed to a Group by selecting a Group output in the output routing menu. If required, Group channels themselves may be routed to other Group channels.

Groups are extremely useful for dividing your mix into separate sub-mixes. For example, if you were mixing four channels of backing vocals and wanted to apply the same compression, EQ and reverberation to all of them, it is easier to mix them to a Group first and apply the treatment from there. This also minimises the load on the CPU. Likewise, once you have established a drum mix, it is easier to balance its level with the rest of the mix by sending it to a Group. In both these cases, it is also easier to arrange the stereo pan position of each voice / instrument by soloing the Group to listen to it in isolation from the rest of the mix. Where appropriate, any mix might be broken down into its constituent parts and each sent to a different Group. These might include stereo kit, vocals, rhythm instruments, pads, strings and so on.

VST Instrument channels are also shown in the Mixer. In order to be displayed a VST instrument must first be activated in the VST Instruments panel. The VST Instruments panel is opened by selecting Devices / VST Instruments or pressing F11 on the computer keyboard. An instrument is activated when you make a selection from the pop-up menu which appears when you click in one of the slots. The general operation of VST Instrument channels is similar to regular Audio channels, with the exception of the record enable and monitor buttons which are not present. VST Instrument channels feature an additional edit button below the regular buttons which directly opens the GUI for the instrument.

Rewire channels are displayed in the Mixer when the audio channels from a Rewire equipped application (such as Propellerhead Reason) are directed to Cubase via Rewire. Rewire allows the real-time streaming of digital audio into Cubase from such things as software synthesizers and drum modules. The function buttons and general operation of Rewire channels are similar to regular Audio channels, with the exception of the record enable and monitor buttons which are not present.

Tip

Group channels can be used to quickly create stems of the main elements within your mix. Stems are separate audio files of these main elements. To create stems in Cubase, assign the chosen Group channels as the input sources for an appropriate number of empty audio channels. Record enable these audio channels and press the Transport record button to record all the stems in one pass.

Tip

Open the graphical user interface for a VST Instrument directly from the Mixer by clicking on the VSTi edit button in an Instrument or VST Instrument channel strip.

Channel controls

The channel insert, EQ and send controls are adjusted in a number of locations, including in the extended section of the Mixer and in the Channel Settings window. The channel controls may also be adjusted in the Inspector (see Chapter 4 for details).

1 Adjusting the controls in the extended section of the Mixer

The insert / send assignments and EQ configuration can be immediately viewed and edited on any channel by activating the extended Mixer. The channel must be in wide mode in order to view the extended channel strip. You can choose what to view in each channel's pop-up options menu (Figure 12.5) or globally for all channels by clicking on the appropriate symbol in the Common panel.

Figure 12.5
Choose what to view in the extended part of the Mixer using the channel's pop-up options menu

Inserts in the extended Mixer

Audio insert effects are activated individually in the inserts section for each channel. Insert effects are assigned by clicking in one of the insert effects slots and choosing an effect from the pop-up menu (Figure 12.6). There are a total of eight insert effects slots. Insert effects are arranged in series i.e. the signal passes through each effect in turn. The output of each effect provides the input for the next effect in the following slot. However, inserts 1-6 are pre-fader and inserts 7-8 are post-fader. The post-fader inserts are intended for processing which is best applied after the channel's fader, such as limiting for peak level control.

Figure 12.6
Assigning an audio channel insert effect

To move the contents of any insert slot to another, drag from the source insert slot number and release over the target slot. Hold Alt to copy rather than move the contents. This gives total freedom to change the order of effects at any time during the mix and also allows you to copy effects between channels.

Sends in the extended Mixer

Send controls are available in the extended Mixer for sending the channel signal to effects, effects side chains, groups and output busses. Before a destination is available to the send control it must first be active. For example, to

Figure12.7
Setting the level of an audio channel
auxiliary send

activate a standard send effect first create an FX channel using Project / Add track / FX channel. You may then assign a send control to the effect by selecting it from the pop-up menu which appears when you click on a send effect slot in the extended Mixer. To send the channel signal to the effect, increase the corresponding send mini-fader level (Figure 12.7). There are a total of eight send effects slots. Send effects are arranged in parallel i.e. they are added to the original signal. The relative levels of the original (dry) and effected (wet) signals are carefully mixed together for the desired result.

EQ in the extended Mixer

The EQ for audio channels may be adjusted in the extended part of the Mixer using the built-in 4-band EQ sections. These are arranged in a similar manner to a real-world mixing console. EQ is outlined in more detail below.

MIDI effects in the extended Mixer

The MIDI insert and send effects sections of the extended Mixer are implemented in a similar manner to the Audio effects sections. Clicking once in any of the insert or send effects fields in the MIDI insert or send sections opens a pop-up menu from which you can choose one of the available MIDI effects (Figure 12.8). Here, you need to bear in mind that you are affecting MIDI data and not audio signals, but the logical structure of applying the effects remains very similar to the audio equivalent. There are four insert effect and four send effect slots.

2 Adjusting the controls in the Channel Settings windows

For detailed management of all the controls of a single channel, Cubase provides the Channel Settings window. To open the Channel Settings window click on the channel edit button ('e'). The main advantages of the Channel Settings window is that you can see all of the parameters simultaneously and, for audio-based channels, the EQ section features an EQ curve display where you can make adjustments graphically. You can also customise what is visible in the Channel settings window so that it shows only what you really need to see.

Figure 12.8
Assigning insert and send effects on
MIDI channels is handled in a similar
manner to Audio channel effects

Audio channel Settings

For Audio, Instrument, Group, FX, VSTi and Rewire channels, the Channel Settings window (Figure 12.9) features a duplicate of the channel fader, insert effects, EQ section, send effects section and all other parameters associated with the channel. This is ideal for detailed work. The channel fader, insert and send sections function in similar manner to the main Mixer. The EQ section features an EQ curve display in which you can quickly create custom curves, and a useful EQ presets menu (see the 'EQ' section, below, for more details). Also worthy of mention is the 'Choose edit channel' menu which allows you to switch between channels of any type in the same open window.

MIDI Channel Settings

Similar to the Audio Channel Settings window, the MIDI Channel Settings window features a duplicate of the channel fader, MIDI insert effects, MIDI send effects and all other MIDI channel parameters. And similar to the Audio Channel Settings window, the main advantage of the MIDI Channel Settings window is that you can

Figure 12.9
Audio channel settings window

see multiple parameters simultaneously. All parameters function in a similar manner to the main Mixer window. The 'Choose edit channel' menu allows you to switch between channels of any type in the same open window.

Figure 12.10
MIDI Channel Settings window

Input and output busses

The main input and output busses appear on either side of the regular channels in the Mixer (input busses on the left and output busses on the right, as shown in Figure 12.11). Input busses provide control of any incoming signals from the audio hardware's inputs while output busses provide control of sig-

Figure 12.11
The input and output busses to the left and right of the regular Mixer channels

Figure 12.12
Main mix buss with inserts section set up for a stereo mix

nals which are being routed back out via the audio hardware's outputs. The manner in which the input and output busses are connected to the audio hardware is managed in the VST Connections window. The input and output busses may be mono, stereo or multiple channel format.

Input busses are used primarily for the recording of input signals (see Chapter 3 for details of setting up an input buss for recording). The remainder of this section is concerned with the use of output busses.

By default, the regular Mixer channels are routed to the first stereo output buss which, in turn, is usually assigned to the first pair of stereo outputs in the audio hardware. The output routing for regular Mixer channels is chosen in the input / output routing menus above each channel. When mixing to stereo most of the output routing menus of the regular channels are set to the same stereo master output buss (sometimes referred to as the Main Mix buss). The channel fader on this buss provides the master fader for the whole mix (Figure 12.12).

By activating the extended Mixer you can see the inserts section for the stereo master output buss. Using the inserts section, you can implement effects and processing which affect the whole mix. The output buss insert effects routing is similar to that of regular channels i.e. the signal passes through each effect in the slots in descending order. However, the insert effects slots on an output buss are primarily intended for processing which is suitable for a final stereo mix or mastering. This includes such things as limiters, compressors, loudness maximisers, noise reduction processors and denoisers. Inserts 1-6 are pre-fader and inserts 7-8 are post-fader. The post-fader inserts are intended for processing which is best applied at the very end of the signal chain after the fader, such as limiting and dithering.

Multiple buss and surround configurations

Users with multiple I/O hardware may configure their system for surround sound or other multiple input / output configurations. Multiple channel surround busses or a number of extra busses may be added to the system in the VST Connections window. I/O busses added in the VST Connections window appear in the Mixer to the left (for input busses) and to the right (for output busses) of the regular audio, MIDI and other channel types.

Figure 12.13
After having been activated in the VST Connections window, additional output busses appear in the Mixer to the right of the regular channels

Input busses are mainly used for recording purposes and are outlined in chapters 2 and 3. Output buss assignments might involve surround configurations, where a single buss is all that is needed to control a 5.1 surround output, or multiple output configurations where additional mono or stereo busses are used to route signals to other parts of your audio system (see Figure 12.13).

Once activated, additional output busses are available in other parts of the system. For example, any Audio channel can be assigned to any of the available output busses in the output routing menu of the channel strip.

EQ

EQ is an abbreviation for 'equalisation'. This involves increasing or decreasing the levels of different frequency bands within a sound signal for corrective or creative purposes. Essentially, EQ combines the actions of various types of filters but, whereas filters are normally concerned with removing frequencies, EQ involves both reducing and boosting frequencies within the signal. One of the most popular implementations of EQ is known as parametric EQ. This allows you to select a frequency band within the signal, adjust the width of this frequency band and increase or decrease its level. Cubase provides four bands of built-in parametric EQ per channel. These are arranged as modules which can be viewed and adjusted in the extended part of the Mixer, in the Channel Settings window, or in the Inspector.

EQ in the Mixer window

In the Mixer, the layout of the EQ controls resembles that of a classic real-world console. Here, you have the choice of viewing the parameters as mini-faders or as controls with a curve display (Figure 12.14). The advantage of viewing the EQ section in the extended Mixer is that you can adjust the EQ for a number of related tracks simultaneously and you maintain a good overview of your EQ settings. This is similar to how you might work with a real-world console.

Tip

Understanding filters helps understand EQ. For information about filters see the section entitled 'Filtering' in Chapter 13.

Figure 12.14
Mixer EQ sections displayed with a curve display and with mini-faders

EQ in the Channel Settings window

To open the Channel Settings window for a channel, click on the channel edit button ('e'). The Channel Settings window shows the EQ section as four modules with an EQ curve display in the central area of the window (Figure 12.15).

The EQ curve display provides visual feedback of the EQ settings. Frequency is shown on the horizontal axis and gain on the vertical axis. Clicking in the display activates a numbered handle and its corresponding module. The handle can be freely dragged to any position and allows the adjustment of frequency and gain simultaneously. Double-clicking on a handle deletes it and de-activates its corresponding module. Moving the handles in the EQ curve display is a great way of intuitively adjusting the EQ while listening to the sound. This is the main advantage of adjusting EQ in the Channel Settings window.

Figure 12.15
The EQ section in the Channel Settings window

Tip

In the EQ curve display, press Ctrl / Command while dragging a handle to change the gain only, press Alt while dragging a handle to change the frequency only, or press Shift while dragging a handle to change the Q only.

EQ details

EQ controls

To help you understand the EQ section in more detail, Figure 12.16 shows the functions of one EQ module in isolation.

EQ Modules 1 and 4 may be set to parametric, shelving, high-pass or low-pass types. EQ modules 2 and 3 may be set to two parametric types only. The modes are chosen in the type menus for each band. The EQ controls include the following:

- Band pass 1-2 - standard parametric EQ providing centre frequency, bandwidth and level boost or cut parameters. Two types of curve response are provided.
- Low shelf 1-4 – a low shelving filter providing overall low frequency boost or cut below the selected frequency cut-off point. Four contrasting response curves are provided.

EQ module on/off button

boost/cut amount indicator and mini-fader

frequency selector. Sets centre frequency (cut-off point)

EQ type selector

Q value indicator and Q control

Figure 12.16
EQ control functions

- High-pass 1-2 – a high pass cut-off filter where all frequencies below the selected frequency cut-off point are significantly reduced and all those above pass through unchanged. Two contrasting response curves are provided.
- High shelf 1-4 – a high shelving filter, providing overall high frequency boost or cut above the selected frequency cut-off point. The opposite of the low shelf filter. Four contrasting response curves are provided.
- Low-pass 1-2 – a low pass cut-off filter where all frequencies above the selected frequency cut-off point are significantly reduced and all those below pass through unchanged. The opposite of high-pass mode. Two contrasting response curves are provided.

The EQ section, as displayed in the Channel Settings window, features two other useful parameters as follows:

- Preset management menu – for the storage and recall of EQ presets.
- Invert equaliser button – for inverting the EQ curve. This is useful for finding an unwanted frequency range by first boosting it so that you are certain you have found it and then cutting it by selecting the invert button.

Parametric EQ in theory

This section quickly outlines the theory behind parametric EQ. This is of value to those who are new to EQ'ing. The essential pre-requisites for a parametric EQ are a gain control, a centre frequency selector and a Q control. The frequency selector allows you to tune the EQ to the frequency band you wish to process and the Q control governs the width of this band, (otherwise known as the bandwidth). The gain control provides the means to boost or cut the chosen frequencies. Figure 12.17 shows a graphical view of these main controls.

Figure 12.17
Parametric EQ controls

Frequency control

Gain control

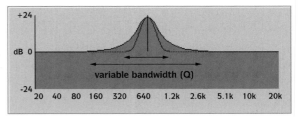

Q control

Parametric EQ in practice

Now, bearing the theory in mind, let's conduct an experiment with a single Cubase EQ module. Try the following:

- Activate a single EQ module while playing a complex signal through the chosen audio channel (try a rhythm guitar or a drum performance).
- Select Band Pass I mode.
- Set the gain control to -24dB to radically cut the chosen frequencies.
- Set the Q control to 6.0.
- Slowly sweep the frequency selector from the maximum to the minimum position

As you sweep the frequency selector you notice the change in the sound as the cut frequency band sweeps down through the spectrum. The effect is particularly apparent between 100Hz and 5kHz. As you reach the lower part of the frequency range the sound becomes more treble biased as the bass and lower-mid frequencies are reduced in level. Using a more moderate version of this technique you can, for example, tune into unwanted frequencies to correct a sound which was recorded with too much lower middle, or too much bass. Try the same experiment with the Q control set to different values.

EQ Summary

Cubase's EQ section provides a convenient means of shaping your sounds for both corrective and creative purposes. The inclusion of parametric EQ, high and low pass cut-off filters and high and low shelving filters means that Cubase's EQ section matches the performance of that found on many real-world mixing consoles. The preset storage facilities are particularly welcome since any EQ configuration can be saved for later recall and instant comparisons can be made between different settings. For further tips on using EQ see the 'EQ Hot Zone' charts and 'Mixing decisions' sections, below.

Tip

To make A/B comparisons between the equalised and unequalised signal, click on the channel's EQ state button (green = EQ enabled, yellow = EQ disabled).

EQ Hot Zones

This section highlights the important frequency ranges or 'hot zones' for a number of popular musical instruments in the form of 'EQ Hot Zone' charts. This helps you to tune in to the relevant frequencies for corrective or creative purposes using Cubase's on-board EQ section or a third party developer EQ plug-in effect. EQ is an important tool in any mix but, if your sounds are already well recorded, you shouldn't need to use much EQ to get the desired result. Using EQ in the mix should be more about blending sounds together rather than correcting poor recordings.

How to use the EQ Hot Zone charts

The first thing to bear in mind before using the following EQ Hot Zone charts is that you cannot adjust a chosen frequency band in a sound if that frequency band is not already present in the signal. For example, you cannot enhance the so-called 'air' of a vocal track between 14kHz and 20kHz if this frequency range is not present in the recording. All you add is hiss! Similarly, you cannot easily boost the 80Hz sub-bass region of a bass drum if it was originally recorded with a microphone which did not capture this frequency. Also bear in mind that you cannot make accurate EQ adjustments if your monitoring equipment or headphones are not capable of accurately reproducing the whole of the audible frequency range.

Each EQ Hot Zone chart displays two EQ curves. The upper curve shows the key areas within the frequency spectrum where the chosen instrument may be boosted for specific creative or corrective purposes. The effect of boosting is indicated for each zone. Similarly, the lower curve (the dotted line) shows the key areas within the frequency spectrum where the chosen instrument may be cut for specific creative or corrective purposes. Likewise, the effect of cutting is indicated for each zone. The amount of boost or cut shown for the curves is only a rough (and conservative) estimate and may vary considerably for each treated sound. There are, therefore, no hard and fast rules for the amounts of boost or cut. Going beyond the amounts indicated usually gives more extreme results, which might be suitable for radical creative effects or radical correction. Where appropriate, suitable high-pass or low-pass filter settings are indicated by the lower curve (dotted line).

Above all, the curves shown in the charts are not intended as overall EQ settings which you would want to re-create in their entirety in Cubase's EQ curve display. They merely show those frequency bands which are useful for the specific effects indicated. The EQ Hot Zone curves were created using typical source sounds in each category. However, the accuracy of the curves cannot be guaranteed for all sounds in the same category since the tone colour and spectral components of sounds vary enormously. Mixing cannot be reduced to the sonic

Figure 12.18
Curing a boomy bass drum in Cubase's EQ curve display using the EQ Hot Zone Bass Drum chart

equivalent of painting by numbers. The charts are therefore usable as rough guides to help you quickly tune in to the key frequency ranges of your sounds. You may well need to fine tune the EQ settings for the final result and you must, at all times, use your ears and your own judgement.

Depending on the nature of your creative or corrective task, you might need to use only one part of the curve, as in the case of a boomy bass drum, or several parts of the curve, as in the case of a vocal with too much hard edge and not enough warmth. For a boomy bass drum, try a moderate broad band cut centred around 200-300Hz, (as indicated in the EQ Hot Zone Bass Drum chart in Figure 12.20, below). This corrective EQ setting is easily created in Cubase's EQ section by dragging a handle to the appropriate position in the Channel Settings EQ curve display and setting an appropriate Q value (Figure 12.18). Alternatively, click on the frequency field and type in the centre frequency. Then adjust the gain and Q by ear using the mini faders.

Figure 12.19
Correcting a cold, piercing vocal in Cubase's EQ curve display using the EQ Hot Zone Vocals chart

For a cold, piercing vocal, try a little broad-band boost centred around 250-300Hz and a subtle cut centred around 1.5kHz or perhaps a sharper cut at around 3kHz, (as indicated in the EQ Hot Zone Vocals chart in Figure 12.31). The corrective EQ setting for this vocal problem is easily created in Cubase's EQ section by dragging handles to the appropriate positions in the Channel Settings EQ curve display and setting the appropriate Q values (Figure 12.19). Alternatively, click on the frequency field and type in the centre frequencies. Then adjust the gains and Q controls by ear using the mini faders.

EQ Hot Zone charts

Figures 12.20 to 12.31 show the EQ Hot Zone charts for a selection of popular musical instruments and vocals.

Figure 12.20

Figure 12.21

Figure 12.22

Figure 12.23

Figure 12.24

Figure 12.25

Figure 12.26

Figure 12.27

Figure 12.28

Figure 12.29

Figure 12.30

Figure 12.31

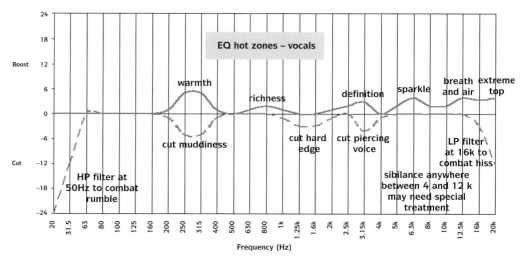

Mixing decisions

At this point in the chapter you should have a good grasp of the parameters involved in the mixing process and how you might use the basic mixing features of Cubase. For more details about real-time effects and processors, see Chapter 13. The mixing tools supplied within Cubase are very high quality and comprehensive but, no matter how many channels or how many effects and processors you have, you still have to actually *do* the mix. Above all, this involves listening very carefully and making a large number of decisions based upon what you hear. The following section focuses on the key elements of your mix and helps you make the right decisions.

Mixing tips

The 'Ten golden rules for recording and mixing', above, help with the basic decisions involved in the recording and mixing process but here are some additional tips to help you create a better mix:

- If you are mixing pop or rock material, the bass drum, snare drum and bass instrument are invariably panned to the centre of the stereo image along with the lead vocal. The bass sounds tend to be mixed fairly dry (i.e. with little or no reverb). Carefully mixing the drum kit and bass first is a good way of laying the foundations for the rest of the mix.
- The different sounds in a drum kit should not be panned excessively wide as this can give the rather odd impression that the drummer has very long arms!
- The lead vocal in your mix is normally panned to the centre of the stereo image and mixed more 'up-front' than the other sounds. It is also often treated with reverberation. The correct balance of the dry (original) and wet (reverberant) signals of the vocal sound and their balance with the rest of the mix is crucial, as is the choice of reverb type. Beware of adding too much reverb.
- The vocal or other lead instrument may be difficult to hear because it is being masked by the frequencies from other instruments. Rather than trying to excessively boost the sound you wish to hear, try instead cutting some of the frequencies of the sounds in the same register. For vocals, try cutting some of the accompanying instruments between 2kHz and 4kHz and slightly boosting the vocal itself in the same frequency range. To add still more presence to the vocal try slightly boosting at around 3kHz.
- Some instrumental and vocal performances produce wildly fluctuating signal levels. These are difficult to mix since sometimes they are too loud and sometimes too soft. Applying mild compression can help control this type of unmanageable signal. The problem can also be resolved by riding the faders as part of a manual or automated mix.
- The perceived distance, location and depth of a sound in the mix is determined by its relative level, its high frequency content and the delay / reverberant characteristics which surround it (especially the early reflections). Cutting the high frequency content and adding subtle early reflections (or delay) can move a sound 'back' in the mix. Reducing the level of the direct sound and adding a slight amount of reverberation can increase the

perceived distance of the sound still further. Careful use of short delays (less than 40ms) on monophonic sources helps give them depth and directional focus. For depth enhancement, avoid surrounding all your sources with excessive reverb. Inevitably, this results in a cloudy, unfocused mix.

- If the mix is sounding muddy attempt to clarify the definition of the main instruments in the mix by slightly boosting their most prominent frequencies. However, beware of boosting multiple instruments at the same frequency range; attempt to differentiate the sounds by giving each instrument its own EQ space. Your mix may also be sounding muddy due to a confused and boomy bass end. In this case, try using some low frequency broad band cut on the bass instruments centred between 200 and 250Hz.

- If the mix is sounding harsh, identify which instruments are producing this harshness and cut the offending frequencies. Upper frequency hard edge usually occurs somewhere between 1kHz and 3kHz so try cutting in this range. Many instruments can be softened by applying a broad band cut centred between 3kHz and 4kHz. To add more warmth, try a moderate broad band boost centred around 200Hz on selected instruments.

- Sounds to which you have applied corrective or creative EQ may sound good within the mix but odd or unnatural when listened to in isolation. This is normal. If it sounds right in the mix then it *is* right. It is standard practice to subtly adjust the EQ for various chosen sounds to help blend them together and provide each instrument with its own EQ space.

- When using EQ, be aware of the internal balance within the sound. Boosting or cutting in one frequency range affects other frequency ranges. For example, adding bass may give the impression that the sound is more dull and cutting bass tends to make the sound brighter. The primary frequency change has a secondary effect. This can be used to great advantage when blending sounds together in a mix since there is more than one way to achieve the same result.

- Broad bandwidths tend to give more natural results than narrow bandwidths when boosting frequencies with parametric EQ. Narrow bandwidths are better tolerated when cutting frequencies.

- *Always* listen to sounds as recorded, before applying any EQ. Only apply EQ if it absolutely necessary. When EQ has been applied, *always* re-check the equalised version against the unequalised version (using the EQ state button) and check both versions with the other tracks in the mix. If the EQ has not improved matters, change the settings or go back to the unequalised version of the sound.

- Do not try to achieve a mix by continually raising levels and boosting EQ frequencies since, not only will it sound like an aural battlefield, you will also quickly run out of headroom on the master faders.

- As you add more sounds to the mix try to keep some kind of focus on the overall sound image you are trying to create. Many engineers listen to one or more mixes of established artists, before and during the mix session, as a point of comparison with their own mix.

- Judging the mix clearly, especially after having worked on it for some time, is not always easy. Some engineers recommend listening to the mix from outside the mixing room with the door open. This technique often shows up faults with the mix which were not obvious when you were in front of the speakers. Strange but true!

- As well as performing the mix in one take, do not be afraid to also try recording the mix in separate sections. These can be edited together at a later stage.
- If your mix is to undergo further editing and processing at a later mastering stage, do not apply noise-shaped dither and truncate to 16-bit at the mixdown stage. Instead, mix to a high-resolution format, such as 32-bit float or 24-bit. Noise-shaped dither is applied later, as the last step in the mastering session, prior to truncation. Global fades in and out are also best left to the mastering session.
- When you have completed the mix, try listening to it on different audio systems such as a regular hi-fi system, a walkman or a car hi-fi system. Try also listening to the mix on high quality headphones. If it sounds like you intended on all systems then you have probably created a good mix.

The above tips help with a number of issues which may be encountered during the course of a mixing session but only knowledge, experience and practice will produce the 'perfect' mix.

Mixing strategies

Designing your own mixing layout in Cubase

The first thing you might like to do before proceeding with a mix is to set up Cubase's working environment so that it is optimised for the kinds of mixing tasks you may need to perform. This is rather like the traditional recording studio when the engineer resets all the faders, dials and buttons on the console before proceeding with mixing. You could open all the relevant windows that you might need for the mixing session, place them in convenient positions on the screen and pre-load your favourite effects and processors. The window layout you design may be saved as a workspace in the Window menu.

Figure 12.32 shows a single screen layout optimised for mixing. A reduced Project window forms part of the layout, where the Marker track has been made larger than the other tracks. The Marker track helps you find your way around the musical arrangement and is especially useful if you have set up cycle markers. Mixer 2 and 3 are displayed next to the Project window, configured to show the FX and Group channels respectively. This provides quick access to the send effects return levels and group levels. The Mixer itself is shown in extended mode for access to multiple EQs, inserts and sends. The ASIO time usage and disk cache usage meters are displayed in the Transport panel for monitoring the system load. This helps when using large numbers of real-time effects where, ideally, the ASIO load should not average much higher than 50 - 60%.

If your mixing layout goes beyond the limits of your screen this is not a big disadvantage since you can always use the main scroll bars to quickly move around. Equally, you can scroll through the channels in the Mixer using the Mixer window's scroll bar when there are too many channels to fit in your Mixer window width. Alternatively, use the left / right arrow keys on the computer keyboard to scroll / select the channels.

Figure 12.32
Cubase mixing layout

Once you have set up a satisfactory layout you can save it as a Workspace (Window / Workspaces / New workspace). Your mix environment may now be recalled at any time from the Organise workspaces dialogue (Alt + Pad 0) or using a key command (by default, Alt + Pad 1 to Pad 9).

Using Group channels

Rather than the usual FX channels, Group channels provide an alternative method of managing send effects returns. Instead of activating an effect in an insert slot of an FX channel, you activate it in an insert slot of a Group channel. You may then route a send signal from the auxiliary send of an Audio channel to the Group channel, in the same manner as you would route it to an FX channel. Using Group channels in this way is good for creative routing techniques. For example, you could route a signal to a Group set up for a delay effect, and then route the delay signal to a Group set up for reverb. This gives you a separate return fader for each effect.

Group channels are also useful for creating stems of the main elements within your mix, such as drums, bass, vocals, guitars, pads, strings, brass, woodwind, dialogue, sound effects and so on. Stems are separate audio files of these main elements. To create stems in Cubase, firstly route the source audio channels to separate Group channels according to their instrument type. Next, assign the Group channels as the inputs for an appropriate number of new empty audio channels. Name these new channels appropriately and set their outputs to 'no bus' to avoid high levels on the stereo output bus. Finally, record enable the new audio channels and press the transport record button to record all the stems in one pass. Stems are commonly used in the film and television industries.

Useful solo functions

When you solo an audio-based channel with an active auxiliary send routed to an FX channel, the FX channel is also automatically soloed. This is helpful when you wish to listen to a soloed track complete with any effects which have been applied to it. If, however, you wish to hear the channel dry, then click on the mute button of the FX channel before activating solo. Any other channels you want to listen to when activating a solo button can be 'protected' from the soloing action using the solo defeat function. To activate solo defeat, hold Alt and click on the solo button of the chosen channel. Now when you activate the solo button of another channel, the 'solo defeated' channel is not muted. To de-activate the solo defeat function, hold Alt and click on the solo button of the 'solo defeated' channel a second time.

Routing signals to side chains

The Mixer allows you to send audio-based channel signals to any active side chain via the auxiliary sends. Before the side chain input is available to the send control, the side chain button must first be activated in the relevant audio effect. For example, activating the side chain button of the supplied Compressor audio effect allows it to be used for ducking. Typically, ducking involves the reduction in the level of a music track according to the presence of a voice-over track (speech), as is often heard on music radio stations. To route a channel signal in this manner, proceed as follows:

- Set up a project with a music track and a voice-over track.
- Activate the Compressor audio effect in an insert slot of the music track.
- Activate the side chain button in the Compressor plug-in.
- Select the Compressor side chain input in a send slot of the voice-over track.
- Activate the side chain send slot and set an appropriate send level.
- Try the Compressor settings in Figure 12.32b. Try ratios between 2 and 8 : 1.

Using the Mixer context menu

Right clicking (PC) / Command clicking (Mac) anywhere on the Mixer display opens the Mixer context menu (Figure 12.33).

The Mixer context menu is a multi-purpose menu for managing the Mixer view, command targets, 'can hide' status, linking channels, adding channels, saving / loading selected channel settings or all the current Mixer settings, and for meter management. The options function as follows:

Figure 12.32b
The Mixer sends allow you to route the audio signal of one channel to the side chain input of an audio effect on another channel for corrective or creative processing

Send 1 routed to Compressor side chain

- Window – allows you to show or hide the extended and routing views of the Mixer.
- Command target – the settings here govern which channels are subject to 'set target channels to can hide' and 'all targets wide' or 'all targets narrow' commands.
- Channel visibility – allows you to set or clear the 'can hide' status on the target channels.

Figure 12.33
The Mixer context menu

- Link / Unlink channels – links two or more channels together so that moving the fader, mute, solo, monitor or record enable controls on one of the linked channels also moves the same controls on all the other linked channels. To link channels, select two or more channels in the Mixer by holding the Shift key on the computer keyboard (alternatively for consecutive channel selections use the left/right arrow keys while holding Shift on the computer keyboard). Select Link Channels in the Mixer context menu to implement the link. Link Channels is immediately useful for grouping channels together for common tasks, such as muting the backing vocals in a mix, lowering the volume of linked string channels while maintaining their relative levels, or soloing all the drum tracks.
- Save / Load Selected channels – saves or loads the current settings of the selected channel(s). All parameters are saved or loaded. When loading a multiple channel file, only the currently selected channels are affected. For example, if you selected six channels when you saved the file then, to load all six channels, you must manually select six channels when you load the file. Good for copying settings between multiple tracks in the same mix or in an alternative version of the same project.
- Save / Load all Mixer settings – saves or loads all the current parameter settings for all channels in the Mixer, including the input and output busses. This is like taking a global snapshot of the whole Mixer. Good for re-initialising the Mixer to your preferred settings prior to commencing a mix and for copying mixes between different versions of the same project. This function does not add channels when there are less channels in the destination Mixer than in the saved file.
- Global Meter Settings – features a number of options for changing the behaviour of the meters. When 'Hold Peaks' is activated a horizontal line at the peak level of the signal remains in the display for a short time. The hold time may be modified in File / Preferences / VST. When 'Hold Forever' is activated the highest peak in the signal is held permanently in the meter display, which is helpful for finding the maximum peak within

Tip

To change a single parameter in a group of linked channels hold Alt on the computer keyboard.

any audio passage. When 'Fast release' is de-activated, the meters react slightly more slowly to changes in the signal allowing you to perceive the average peak level. When 'Fast Release' is activated, the meters behave in a similar manner to peak program meters and react extremely quickly to show all the peaks in the signal. This is good for recording highly dynamic signals where you may wish to monitor the transient peaks more clearly in order to avoid distortion. The 'Meter Input', 'Meter Post-Fader' and 'Meter Post-Panner' settings allow you to see the levels on the channel meters either before the channel fader, after the channel fader (but before the pan control) or, finally, after both the channel fader and the pan control. In Meter Input mode, you are viewing the meter level of the source audio as recorded on hard disk if you are looking at an audio-based channel or of the incoming audio signal if you are looking at an input buss. Meter Input mode is normally used when recording. In Meter Post-Fader mode, you are viewing the level of the signal after it has passed via the channel fader. In Meter Post-Panner mode you are viewing the level of the signal after it has passed via the channel fader and the pan control. Post-Panner mode is relevant to stereo signals only. The pan position you choose is now reflected in the channel meter. Many sound engineers claim that post-panner mode is more intuitive and visually logical to use.

- Reset Meters – resets all meters simultaneously. Helpful if you are measuring levels over a specific passage or checking for clipping.

Other useful Mixer techniques

Other useful Mixer techniques include the following:

- Various simple key commands make life easier when using the Mixer. For example, use the left / right arrow keys on the computer keyboard to select the channels. Hold Shift while pressing the left / right arrow keys to make multiple channel selections. Use the up / down arrow keys to change the fader level of the currently selected channel or a number of selected channels. Use 'M' to mute and 'S' to solo the currently selected channel or a number of selected channels.
- Automatic record enabling of channels upon selection is not convenient for most mixing purposes. To disable automatic record enabling upon channel selection, open File / Preferences / Editing / Project & Mixer and disable 'Enable Record on Selected Track'.
- The settings of one channel can be copied to another using standard copy and paste techniques. Select the channel which you wish to copy from and select Ctrl (PC) / Command (Mac) + C on the computer keyboard to copy the settings. To paste the settings to another channel, select the target channel and select Ctrl (PC) / Command (Mac) + V on the computer keyboard. Settings may be copied from one Project window to another.
- During mixing you are likely to concentrate on specific passages using Cubase in cycle playback mode. To make this quicker and easier, try setting up a number of cycle markers in the Marker track. Hold Ctrl (PC)

/ Command (Mac) and drag with the pointer in the Marker track to insert a cycle marker over the selected range. Open the cycle marker pop-up menu and make a selection from the list to move the left and right locators to the start and end of the chosen cycle marker range. Alternatively, press Shift + G to start immediate loop playback around the currently selected cycle marker.

• When using Send effects, there are times when you do not want the channel fader to affect the level of the signal going to the effect. In these circumstances, use the Pre-fader button (next to the on/off button in the Send effect slots). When the Pre-fader button is in its default *de-activated* state (the *post fader* setting), the channel fader affects the send level. Lowering the channel fader reduces the channel level *and* reduces the signal level which is routed to the effect. When the Pre-fader button is *activated* (the *pre-fader* setting), the channel fader no longer affects the send level. Lowering the channel fader reduces the level of the channel only and the send level is controlled by the send slot's mini-fader only. A pre-fader setting suits autopan effects when you want to hear the effects signal only. Here you would reduce the fader level of the dry signal to its minimum, leaving only the effects signal audible. A pre-fader setting is also good for creative sound effects. For example, try setting up a pre-fader send to a reverb effect and then slowly fade out the dry signal to leave the reverberant signal only. This creates the illusion of the sound disappearing into the distance.

Mixer routing

It is helpful to remember the basic routing order as the signal passes through an audio-based channel. This is as follows:

1 phase switch
2 input gain
3 inserts 1-6
4 EQ
5 pre-fader aux send
6 channel fader
7 inserts 7-8
8 post-fader aux send
9 pan

To help further clarify your mixing tasks, Figure 12.34 shows a flowchart of the signal as it passes through an audio channel and a master stereo output buss and the order in which the effects and EQ are applied.

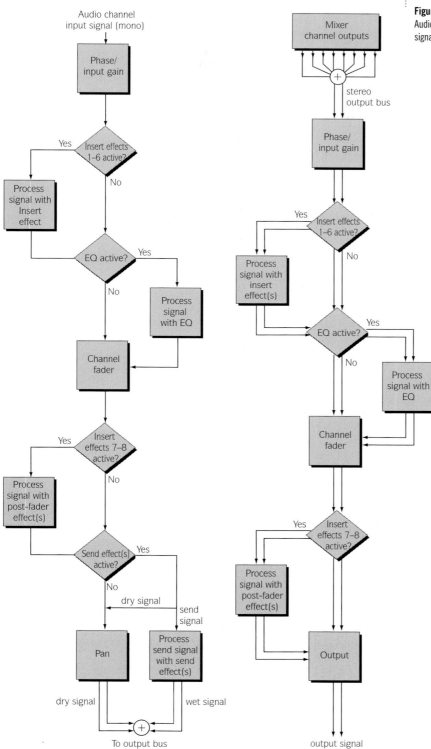

Figure 12.34
Audio channel and stereo output bus
signal flowchart (for stereo mixing)

Mixing down

The final mix

The final mix involves mixing down the multi-track audio into a stereo or multi-channel / surround format. Depending on your preferences and overall system resources, this can occur using a variety of techniques. The main choices are as follows:

- Mixing down via an external console. Here, the signals from the tracks in Cubase are routed to an external console via the digital or analogue outputs of your audio hardware. The final mix takes place using the faders and controls of the external console. The mix is transferred to the final medium, such as analogue tape, DAT or CD recorder, via the outputs of the external mixer.
- Mixing down to external media using the virtual Mixer in Cubase. In this case, the final mix takes place entirely within Cubase. The mix is transferred to the final medium via the analogue or digital outputs of your audio hardware. This technique suits mixing down to analogue tape, DAT or external CD recorder and offers the possibility of an automated mix within Cubase, when your external console does not feature automation.
- Mixing down to an audio file using the virtual Mixer in Cubase and the Export / Audio Mixdown function. The resulting audio file is stored on the hard disk of the host computer. This is often referred to as mixing 'in the box'. In this case, the final mix takes place entirely within Cubase. The mix is transferred directly to the hard disk as an audio file in the format specified in the Export / Audio Mixdown dialogue. This allows you to produce high-resolution audio files suitable for an audio CD or other final media (see below for details of the Export / Audio Mixdown function).

The third option tends to be the most popular choice among Cubase users since it is convenient and helps maintain the quality of the audio. If you are using this option and your mix is to undergo further editing and processing at a later mastering stage, do not apply dithering and do not truncate to 16-bits. Instead, choose a high-resolution audio format in the Export / Audio Mixdown dialogue, such as 32 or 24-bit/44.1, and mix down without dithering. Global fades in and out are also best left to the mastering session. However, if no mastering stage is envisaged, use dithering and choose 16-bit/44.1kHz in the Export / Audio Mixdown dialogue when you wish to produce an audio file which is suitable for burning onto an audio CD.

Integrating the MIDI tracks in your final mix

If you are using option 1, as outlined above, the audio signals from your external MIDI devices are easily integrated into the final mix by routing them into the channels of the external console. However, if you are using Export / Audio Mixdown to export your final mix as an audio file, all MIDI tracks which are triggering external MIDI devices are *not* included in the mix. Cubase has no way of knowing what audio signals your external units are producing. The solution is to bounce the audio outputs of your external MIDI devices onto regular audio tracks within Cubase SX, before proceeding with the final mix. This technique is explained fully in the section entitled 'How do I include my MIDI recordings when I use Export / Audio Mixdown?' in Chapter 5.

Export/Audio Mixdown

Export / Audio Mixdown provides a way of creating a stereo (or surround format) audio file of the whole mix. It also allows you to create an audio file from any passage and any track within your project. A range of file formats are available. The Export / Audio Mixdown dialogue is opened by selecting Export / Audio Mixdown in the File menu (see Figure 12.35).

Export / Audio Mixdown allows you to record your entire mix as heard on the chosen stereo or multichannel output buss to a single audio file. You can also export individual channels. The function operates on all non-muted audio-based channels between the left and right locators. The basic procedure for mixing down using Export / Audio Mixdown is as follows:

- Move the left and right locators to the start and end points of the passage in the project you wish to mix down. This could be a few bars or the whole length of the project. Mute all tracks which you do not wish to include in the mix.
- Carefully audition the selected passage to make sure the mix sounds exactly as required.
- Open the Export / Audio Mixdown dialogue and select the file format, number of channels, bit depth and sample rate for the destination file. Wave is the standard file type in PC systems and AIFF is the standard file type in Mac systems. For internet and website applications, the MPEG1 Layer 3 format is available.
- If you intend to mix down to a final stereo file to be used for the creation of an audio CD, stereo, 16-bit, 44.1 kHz are the correct settings. If it is a final audio file to which no further processing is to be applied, you would also need to apply dithering when truncating the bit depth (reducing the bit-depth from 32 or 24-bit to 16-bit). Dithering is applied in slots 7 or 8 of the chosen output buss.
- If your mix is to undergo further

Figure 12.35
The Export / Audio Mixdown dialogue

editing and processing at a later mastering stage, do not apply noise-shaped dither and truncate to 16-bit at the mixdown stage. Instead, mix to a high-resolution format, such as 32-bit float or 24-bit. Noise-shaped dither is applied later, as the last step in the mastering session, prior to truncation.

- Choose the output buss you wish to mix down in the output section. For mixing down a whole stereo mix, select the main stereo output buss to which all the channels in the Mixer are routed.
- Activate 'Pool' or 'Audio track' in the 'Import into project' section if you wish to import the resulting audio file back into Cubase after it has been created.
- Select a name and folder for the new file and, after verifying that you have made the correct settings in the dialogue, click on the Export button.

In the above procedure, make sure you set the left and right locators to appropriate positions. When placing the right locator, it is preferable to leave a gap of one or two bars *after* the audio tracks have finished to take into account any reverberation tail or other effects which may spill over beyond the end point of the music.

Using Export / Audio Mixdown to create a stereo file of a whole mix results in an audio file which has not suffered any degradation due to being transferred from one medium to another and, if it is a final 16-bit/44.1 audio file, it can be assembled with other similar files to create the tracks for a CD. If you have a CD-R drive, you can burn a sequence of 16-bit/44.1kHz audio files to an audio CD using an audio CD burning application.

If your mix is to undergo further editing and processing at a later mastering stage, you would normally choose a high-resolution audio format, such as 32-bit float or 24-bit, in the Export / Audio Mixdown dialogue. Mastering is often better handled in a specialised mastering and CD burning application like Steinberg Wavelab or Bias Peak, but excellent results may also be obtained using Cubase for the mastering session and a separate CD writing application for burning the CD.

Other possibilities for exporting audio include the creation of:

- MP3 files for multimedia applications
- Multiple-channel interleaved files
- Split stereo or split multi-channel files
- Mono files

If you encounter difficulties when using Export / Audio Mixdown, try activating 'Real Time Export' in the output section. This takes longer but may provide a solution. Also make sure that none of your tracks have their monitor buttons activated, as this blocks transfer of the channel's data during the export process.

Mixer moves

To help you in your various mixing tasks, the following table shows a number of useful key commands and practical mixer moves:

Table 12.1 Mixer moves

Key selected		Mouse action	Result
PC	Mac		
F2	F2	–	opens the Transport panel
F3	F3	–	opens the Mixer
F4	F4	–	opens VST Connections window
F11	F11	–	opens VST Instruments panel
F12	F12	–	opens VST Performance meter
M	M	–	mutes selected channel(s)
S	S	–	solos selected channel(s)
ctrl	cmnd	click once on fader	resets fader to 0dB
ctrl	cmnd	click once on pan control	resets pan position to centre
Shift	Shift	move fader or pan control	changes setting in fine amounts
–	–	click on channel headroom indicator	resets headroom indicator
–	–	double-click on channel strip name	opens channel name entry pop-up
L/R arrow	L/R arrow		selects next consecutive channel
U/D arrow	U/D arrow		changes volume fader level of selected channel

The Control Room Mixer

The Control Room Mixer is a specialised mixer for managing control room monitoring, studio performance area monitoring, headphone mixes, talkback, external equipment interfacing and general signal distribution within your studio environment. The manner in which you use it depends upon what equipment is included in your setup and how many inputs and outputs are included on your audio hardware. For example, at its most basic level you can use it to regulate the listening volume of your main control room monitors. In a more elaborate setup, you could create separate mixes for up to four separate studio destinations, distribute the metronome click among these destinations, patch in up to six different external machines such as CD players, DAT machines and so on, activate multiple, stereo or mono down-mix configurations and switch between main and nearfield monitors in the control room.

Setting up the studio connections

Before you can use the Control Room Mixer you need to set up the inputs and outputs of your audio hardware in the Studio section of the VST Connections window. It is best not to use the same inputs and outputs here that you use for the main Mixer inputs and outputs, as this may lead to logic problems. To assign a studio buss, click on the Add Channel button. Assign the device and outputs for each buss in the Audio Device and Device Port columns.

Figure 12.36 shows an elaborate configuration for connecting talkback microphone, DAT machine and CD player, with two studio sends, control room headphones and main or nearfield monitor connections. This setup only suits multiple I/O audio hardware but shows the wide ranging applications of the Control Room Mixer.

Figure 12.36
VST Connections studio setup

The Control Room Mixer window

When you have assigned the required studio busses in the VST Connections window, open the Control Room Mixer from the Devices menu. Figure 12.37 shows the Control Room Mixer set up in a multiple I/O configuration as described above.

Main functions and controls

The Control Room Mixer can be viewed in extended or reduced mode. The extended view shows either meters or inserts. Click on the Show Meters / Inserts icon to change the view.

The configuration in Figure 12.37 features, from left to right, external equipment inputs, the studio send channels, the control room headphones

Figure 12.37
The Control Room Mixer window

channel, the control room level channel, the common panel with talkback, dim and listen functions, and the monitor channel.

You can select a source for each of the channels using the various buttons above the studio level faders. The external equipment buss allows you to select one source using the numbered buttons. The setup shown here allows you to choose either a CD player or DAT machine. The studio sends feature external, auxiliary or main mix switching, while the control room headphones or main level channels allow you to choose between all possible choices; in this case external, main mix, studio 1 auxiliary, or studio 2 auxiliary. The control room headphones channel is intended for headphone monitoring in the control room and not as a headphone mix for musicians in the performance area.

The talk button engages the talkback mic. This is routed to all those studio sends with their talkback enable buttons activated. The dim button reduces the level in the control room.

The Listen functions

The Control Room Mixer Listen functions allow you to listen to individual channels or any combination of channels in the main Mixer by engaging the Listen enable button of either the Headphone or Control Room channels. This is extremely useful for exclusive monitoring of, for example, a vocal recording as it is taking place. It is equally useful for monitoring different instruments or groups of instruments in isolation when making a multi-track recording. To set up which channels to monitor, go to the main Mixer and activate the listen buttons ('L' buttons) of the desired channels. In the Control Room Mixer, you can monitor the chosen channels in after-fader listen or pre-fader listen modes by activating or de-activating the AFL/PFL button. When you need to set up a different combination of listen enabled channels, you can disable the current listen selection by clicking on the 'De-activate All Listen' button in the Control Room Mixer.

Figure 12.38
Using the Listen enable button in the Control Room Mixer

Setting up the studio sends

The mix in each studio send channel is set up using the auxiliary studio sends in the main mixer. To set up your own studio send mix, open the main mixer in extended mode and select studio sends in the pop-up menus of the appropriate channels (or select the studio sends icon in the Common panel). Each studio send slot features a mini-fader, pan control and pre-fader button (Figure 12.39). Only those sends which are activated in VST Connections are available here. Activate and adjust the levels of the studio sends on the required channels while monitoring the appropriate studio send channel in the Control Room Mixer.

Figure 12.39
Set up the mix for each studio send channel in the studio sends section of the main Mixer

Patching in external equipment

The Control Room Mixer makes it easy to patch in external equipment like CD players, mini-disc players or DAT machines. All you do is connect your external equipment to the appropriate inputs of your Cubase system's audio hardware and then assign these to the external inputs in the studio section of the VST Connections window. Once connected and assigned, you can select any one of these in the Control Room Mixer left-most channel using

Tip

Use the down-mix preset buttons in the Control Room Mixer monitor channel to quickly compare stereo and mono playback of the current mix.

the numbered buttons. Opening the Control Room Mixer in extended mode reveals an input gain dial for regulating the level. This is useful for matching the relative levels when comparing your own mix in Cubase to a commercially released CD.

Using the Control Room Mixer to manage your control room monitors

For studios with separate full range and nearfield control room monitors (or more complicated systems), the Control Room Mixer allows you to effortlessly switch between them. To configure your setup, assign the required number of monitor busses to the appropriate outputs in the studio section of the VST Connections window. You can now choose which monitors you are listening to by switching between the monitor selection buttons in the lower section of the monitor channel (the right-most channel strip).

Audio effects

Cubase is supplied with a wide range of audio effects and processors. These are found in the Plug-ins sub-menu of the Audio menu or in the pop-up menus of the audio-based channel insert slots and are designed principally for real-time processing. Real-time processing is that which takes place at the same time as the music is playing, as opposed to the off-line processing available in the Process menu, which takes place when you are not in playback mode. However, to maximise the flexibility of the program, all plug-in effects may also be applied as off-line processes.

Plug-in audio effects and processing devices may be loaded in the effects panels of Cubase when you need them. They do not usually function as stand-alone programs and, therefore, always require a host (like Cubase) in which to run. As well as the plug-ins supplied with the program, you can add additional Steinberg and third party developer plug-ins.

Because of its open-ended nature, the plug-in concept offers possibilities beyond the normal confines of the core program. Plug-ins open up whole new worlds of audio processing to the Cubase user and endow the program with a large degree of expandability and flexibility within a single software environment. This allows users to build their own virtual studio according to their budget, their system resources, and the kind of project they are working on.

Plug-in formats and standards

Plug-ins are supplied in a number of different formats such as AU, Direct X, RTAS, and VST, each of which suits the host program in which they are intended to run. The format relevant to Cubase is the popular VST plug-in standard which runs under Windows and Mac OS X. VST plug-ins run in all VST compatible applications including, of course, Cubase. However, the plug-ins supplied with Cubase are designed to run in Cubase alone and cannot be used in other programs.

A VST plug-in normally features a graphical user interface (GUI). This is where you manipulate the control parameters for the device and save and load presets. Most plug-ins are software-only but a small number are supplied as hybrid software / hardware units. This usually means that the GUI appears within Cubase like a normal VST plug-in but the audio processing takes place within the associated hardware. This is advantageous since it reduces the load on the CPU of the host computer.

Audio effects in theory

In the quest for instant results, the theoretical aspects of audio signal processing are often forgotten. However, taking some time to understand the theory can help you achieve better results. This section, therefore, covers the theoretical aspects of the main effects and processing techniques you are likely to encounter in your use of Cubase.

Audio effects and audio processing refer to a number of methods by which you can modify an audio signal for creative or corrective purposes. Effects are generally those techniques which modify the sound for creative purposes and often involve adding elements to the signal (such as reverb, delay and chorus). Processing tends to mean the modification of signals for corrective purposes and often involves subtracting elements from the signal (such as compression, gating and filtering). However, these too can be used for creative effects. For the sake of convenience, 'audio effects' as used in this text is taken to mean all types of audio effects and audio processing. The essential thing to remember is that all effects and processing involve the modification of the original sound in some way.

Audio effects can be divided into a number of sub-categories like delay, distortion, dynamics, filtering, modulation and reverb. The theoretical aspects of these are outlined in the following sections.

Delay

Delay is the replication of a signal which occurs at a set time after the original. When the delayed signal is clearly distinguishable from the original, this is classed as a particular type of delay known as echo. Delay effects often involve repeating echoes, produced by adding an amount of feedback to the delay circuit. Delay is also an essential element when producing modulation effects like chorus and flanging and plays a part in reverb devices where a pre-delay controls the length of time between the original sound and the onset of the reverberation effect.

The concept of delay is easily understood by the majority of users but, nowadays, surrounded by ever more exotic effects, it tends to be under-valued. In sound processing, delay and echo are terms which essentially refer to the same thing but, strictly speaking, an echo is a sound reflection separated from the original sound by more than 30ms. Before 30ms the ear perceives the reflections as part of the original sound and the whole sound is fused into one. After 30ms the ear begins to differentiate the original and the delayed signal. This is important to remember since it can help you achieve the desired effect when programming the delay devices supplied with Cubase.

Delay devices feature a relatively simple set of controls which usually include the following parameters:

- Delay time – sets the time delay for the replication of the signal, usually measured in milliseconds.
- Feedback – determines the proportion of the delay which is fed back to the input, thereby controlling the number of repeats for the delay line.

- Pan – pans the delayed signal to different positions in the stereo image (in a stereo delay device).
- Mix – controls the mix of the original (dry) signal and the effects (wet) signal.

Bearing in mind the 30ms threshold, ADT effects (Automatic Double Tracking) are created using delay times of around 30 to 60ms with no, or very little, feedback. ADT simulates the effect of doubling the sound, since the ear perceives the delayed signal as a separate event but the delay time is not great enough for it to become detached from the original sound. As you increase the delay time beyond 50-60ms and increase the feedback, other kinds of effects, such as slap-back echo, are possible. Here we begin to clearly differentiate the original and the delayed signal. If you also manipulate the stereo imagery by delaying one channel by a different amount to the other you can create pseudo-stereo effects. As you increase the delay time still further, special effects such as ping pong echoes and multiple echo effects become possible. Ping pong is the term applied to an echo which bounces a number of times between each channel of the stereo image. With longer delay times, all kinds of special effects can be created and, in Cubase, the timing of the echoes can be tuned to the tempo of the music using the tempo sync features.

If needed, you can also work out the delay times for any given tempo with a calculator, using the following equation:

delay (in seconds) = (240 / current tempo) / note value

where note value equals four for a quarter note, eight for an eighth note, sixteen for a sixteenth note and so on.

Distortion

Distortion is the adding of extra frequencies to a sound signal using a non-linear audio process. This results in a change in the waveform. Distortion can be of the unwanted type, such as that encountered when you record at too high a level, or it can be of the wanted type, such as the warm characteristics of tube amplifiers or mildly overdriven analogue tape. Distortion of the wanted type usually involves the adding of extra harmonics based upon the most prominent frequency components in the original signal. Distortion is referred to by a number of different names including saturation, overdrive and fuzz.

Distortion effects range from subtle simulated tape saturation and mild distortion to extreme overdrive. Simulated tape saturation effects often use only small amounts of low order odd harmonic distortion (especially third-harmonic distortion) and apply this distortion to the loudest peaks in the signal. Tube simulations or overdrive type effects use combinations of both odd and even numbered harmonics added in greater amounts to the signal, where lower-order harmonics (second, third, fourth and fifth) produce a musical thickening of the sound and the addition of higher-order harmonics produces more metallic results.

Info

Cubase is supplied with mono, stereo and ping pong delay plug-ins and a special delay device named ModMachine which combines delay modulation with filter frequency and resonance modulation for some highly creative effects.

Info

The phenomenon that delays of less than 30–40 ms are fused with the direct sound is known as the Haas effect (discovered by Helmut Haas in 1951). Haas also found that short delays help the ear locate the direction of the original source, like the early reflections in a reverberant space. The careful use of short delays across the stereo sound field therefore helps place mono sources at specific positions within the stereo image and adds depth and focus to the mix.

Figure 13.1
The effect of changing the amplifier tube settings in AmpSimulator's 'Studio Clean 1' preset. A clean guitar signal (left) is treated with 1 tube, 2 tube and 3 tube amplifier settings, progressively distorting the signal into a more square-like waveform.

Info

Simulated tape saturation is available in the supplied SoftClipper plug-in, which allows you to regulate the amount of second and third harmonic distortion. Overdive and extreme fuzz effects are available in the supplied AmpSimulator plug-in.

Since distortion often involves an obvious change in the waveform of the signal, it is useful to view exactly how in a graphical representation. The results vary enormously between different distortion effects. Some distort the signal into triangular-like or sawtooth-like waveshapes while others produce square wave characteristics. Figure 13.1 shows how the amplifier tube settings of the supplied AmpSimulator plug-in progressively distort the waveform into a square-like shape, suggesting the addition of predominantly odd harmonics for this particular effect.

Dynamics

Dynamics processing involves the automatic control of the level of the signal in various ways and includes the techniques of compression, limiting, expansion and gating. These are important concepts in audio processing and it is therefore worth persevering with the theory if you are not already familiar.

In classic compression and expansion, when you compress a signal, loud parts become quieter and quiet parts become louder; compression converts a large dynamic range into a smaller dynamic range. When you expand a signal, loud parts become louder and quiet parts become quieter; expansion converts a small dynamic range into a larger dynamic range. Compressors and expanders are automatic gain control devices. Compressors start to reduce the gain of an audio signal when the level rises above a set threshold and expanders reduce the gain as the level falls below a set threshold.

The amount of compression or expansion is usually described in terms of a ratio, (e.g. 2:1, 10:1 20:1, infinity:1). When an infinitely high ratio of compression is applied to an input signal, the output does not increase above the threshold no matter how much level is applied at the input. This is a particular type of compression known as limiting. When an infinitely high ratio of expansion is applied to an input signal, the output reduces to zero as soon as the input drops below the threshold. This is a particular type of expansion known as gating, (also known as noise gating). Therefore, compression and limiting can be grouped into the same category, and expansion and gating can be grouped into another.

Compression and limiting

There are normally a number of standard controls which govern the compressor/limiter process and these are as follows:

- Threshold – sets the level at which compression begins to occur. When the input signal goes above the threshold, the output signal from the device is attenuated, (reduced in level), according to the ratio set with the ratio control.

- Ratio – varies the amount of gain reduction. A ratio of 2:1 indicates that for every 2dB the input level rises above the threshold level there will be a 1dB increase in the output level. A ratio of 10:1 indicates that for every 10dB the input level rises above the threshold level there will be a 1dB increase in the output level and so on. Note that a ratio of 1:1 indicates that there is no change in gain between the input and output levels.
- Attack time – determines the rate at which the compressor attenuates the output level after the threshold has been exceeded.
- Release time – determines the rate at which the compressor returns to its normal output gain after the input signal has fallen below the threshold level.
- Gain makeup – since compression often involves an overall reduction in output level a 'makeup' control is provided to increase the level after compression.

Compressor/limiters also generally feature soft-knee or hard-knee characteristics. Soft-knee is when compression begins gradually a number of dB's below the threshold, whereas hard-knee is when the compression begins more suddenly at the threshold level. Soft-knee compression tends to sound more natural and transparent to the listener whereas hard-knee compression produces a more obvious effect.

The relationship between the input level, output level and ratio is best viewed in diagrammatic form as in Figure 13.2. The various compressor graphical displays in Cubase resemble this same format. Figure 13.2 shows the threshold set at –20dB. When the ratio is set at 2:1, an input level exceeding the threshold by 10dB results in a 5dB attenuation in the output level. When the ratio is set at infinity:1 the output level remains at –20dB no matter how high the input level rises above the threshold.

Settings for the threshold and ratio vary enormously depending on the input signal and the effect you are attempting to achieve. As an initial starting point for classic downward compression, a gain reduction of around 5–10dB might be expected. To achieve this, try setting the threshold to around 10–15dB below the maximum peaks in the signal and the ratio to between 2:1 and 10:1. Set the gain makeup to bring the output back up to the required level.

The attack and release times are very important for the resulting characteristics of the compressed signal and can be used for a variety of creative effects. For example, setting a slow attack time (20-50ms) on a bass guitar or lead guitar allows the initial impact of each note to pass through unhindered before the compression takes effect. This maintains the original attack characteristics of the sound while still compressing the body of the signal, adding punch and allowing it to cut through in the mix. For this effect, try release times around 20-50ms and ratios between 5:1 and 15:1.

Figure 13.2
Compressor/limiter input and output levels for different ratios

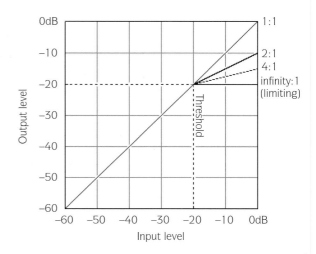

Tip

Deliberately setting both the attack and release time of a compressor very fast (less than 1-2ms), together with a threshold set for the peaks in the signal, can produce desirable distortion in the individual cycles of the waveform. Try ratios between 2:1 and 6:1. Used in a very subtle manner, this can simulate the effect of tape saturation, adding warmth to the signal.

Tip

As well as controlling the wanted parts of the signal, compression may also result in an increase in the level of some of the unwanted parts of the signal, such as interference or headphone spill between sung vocal lines. To avoid this effect, try firstly using expansion / gating to reduce the level of the interference and then apply the compression.

Info

Cubase is well stocked with compressors and limiters featuring Compressor, Vintage Compressor, Multiband Compressor and Limiter plug-ins. Combined gating, compression and limiting is available in the VST Dynamics plug-in.

Conversely, a slow attack time on a rock vocal sound, which you are attempting to level out, might not be appropriate. The slow attack may allow too many of the initial transients to pass through unhindered, thereby negating the levelling effect you are trying to achieve. For many vocal applications, a faster attack (5-15ms) may be more suitable. Combine this with release times around 100ms and ratios between 3:1 and 6:1.

The choice of release time is also paramount in creating the desired effect. Too short or too long a release time can result in undesirable audible pumping or breathing side-effects, so the release time must be set carefully. A fast release time (less than around 20ms) can increase the perceived level of the natural decay of an instrument. This can be used to increase the body of a drum sound. Conversely, you may wish to emphasise the actual hit of the drum, in which case you would set a slow release time combined with a moderately slow attack time.

Compressors are often used to increase the average signal level to make sounds and mixes seem louder and to even out the level of wildly fluctuating signals so that they can be managed more easily in the mix. However, the parameters must be set very carefully in order to avoid unwanted side-effects. This is especially true when compressing a whole mix, where one dominant instrument may produce undesirable level reduction in the rest of the mix. In addition, using the gain makeup control to increase the level after compression also increases the noise floor by the same amount. This is an unavoidable side-effect of compression which can sometimes become obtrusive, particularly if the original signal already contains high levels of background noise.

Compressors and limiters are often found in the same device but the applications of pure limiting are different from those of compression. Limiters are generally used to stop a signal passing above a set threshold, no matter how loud the input becomes, (sometimes referred to as 'brickwall' limiting). Limiting devices are characterised by very fast attack and release times, so that fast transients can be detected and corrected very quickly. The threshold for limiting is normally set quite high, so that only the transient peaks are attenuated while the rest of the signal passes through unaffected.

Expansion and gating

Expansion and gating are the opposites of compression and limiting and, once again, the precise characteristics are best viewed in diagrammatic form (see Figure 13.3).

Although expanders have their uses, most of this section concentrates on the use of one particular kind of expander, commonly known as the noise gate. A noise gate is a very high ratio expander. If the input signal falls below a preset threshold the output is radically attenuated. This is extremely useful for eliminating the unwanted noise and interference which may be present in between the wanted sections of a musical performance. Figure 13.3 shows the behaviour of an expander/noise gate whose threshold has been set at −20dB.

Typically, expander/noise gates feature the following control features:

• Threshold – sets the level at which expansion begins to occur or the gate begins to close. When the input signal goes below the threshold, the output signal from the device is attenuated according to the ratio set with the ratio control.

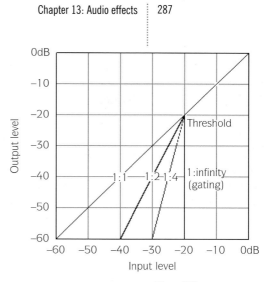

- Ratio – varies the amount of gain change. A ratio of 1:2 indicates that for every 1dB the input falls below the threshold there is a 2dB decrease in the output. A ratio of 1:infinity indicates that as soon as the input falls below the threshold the output is radically attenuated (i.e. the signal is gated). Classic gating devices feature fixed infinite ratios with no ratio controls. Instead, the gating action is regulated with a threshold (as above) and sometimes a floor or gain control which determines by how many dB the signal is attenuated when it falls below the threshold.

Figure 13.3
Expander/gate input and output levels for different ratios

- Attack time – determines the rate at which the expander/noise gate opens (to allow the signal through) when the signal rises above the threshold.
- Release time – determines the rate of attenuation when the signal has fallen below the threshold.
- Hold time – controls the length of time for which the level of the signal is guaranteed to be held before attenuation occurs.

The attack control of noise gates are normally endowed with very fast attack times in order to be able to cope with sounds which have rapid attack transients such as drum and percussion sounds. This ensures that the first part of the sound opens the gate quickly enough so that it passes through unhindered. However, sounds with slower attack characteristics benefit from slower noise gate attack times in order to avoid the audible click which can sometimes occur when the gate is opened abruptly. The hold time is used to determine how long the gate remains open and, once it starts to close, the release time determines the rate at which the signal fades away.

As well as their usual noise elimination function, noise gates can also be used creatively to modify the envelope of the signal. For example, special effects can be created by intentionally slowing down the attack portion of a sound using a slow attack setting, or the body of the sound can be attenuated with a fast release time to produce staccato effects.

Info

Frequency-conscious gating, as implemented in Cubase's Gate and VST Dynamics plug-ins, is particularly useful for gating live drum recordings which are suffering from leakage between microphones. This involves filtering the side-chain signal which triggers the gate so that it emphasises only the frequency range of the wanted instrument. For example, tuning the filter to the frequency bandwidth of the bass drum makes the gate sensitive to the bass drum alone. This means that the gate only opens when the bass drum is playing and any leakage into the bass drum mic from the snare and hi-hats is minimised.

Filtering

A filter is a device which attenuates one or more chosen frequency bands within a sound while allowing the others to pass through unchanged. In the same way as a coffee filter 'filters' the larger particles of coffee from the source coffee mixture, or an air filter 'filters' the larger particles of air-born dust from the air, a sound filter 'filters' various sound particles (harmonics) from the raw source sound which passes through it. Various types of sound filter are available but the essential idea of all sound filters is that of a device which modifies the harmonic structure of the treated sound.

The filter type determines what kind of filtering action takes place on the source signal. Each filter type has specific characteristics which are fundamental to the manner in which the filtering action takes place. The main filter types include low pass, high-pass, band-pass and band-reject. Each filter features a cut-off frequency. This determines the frequency at which the filter begins to have an effect. In the case of a low-pass filter those frequencies below the cut-off point are allowed to pass through unchanged while those above are significantly reduced. The cut-off point of a low-pass filter therefore regulates the overall brightness of the tone. Resonance is another attribute of most filters and this is also referred to as Q or emphasis. This modifies the frequencies around the cut-off point, regulating the sharpness or resonant character of the tone. Other aspects of filter design include filter slope characteristics, phase response and the implementation of envelope generators to control the action of the cut-off frequency.

Filter types

The four basic types of filter are low-pass, high-pass, band-pass and band-reject. Variations and combinations of these are known by different names such as notch filtering and parametric EQ. The use of filters in the pure sense implies the cutting of frequencies, whereas EQ implies the cutting and the boosting of the chosen frequencies. Understanding the action of the four basic filter types can lead to a better understanding of EQ and is the first step in becoming familiar with filtering in general.

Filter types are generally recognised by their amplitude response. This is shown on a graph of amplitude against frequency (see Figures 13.4 to 13.7, below). Each filter type is characterised by one part of the frequency spectrum which is allowed to pass through, known as the pass band, and another part of the spectrum which is significantly reduced, known as the stop band. The point at which the filtering action begins, (when the amplitude response passes from the pass band to the stop band), is known as the cut-off frequency (or cut-off point). There is always a transitional area between the pass band and the stop band. The rule for defining the exact point for the cut-off frequency is generally accepted as that point where the signal has fallen 3dB below the level of the pass band. It is, therefore, true to say that a significant number of frequencies below (or above) the cut-off point will have already been attenuated (cut) before the cut-off point itself is reached.

Low-pass

A low-pass filter allows those frequencies below the cut-off point to pass through with little change while those above are significantly reduced.

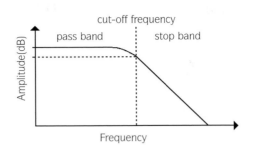

Figure 13.4
Amplitude response of a low-pass filter

High-pass

A high-pass filter significantly reduces those frequencies below the cut-off point while those above are allowed to pass through with little change (the opposite of the low-pass filter).

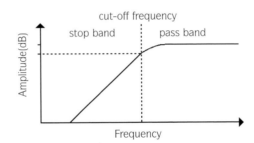

Figure 13.5
Amplitude response of a high-pass filter

Band-pass

A band-pass filter allows a band of frequencies to pass through between two cut-off points while significantly reducing frequencies both above and below the pass band. The mid-point of the amplitude response curve is referred to as the centre frequency and the frequency range between the lower and upper cut-off points is known as the bandwidth.

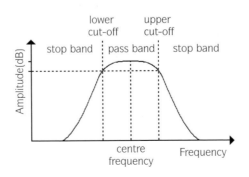

Figure 13.6
Amplitude response of a band-pass filter

Band-reject

A band-reject filter attenuates (rejects) a band of frequencies between two cut-off points while allowing the rest of the signal to pass through with little change (the opposite of the band-pass filter). The mid-point of the amplitude response curve is referred to as the centre frequency and the frequency range between the lower and upper cut-off points is known as the bandwidth.

Figure 13.7
Amplitude response of a band-reject filter

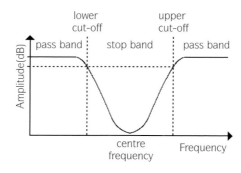

In its most basic form, a low-pass filter (for example) is regulated using a single parameter, the cut-off frequency. This governs the point at which the upper frequencies in the sound begin to be reduced, (attenuated), thereby controlling how the spectrum is modified. However, this attenuation takes place according to a slope as the filter passes between the pass band and the stop band. This slope describes the rate at which the upper frequencies are attenuated and is generally measured in terms of dBs per octave. The slope varies according to the manner in which the filter has been designed. In voltage-controlled circuitry, for example, the rate is governed, among other things, by the number of resistors and capacitors used in the circuit. A simple passive filter with one resistor and one capacitor in the circuit is known as an RC filter and this has an attenuation slope of 6dB per octave. Other common rates include 12dB per octave, 18dB per octave and 24dB per octave. These slopes can be plotted graphically in terms of relative attenuation against frequency.

Info

The filter section of the supplied plug-ins contains just two devices, ToneBooster and Wah Wah, but filtering is an important element within a large number of the other supplied plug-ins. It forms the basis of the StepFilter, Metalizer and Tonic plug-ins from the earlier VST plug-ins collection and is an essential part of ModMachine and the EQ plug-ins.

Filter resonance (emphasis)

Resonance can be defined as the frequency or frequencies at which an object vibrates in sympathy with itself or with external vibrational phenomena. Filters, too, can be endowed with this kind of behaviour. Passive RC filters have no resonant frequencies and simply filter the source according to their amplitude and phase response. However, active filters are often designed to produce a boost in the response around the cut-off frequency. Some filtering plug-ins include a parameter which is used to regulate the amount of resonance (see StepFilter and Tonic). The parameter is commonly referred to as resonance, emphasis or Q. Figure 13.8 shows what happens to a low-pass filter's amplitude response for low, high and maximum resonance values.

When the resonance control parameter is set to low or medium positions the bandwidth of the emphasised frequencies is quite wide and they are only boosted by a small amount (Figure 13.8a). For higher resonance values the bandwidth of the emphasised frequencies is quite narrow and they are boosted by a large amount (Figure 13.8b). As the resonance is increased the lower frequencies are progressively attenuated. At maximum resonance the lower and upper frequencies virtually disappear from the filtered signal leaving a single harmonic which oscillates at the cut-off frequency (Figure 13.8c). In the latter case, an amount of the source signal normally still passes through.

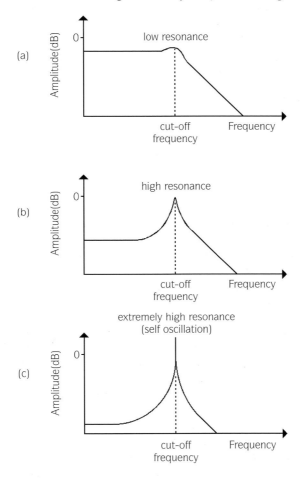

Figure 13.8
The effect of resonance on a low-pass filter's amplitude response

The effect of resonance can be summarised as follows: resonance results in the emphasising of a narrow band of frequencies (harmonics) located around the cut-off point. This narrow band can be moved around within the frequency spectrum by changing the frequency of the cut-off point. This results in effects which are particularly pleasing to the ear. At extreme resonance values, when the filter enters a state of self-oscillation (as in Figure 13.8c), special effects and pitched tones can be produced.

The resonant low-pass filter has, more than any other filter type, been responsible for some classic subtractive synthesis effects and is excellent for producing the filter sweeps commonly used in dance music. Cubase's Step Filter plug-in allows the simultaneous changing of both the cut-off frequency and the resonance in synchronisation with the current tempo of the project. Setting up a medium to high resonance level and then sweeping the cut-off frequency up and down has been used in innumerable synth patches and dance tracks.

Using filters

In addition to the sweeping effects described above, filters may be used to produce pseudo-stereo effects, comb-filter effects, wah-wah effects and such things as AM radio and telephone simulations. In a corrective sense, filters are particularly useful for hum and hiss removal and band-limiting. Filters are, of course, essential to all EQ.

Modulation

Modulation encompasses a wide range of effects including chorus, flanging, and phasing and the, perhaps slightly lesser known, techniques of amplitude modulation, frequency modulation and ring modulation. Modulation is the modification of the characteristics of one signal using a second signal. The modulating signal could be an LFO (a low frequency oscillator) or some other kind of signal somewhere in the audible range. For example, simple modulation effects include vibrato and tremolo. Vibrato is a form of frequency modulation where the frequency (or pitch) of the target signal is modulated by an LFO. Tremolo is a form of amplitude modulation where the amplitude level of the target signal is modulated by an LFO.

Chorus, flanging and phasing

Although the classic modulation effects like chorus, flanging and phasing are easily recognisable, the ways in which they are produced in modern effects devices may not be so obvious.

Chorus is an effect produced by passing a signal through one or more delay lines and modulating the delay time(s) with an LFO. The result is mixed with the original signal. The modulation of the delay times produces phase cancellation effects and changes in the perceived pitch and timing, creating the illusion of an ensemble of sound sources. Comparatively short delay times are used. It was first conceived as a means of attempting to make a single musical performance sound like more than one performer.

Flanging is a similar effect created by mixing a delayed version of a signal with the original and modulating the delay time with an LFO whilst also applying an amount of feedback. Comparatively short delay times are used. This produces phase cancellation effects which are heard as a comb filter effect sweeping up and down within the frequency spectrum.

Phasing is created by mixing a phase-shifted version of a signal with the original and modulating the phase shifting with an LFO whilst also applying an amount of feedback. Similar to flanging, phasing is also perceived as a comb filter effect weeping up and down within the frequency spectrum, but the swept frequency bands are not always harmonically related to the target signal.

Amplitude modulation, frequency modulation and ring modulation

Amplitude modulation, frequency modulation and ring modulation tend towards more esoteric effects and are implemented in sound synthesis, as well as sound effects devices.

Amplitude Modulation is achieved by modulating the amplitude of one audio signal by another signal where both signals are in the audible range. Using simple sine waves for the modulator produces a signal containing the target signal and two side-bands which are the sum and difference frequencies of the target signal and the modulating signal. Applying amplitude modulation where the modulating signal is an LFO produces tremolo effects. When the modulator is not an LFO (i.e. when it is in the audible range), the result tends towards densely packed inharmonic frequencies added to the signal.

Frequency modulation is probably better known for its uses in sound synthesis. In FM, the frequency of one signal is modulated by another. Applying frequency modulation where the modulating signal is an LFO produces vibrato effects. When the modulator is not an LFO (i.e. when it is in the audible range), multiple frequencies known as side-bands are added to the signal.

Ring modulation is a special kind of amplitude modulation where the target signal and the modulating signal are multiplied to produce the sum and difference of their frequencies in the output. Unlike amplitude and frequency modulation, the original frequency of the source signal is not present in the output. Typically, this produces 'alien' effects for speech and metallic tones for pitched sounds.

Reverb

Reverb is an abbreviation for reverberation. Reverberation is an effect produced by a multiple series of echoes occurring after the original sound in an acoustic space. It is characterised by three distinct phases, as shown in Figure 13.9. Reverberation is found in virtually every acoustic space and its characteristics vary enormously depending on the size of the space and the kinds of materials and objects found therein.

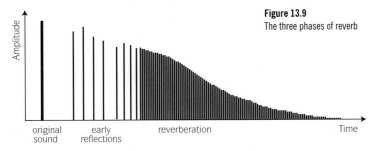

Figure 13.9
The three phases of reverb

Figure 13.9 approximates what takes place in a real reverberant space. Firstly, the original sound arrives directly from the source to the listener's ear. After a short pause the first reflections from the surfaces of the room (or other acoustic space) are heard; these are known as early reflections. This is followed by a complex mass of multiple reflections as the reflected sounds continue to bounce off the various surfaces. The amplitude of these multiple reflections decays exponentially to form what is commonly known as the reverb tail. In real reverberant spaces (especially in large ones), the upper frequencies decay at a faster rate than the rest of the signal.

Info

Cubase is supplied with a wide range of modulation effects including auto-pan, chorus, flanging, phasing, tremolo, vibrato and others.

Info

The early reflections within reverberation are crucial in giving the treated sound a sense of depth and focus, and clarify the location of the direct sound. Careful manipulation of early reflections can enhance the clarity, shape and depth of sounds within the mix.

The aim with virtual reverb plug-ins is to re-create the same kind of behaviour. However, the first thing you may notice when comparing different devices is that reverb units are not all created equal. Convincing reverberation remains difficult to replicate artificially and requires a large amount of processing power to achieve the best results. Among the best attempts are those using convolution techniques. Convolution uses impulse responses from real reverberant spaces thus producing highly convincing results.

Other

There are of course a multitude of other effects which do not necessarily fit neatly into any particular category. These include such devices as Cubase's earlier Grungelizer plug-in, which adds crackle, noise and distortion to your signals, and Bitcrusher, which adds distortion to signals by truncating the bit resolution.

Other miscellaneous effects and processing techniques include bass maximisation, click and hum removal, harmonic excitement, loudness maximisation, pitch processing, psychoacoustic enhancement, spatial processing, stereo enhancement, sonic optimisation, tape saturation emulation, and vocoding.

Setting up audio effects in Cubase

In Cubase, real-time audio effects may be assigned as insert effects or send effects. There are no strict rules about which effects are assigned to which kind of effects slots but, for example, not all effects are suitable for use as insert effects, and reverb effects are almost always assigned as send effects. The effects routing structure of the Mixer is similar to that found in a classic real world console (see Info box).

Insert effects

Insert effects are assigned by clicking in any of the Insert effects slots of an audio-based channel or an input / output buss, at which time a pop-up menu appears containing the plug-ins available in your system (Figure 13.10).

Insert effect assignments are unique for each channel and each time you activate an insert effect you also activate an additional instance of the chosen plug-in effect. This, of course, uses pro-

Figure 13.10
Assigning an effect in an Insert effects slot

cessing power so, while insert effects are invaluable, they tend to use more system resources than send effects. Each channel in the Mixer has a total of eight insert slots. Effects are assigned to the insert slots in the extended channel strips in the Mixer, in the Channel Settings window or in the Inspector. The order of effects can be freely modified by dragging and dropping between slots.

With insert effects, the signal passes directly *through* the effects in series in descending order (see Figure 13.11). The channel audio signal is routed directly to the first insert effect's input. This means that it has not yet passed via the channel fader and is commonly known as the 'pre fader' signal. If necessary, the level of this signal may still be changed using the input gain control for the channel. The insert slots themselves do not feature any level controls.

After having passed through one or more of insert effects slots 1-6, the output from the effect(s) is routed via the EQ section (if active), channel fader, inserts 7 and 8, and pan control to the chosen output buss. The signal level going into insert effects 1-6 is *not* affected by the channel fader level since they are pre-fader. Inserts 7 and 8 are special case post-fader slots which are suitable for processing which benefits from coming after the channel fader, such as limiting. Slots 7 and 8 are particularly useful when used in an output buss for final limiting, loudness maximisation or dithering during a mix or mastering session.

In general, insert effects are best suited to processing like compression, distortion, EQ, expansion, filtering, limiting and noise gating. Chorus, flanging and phasing also work well as insert effects.

Audio channel

Figure 13.11
The routing configuration for Insert effects (slots 1-6)

Send effects

Send effects are managed using FX channels. The effect is actually assigned as an insert effect on the FX channel, which may at first seem confusing. The first thing to do when setting up a send effect is to add an FX channel to the project. This is achieved in the same way as for other channel types by using the Add function (Project menu). The Add FX channel dialogue allows you to choose an effect for the new FX channel (Figure 13.12). The effect for the channel may be changed at a later time, or other effects may be added, in the remaining Insert slots of the FX channel.

Once an FX channel is activated in the project, you can send signals to it for processing from the auxiliary send slots of any of the audio-based channels. Send effects are assigned by clicking in any of the send slots for the channel, at which time a pop-up menu appears containing the FX channels

Figure 13.12
Choosing an effect for an FX channel in the Add FX channel dialogue

Info

The number of effects which are used within a project is restricted only by the processing power of your computer. Sophisticated high-end plug-ins use substantial amounts of CPU power and using a large number of these simultaneously could slow down system performance. Open the VST Performance window (Devices menu) to monitor the current load on your CPU. Aim for no more than 50 – 60% average load on the ASIO meter.

Figure 13.13
Assigning a send effect in a send effects slotslot

and other routing destinations (Figure 13.13). The send level is regulated using the mini-fader of the effects slot. Send effects can be chosen on as many audio-based channels as required, in any order, and with unique send levels for each slot. This saves on processing power since, for example, any number of audio channel sends can use the same reverb effect which you have activated only once in a single FX channel.

Each channel in the Mixer has a total of eight send slots. The send slots are assigned in the extended channel strip in the Mixer, in the Channel Settings window or in the Inspector. The routing configuration for send effects is similar to a traditional mixing console. Figure 13.14 traces the signal as it is split between the 'dry' and the 'wet' signal paths, in a typical post-fader send configuration. The dry signal passes through the pan control of the channel strip, as usual, and is routed to the chosen output buss. The send signal is routed post-fader via the send level and the send effect to the chosen output buss. This wet signal joins the dry signal in the mix. The FX channel fader controls the level of the effects return.

Audio channel

Signal

Phase
Input gain

M In 1
S Out 1

Dry signal to output bus

Pan

Dry signal

C

Level

Send signal

Send 1

FX 3-...Works
-2.60

-3.8
0.00

CleanElec GTR

FX channel

Send signal

Phase
Input gain

S Out 1

Wet signal to output bus

FX channel
Insert 1

RoomWorks

Level

Pan

Through signal

C

FX channel
Insert 2

EQ

eq 1
2.1
793.1 Hz
6.2

-oo
0.00

FX 3-RoomWor

Figure 13.14
Typical routing configuration for send effects

With FX channels, the effect (or wet) signal is added 'in parallel' to the dry signal in the mix via the FX channel fader, which is usually routed to the same output buss as the dry signal. A suitable mix between the dry and wet signals is achieved by carefully balancing the fader level of the source channel with the fader level of the FX channel. Under normal circumstances, the 'mix' control in the user interface of the effect in the FX channel is set to 100% wet. This ensures that the FX channel governs only the wet signal and the source channel governs only the dry signal.

Each send is routed either pre or post-fader. If it is pre-fader, the signal is routed to the FX channel before it arrives at the channel fader. In this case, the channel fader level does *not* influence the send level. If it is post-fader, the signal passes via the channel fader before it is routed to the FX channel. In this case, the channel fader level influences the send level. Post-fader is the default setting.

You may wonder how the pre-fader switch might be useful. Practical uses include occasions when the channel fader has been set rather low and does not provide enough signal for the effect send; in this case the pre-fader signal provides more level. The pre-fader switch also allows you to fade a signal in the mix without also fading any effect applied to it. This can be used for special mixing techniques like fading a sound which has pre-fader reverb added to it. The result gives the impression that the sound is disappearing into the distance as the dry signal fades away whilst the reverberation signal remains.

In general, send effects are best suited to reverb, delay, chorus, flanging and phasing.

Common GUI functions for audio effects

The graphical user interface (GUI) for any of the currently active effects can be opened by clicking on the edit button of the slot corresponding to the effect. The edit buttons are labelled with a lower case 'e' and are found in all channel effects slots in the Mixer, in the Channel Settings window and in the Inspector. All GUIs for the effects open in a separate window similar to that shown in Figure 13.15.

Basic GUI functions

The GUI parameters common to most effects include an On button, automation read and write buttons, presets management functions and, where appropriate, an output and/or mix control. An effect is activated by clicking the On button, at which time it is illuminated in blue. Clicking on the presets field opens the presets browser which automatically searches for the presets relevant to the chosen effect. If desired, the presets browser may be resized to show only the list of presets in the viewer, as shown in Figure 13.16. There are also load and save presets functions which open the browser at a separate location within your screen space.

Figure 13.15
The graphical user interface for the supplied Flanger effect

Figure 13.16
Opening the presets browser

Figure 13.17
Use the mix dial to set the proportion of wet and dry signal

Figure 13.18
In tempo sync mode control values are shown as note values instead of numerical values

Figure 13.18b
Use the side chain button for a wide range of creative effects

The output control is for setting an appropriate level for the output of the effects device. This varies according to the application. The mix dial determines the mix between the wet and dry signal which passes to the output (Figure 13.17). When used as a send effect, the mix dial is normally best set to 100% wet and, when used as an insert effect the wet and dry signals might be provisionally set to equal proportions.

The general rule is that all visible parameters can be manipulated in some way by clicking and dragging with the mouse. All parameter changes made as part of a mix can be automated by activating the Read and Write buttons found next to the On button.

Tempo sync controls

Where applicable, the supplied effects feature tempo sync controls. These allow the synchronisation of various parameters (such as LFOs and delay times) to the current tempo of Cubase. Activating the tempo sync button changes the relevant control to note values instead of numerical values (Figure 13.18).

The note values determine the division of the bar which Cubase uses for synchronisation purposes. For example, setting a value of 1/8 where a delay time is concerned produces repeated delays at 1/8 note intervals, or setting a value of 1/1 where an LFO controlling auto pan is concerned produces a panning effect which occurs once in each bar.

Side chain buttons

Where appropriate, the supplied VST3 plug-ins feature side chain buttons at the top of the GUI next to the automation read and write buttons. This concerns a number of delay, dynamics and modulation effects. An active side chain disengages the source signal which normally feeds the side chain and instead allows you to send a second signal to control some element within the effect. When activated, the side chain inputs become available in the auxiliary sends of audio channels or, if preferred, you can send a signal directly to the side chain using the output routing menu for the channel.

Side chains may be used in a wide range of creative and corrective audio processing techniques. For example, activating the side chain for a delay effect allows you to mute the delay when the side chain signal rises above a fixed threshold. When used with a compressor effect you could apply compression to a bass guitar according to the presence of a kick drum signal in the side chain, or apply ducking to a musical signal according to the presence of a voice-over signal . When used with a gate effect you could rhythmically open and close the gate on a sustained synth pad according to a percussive signal in the side chain. For modulation, you could control the LFO of a chorus effect according to the amplitude envelope of the side chain signal. There are many possibilities.

Audio effects in practice

There now follow descriptions and practical uses of a selection of the VST3 audio effects supplied with the program and, where appropriate, alternatives from other developers. The plug-ins are covered in a similar order to that of the plug-ins pop-up menu and are therefore arranged in similar categories.

Delay effects

Delay – supplied plug-ins

Cubase is supplied with MonoDelay, PingPongDelay and StereoDelay for standard delay effects such as ADT, slapback, ping pong and echo effects. For more advanced delay effects, ModMachine combines the modulation of delay time, filter frequency and filter Q to allow the creation of some unique filtered chorus and delay effects.

MonoDelay for ADT and slapback echo effects

ADT (Automatic Double Tracking) involves mixing the source signal with a delayed copy using delay times of around 30-60ms. This is good for thickening or enlivening the source and particularly suits vocals, guitars and saxophones. MonoDelay is suitable for simple delay effects of this type. In addition to the standard delay parameters MonoDelay features filtering which helps separate the delayed signal from the source (when required). For

Figure 13.19 (left)
MonoDelay ADT effect

Figure 13.20 (right)
MonoDelay slapback echo effect

example, adjusting MonoDelay to the settings shown in Figure 13.19 produces a filtered 'shadow' which sits behind the original signal and tends to lift the sound. The 'Lo' roll-off filter reduces frequencies below 480Hz while the 'Hi' roll-off filter reduces frequencies above 10kHz in the delay signal path. This combined with a 40ms delay and minimal feedback produces the desired ADT effect.

Figure 13.21
ModMachine chorus effect with no filter modulation

Slapback echo relies upon similar principles to ADT but usually increases the delay time to beyond 60ms. Figure 13.20 shows an example where the delay time is extended to 125ms with a narrower frequency band for the filtering.

ModMachine

ModMachine is capable of producing esoteric filtered delay and chorus effects, but to get to know the parameters it is best to first use it in a simple capacity. To this end, try setting up ModMachine for a chorus effect which uses no filter modulation, as shown in Figure 13.21. This uses a minimal delay time with subtle delay time modulation, medium modulation width and no feedback. To modify this setup for a classic delay effect, try increasing the delay time to 125ms, increase the feedback to around 40 and decrease the mix to around 20. Even though this setup uses no filter modulation, the filter remains in the signal path

Figure 13.22
ModMachine filtered delay effect with the filter placed in the feedback loop

after the delay feedback loop and just before the output (output mode). To hear the delay effect you should select highpass as the filter type to allow the signal through.

The filter controls of ModMachine are arranged in two sections. The upper section manages the filter frequency while the lower section manages the filter Q. When the speed dials are set to zero and the sync buttons are de-activated, the Lo and Hi parameters become inactive. In this mode, the filter becomes a static filter where the frequency dial governs the centre frequency and the Q-Factor dial governs the resonance. Figure 13.22 shows ModMachine set up in this manner with the filter placed in the feedback loop (loop mode) and set to lowpass. In this configuration, there is no filter modulation but the filter has a dampening effect on the delayed signal as it passes through the feedback loop. This is helpful for emulating the dampening effect of analogue tape delay units where the delay signal progressively loses more high frequencies each time the tape loop passes over the playback heads. Also try this setup with longer delay times and modify the mix dial as desired.

For filter modulation, start with the overall settings shown in Figure 13.22 and modify the filter sections to match the settings shown in Figure 13.23. Select the output position and bandpass type for the filter and try increasing

Figure 13.23
ModMachine filter modulation settings designed for the filter placed at the output in bandpass mode

the delay time to around 1000ms and the mix to around 30%. Here the bandpass filter centre frequency modulates between the Lo and Hi values while the filter Q simultaneously modulates between its Lo and Hi values. The spatial parameters distribute the delay effects around the stereo image.

Delay – alternatives

There are a wide range of delay alternatives available. Notable among these are Native Instruments Reaktor Echomania and Fusion Reflections; Native Instruments Spektral Delay; PSP Audioware 608 Multi Delay, PSP42 and PSP84; Steinberg Karlette; and Waves Supertap. If you are already an owner of Reaktor and are looking for delay effects with a difference, Echomania and Fusion Reflections are well worth exploring. Fusion Reflections combines chorus and delay with delay modulation, stereo spread and diffusion controls. Echomania combines delay and EQ with delay modulation, EQ modulation and distortion. Steinberg Karlette is an earlier plug-in which emulates a tape loop echo unit. This is a multi-tap device featuring four delay lines with traditional delay time, dampening, pan, feedback and sync controls. Waves Supertap is a high-precision multi-tap device combining up to six delay lines with delay modulation and EQ controls.

PSP84

PSP Audioware developed the PSP84 delay plug-in as a more elaborate version of their Lexicon PSP42, which is an emulation of the legendary Lexicon

Tip

To appreciate the full range of third party developer VST plug-ins available in any category, search the KVR Audio website on the internet at www.kvraudio.com

PCM42 hardware delay unit. The PSP84 (Figure 13.24) features two independent delay lines with channel link button, wet signal and feedback loop phase inversion buttons, pan controls, switchable low pass, band pass or high pass resonant filter, and modulation of delay times and filter cut-off frequency. In addition, there is tape saturation emulation and vintage spring or plate reverberation. All this adds up to a delay unit of exceptional character, warmth and creative potential.

Delay times up to 5secs per channel are available and times may be set in milliseconds or, for tempo sync operation, in note values. The delay and feedback inversion buttons are helpful for deep flanging and pseudo stereo effects. The filter may be placed at the input, in the delay feedback loop or in the wet signal path just before the output. When placed in the feedback loop, progressively greater high frequency dampening of the feedback signal can be achieved to emulate the dampening action of traditional tape loop echo units. Modulation of the filter cut-off frequency combined with low delay times produces warm chorus and flanging. Setting the filter to input mode while modulating the cut-off frequency in band pass mode produces excellent auto wah-wah effects. The LFO modulation may be set in frequency values or synchronised to the tempo of Cubase. The reverb section takes its feed from either the wet signal alone or the combined wet and dry output mix, and makes a valuable addition to the vintage sound.

The PSP84 is excellent for tracking and mixing and is particularly suited to guitar and vocal effects and drum loop mangling. Its effects arsenal spans traditional echo and delay to sumptuous chorus and flanging. The unit can sound crystal clean, glowingly warm or analogue dirty and when required can produce totally wacky, weird and wonderful effects and soundscapes. Despite its power PSP84 remains easy to use, combining intuitive parameter manipulation with an intelligent user interface.

If you need a simpler version with the same sound character try PSP84's little brother, the Lexicon PSP42. Alternatively, PSP supply the powerful PSP 608MD multi-tap delay, featuring up to 8 delay lines.

Figure 13.24
PSP84 delay unit. An ideal alternative to Cubase's supplied delay plug-ins.

Distortion effects

Distortion – supplied plug-ins
There are two distortion plug-ins supplied with Cubase: AmpSimulator and SoftClipper.

AmpSimulator

AmpSimulator simulates the warmth and distortion associated with guitar amplifiers, ranging from mild distortion through to extreme overload. The heart of the plug-in is in the Amplifier and Cabinet menus. These define the essential character of the distortion. The amplifier models include: Clean, American Clean, Jazz and Tube settings for moderate distortion; Lead set-

Figure 13.25
AmpSimulator

tings for smooth lead guitar; and Crunch and Modern set-tings for extreme overdrive. The character of each may be subtly modified by the cabinet setting and the sound of the cabinet itself may be filtered using the Lo and Hi damping controls.

Finally, the Drive dial governs the amount of distortion and the Low, Mid And High tone controls and Presence dial allow you to fine tune the overall result. AmpSimulator is designed mainly for guitar processing but also has its uses for enlivening synth sounds.

SoftClipper

SoftClipper is a relatively simple device featuring separate second and third harmonic controls. These allow the harmonics to be added to the signal in varying proportions. This suits the simulation of mild tube distortion and tape saturation where adding very subtle distortion enhances detail and warmth. The saturation effect may be emphasised by increasing the input above 0dB. Try the settings in Figure 13.26 to give guitar and other sounds a subtle high frequency edge.

Figure 13.26
SoftClipper

Distortion – alternatives

Notable distortion plug-in alternatives include IK Multimedia Amplitube, Native Instruments Guitar Rig and Steinberg Quadrafuzz. Quadrafuzz is out-lined in the section entitled 'Additional Supplied Effects', below.

Dynamics effects

Dynamics – supplied plug-ins

Cubase is well-stocked with dynamics processors including Compressor, EnvelopeShaper, Expander, Gate, Limiter, Maximizer, MultiCompressor, VintageCompressor and VST Dynamics. However, using any dynamics pro-cessor requires a good understanding of the parameters and an in-depth knowledge of how the settings are likely to affect the target signal.

Having a clear idea of the difference between peak and average levels in music helps understand what gets affected when you manipulate dynamics. Peak levels are brief transients which register momentarily on a peak level meter at the highest positions and average level is the energy contained with-in the main body of the signal. The energy in each transient peak is very small in isolation but in greater numbers contributes to the impact and clarity of the sound. However, it is the average level which gives the main indication of the perceived loudness of the signal. Dynamics processing can therefore be set to control only the highest transient peaks or it can be set to act upon the main body of the music where most of the energy is found. The former may have little or no initial effect on the perceived loudness whereas the latter is likely to radically affect the perceived loudness and 'shape' of the signal. Of course, compressors and expanders can be set to act at any given threshold between the high and low points in the signal.

Dynamics processing, therefore, is concerned with manipulations of the peak and average levels within audio signals, for example: to control transient peaks (peak limiting), to gently reduce the loudest sections (classic downward compression), to enhance the lower level details of the music (low or mid-level upward compression), to increase the level of the loudest sections (upward expansion) or to reduce low-level sections in the signal (downward expansion/gating). Much of this can be achieved with the supplied dynamics plug-ins.

Peak limiting with Limiter

Classic peak limiting involves setting a 'brick wall' level above which the loudest peaks in the input signal do not pass to the output, no matter how high they rise above the threshold. In Limiter, this brick wall is set with the output parameter. In Figure 13.27 the output is set to -0.3dBFS to ensure no transient clipping when limiting a mix. When used in this capacity, Limiter is best inserted as a post-fader effect in slots 7 or 8 of the main stereo output buss.

Limiter is pre-set to a very fast attack time so that transient peaks are brought under control instantaneously. The input parameter allows you to boost the input to achieve loudness maximisation effects and the release parameter governs the time it takes to return to a normal level after gain reduction. For the most natural results, set this to auto (program dependent release).

Figure 13.27
Limiter set for limiting transient peaks to -0.3dBFS

Classic downward compression with Compressor

Classic downward compression pushes down the rising attack energy in the signal while emphasising the release. This fattens the sound and brings out detail but may also dull the high frequency content. Classic ratios produce a subtle curve. The configuration shown in Figure 13.28 uses a 4 : 1 ratio with a soft knee setting. Try starting with the attack at 50ms and release at 100ms and adjust to taste. In contrast to the limiting settings outlined above, here we are starting to lower the threshold into the body of the signal. Set shorter attack times if you wish to squash more transients and adjust the release time to avoid pumping effects. Appropriate settings are highly dependent upon the characteristics of the input signal and the desired result.

Figure 13.28
Classic downward compression using the supplied Compressor plug-in

Figure 13.29
Mid-level upward compression

Mid-level upward compression with Compressor

Mid-level upward compression uses a comparatively low threshold, a subtle ratio and sufficient makeup gain to push up the lower and mid-level detail in the signal. The louder parts of the signal remain unchanged. For this kind of processing, try the Compressor plug-in settings shown in Figure 13.29. This uses a gentle 1.3 : 1 ratio with the threshold at -45dB and 6dB of makeup gain. A fairly fast attack at 4ms and a hard knee setting keeps the input sig-

nal under control. Try a soft knee setting for a more natural effect. These settings bring out the inner detail of a recording and increase the density of the sound. Try this on strummed acoustic guitar and you should hear the rhythmic and percussive elements emphasised. For a slightly more exaggerated effect try decreasing the threshold still further to around -56dB, combined with a 1.68 : 1 ratio, 20ms attack and around 13dB of makeup gain.

Classic noise gating with Gate

Gating involves a radical drop in output level once the input falls below a set threshold. To reduce background noise, the threshold is set just above the noise level. Figure 13.30 shows the Gate plug-in set up for classic noise gating. Here the threshold is set at -35dB but this must be adjusted according to the noise level in the signal you are gating. Careful adjustment of the attack, release and hold parameters ensures a natural transition between the gated and ungated signal. Try starting with an attack of 2ms and a release of 250ms. A fairly fast attack ensures that the gate opens fast enough when the wanted part of the signal

Figure 13.30
Gate set up for classic noise gating

rises above the threshold. A long release ensures a natural attenuation to silence since radical cuts between the signal and absolute silence are not always desirable. For this setup, the side-chain filter is switched out.

Frequency conscious gating with Gate

A popular technique in live drum recording is the gating of individual instruments within the kit to reduce leakage between microphones. For example, it is very often the case that the sounds of the cymbals and the bass drum leak into the snare drum microphone and vice versa. 'Frequency conscious' gating is highly appropriate for curing this kind of problem. The essential idea is the setting up of a gate which is tuned to open only when the frequencies of the wanted instrument are present. The technique can be extended to any occasion when you need to separate a wanted sound from background interference. In the Gate plug-in, this is achieved using the side-chain filter.

Info

Frequency conscious gating of drums presents few problems if the parameters are set up very carefully. However, make sure that you are not losing the initial transients in the attack phase of the sound. It is this part of the signal which endows drums with their impact and clarity. When attacks are set too slow or thresholds are set too high the initial impact is easily lost.

Figure 13.31 shows the Gate plug-in set up for frequency conscious gating of a bass drum. This uses the side-chain filter set to band pass mode with a very narrow Q. The frequency is tuned to the dominant band in the bass drum which, in this case, is 73Hz. You can find this by ear by engaging the side-chain filter monitor button while in playback. A very fast 0.1ms attack ensures the capture of the click of the bass drum and a medium fast release of 73ms with a hold of 25ms captures the body. The analysis is set to the peaks of the incoming signal and the Live button is de-activated to engage the default look-ahead behaviour of the gate. The threshold setting must be precisely adjusted to allow only the bass drum to pass through. Also see the supplied 'Isolate BD' presets which use the side-chain filter in the more orthodox low pass mode.

Similarly, Figure 13.32 shows the Gate plug-in set up for the frequency conscious gating of a snare drum. The side-chain filter is set to band pass mode and the centre frequency is tuned to the 'crack' of the snare with a fairly wide Q setting. The attack, release and hold settings are similar to those for the bass drum example, above. The threshold setting must be precisely adjusted to allow only the snare drum to pass through.

Tip

Drums and percussion which vary greatly in dynamics may prove difficult to treat with frequency conscious or any other kind of gating. In these cases, gentle downward expansion may be more appropriate than hard gating.

Figure 13.31 (left)
Frequency conscious bass drum gate

Figure 13.32 (right)
Frequency conscious snare drum gate

Punch with VintageCompressor

The supplied VintageCompressor simulates the action of older style compressors. Here, you regulate the amount of compression by pushing up the input until you see gain reduction taking place in the gain reduction meter. Gain reduction starts when the input signal reaches around +6dB. Once you have applied input gain you must normally apply a corresponding amount of cut with the output control to bring the signal back down to a reasonable level. The attack and release controls are set in a similar manner to the

Figure 13.33
Try these VintageCompressor settings on a snare or a whole drum kit

Compressor plug-in described above. Activating the punch button ensures that the attack of the compressed sound cuts through regardless of how short an attack time you set. This is good for adding punch to drums, bass and percussive instruments. Try the settings in Figure 13.33 to add punch to a snare or a whole drum kit.

Dynamics – alternatives

There are a wide range of dynamics plug-in alternatives available. High on the list are the Chandler EMI TG12413 Limiter, Izotope Ozone mastering suite, PSP Master Compressor, PSP Vintage Warmer, PSP Xenon Limiter, Sonnox Oxford Dynamics and Oxford Limiter, SSL LMC-1, TC Powercore Brick Wall Limiter, Universal Audio UAD 1176LN, URS Classic Compressors, and Waves Ultramaximizer, C1 Compressor / Gate, C4 Multiband Compressor, and Renaissance Compressor.

EMI TG12413 Limiter

The Chandler Limited EMI TG12413 Limiter (Figure 13.34) provides authentic vintage-style compression and limiting based upon the original EMI limiters of the EMI TG12345 and TG12413 consoles used at Abbey Road Studios in the late 60s and early 70s. These consoles were used to record classic albums such as the Beatles' Abbey Road and Pink Floyd's Dark Side of the Moon. The TG12413 includes two modules: the 1969, for an authentic emulation of the original TG12345 hardware, and the 2005, based upon the hardware reissue TG1 Limiter supplied by Chandler Limited. Both modules provide transparent control of transients while also adding warmth and character. These plug-ins are remarkable for their fuss-free GUIs which include just four control parameters. The apparent simplicity of the interface

Figure 13.34
The EMI TG12413 1969 version, providing high-quality vintage compression and limiting within a fuss-free interface

belies the range of processing possibilities. The TG12413 is full of character, can flatter almost any audio signal and, where appropriate, can produce extreme and intentionally audible compression effects.

EQ effects

EQ – supplied plug-ins

In addition to the built-in EQ of the Mixer, Cubase is supplied with the StudioEQ, GEQ-10 and GEQ-30 plug-ins. StudioEQ operates in a very similar manner to the built-in EQ (see Chapter 12 for details). The GEQ-10 and GEQ-30 are 10 band and 30 band graphic EQ units.

GEQ30 graphic equaliser

The GEQ30 plug-in (Figure 13.35) is a 30 band graphic equaliser divided into the usual thirty third-octave frequency bands. Like its hardware counterparts the GEQ30 is very easy to set up. All you need do is drag the faders in each band to the desired level. The GEQ30 provides 12dB of cut or boost in each band. Of course, the disadvantage of graphic EQs is their inability to change the centre frequency for each band. However, this does not detract from the fact that the GEQ30 is often extremely useful. For example, it is quick and easy to find problem resonances within a sound and reduce them, and by clicking on one slider and then dragging across the GUI you can quickly set the levels of all faders. Moreover, once you have set up an EQ curve you can modify the overall effect using the Range dial. This reduces the overall depth of the curve. The character of the EQ may be further modified using the filter response menu. Here, you can choose between a true response and various resonant modes for the filter bands. For example, it is worth trying Resonant mode where applying gain to any band also applies an amount of cut to the adjacent bands, or the musical sounding Variable Q mode where the resonance is decreased as the gain is increased and vice versa. Overall, the GEQ-30 and its little brother, the GEQ-10, make a refreshing change to the usual parametric EQs to which we have become so accustomed.

Figure 13.35
GEQ-30 graphic EQ

EQ – alternatives

It is worth having a number of EQ plug-ins from different developers in your collection. Each tends to impose a slightly different character on the treated sound and having a choice helps you find the most suitable EQ for each equalisation task. Among those worth exploring are Eiosis Air EQ, Kjaerhus GEQ7 Golden EQ, PSP MasterQ, PSP Neon, Sonalksis SV-517 equaliser, Sonnox Oxford EQ, TC Electronic Assimilator, UAD Cambridge EQ, UAD Neve 1073 EQ, Waves Linear Phase EQ and Waves Renaissance EQ.

Eiosis Air EQ

Eiosis Air EQ challenges traditional approaches to plug-in EQing. Most obvious is the absence of an EQ curve display. This avoids visual distractions and encourages you to listen to the sound in more detail. You may also choose to hide all frequency, gain, and Q indicators, and generally re-configure the interface to your own preferences.

Figure 13.36a
Eiosis Air EQ is especially suitable for tracking and mixing in Cubase

Air EQ includes 7 bands of EQ plus the 'air' EQ control itself. The main bands feature low and high pass filters in the lowest and uppermost positions with five parametric EQs in between. The lowest and highest of the latter may be switched between parametric or low / high shelving filters. The special 'air' band is designed to restore life into uninteresting sounds and add brightness and character without harshness. The supplied presets bank features combinations of EQ bands set up for specific instruments and tasks. Most presets feature each band labelled according to task rather than frequency with names such as density, presence, clarity, body, string noise, click and so on. This encourages intuitive use of the controls and helps you to quickly tune in to the desired part of the spectrum. Air EQ excels at boosting mid and upper frequencies and is good for sweetening and enlivening vocals and acoustic guitars. This plug-in uses very little CPU power and has zero latency, so it is especially suitable for tracking and mixing in Cubase.

Sonnox Oxford EQ

Among the EQ alternatives, the Sonnox Oxford EQ plug-in remains one of the most flexible. The Oxford EQ is based upon the EQ section of the renowned OXF-R3 console. The controls feature: variable slope high and low pass filters; low and high EQ switchable between shelving and parametric control; and low-mid, mid and high-mid parametric EQ. The overall characteristics may be modified using a four-position EQ type selector featuring: 1) clinical style EQ emulating the SSL 4000 series; 2) unsymmetrical boost / cut EQ curves suited to drums and percussion; 3) musical style EQ similar to Neve and SSL G series consoles; and 4) soft and gentle EQ for mastering and other applications.

Figure 13.36b
Sonnox Oxford EQ. High precision EQ for mixing and mastering

Filter effects

Filter – supplied plug-ins

ToneBooster

ToneBooster is a basic filter with centre frequency (tone), gain and width controls. It operates in either peak or bandpass mode. This is similar to a parametric EQ except that the gain control does not allow you to attenuate the level. Peak mode allows you to boost a single band within the signal and when width is set quite narrow (low values) produces resonant effects. Bandpass mode allows only those frequencies within the chosen bandwidth to pass through. This allows you to band limit sounds to specific frequency ranges which is occasionally useful for guitar, pad and synth sounds.

Figure 13.37
ToneBooster

WahWah

As the name suggests, the WahWah plug-in is specialised in the production of wah wah effects. Wah wah is created by sweeping a peak or bandpass filter up and down within the frequency spectrum. In WahWah the sweeping effect is created using the pedal control. This mimics the action of a real wah wah pedal. The low and high frequencies, bandwidth and gain change resulting from moving the pedal are regulated using the respective Lo and Hi controls. To get started, try selecting the 'Warm Wah' preset and then choose one of the following techniques for recording your pedal manipulations:

1 Select 'automation' in the menu below the pedal dial and activate the Write automation button of the plug-in. Commence playback and move the pedal dial as desired using the mouse. Stop playback when you have completed your automation recording. De-activate the Write button and activate the Read button. Commence playback again to hear the results.

2 Select 'modulation' in the menu below the pedal dial and select the WahWah plug-in as the output on a spare MIDI track. Record enable the chosen MIDI track. The pedal dial may now be controlled via the modulation wheel of your MIDI keyboard. Commence recording and move the pedal dial as desired. Replay the passage after recording to hear the results. After recording MIDI modulation data in this way, you may wish to edit it in one of the MIDI editors. Redrawing the curve with greater resolution gives a smoother wah wah effect.

Figure 13.38
WahWah plug-in and pedal automation curve in the project window

Filter – alternatives

There are a wide range of filter plug-in alternatives available including Native Instruments Reaktor Analogic Filter, Ohm Force Predatohm, PSP Nitro and Steinberg Metalizer, StepFilter and Tonic. See 'Additional Supplied Effects' below, for detailed coverage of Metalizer and StepFilter.

Modulation effects

Modulation – supplied plug-ins

Almost all the plug-ins in the modulation range may be synchronised to the tempo of Cubase. Overall, they are versatile effects which may be used on a wide variety of sounds. They are often the first choice for adding movement and excitement and are always worth trying in combination with other effects. Modulation effects are popular for guitar, bass, strings, organ and electric piano, and help thicken or sweeten almost anything in the mix. However, like most other effects they are best when not overused. There now follows more detailed descriptions of the Cloner and StudioChorus plug-ins.

Cloner

Cloner produces up to four copies of the input signal (known as voices) each of which can be delayed or detuned. The delay and detune sliders govern the relative proportions of delay and detune for each voice while the overall delay and detune depth is governed by the global delay and detune dials. The global delay and detune dial values may be 'humanised', meaning that subtle variations are introduced into the settings. The overall effect is spread across the stereo image using the spatial control. Cloner produces particularly clean and rich chorus effects which are difficult to match with traditional chorus devices. It is recommended for guitar, bass and voice doubling effects. Try the settings shown in Figure 13.39 for a voice doubling effect.

Figure 13.39
Cloner

StudioChorus

StudioChorus features two chorus units arranged in series, each with rate, width, spatial, mix, delay and low and high frequency roll-off filters. The delay control sets the basic delay value, rate governs the rate of an LFO which modulates the delay time, and width governs the depth of the effect. The LFO may be set to a sine or triangular wave and the rate may be synced to the tempo of Cubase. Cascading two units in series allows for the creation of some very rich chorus effects. Try the settings in Figure 13.40 for bass guitar.

Figure 13.40
StudioChorus

Modulation - alternatives

Modulation plug-in alternatives include Audio Ease Deep Phase Nine, Ohm Force Mobilohm, Universal Audio UAD-1 Dimension D, Voxengo Vintage Modulator, Waves MondoMod and Waves MetaFlanger, and many others. The UAD-1 Dimension D, for example, is an emulation of the original Roland Dimension D, a unique device with only four control buttons which may be activated in various combinations to produce warm and characterful chorus.

Other effects

Others – supplied plug-ins

Cubase provides Octaver and Tuner in the Others category. Octaver features only three controls: direct level, and octave 1 and 2 dials. The octave dials provide transposed copies of the input, one and two octaves down in pitch. Octaver might provide a solution when you wish to thicken synth sequences or simulate a bass line using a guitar.

Tuner is a pitch monitoring device which analyses the input and gives a reading of its pitch in terms of note value, frequency and octave. Deviations from the centre pitch position are measured in cents. This plug-in is intended as a software replacement for a guitar tuner and is therefore useful for tuning guitars and any other stringed instrument. The string is in tune when the two arrows are in the centre position pointing at the pitch value and the cent value equals zero.

Figure 13.41
Tuner. A software guitar tuner.

Others – alternatives

Plug-ins which fit into the 'others' category are often hybrid effects which combine techniques from the other more conventional processing techniques to produce something unique. Such is the case with Noveltech's Character and Vocal Enhancer plug-ins which run on the TC Powercore system. These allow you to capture the identity of a sound and then enhance this identity to make it stand out in the mix.

Also in the 'others' category are restoration and tape saturation emulation. For restoration, Bias Soundsoap, Steinberg De-noiser, Steinberg De-clicker and Waves X-noise come high on the list, and if you have the budget, the Cedar Audio restoration tools give excellent results. Tape saturation emulation is of great value to digital audio since it can add character and warmth when a digital recording sounds cold and lifeless. Tape saturation emulation has proved difficult to reproduce digitally. Among the finest efforts among VST plug-ins are the PSP Vintage Warmer and Voxengo AnalogFlux Tape Bus.

PSP Vintage Warmer

Vintage Warmer (Figure 13.42) combines compression, limiting, and tape saturation emulation. It may be used as a single or multi-band compressor, or as a brick-wall limiter, so it is equally at home in the dynamics category of plug-ins. Its overload characteristics produce warm saturation reminiscent of analogue tape. This can help remedy the problems of Cubase users suffering from cold, brittle or characterless digital recordings.

Figure 13.42
PSP Vintage Warmer

The heart of the device is in the drive, knee and speed dials. Drive regulates the amount of input gain, allowing you to boost or attenuate the signal passing to the compressor / limiter. Knee sets up the characteristics of the compressor / limiter where low settings produce hard knee limiting effects while higher settings produce fast soft knee compression. Knee dial settings around 50% are often the best for tape saturation emulation. The speed dial produces slower attack / release behaviour at low settings and faster attack / release behaviour at higher settings. The other controls include a release multiplier dial which modifies the release time established with the speed dial according to a multiplication factor, a ceiling control which sets the peak level above which the output signal is not allowed to pass, and low / high shelving EQ (single band mode) or three-band pre-limiter level adjustment (multi-band mode). Vintage style VU / PPM meters and toggle switches for single-band / multi-band, stereo / mono and stereo link on / off modes complete the picture.

Vintage Warmer works equally well on individual tracks, whole mixes or as a mastering effect. To become familiar with its operation, try moving the controls in broad strokes at first, and then back off the effect until it is just noticeable. The knee dial can have a dramatic effect on the density, punch and impact of the sound. Take care to not overdo the effect.

Voxengo AnalogFlux Tape Bus

Voxengo's AnalogFlux series of plug-ins are all about emulating analogue warmth and one of the best in the collection is Tape Bus which emulates analogue tape. Seven tape impulses are provided, each of which imposes a different tape-style colouration upon the signal. Other controls include record gain, low and high EQ, a saturation curve dial for regulating the harmonic

Figure 13.43
Voxengo AnalogFlux Tape Bus

content of the saturation, and frequency and gain dials for the pre-emphasis high-shelf filter. Push the record gain up to achieve more saturation. The distortion meter between the Out and Curve controls gives an indication of how much saturation is taking place. Try the settings in Figure 13.43 to enliven dull-sounding drum kits and loops.

Reverb effects

Reverb – supplied plug-ins
At the time of writing the main reverb plug-in supplied with Cubase is Roomworks. This provides good results with drums and other sounds which need to be placed in small to medium size acoustic spaces.

Roomworks
Roomworks is a reverberation device for the simulation of rooms and acoustic spaces (Figure 13.44). The interface includes the following parameters:

• Low shelf input filter – provides low frequency cut or boost (-18dB to +6dB) below the selected frequency cut-off point (25Hz – 6kHz). This filtering is pre-reverb.
• High shelf input filter – provides high frequency cut or boost (-18dB to +6dB) above the selected frequency cut-off point (250Hz – 22kHz). This filtering is pre-reverb.
• pre-delay – sets the delay between the initial sound and the onset of the reverb (0-500ms).
• Reverb Time – sets the duration of the reverb (100ms – 20s).
• Size – governs the size of the simulated room (20 – 250 cubic metres).

Figure 13.44
Roomworks

- Diffusion – determines the amount of diffusion in the simulated room (0 – 100%).
- Width – governs the width of the stereo effect of the reverb (0 – 100%).
- Variation button – each time this button is pressed a new variable is introduced into the reverb algorithm to create a slightly different sound.
- Hold button – when enabled, holds the reverb effect infinitely.
- Low frequency damping filter – dampens or emphasises the low frequency content (10% – 400%) around the chosen cut-off point (25Hz – 1kHz). This filtering is post-reverb.
- High frequency damping filter – dampens or emphasises the high frequency content (10% – 400%) around the chosen cut-off point (500Hz – 22kHz). This filtering is post-reverb.
- Envelope amount, attack and release controls – trims the overall contour of the reverberation result.
- Mix – determines the proportion of wet and dry signals at the output (0% = dry, 100% = wet). If you are using the unit as a send effect, activate the 'wet only' button which locks the mix output at 100% wet.
- Efficiency – determines the liveliness (amount of absorption) in the simulated room (0-100%).
- Export button – when enabled, optimises the reverb signal for maximum quality during Export / Audio Mixdown operations.

Roomworks' main strengths are the pre and post reverb filtering which allow excellent fine tuning of the character of the reverb. After setting up the pre-delay, time, size and diffusion parameters to achieve a basic sound, the real soul of Roomworks is found in the low and high damping controls. Juggling the four parameters of the damping section allows the creation of a wide range of effects. The overall shape of the results can be still further modified using the controls in the envelope section.

The unit is supplied with a good range of presets. It works particularly well with drums and can place snares and overall kits in a variety of reverberant spaces with convincing ease. It excels at producing small and medium sized room simulations and provides adequate results for vocals if you do not have access to a high end hardware unit or convolution plug-in. Roomworks would normally be used as a Send effect and in this capacity the wet only button would usually be activated to provide a 100% wet signal from the unit.

Reverb – alternatives

Reverb is an essential effect in any studio setup and many Cubase users seek out units from other developers. The main categories include hardware units, convolution software plug-ins, or algorithmic software plug-ins (non-convolution). Hardware units have the advantage of greater DSP power for the complex processing needed to simulate reverb and this takes place without use of the CPU in the host computer. Software convolution reverb plug-ins use impulse responses taken from real acoustic spaces and produce very convincing results. Algorithmic software reverb plug-ins use similar processing techniques to conventional hardware units. Both of the latter techniques use the host CPU for all processing, which might be disadvantageous if you have limited CPU power.

There are a wide range of reverb devices available. In the hardware category, the Lexicon MX300, MX500 and other Lexicon units are worth considering. Of particular note in the software category are Audio Ease Altiverb, Sir Convolution reverb, Sonnox Oxford Reverb, Universal Audio UAD Plate 140 and Voxengo Pristine Space Convolution Processor. Sir is a free download and, for those on a tight budget, neatly compensates for the lack of convolution reverb in Cubase. The Universal Audio Plate 140 is one of the better non-convolution software reverbs providing a highly convincing emulation of the original EMT 140 plate reverb (this requires a UAD-1 card installed in the host computer). Altiverb and Pristine Space are worth covering here in more detail.

Audio Ease Altiverb

Altiverb is renowned as the industry standard convolution reverb plug-in. The GUI is laid out like a classic rackmount unit with a centrally placed display showing either an impulse response browser, a waterfall diagram or a waveform diagram. Its main control parameters include reverb length, room size, wet / dry mix, damping, early reflections, reverb tail, stage position and EQ.

Audio Ease encourage you to think of Altiverb as an echo chamber where the input to the unit passes through one or two speakers placed in the chamber and the output is produced via microphones which pick up the reverberation in the chamber. This set up is indeed how most of the impulse responses are recorded and Altiverb allows you to view a diagram of the placement of the speakers and microphones within the chosen acoustic space. Furthermore, you can modify the position of the speakers relative to the microphones using the stage position controls, thus producing a corresponding modification in the reverberation. In addition to all this, a virtual reality movie, photographs and detailed recording information are provided for each acoustic space which help you gain a real appreciation of the kind of space in which you are placing your material.

Figure 13.45
Audio Ease Altiverb. Probably the ultimate convolution reverb.

The essential strength of Altiverb is its vast library of impulse responses and the precision with which they are recorded. The library features a wide range of cathedrals, churches, halls, small rooms, scoring stages, and stadiums as well as vintage reverb device and abstract sound design impulses. The locations range from the Mechanics Hall, Worcester, USA to the Antwerp Sports Stadium, Belgium to the Vienna Konzerthaus Mozart Hall, Austria to the Sydney Opera House, Australia, so you can literally travel the world of reverberation.

Like all convolution reverb plug-ins, using Altiverb may result in slightly more load on the CPU of the host computer, when compared to an average plug-in. It may also take a few seconds to read the impulse response cache file each time you activate it. However, these are extremely small issues and Altiverb is no ordinary plug-in. Overall, Altiverb offers access to a whole new world of reverberation treasures and could justifiably be described as the ultimate convolution reverb plug-in. It is particularly suitable for those seeking convincing emulation of the reverberant behaviour of real acoustic spaces. In Cubase, it is best used as a send effect.

Voxengo Pristine Space

Voxengo Pristine Space is an 8-channel convolution reverb processor. Its multi-channel capability means that you can implement simultaneous multiple reverb effects. For example, this allows you to mix the early reflection part

Figure 13.46
Voxengo Pristine Space

of one impulse response with the reverb tail of another, or simulate the effect of overhead mics and ambient room mics for an acoustic drum kit using two different impulses. For sound design and special effects, you can arrange a number of reverb effects in series.

Pristine Space provides control curves for the time-based modification of volume, stereo width, pan position, high and low pass filtering and overall EQ. This is achieved using multiple breakpoint envelopes in a graphical display. In addition, offset, length, delay, gain and reverse controls are provided for each impulse response. The eight channels are normally arranged in four stereo pairs. Preset configurations are supplied for true stereo reverb insert, true stereo reverb send, 2-step 2-channel serial insert and so on, which helps you quickly set up the device for use as an insert or send effect in Cubase. The impulse responses are loaded into one of eight slots and each slot is colour-coded, which helps clarify what you are editing when working with multiple reverbs.

Overall, Pristine Space is an excellent reverb alternative for Cubase users and is particularly good for experimental work and sound design. It is not supplied with its own library of impulse responses. Instead, it relies upon the free IR files available for download on the internet or you can design your own using Voxengo's Impulse Modeller plug-in. Similar to other software convolution reverb plug-ins Pristine Space may result in slightly more load on the CPU of the host computer, when compared to an average plug-in. For this reason, it is best activated in a single instance as a send effect.

Additional supplied effects

A number of additional effects are supplied in the Additional Content folder of the installation DVD. You also have the option of installing older plug-ins from previous versions of Cubase if they are still present on your hard disk. The following outlines the operation of three of the best of the earlier range of plug-ins: Metalizer, Quadrafuzz and StepFilter.

Metalizer

Metalizer is a variable band-pass filtering device with tempo or time based frequency band modulation (Figure 13.47). The GUI includes the following parameters:

- Feedback – regulates the resonance of the effect. Higher settings produce more resonance. Range 0 – 100%.
- Sharpness – governs the narrowness of the bandpass filter. Higher settings produce a narrower pass band and thus a sharper tone. Range 0 – 100%.
- Tone – regulates the frequency content of the effect. Lower settings emphasise the mid-range frequencies while higher settings emphasise the upper frequencies. Range 0 – 100%.
- Modulation on/off button – when activated, moves the band-pass filter up and down the frequency axis to produce 'wah-wah' effects.
- Modulation speed dial – regulates the speed of the modulation

Figure 13.47
Metalizer

effect according to a frequency in Hertz, if the sync button is de-activated (Range: 0 – 10Hz), or according to a note division of the bar, if the sync button is activated.

- Tempo sync pop-up – offers a choice of tempo synchronised note value settings in tempo sync mode, providing a way of matching the modulation effect to the tempo of the music. Range: whole note to 1/32 note, whole note triplets to 1/32 note triplets, dotted whole note to dotted 1/32 note.
- Sync button – activates/de-activates tempo synchronisation.
- Mono/stereo button – toggles between mono or stereo output.
- Output slider – regulates the level of the output signal. Range: 0 – 100%.
- Mix slider – determines the proportion of wet and dry signal output from the effect where 0% is no effect and 100% is fully wet. Range: 0 – 100%

Metalizer produces a range of effects from flange-like sounds and wah-wah to extreme notch filtering effects. The heart of Metalizer is the sharpness dial. This governs the essential quality of the effect and the higher its setting the narrower the band-pass filter, as shown in the graphic display. The tone and feedback dials affect the high frequency and resonant content of the effect and this is reflected in the display by the density and brightness of the wave-form inside the filter curve. Switching in the filter band modulation allows time or tempo-based modulation of the filtered frequency band up and down the frequency axis for the production of classic wah-wah and other swept filter effects. The mono/stereo button is a welcome feature since it helps create simple centred monophonic effects as well as those which are swept across the stereo image. Clicking and dragging directly in the graphic display allows the simultaneous adjustment of the sharpness and tone controls. Metalizer is excellent for wah-wah and other filtering effects and is particularly suitable for the production of special effects. It works best on harmonically rich sound sources like strings, distortion guitars and complex synth sounds. Metalizer is suitable for use as an insert or send effect.

QuadraFuzz

QuadraFuzz is a multi-band distortion device providing level control in four frequency bands both before and after distortion. In addition, the width of each frequency band is user-configurable (Figure 13.48).

The interface features the following parameters:

Figure 13.48
QuadraFuzz

Main section

- Gain dial – determines the overall input gain for the device. The 'Over' clipping LED is illuminated if you apply too much input gain. Range: –20dB to +20dB.
- Low, Low mid, High mid, High dials – regulate the outputs from the four frequency bands after distortion. Range: –12dB to +12dB.
- Output dial – regulates the overall output level. –20dB to +20dB.
- Preset slider – allows the selection of the available presets in the current bank.
- Edit button – opens the extended editing section (see below).

Extended section

- Dual function input level / frequency band selector display – the frequency spectrum is divided into four zones according to the positions of four user-configurable selector bands. These bands act upon the input signal before distortion. The level of each band is changed by dragging the top handle vertically. Note that this level affects the overall gain set with the main panel's Gain control and can therefore cause clipping, (indicated by the the 'Over' clipping LED). The frequency crossover points for each band is adjusted by dragging the lower handles horizontally. Scale: –20dB to +20dB (vertical), 25Hz to 22kHz (horizontal).
- Transfer shape selector buttons – determine the transfer function which produces the distortion effect (five buttons).
- Delete button – deletes the currently selected preset.
- Create button – stores the current settings as a preset. All presets are saved with the project.
- Solo button – solos the currently selected frequency band allowing you to hear the distortion effect in one band alone.

QuadraFuzz was originally a hardware circuit designed by Craig Anderton, hence the Craig Anderton signature on the front panel. Spectral Design have expanded on the original concept by providing control over the width of the frequency bands before distortion. This, coupled with the fact that you have control over the level of the frequency bands both before and after distortion, produces a distortion device of extremely wide ranging capabilities.

You can use QuadraFuzz as mainly a preset device by operating in the main window only, and testing the unit with the supplied presets shows how you can create effects of extreme subtlety through to manic overdrive. The heart of the device is in the edit window and this is where you need to go if you want to radically change the existing presets or create your own. Like many distortion devices, you need to maintain a balance between the input and output stages since applying radical distortion can create radical level changes. Try using the solo button while making changes in the frequency band selector display. This helps you judge more precisely the result of each change you make. The distortion itself is applied to the signal according to your choice of transfer function (Shape button). A transfer function is a function which governs the relationship between the amplitude of an input and output signal which pass through it.

Changing the shape of this function affects the waveform of the output signal in various ways, producing different types of distortion. The shapes you see on each button give a rough indication of the kind of transfer function which has been used and the lower the button you select the more harmonics are added to the signal. The point to remember here is that the harmonic distortion is only added to those parts of the signal you choose using the frequency selectors, and how much distortion applied to each band depends on the levels you set. QuadraFuzz is, of course, well suited to the production of all types of fuzz guitar effects but it is also excellent for synth sounds and for subtly highlighting or completely mangling drum and percussion sounds. It might also be used for adding subtle warmth and character to certain frequencies within a mix. QuadraFuzz is suitable for use as an insert effect or a send effect and, for subtle treatments within a mix, might occasionally be used as an insert on the stereo output buss.

StepFilter

StepFilter is versatile step-based and static filter device suitable for rhythmic, tempo-linked and traditional filtering effects (Figure 13.49).

The interface features the following parameters:

- Cut-off point step display – a 16 step entry grid which functions when the tempo synchronisation button (Sync button) is activated. The horizontal axis represents 16 note divisions at the resolution chosen in the tempo sync field (see below). The vertical axis represents the cut-off frequency setting which is chosen using a draggable blue marker.
- Resonance step display – a 16 step entry grid which functions when the tempo synchronisation button (Sync button) is activated. The horizontal axis represents 16 note divisions at the resolution chosen in the tempo sync field (see below). The vertical axis represents the resonance setting which is chosen using a draggable blue marker.
- Base cut-off dial – determines the base frequency for the cut-off frequency i.e. the values shown in the cut-off point step display are relative to the value chosen here. Range: 0-100.
- Base Resonance dial – determines the base value for the resonance amount i.e. the values shown in the resonance step display are relative to the value chosen here. Range: 0-100.
- Glide dial – implements smooth transitions between each filter step. Range: 0 – 100%.
- Filter mode slider – selects low-pass, band-pass and high-pass filter types, (see the section entitled 'Audio effects in theory' at the beginning of this chapter for more details about filter types).
- Pattern selector – provides eight internal storage slots for the saving of cut-off and resonance patterns. These are saved with the current project but for global availability you must save them with the file save options at the top of the window.
- Copy and Paste buttons – provide copy and paste functions for copying cut-off and resonance patterns. This helps build up variations on the same theme.
- Sync button – activates/de-activates tempo synchronisation.

- Tempo sync field – offers a choice of tempo synchronised note value settings which determine the resolution of the cut-off point step display and resonance step display. Click on the tempo sync field to open the pop-up menu. Range: whole note to 1/32 note, whole note triplets to 1/32 note triplets, dotted whole note to dotted 1/32 note.
- Output slider – regulates the level of the output signal. Range: 0 – 100%.
- Mix slider – determines the proportion of wet and dry signal output from the effect where 0% is no effect and 100% is fully wet. Range: 0-100%

Figure 13.49
StepFilter

The first thing to try with StepFilter is to play a drum loop in cycle playback mode and check out the various patterns in the Examples preset. Try changing the tempo sync value to 1/8, 1/16 and 1/32 notes with pattern 1 selected. Next, listen to the effect of changing the base cut-off and base resonance dials. Be careful with your speakers and your ears! At high resonance levels this can produce piercing ringing effects. Now move on to the cut-off and resonance displays themselves. Simply drag the mouse in the displays to set up your own patterns. The cut-off and resonance values of the two displays are stepped through simultaneously. If you want just straight filtering, de-activate the sync button. At this point in time, all step sequencing functions are de-activated. However, the first markers in each of the cut-off and resonance displays remain active as do the base dials and the filter type slider. StepFilter is an extremely expressive and responsive device, even in this static mode and, if you wish, the movements you make can be automated by activating the Read and Write buttons. StepFilter is superb for setting up filtering effects on dance tracks and works wonders with drum loops. Virtually any other kind of material can also be processed. StepFilter is normally used as an insert effect.

Powered plug-ins

There are a number of so-called powered plug-ins available which are worth considering for use with Cubase. These take the form of software plug-ins, which appear within Cubase in the usual manner, combined with a hardware component like a rackmount unit or PCI / PC Express card. The hardware takes care of most of the digital signal processing, thus relieving the host CPU of the burden, and simultaneously doubles as a copy protection device. Devices included in this category are the UAD powered plug-ins, which run on a dedicated PCI or PCI Express card and the TC Electronics Powercore system which is run using a PCI card or an external unit connected by Firewire. Similarly, the SSL Duende system features a rackmount unit connected to the host computer via a Firewire cable providing up to 32 channels of high-end SSL EQ and dynamics processing.

Powered plug-ins are a good choice for those who wish to use high-end plug-ins without unnecessary load on the CPU of the host computer. Any of the solutions mentioned here are compatible with Cubase.

Integrating external hardware effects units

While the supplied plug-in effects are good, processing such as reverb is still often best handled using an external unit. A common requirement is the need to integrate the external unit into the mixer of Cubase so that you can use it in much the same way as an internal plug-in. Luckily, Cubase features a special External FX plug-in module designed specifically to make the integration of external effects a painless process. This is possible only if you have audio hardware with multiple inputs and outputs, since you need to route the effects signal out of and back into Cubase via additional busses, (separate from the main input / output busses). To integrate an external send effect, proceed as follows:

- Open the VST Connections window (Devices menu or press F4) and select the External FX tab. Add a new External FX buss and activate the desired input and output ports corresponding to the physical inputs and outputs to which you are connecting the external unit. Name the new buss as appropriate. Leave the delay, send gain and return gain columns at their default zero settings (Figure 13.50)

Figure 13.50
Set up the external FX buss in the VST Connections window

- Connect your external effects device to the physical inputs and outputs associated with the new External FX buss you created in the previous step.
- In the Mixer, add a new FX channel (Project / Add track / FX channel). In the pop-up dialogue which appears adjust the configuration to match the number of channels on the external unit (usually mono or stereo). Select the External plug-ins sub-menu and choose the appropriate external effect from the list (Figure 13.51). You have now created a send effect which routes the send and return signals to/from the external device.
- When the external FX channel is first created, the External FX interface appears automatically on the screen (Figure 13.52). Here you can adjust the send and return levels and, if necessary, configure the delay time so that Cubase can compensate during playback. A delay time may be required if your external unit introduces latency into the signal path. (Note that the

Figure 13.51
Create a new External FX channel

Figure 13.52
Set up the external FX settings in the
External FX interface

latency of your audio hardware has already been taken into account in this
process and should not be entered here). Typically, the latency time is 0ms
or values between 0.5 and 2ms, depending upon the external device.
Compressor/limiters are likely to introduce slight latencies and should be set
up carefully. To help find out the exact time required, the interface features a
'ping' button. This sends a short pulse to your external unit and measures
the time it takes to come back via the return line. When measuring the
latency in this way, temporarily reduce all delay parameters in your external
unit to zero or use a bypass button (if available) to avoid measuring the
delay in the effect rather than the latency in the signal path.

- If the external unit is a reverb device you would normally set it up to
produce a 100% wet signal at its output since, here, we have created a
send effect.
- You can now send a signal to the external effect in exactly the same way
as you would for an internal send effect. Choose an audio-based track to
which you wish to apply the effect and open its send panel. Activate the
External effect in one of the send slots. Adjust the send level using the
mini-fader in the send slot. Insert effects are set up in a similar manner.

Info

Unlike conventional plug-ins, only
one instance of each external
hardware effect may be activated in
the Mixer. For this reason, the
integration of external hardware
devices is best suited to effects like
reverb, which can be set up as a
single-instance auxiliary send on an
FX channel, or mastering
processing, which can be set up as
a single-instance insert on the main
stereo output buss.

Combination processing

If you have enough processing power you can achieve some creative effects by
using more than one unit as an insert effect. Try the following combinations:

- Compression followed by overdrive distortion (typically used by guitarists
to achieve more sustain).
- Compression followed by filtering.
- Delay followed by chorus/flange.
- Distortion followed by chorus/flange.
- Phasing followed by wah wah.
- Tremolo followed by autopan.
- Reverb followed by phasing.
- Filtering followed by delay.

Experimentation can yield some surprisingly good effects and if you are feel-
ing really adventurous try using combinations of three or four effects / pro-

cessors. In addition to using insert effects, you could also simultaneously incorporate one or more send effects.

Plug-in information

To see an overview of all the plug-ins installed in your system, select 'Plugin Information' from the Devices menu. This opens the Plug-in Information window (Figure 13.53) where the plug-ins are arranged in a list with columns showing the important characteristics of each device. Here, you can check out the number of inputs and outputs, the latency, category, version number and so on, for each plug-in. The leftmost column allows you to de-activate those plug-ins you never use by unchecking the tick box. This de-activates the plug-in in Cubase but it remains installed on your computer. You can, at any time in the future, re-activate it. Using the tabs at the top of the window you can view the different types of plug-ins currently installed within Cubase.

Figure 13.53
Plug-in Information window

A	In	↗	Name	Vendor	File	Path	Category	I/O	SDK	Latency	V
✔	1		Altiverb 6	Audio Ease	Altiverb 6.dll	C:\Program Files\Steinberg\VstPlugins\Audio Ease	Fx\Reverb	5.1 / 5.1	VST 2.3	-	
✔	1		AmpSimulator	Steinberg Media Technologies	Cubase Plug-in Set.vst3	C:\Program Files\Steinberg\Cubase 4\VST3	Fx\Distortion	Stereo / Stereo	VST 3.0	-	
✔	-		AudioTrack	Waves	WaveShell.dll	C:\Program Files\Steinberg\VstPlugins	Fx	Stereo / Stereo	VST 2.3		
✔	-		AudioTrack Mono	Waves	WaveShell.dll	C:\Program Files\Steinberg\VstPlugins	Fx	Mono / Mono	VST 2.3		
✔	-		AutoPan	Unknown	AutoPan.dll	C:\Program Files\Steinberg\VstPlugins	Fx	Mono / Stereo	VST 1.0		
✔	-		AutoPan	Steinberg Media Technologies	Cubase Plug-in Set.vst3	C:\Program Files\Steinberg\Cubase 4\VST3	Fx\Modulation	Stereo / Stereo	VST 3.0	-	
✔	-		B4	Native Instruments	B4.DLL	C:\Program Files\Steinberg\VstPlugins\02 NI	Instrument	Stereo	VST 2.1	-	
✔	-		B4fx	Native Instruments	B4fx.dll	C:\Program Files\Steinberg\VstPlugins\02 NI	Fx	Mono / Stereo	VST 2.1	-	
✔	-		Battery	Native Instruments	Battery.dll	C:\Program Files\Steinberg\VstPlugins\02 NI	Instrument	Multi (10)	VST 2.1	-	
✔	-		BitCrusher	Steinberg Media Technologies	BitCrusher.dll	C:\Program Files\Steinberg\Cubase 4\VSTPlugins\Other	Fx	Stereo / Stereo	VST 2.4	-	
✔	1		C1 comp	Waves	WaveShell.dll	C:\Program Files\Steinberg\VstPlugins	Fx	Stereo / Stereo	VST 2.3		
✔	-		C1 comp Mono	Waves	WaveShell.dll	C:\Program Files\Steinberg\VstPlugins	Fx	Mono / Mono	VST 2.3		
✔	-		C1 comp-gate	Waves	WaveShell.dll	C:\Program Files\Steinberg\VstPlugins	Fx	Stereo / Stereo	VST 2.3	340	
✔	-		C1 comp-gate Mono	Waves	WaveShell.dll	C:\Program Files\Steinberg\VstPlugins	Fx	Mono / Mono	VST 2.3	340	
✔	-		C1 comp-sc	Waves	WaveShell.dll	C:\Program Files\Steinberg\VstPlugins	Fx	Stereo / Stereo	VST 2.3	340	
✔	-		C1 comp-sc Mono	Waves	WaveShell.dll	C:\Program Files\Steinberg\VstPlugins	Fx	Mono / Mono	VST 2.3	340	
✔	1		C1 gate	Waves	WaveShell.dll	C:\Program Files\Steinberg\VstPlugins	Fx	Stereo / Stereo	VST 2.3	-	
✔	-		C1 gate Mono	Waves	WaveShell.dll	C:\Program Files\Steinberg\VstPlugins	Fx	Mono / Mono	VST 2.3	-	
✔	-		C4	Waves	WaveShell.dll	C:\Program Files\Steinberg\VstPlugins	Fx	Stereo / Stereo	VST 2.3	64	
✔	-		C4 Mono	Waves	WaveShell.dll	C:\Program Files\Steinberg\VstPlugins	Fx	Mono / Mono	VST 2.3	64	
✔	-		Choirus2	Unknown	Choirus2.dll	C:\Program Files\Steinberg\VstPlugins	Fx	Mono / Stereo	VST 1.0	-	
✔	-		Chopper	Steinberg Media Technologies	Chopper.dll	C:\Program Files\Steinberg\Cubase 4\VSTPlugins\Other	Fx	Stereo / Stereo	VST 2.4	-	
✔	-		CleanComp	Unknown	CleanComp.dll	C:\Program Files\Steinberg\Cubase 4\VST3	Fx	Stereo / Stereo	VST 2.3	5511	
✔	1		Cloner	Steinberg Media Technologies	Cubase Plug-in Set.vst3	C:\Program Files\Steinberg\Cubase 4\VST3	Fx\Modulation	Stereo / Stereo	VST 3.0	4410	
✔	1		Compressor	Steinberg Media Technologies	Cubase Plug-in Set.vst3	C:\Program Files\Steinberg\Cubase 4\VST3	Fx\Dynamics	Stereo / Stereo	VST 3.0	88	
✔	-		DaTube	Steinberg Media Technologies	DaTube.dll	C:\Program Files\Steinberg\Cubase 4\VSTPlugins\Distortion	Fx	Stereo / Stereo	VST 2.4	-	
✔	-		DeEsser	Steinberg Media Technologies	DeEsser.dll	C:\Program Files\Steinberg\Cubase 4\VSTPlugins\Dynamics	Fx\Mastering	Stereo / Stereo	VST 2.2	683	
✔	-		DeEsser	Waves	WaveShell.dll	C:\Program Files\Steinberg\VstPlugins	Fx	Stereo / Stereo	VST 2.3	-	
✔	-		DeEsser Mono	Waves	WaveShell.dll	C:\Program Files\Steinberg\VstPlugins	Fx	Mono / Mono	VST 2.3	-	
✔	-		Doppler	Waves	WaveShell.dll	C:\Program Files\Steinberg\VstPlugins	Fx	Stereo / Stereo	VST 2.3	-	
✔	-		Doppler m/s	Waves	WaveShell.dll	C:\Program Files\Steinberg\VstPlugins	Fx	Mono / Stereo	VST 2.3	-	
✔	-		Embracer	Steinberg Media Technologies	Embracer.dll	C:\Program Files\Steinberg\Cubase 4\VSTPlugins\Synth	Instrument	Multi (2)	VST 2.3	-	

Mastering

What is mastering and what is a master?

'Mastering' is a final editing and processing stage which comes after mixing. Officially, this stage is referred to as 'pre-mastering', since it takes place before the 'real' master (the glass master) is produced at the CD duplication factory. For most of us, mastering is understood to mean the same as pre-mastering. Here, you might adjust the final sound quality using any combination of EQ, filtering, compression, expansion, loudness maximisation, stereo processing, harmonic excitation, dithering or other processes, and you might also adjust the order, spacing, lengths and levels for a group of mixes intended as the tracks for a CD.

In broad terms, a 'master' is a final high quality recording from which copies can be made. This could be a master produced within Cubase, or the master produced after a final mastering stage in other software or in a professional mastering house. A master may also be referred to as a 'pre-master'.

For commercial releases, the mastering stage often takes place under the direction of a highly experienced professional mastering engineer. While professional mastering of your mixes is likely to give better quality results, doing it yourself and producing your own factory-ready CD master is certainly possible (CD duplication plants readily accept masters in red-book CD audio format).

Mastering decisions

The way you approach mastering is highly dependent upon the nature of your project and your personal preferences, but assembling the tracks for a CD master would normally involve the following steps:

- General editing decisions such as removing clicks, topping and tailing and adjusting track lengths
- Deciding the track order and the spacing between tracks
- Expansion / compression, equalisation and other sound processing decisions
- Fading, levelling and limiting decisions
- Dithering and truncating the bit-depth to 16-bit
- CD track indexing and burning of the final Red Book audio CD

Info

Mastering is the final stage in a chain of processes which contribute to the production of a finished musical work or recording project. These processes include: composition, arrangement, performance, recording, mixing and mastering.

Info

Many professional mastering houses master to DDP (Disc Description Protocol) on Exabyte tape. This helps optimise results since DDP is not subject to the same error rate and handling difficulties as CDR.

The mastering stage may be the first time that you hear your group of finished mixes one after the other and at this point you may hear some surprising differences between the overall sound quality and perceived loudness of each track. These are the kinds of elements which need correction during the mastering session, so that you finish up with a homogenous set of tracks. However, it is important to bear in mind that the way in which you use sound processing in a stereo mix at the mastering stage is very different to the way in which you use it on individual instruments at the mixing stage. For example, emphasising the snare using EQ also affects the vocal and bringing out the bass drum may also affect the bass guitar. The sound processing settings for mastering, therefore, are likely to be far less radical. In this context, it is vitally important that you use an accurate monitoring system in an acoustically balanced listening space, otherwise the subtleties of the mastering process cannot be judged correctly.

If your mixes are already sounding exactly the way you wish then further modification with mastering processing may no longer be necessary. In this case, the remaining mastering decisions would involve the track order and spacings, dithering and truncating to 16-bit and indexing and burning the CD.

Mastering in Cubase

Although it may be preferable to use a specialised program for mastering (such as Steinberg Wavelab or Bias Peak), almost all of the mastering steps suggested above can be applied within Cubase. The one exception is the final step of creating track indexes and burning the CD. Cubase is not designed for the detailed preparation of the track list for a CD and integrated CD burning is not included. For some suggestions about how to approach CD burning, see 'Burning the CD', below.

The remainder of this section details how to set up Cubase for a mastering session and suggests some mastering plug-in chains for the insert slots of the stereo master output bus.

Creating a mastering template

Cubase is supplied with a mastering template but it is a good idea to create your own personalised version which you can use to start each mastering session. This streamlines the project for the usual mastering operations. Try the following:

- Select 'New Project' in the File menu.
- In the dialogue which appears, click on 'Empty'. Select the directory where you wish to create the folder for the project and click on the 'Create' button. Enter a name for the new project folder in the 'Create new directory' pop-up box which appears. Click on OK to open the empty project.
- In the Project Setup dialogue (Project menu), enter a suitable length for the project in the Length field. If you expect to work with the standard audio CD format you might like to enter the normal audio CD duration (74 minutes). Select 'seconds' in the Display format field. Enter your preferred sample rate and record format in the respective fields (24-bit or 32-bit float is normally appropriate).

Figure 14.1
Stereo mastering template in Cubase

- Open the Control Room Mixer in extended mode, configured to show only the control room headphones and monitor levels with the large-scale meters displayed in the extended section. This provides a clearly visible stereo level meter and mono/stereo compatibility switching using the cycle downmix preset selection button. Place the Control Room Mixer to the right of a suitably sized Project window as shown in Figure 14.1.
- Add two stereo audio tracks in the Project window. Name the first track 'CD tracks' and the second 'Editing' (for example). The first track is for your CD tracks and the second is for rough editing purposes. This is assuming that you intend to pass all the CD tracks through the same mastering processing of the stereo master output buss. However, if it is your intention to apply separate real-time processing on each CD track then you may need to put each song on a different audio track in the Project window. Alternatively, you could automate the processing. If desired, add the Marker track for navigation purposes.
- Resize all tracks as appropriate and select seconds in the Project window ruler. Activate the overview button to help with zooming and navigating within your mastering project. Try setting the Snap mode to Shuffle. In Shuffle mode, all events on a track are tightly snapped one against the other and the order may be changed by dragging one event in between

two others. This is excellent for quickly re-ordering CD tracks.

- For spacing, try preparing empty audio events of various lengths (1, 2 and 3secs, for example) and store these on the rough editing track. In shuffle mode these can be inserted between two CD tracks at any time by holding Alt and dragging a copy of the event to the desired join between two tracks. A green insert marker is displayed.
- Click on the edit button of either of the tracks to open the Channel settings window. Arrange the Channel settings window below the Project window as shown in Figure 14.1. Customise the view to show inserts, EQ and fader.
- In the 'Choose edit channel' menu of the Channel settings window select the main stereo output buss. Set up your chain of mastering plug-ins in the insert slots. You might like to activate the Limiter and UV22HR in slots 7 and 8. For CD mastering set the UV22HR to Normal / 16-bit. If desired, add other processors in the remaining slots.
- Arrange the Transport panel and the GUIs for your plug-ins in the remaining screen space. If required, activate the large-scale time display and VST performance windows from the Device menu. A large-scale time display is easier to see and the VST performance window helps you keep an eye on the current CPU overhead.
- Save the project as a template using 'Save as template' (File menu). Enter a name such as 'stereo mastering' into the pop-up dialogue to save the project in the Templates folder. Now, whenever it is your intention to do a mastering session, you can load your mastering template from the list of templates which appears when you select 'New Project' (File menu).

Typical mastering plug-in processing chains

The processing chains shown below might typically be found in the insert slots of the stereo master output buss during a mastering session. While it is possible to use various of the supplied plug-ins for mastering purposes, mastering quality EQ, compression and limiting normally requires high precision plug-ins designed specifically for the purpose. Therefore, some of the plug ins shown in these examples are from alternative plug-in developers. To get started with mastering try the following processing chains:

1 High quality mastering

A high-quality mastering chain featuring linear phase equalisation, linear phase multi-band compression, loudness maximisation, limiting, and dithering (Figure 14.2). Alternatives from the plug-ins supplied with Cubase are shown in brackets.

- Slot 1: PSP Audioware Neon EQ (or the supplied Studio EQ)
- Slot 2: Waves Linear Phase Multiband Compressor (or the supplied MultibandCompressor)
- Slot 7: Waves L1 or L2 Ultramiximiser (or the supplied Limiter in slot 7 and UV22HR in slot 8)

Figure 14.2
High quality mastering plug-in chain

2 Classic mastering chain for adding warmth and character

A digital mix suffering from a cold, brittle quality might benefit from the analogue-like characteristics of the PSP Neon Linear Phase EQ or Waves
Renaissance EQ. PSP Vintage Warmer or Voxengo Tape Bus may help add
warmth to the signal. Overall, this chain includes equalisation, compression,
tape saturation emulation and limiting. If you are using the supplied Limiter
plug-in, make sure you are limiting only the peaks in the signal (i.e. only
occasional activity in the gain reduction meter).

- Slot 1: PSP Neon EQ (or the supplied Studio EQ)
- Slot 2: VintageCompressor
- Slot 3: Voxengo Tape Bus (or the supplied SoftClipper)
- Slot 7: PSP Vintage Warmer (or the supplied Limiter)
- Slot 8: Apogee UV22 HR dithering

All stages in these mastering chains are optional and individual plug-ins can be
bypassed using their respective bypass buttons. Depending upon the desired result,
the order of the EQ and compressor plug-ins may be reversed, and tape saturation
may sound better as the first process in the chain. Unless you wish to impose radical
changes upon your mixes for creative effect, the settings for most mastering processors must be set with great subtlety and precision. Be aware of undesirable interaction between the processes. If the mix is already sounding exactly as you want to hear
it, then it may not need any mastering processing at all (except for dithering).

Mastering processing settings

This section briefly covers the kinds of settings you might need when using plug-
ins for mastering purposes (bear in mind that appropriate settings depend entirely upon the signal you are processing). Due to the often specialist requirements
of mastering, reference is also made to plug-ins from other developers. These are
not supplied as part of Cubase. The settings for plug-ins when used in mastering
applications are likely to be far less radical than those used for processing during
the tracking and mixing stages. This is especially true of EQ, compressor and limiter settings. Let's examine how you might adjust the controls in a mastering
chain featuring EQ, compressor and limiter plug-ins.

EQ settings for mastering

Flattering the mix

A dull mix may need to be flattered at the mastering stage, either to reinforce a
weak bass end or to bring out the detail and 'air' in the upper frequencies, or
both. A common problem is that the mix has too much activity in the mid frequencies. This tends to mask the other frequencies in the signal and may also
result in a harsh sounding mix. Correcting these issues might involve slightly
boosting the lower and upper frequencies whilst also attenuating the mid frequency band (or it may require just one of these measures). The target low frequency band is usually that below around 150Hz. Boosting here should always
be approached with great subtlety since too much bass just adds boominess. The
'air' frequencies are in the region between 15kHz to 20 kHz but beware of boosting too much as this may give the impression that your mix is now sounding thin.

Figure 14.3
Mastering plug-in chain for warmth and
character

Info

The examples used in this
section are available for
download from the PC Publishing
website at:
www.pc-publishing.com

Info

Appropriate sound processing
settings depend entirely upon
the nature of the source signal.
The suggestions outlined in this
section are only starting points
and must be fine tuned to your
own source material.

Figure 14.4
Subtle curve for flattering the mix in the supplied Studio EQ plug-in

Attenuating the mid frequencies might involve a wide and extremely subtle curve somewhere between 1 and 6kHz. Beware of cutting the frequencies too much as this can seriously upset the balance. Any adjustments to the all-important mid-frequencies should always be kept to an absolute minimum. These measures sometimes produce an EQ curve which resembles a smile, hence this kind of EQ is sometimes referred to as a 'smile curve'. Try the settings shown in Figure 14.4.

Adding warmth

One undesirable side-effect inherent in EQ plug-ins is phase shifting between the different frequency bands. This results in loss of clarity and harshness. Digital mixes sometimes suffer from a cold, brittle quality to the sound, so the last thing you want to do is process the signal with an EQ which adds still more harshness. Linear phase EQ devices provide a solution. One outstanding example in this category is PSP Audioware's Neon Linear Phase EQ. This produces warm, analogue-like results. Even if you impose a fairly radical EQ curve, any undesirable side-effects are likely to be minimal in linear phase mode. The high resolution version

Figure 14.5
PSP Neon HR Linear Phase EQ for warm, transparent, analogue-like EQ control

of the plug-in features PSP's proprietary FAT mode (Frequency Authentication Technique) which ensures a smooth high frequency response. To warm up your mix, try matching the PSP Neon curve to that shown in Figure 14.5 (bands one to five only are active). This resembles the smile curve shown above but is a more radical curve designed to add warmth and air to a harsh, congested mix. Flatten the curve slightly if the settings are too radical for your own mix.

Compression settings for mastering

Wideband compression

Classic wideband compression devices may be used to add punch and dynamic movement to a mix whilst also controlling the average level of the signal. When using Waves Renaissance Compressor, Waves C1 or the supplied Dynamics plug-ins for mastering, try very gentle ratios between 1.01 and 1.5 : 1 with thresholds between -30 and -50dBFS to add coherence and density. Gentle control can also be achieved with slightly higher ratios between 1.1 and 3 : 1 and a high threshold between -3 and -5dBFS. Try starting with an attack of around 100ms and a release of 250ms and then adjust to taste. In the case of the Waves Renaissance Compressor plug-in try the 'Mastering Opto 1' preset as a starting point. Try setting a threshold of around -15dB, lower the release to around 250ms and add around 3dB of gain. Leave all other controls in their default positions. This is good for density and punch. Alternatively, try the Compressor plug-in supplied with Cubase with the following compressor settings. threshold: between -20 and -30dB, ratio: 1.3 : 1, soft knee: active, attack: 100ms, release: auto, and makeup gain: +2dB. Try following this with the Limiter plug-in with its threshold set to -0.5dB and auto release active. This ensures transient peak control.

Subtle compression can often be applied in a fairly transparent manner. However, undesirable side-effects include a blurring of the transients and a dulling of the overall sound. It is also true to say that the lower frequencies in a composite signal tend to dominate the attack and release of the compression. This can produce an undesirable effect where, for example, the bass line dictates the dynamic changes in the upper frequencies. A still worse effect of this is 'hole punching' where sudden low frequency energy may severely reduce the level of the rest of the signal, producing a virtual drop-out in the perceived loudness of the signal.

Multi-band compression

Multi-band compressors may help overcome some of the undesirable effects of wide-band compression. Multi-band compressors split the input signal into a number of frequency bands so that you can apply a different amount of compression / expansion to each band. However, these devices are more difficult to use and can easily ruin a good mix if set up incorrectly.

Using multiband compression for frequency selective dynamics processing

This example uses the supplied Multiband Compressor to increase the level of a bass drum which was mixed too low and reduce the high frequency level of a vocal which becomes harsh during loudly sung passages. Ordinary EQ or wideband compression are not ideal for these kinds of tasks. However, using multiband compression, you can dial in to the frequency range of the problem instrument or voice and expand or compress to emphasise or de-emphasise the sound as required. Assuming that the above two problems are occurring in the same mix, proceed as follows:

- Open the Multiband Compressor in an appropriate insert slot in the master bus inserts panel.

Info

Any processing which affects the crucial mid-band frequencies in the mix (between around 250Hz and 6kHz) should be approached with subtlety and caution, since it is easy to disturb the natural internal balance of the main instruments if you use radical or inappropriate settings.

- In the user interface, load the preset named 'Reset'. Activate the bypass buttons of the second and fourth frequency bands.
- In the upper part of the display, adjust the upper split point of the low frequency band to around 100 to 120Hz and the split points of the third frequency band to give a range of 6kHz to 12kHz (see Figure 14.6).
- Adjust the compression settings of the low frequency band to ratio: 1.33, attack: 13.5, and release: auto. Raise the level of the lower frequency band to +7dB. Adjust the threshold while listening to the mix until you hear the bass drum emphasised. Here you are applying low level upward compression. The objective is to lift the bass drum slightly out of the mix. You could try narrowing the frequency range of the lower band to tune in to the bass drum more precisely. The net effect is more bass drum without processing the other frequency ranges in the mix.
- Now adjust the compression settings of the third frequency band to ratio: 4, attack: 1, and release: auto. Adjust the threshold while listening to the mix. Here you are applying downward compression near the threshold where the vocal becomes harsh during the loud passages. Whenever the vocal becomes loud and harsh the upper frequencies are compressed downwards, hopefully without an obvious effect on the other instruments in the mix.
- Notice how we have achieved the above effects without processing the mid band and the upper band. This is helpful, since the mid band is responsible for the main body of a mix, including the natural internal balance of the vocals, snare and dominant instruments. If the mid-band is already sounding right it is best not to touch it. The upper band is responsible for the 'air' in the mix and this may also be best left untouched.

Figure 14.6
Multiband Compressor settings to simultaneously emphasise a bass drum and tame a harsh vocal

Info

When setting up the split points of your multiband compressor, try to avoid points which split the frequency bandwidth of any dominant instrument in two, since this means that you may end up applying different compression settings to two frequency ranges of the same instrument. This is not particularly desirable.

Using multiband compression to add punch and density

This example uses the Waves Linear Phase Multiband Compressor to add overall punch to a mix using upward compression. It is assumed here that you are processing rock or pop music which features a drum kit mixed slightly too low. The idea is to attempt to bring out the kit and add punch to the overall mix. Proceed as follows:

- Activate the LinMB plug-in in a slot in the stereo output bus. Load the 'Upward Compressor +3dB' preset from the factory presets.
- Switch off ARC.
- Using the Gain master control, increase the gain of all frequency bands to +5.
- Using the Range master control, reduce the range of all frequency bands to -5.
- Using the Attack master control while observing the mid frequency band, adjust the mid frequency band attack to approximately 43ms. All other bands are adjusted relative to this value.
- Using the Release master control while observing the mid frequency band, adjust the mid frequency band release to approximately 150ms. All other bands are adjusted relative to this value.
- While listening to the mix, lower the threshold of all bands simultaneously using the Threshold master control. Try settings between around -25 and -15dB.
- If the red LEDs above the LinMB's master faders become illuminated, click on the Trim button to reduce the output level. Alternatively, adjust the output level manually. The LinMB should now resemble Figure 14.7.

Figure 14.7
Waves Linear Multiband upward compression for adding punch and density to a mix

For a successful result you need to tweak the above settings to match the characteristics of your own mix. Try setting the attack and release times so that the compression line in the display moves up and down in rhythm with the music. A moderate attack time allows the transients of the drums and percussion to cut through thereby emphasising the rhythm. To increase the emphasis on the rhythm you may need to increase the attack time still further. You can achieve similar results using the above values in the Waves C4 Multiband Parametric processor.

Limiting and loudness maximisation settings for mastering

Limiting is generally used to manage the highest peaks in the signal. The threshold for limiting is usually set quite high, and attack times are typically set extremely fast to ensure brief transients are kept under control. For maximum transparency and preservation of the natural dynamics of the signal, peak gain reduction of no more than around 6dB is recommended. After this the effect starts to draw attention to itself. By controlling the peaks and simultaneously applying gain to the overall signal, a significant increase in the average level can be achieved, resulting in greater perceived loudness. This is commonly known as loudness maximisation. The trick with loudness maximisation is to increase the perceived loudness while also preserving the natural dynamics within the signal. Extreme loudness maximisation results in various distortions in the signal but may suit club and hard rock mixes.

Peak control and loudness maximisation without excessive loss of transient and dynamic detail is the primary purpose of the Sonnox Oxford Limiter (Figure 14.8a). The Oxford Limiter features a two-stage processing design. The first stage is a pre-process section where gain envelope compensation and compression is applied. The second stage includes peak overshoot control and enhancement. The threshold for dynamic gain control action is fixed at 0dBr. However, gain envelope compensation begins below the threshold, reducing exponentially to insignificant at lower levels. Up to 18dB of gain may be applied to increase the effect of the processing using the input gain fader. The pre-process section is unusual for its inclusion of a variable attack parameter. Setting the attack to relatively slow values allows peak transients to pass through the first stage and escape the effects of hard limiting. Any sample overshoots in these peaks may subsequently be controlled in the sec-

Figure 14.8a
Typical Sonnox Oxford Limiter CD mastering setup

Figure 14.8b
PSP Audioware Xenon for limiting and loudness maximisation, featuring high-precision metering with K-system options

ond stage by engaging Safe mode or setting the enhancement control to 100%. The latter ensure zero sample overloads in the output. This whole process allows you to avoid the harshness associated with fast limiting. The enhancement fader may be used to maximise the signal still further and any potential inter-sample peak reconstruction errors which could occur during D/A conversion may be corrected using the auto-compensation function. Used carefully, the Oxford Limiter can match the levels of your own productions to those of commercial releases. For mastering within Cubase, it is best placed in the last plug-in slot (slot 8) on the stereo master buss (i.e. after the main faders).

Where ultimate transparency and pristine audio quality is required PSP Audioware's Xenon Limiter (Figure 14.8b) is an excellent choice. This features 64-bit precision throughout its internal signal path and operates at sample rates up to 192kHz. It features two processing stages including, in the first stage, a transient control which governs how much of the transients pass through, along with a release control which affects perceived loudness and, in the second stage, three transient buttons which govern brick wall limiting behaviour using lookahead processing and Finite Impulse Response envelope detectors. Other features include: an Oversample button which oversamples the limiter envelope detector to avoid inter-sample peak reconstruction errors in the D/A converter; a Leveller parameter which applies gradual gain reduction to loud passages before limiting is applied for natural dynamic changes between quiet and loud passages; and a Link dial which governs how much the stereo image is affected by the processing where 0% allows greater loudness at the expense of potential stereo image fluctuations, and 100% ensures the greatest stability in the stereo image at the expense of less perceived loudness. Finally, Xenon uses TPDF generated noise for dithering, with three styles of noise shaping following the izophonic curves of

Info

Loudness maximisation and limiting are normally placed *after* the master output bus faders. In Cubase, this means slots 7 or 8.

Info

Mastering constitutes a whole separate branch of audio processing in its own right and cannot be covered fully in this text. Those seeking more in-depth coverage are advised to consult specialist books on the subject (see Recommended Reading at the back of this book).

the human hearing system. Excellent meters featuring standard peak and K-system designs (K-12, K-14, K-20) complete the picture. Xenon is suitable for all kinds of audio material. It preserves internal detail and stereo image, and minimises transient smearing. For mastering within Cubase, it is best placed in the last plug-in slot (slot 8) on the stereo master buss (i.e. after the main faders).

Cubase itself provides limiting and dithering in the supplied Limiter and UV22HR plug-ins. For mastering purposes these are best placed in the 7th and 8th slots of the stereo master buss inserts (both after the main faders). Make sure there is only occasional activity in the gain reduction meters of the Limiter plug-in since this indicates that you are limiting only the extreme peaks in the signal. When using the Limiter plug-in for mastering, DO NOT push the final output level to the absolute maximum 0dBFS point. An out ceiling of between -3dB and -0.3dB is more appropriate. This helps avoid potential inter-sample peak reconstruction errors which may occur during D/A conversion.

Dithering

What is dithering?

A reduction in the bit depth of a digital audio signal means that you are now expressing the audio with shorter wordlength samples. This results in a slight loss in the definition of low level signals, since reducing the wordlength means that you have had to throw away some of the least significant bits. Without processing, this manifests itself as a particular kind of low level non-linear distortion known as quantisation noise. Dithering involves adding a low level controlled noise to the signal and takes into account the least significant bits before they are discarded. This converts the low-level distortion into a more friendly linear noise or 'hiss' and preserves some of the integrity of the original signal. Using a process known as noise shaping, the more friendly noise is re-distributed to parts of the audio spectrum where it is less obvious to the ear. The net result is enhanced clarity and spaciousness.

Dithering is most often applied at the point just before you convert a high resolution file (such as 24-bit) to a lower resolution file (such as 16-bit). For CD mastering purposes in Cubase, this is normally when you are producing the final 16-bit master audio file using Export/Audio Mixdown.

When to use dithering in Cubase

All internal audio processing in Cubase is performed at 32-bit float resolution, so if you are using the Export/Audio Mixdown function to create an audio file of lesser resolution then you may need to use the dithering options supplied with Cubase (or those included with other plug-ins such as the Waves L1 or L2). To be exact, dithering should be applied in the following cases:

• When using the Export/Audio Mixdown function (File menu) to create a final master audio file of any bit depth less than 32-bit float (i.e. 24-bit, 16-bit or 8-bit).
• When mixing down to an external medium, such as DAT, (where the standard bit depth is 16-bit).

When truncating the bit depth from 32-bit float to 24-bit as an interim process, some experts recommend using dither without noise shaping and preferably TPDF dither, although Steinberg consider this to be rather a matter of taste than necessity. At the mixing stage, if it is your intention to perform a final mastering stage at a later date, mix down without dither to a high resolution file. Apply noise-shaped dither only as the last step before truncation during the mastering session.

Loading a dithering plug-in

Cubase is supplied with the Apogee UV22 HR dithering plug-in which supports dithering to all the popular bit resolutions. Dithering is always applied after the master faders. This means loading the dither device in insert slots 7 or 8 of the stereo master output bus. To load the Apogee UV22 HR plug-in proceed as follows:

- Open the extended Mixer and activate the stereo master output bus channel strip inserts panel.
- Click in the name field of slot 8 and select 'UV22 HR' from the appropriate effects pop-up menu.
- Upon selecting the UV22 HR plug-in, the graphical user interface is opened automatically (Figure 14.9).

Figure 14.9
The Apogee UV22 HR plug-in

Apogee UV22 HR dithering functions

The UV22 HR dithering plug-in incorporates an advanced dithering algorithm developed by Apogee. It features the following parameters:

- Normal – this provides an all-round type of dithering which is often the best compromise.
- Low – applies a lower level of dither noise to the signal.
- Autoblack – when activated, the dither noise is muted when there are silent passages in the signal.
- Bit Resolution – specifies the intended bit resolution of the final audio result. The choice is between 8, 16, 20 and 24-bit.

Using dithering

As with any processing, you must use your ears to decide if the dithering settings you have chosen give the desired result. However, given that dithering is intentionally an extremely subtle kind of processing, it may be difficult to perceive the results. To get a feel for what dithering can do for you, try a test procedure of

Important

Noise-shaped dithering is normally a once-only operation performed as the very last step in the mastering process. It is best not to re-apply noise-shaped dither to audio that has already been subject to this process. If you intend to conduct a final mastering stage in a specialised mastering application (or in Cubase) do not apply noise-shaped dither at the mixing stage. Instead, mix down to a high-resolution file without dither (24-bit or 32-bit float). At the mastering stage, import this file into the mastering application and apply noise-shaped dither as the very last process just before truncation to produce the final 16-bit master audio file.

producing an audio mixdown file (File / Export / Audio Mixdown) at a resolution of 8-bits both with and without dithering. Preferably, use an audio file which includes some low level material. Listen to the difference between the two files. Now try the same experiment with 16-bit files. The most important thing to remember when you use dithering is that the bit depth should be matched to the intended bit-resolution of the final file.

For CD mastering, set the Apogee UV22 HR plug-in to normal / 16-bit. If you are using the Waves L1 or L2 Ultramaximizers, Waves recommend a number of combinations of IDR dither and noise shaping. The most important of these are as follows:

- type 1, normal (24, 20, or 16-bit) - general purpose high-quality use (standard CD mastering, may be edited or EQ'ed at a later stage)
- type 1, ultra (16-bit) - high resolution CD master (no further editing)
- type 2, ultra (24, 20 or 16-bit) - low noise/high resolution

Recommended order of use of plug-ins for mastering

Placing plug-ins in a chain may result in undesirable interaction between the different processes. The following is a suggested order for some of the common pre-mastering processing steps to avoid problems and to arrive at a final version of the recording which is suitable for duplication or manufacture:

- De-essing
- Equalisation
- Expansion / compression
- Harmonic excitement
- Reverberation
- Stereo imaging / MS processing
- Sample rate conversion (e.g. downsampling from 88.2kHz to 44.1kHz)
- Limiting / level maximisation
- Dithering
- Truncation (e.g. reduction of the bit depth from 24-bit to 16-bit)

Info

Not all of the mastering processes shown here are covered by the supplied plug-ins. Although Cubase may be used for mastering, Steinberg Wavelab, Bias Peak (or similar) are preferable for dedicated mastering and CD burning tasks.

This list is certainly not the only way of ordering the processes. For example, depending on the application, the order of equalisation and expansion / compression might be reversed. Compressing after EQ produces a smoother result but may undo some of the settings of the EQ if the threshold is set inappropriately. EQing after compression allows you to adjust the EQ parameters with more clarity, knowing that EQ changes are not changing the action of the compressor. Limiting is often placed after sample rate conversion since the conversion process can result in slight level increases. Of course, for many projects you do not need to downsample and so you can ignore the latter issues. As for dithering and bit reduction, take care that you do not confuse these processes with sample rate conversion! The most important rule for dithering is that it is normally a once-only final step just before bit reduction.

Downsampling issues

Using Cubase for downsampling (using the 'Sample Rate' field in the Export Audio Mixdown dialogue) is not advisable if limiting and dithering are at the end of your mastering chain, since this places sample rate conversion AFTER limiting and dithering. It may be better to do the downsampling in one pass WITHOUT limiting, dithering and truncation, and then re-import the down-sampled audio file for these final stages in a second pass. If your project is destined to be duplicated on CD, try starting off with the standard CD sample rate of 44.1kHz and maintain this sample rate throughout the project. In this way you do not subject your file to the possible damage caused by poor quality sample rate conversion.

The quality of Cubase's sample rate conversion when using Export Audio Mixdown is not adequate for all professional applications. For the best quality you are advised to use a dedicated sample rate conversion plug-in at the appropriate position within the chain, or to do the final stages of your mastering processing in an external editor. Wavelab features a high quality sample rate conversion plug-in known as the Crystal Resampler. Alternatively, try a stand-alone application like Voxengo's r8brain Pro.

Quality control

Overusing plug-in effects can damage the pristine quality of your digital recordings, especially if you are working with 16-bit files. Almost all audio processing (even simple gain changes) increases the wordlength of the audio, (e.g. after processing, a 16-bit signal might be expressed in 32-bit float resolution). If you were to print this processed signal back to 16-bit, bit reduction and loss of low level detail results. Do this once and the effect is, admittedly, minimal. Do it a number of times to a number of signals and the cumulative effect results in a slight loss of transparency and detail.

To help maintain quality, start with high resolution sources (e.g. 24-bit / 44.1kHz) and try to maintain this high resolution for as long as possible throughout the processing chain. Avoid printing effects one at a time to the same audio file. Multiple effects processing is best applied in a single pass. Where possible, keep effects in real-time until the final mix (if your computer's processing power permits). Of course, the latter is not possible when you are using the off-line processing in the Processing menu. Use only high quality plug-ins which have at least a 32-bit float internal resolution. If it is your intention to carry out a final mastering stage in Cubase or other software, do not truncate the bit-depth or use noise-shaped dither at the mixing stage. Instead, mix to a high resolution file without noise-shaped dither (try 32-bit float). Avoid applying noise-shaped dither more than once in the same project.

These steps help you get a better result when you finally arrive at the mastering stage. With mastering you are aiming to squeeze the final 10% of quality out of your completed stereo mixes but remember; if a mix is already sounding excellent then it may need no further processing other than dithering and truncation to 16-bit. One of the greatest skills of mastering engineers is knowing just how much processing is required and when to leave a mix alone.

Info

Red Book refers to the technical specifications which govern the correct creation and manufacture of an audio CD, as defined by Sony and Philips. An actual copy of the Red Book is usually only available to CD manufacturing plants. Other CD types have similar colour coded books which govern their creation, such as Yellow Book for CD-ROM, Green Book for CD-i, Orange Book for write-once CD-R, White Book for video CD and Blue Book for CD-Extra.

Info

For serious CD pre-mastering and duplication purposes, CD writers manufactured by Plextor are highly recommended.

Burning the CD

As outlined above, Cubase does not include integrated track indexing and CD burning functions. You must therefore conduct the final burning and organisation of the CD in other software (e.g. Steinberg Wavelab, Bias Peak, Ahead Software Nero, Roxio Easy CD Creator, Roxio Jam and others). The chosen software must be capable of burning the final CD in the standard Red Book audio CD format.

The first dilemna is deciding exactly how you are going to mix down the final 16-bit audio; as one long audio file containing all the tracks, or as separate files, one for each track on the CD. This decision is largely dictated by the capabilities of your chosen CD editing and burning software. Some applications allow you to split a single audio file into a number of tracks, others require each track as a separate file. In both cases, if you have carefully spaced your tracks in Cubase you will need to duplicate this in the burning software. One approach is to make a careful note of the intended pauses between each track and enter these manually. Most CD burning software allows you to adjust the pauses. However, bear in mind that the data on audio CDs is divided up into frames, where there are 75 frames per second and each frame contains 588 stereo samples. On an audio CD you can only ever start a CD track at the beginning of a frame. This can lead to subtle problems when adjusting start times and pauses between tracks. Normally, small amounts of silence are inserted to ensure that track starts and ends do not get cut off when the CD is played. Luckily, most CD burning software takes care of these finer points automatically, as long as the timing requirements of your CD remain relatively simple (if in doubt stick to spacings of whole seconds).

Once the track list and suitable pauses have been entered you should carefully audition the material once more to make sure that it sounds as intended. When you proceed to the actual burning of the CD, ALWAYS use disc-at-once mode since this ensures that the CD is recorded in one pass without interruption (as opposed to track-at-once which results in the writing laser being turned off between each track). Also, experts recommend the use of 2 x or 4 x burning speed to minimise writing errors.

If you intend to produce a production master CD yourself, bear in mind that the CD writing process is prone to error, especially if you use a poor quality CD recorder and poor quality media. To avoid errors, always use a high quality CD recorder and the best media. Also, work in a clean, dust-free atmosphere and never touch the surface of the master compact disc. If you are duplicating your own audio CDs for demo purposes, it is still worth working within strict guidelines to avoid problems.

MIDI effects

As well as audio effects, Cubase is supplied with a range of real-time MIDI effects. These are found in the Send and Insert panels of each MIDI channel. MIDI editing has traditionally been an off-line ('permanent') process but, with MIDI effects, the emphasis has changed. The modification of MIDI data has traditionally been an off-line editing process but, with MIDI effects, the emphasis has changed. Like their audio counterparts, MIDI effects are plug-in modules which can be added to the effects panels of MIDI channels when you need them.

The difference between MIDI effects and audio effects

The MIDI effects structure and routing is similar to that found with audio effects but with the following very important differences:

- MIDI effects are for the real-time processing of MIDI data. They do NOT act upon audio data in any way.
- Unlike audio Send effects, MIDI Send effects are unique to each MIDI track and are not assigned for global use by all MIDI channels. There is no send level involved with MIDI Send effects.
- Since you are processing a sequence of digital instructions rather than an audio signal, the results of certain effects may not be directly comparable to their audio counterpart.

Setting up MIDI effects in Cubase

In Cubase, real-time MIDI effects may be assigned as Insert or Send effects. There are no strict rules about which effects are assigned to which kind of effects slots but, for example, if real-time compression or quantizing of a MIDI track were required, the Compress or Quantizer plug-ins would normally be assigned as MIDI Insert effects. Send effects might suit those occasions when you wish to route the Send data to a different MIDI device to the source, since you can assign the target MIDI device separately in the Send effects slots.

MIDI Insert effects
MIDI Insert effects are assigned in the Insert panel of a MIDI channel strip in the expanded Mixer, in the MIDI Channel Settings window or in the Inspector

Figure 15.1
MIDI Insert effects are assigned using the Insert slots in the Insert panel of a MIDI channel

(Figure 15.1). Each MIDI track has a total of four Insert slots. Click on an Insert effect field to open the MIDI effects pop-up menu.

MIDI Insert effects differ from MIDI Send effects in the manner in which the data is routed. There is no separation of the track and effect data. Instead, the MIDI data passes through the effects *in series* (see Figure 15.2). When more than one insert effect is activated, the signal passes through each in turn, in descending order. The destination MIDI device is that which is assigned for the MIDI track. Note that, with multiple Insert effects, the data received by each effect is that which is output by the preceding effect in the panel. Therefore, depending on the effects used, the final output may not resemble the original input data at all.

MIDI Insert effects are suited to almost all MIDI effects but, of course, the suitability depends upon the intended result. There are no hard and fast rules.

Figure 15.2
The routing configuration for MIDI Insert effects

MIDI Send effects

MIDI Send effects are assigned in the Send panel of a MIDI channel in the expanded Mixer, in the MIDI Channel Settings window or in the Inspector (Figure 15.3). Each MIDI track has a total of four Send slots. Click on a Send effect field to open the MIDI effects pop-up menu.

With MIDI Send effects, the MIDI track's data is routed to the destination MIDI device as usual (via the MIDI output port) and a copy of the data is also sent *in parallel* to the MIDI effect. The data produced by the effect is routed to a destination device according to the MIDI port and MIDI channel chosen in the Send effects slot (Figure 15.4). The destination device for the Send effect data may be the same device as the MIDI track or any other MIDI device in your system.

MIDI input data

Channel data

Send data

Figure 15.3 (above)
MIDI Send effects are assigned using the Send slots in the Send panel of a MIDI channel

MIDI device   MIDI device

Figure 15.4 (left)
The routing configuration for MIDI Send effects

It is not always appropriate for the data from the Send effect to be sent to the same MIDI device as the MIDI track since the effects data may cancel out or interfere with the source MIDI data. Such a case may occur with the MidiEcho effect, where the MIDI echo data may coincide unfavourably with the source data, producing double notes, phasing and cancellation effects. If such phenomena become problematic, try routing the Send effect data on a separate MIDI channel assigned to the same sound or, in the case of VST instruments, try activatng a second instance of the instrument. Using the Send effects to route the MIDI data to a completely different device and sound patch is, of course, valuable for creative purposes.

MIDI Send effects are best suited to MIDI plug-ins like MidiEcho, Micro Tuner, Track FX and Transformer but there are no hard and fast rules.

Common graphical user interface functions for MIDI effects

The graphical user interface (GUI) for any of the currently active MIDI effects can be opened by clicking on the edit button of the slot corresponding to the effect. The edit buttons are labelled with a lower case 'e' and are found in all effects slots in the Mixer, in the MIDI Channel Settings window and in the Inspector. Most GUIs for the MIDI effects open in a separate window similar to that shown in Figure 15.5. When opened from the Inspector, some of the effects open within the Inspector itself. If required, you can force these kind of effects to open in a separate window by pressing Alt while making an effects selection.

Info

Like audio effects, MIDI effects use the processing power of your computer, albeit a smaller amount than their audio counterparts. However, generating large amounts of additional MIDI data can result in MIDI bottlenecks so, depending upon your MIDI interface and the polyphony of your MIDI devices, there are limits to the number of MIDI effects which can be run simultaneously.

Figure 15.5
The graphical user interface for the MidiEcho effect

Basic GUI functions

Many MIDI effects include a Presets menu which is opened by clicking on the downward pointing arrow next to the Presets field (Figure 15.6). You can add your own presets by clicking on the plus (+) folder symbol next to the Presets menu and you can delete the currently chosen preset by clicking on the minus (-) symbol folder. Any stored presets are globally available to all projects.

MIDI Effects are active as soon as they are selected in the Inserts or Sends sections and therefore do not feature an On button. Another common attribute are dual action value fields which feature a slider control or up/down arrows for changing the settings. The slider control is helpful for changing values in small incre-

Figure 15.6
Use the Presets menu to store and recall MIDI effects presets

Figure 15.7
Make adjustments in the MIDI effect value fields using the up/down arrows (left) or the slider control (right).

ments while the up/down arrows help set the parameters to note values.

The supplied MIDI effects

There now follows descriptions of a number of the most popular MIDI effects. Please consult the user documentation for full details of all other MIDI effects.

Arpache 5

Arpache 5 is an arpeggiator MIDI plug-in. Typically, an arpeggiator is a device which automatically steps through the notes in a held chord. The speed and order of the playback of the notes are regulated by various settings on the device. Arpache 5 generates arpeggios by transforming MIDI input data. The parameters allow the creation of standard arpeggios, random arpeggios and arpeggios which follow a user-specified note order.

Figure 15.8
Arpache 5

Arpache 5 features the following parameters:

- Playmode buttons – determine the playback order for the arpeggio. The options include up, down, down + up, up + down, random ('?') and Order. The Order button allows you to set the playback order according to the settings in the Play Order fields (see below).
- Quantize – determines the playback speed according to a note value. The value can be changed using the mini slider or the up/down arrows. Range: 1/32 note triplets to whole note values.
- Length – regulates the length of each playback note according to a note value. The value can be changed using the mini slider or the up/down arrows. Range: 1/32 note triplets to whole note values.
- Semi-Range – determines the pitch range of the playback in semitones starting from the lowest input note. For example, a setting of 12 ensures that all arpeggiated notes are within the same octave (12 semitones) and any higher notes are transposed down. A setting of 24 allows the arpeggio to be automatically transposed in as many octaves as are available within the range.
- Thru – when activated, all notes arriving at the input of the arpeggiator are passed through to the output. When de-activated, the input notes are not passed through to the output. For standard arpeggio behaviour, thru would be de-activated.
- Play Order – when the Order button is activated (illuminated) the playback order is determined according to the settings in the play order fields which represent each step in the arpeggio in incremental time position order. The numbers you choose for each field specify which note from the input chord is allocated to each time position step, counting from the lowest note in the chord.

Info

For more elaborate arpeggiator effects, try the 'Arpache SX' MIDI plug-in supplied with the program. Arpache SX features advanced velocity and sorting modes as well as a special sequencer mode which allows you to use the interaction between a MIDI part and the MIDI input as the basis for the arpeggio.

User guide

To set up Arpache 5 for standard arpeggiator purposes proceed as follows:

- Select a MIDI track and activate the Record Enable or Monitor buttons so that you can play live through the track.
- Set the output port of the MIDI track to an appropriate MIDI device. Select a suitable sound. Try using the supplied Prologue VST Instrument set to the 'Classic Ana' preset.
- Activate the Arpache 5 MIDI plug-in as an Insert effect on the chosen MIDI track. In its traditional role as a regular arpeggiator, Arpache is normally assigned as an Insert.
- In the Arpache 5 interface, activate the up + down button, set Quantize to 8, Length to 32 and Semi-Range to 11.
- Hold down a three note chord comprising C3, E3 and G3 (or any other three note chord). The settings in 4) above produce an arpeggio which steps through the notes in the held chord in ascending and descending order, at a speed corresponding to 1/8th note intervals at the current project tempo. Each playback note has a 1/32nd note duration.
- Try changing the Semi-Range to 12. This causes the lowest note to step

up an octave on each cycle of the arpeggio. Try changing the speed by
setting the Quantize value to 16.

- Try activating the random ('?') button to produce a randomised playback
order.
- Check out the effect of the other Playmode buttons and try setting up
your own custom playback order by activating the Order button and
entering values into the Play Order fields (values of 1, 2, 1, 3, 1, 2, 2, 1
give good results with three note chords).

AutoPan

AutoPan is an LFO-like oscillation
device for MIDI Controller data. It
allows the continuous modulation
of any chosen Controller between
a specified value range. Autopan
is suitable for producing automatic MIDI panning effects (the continuous modulation of MIDI
Controller 10). It might also be
applied to the modulation of
Controllers 71 and 74 which con-

Figure 15.9
AutoPan

trol cut-off and resonance in many MIDI devices. In this way, you can set up automated tempo related modulations of the cut-off and resonance parameters of a
synthesizer.

AutoPan features the following parameters:

- Waveform selector buttons – determine the modulation waveforms
applied to the chosen MIDI Controller. The range of these waveforms is
scaled according to the minimum and maximum parameters. The first
five buttons apply the wave shapes as indicated on the button. The sixth
button applies a random shape. The seventh and eighth buttons apply
ascending and descending periodical envelopes respectively, where the
duration of each section of the curve follows the value chosen in the
period parameter.
- Period – determines the speed of one modulation cycle. For example, if
you set this to '4th', a modulation cycle is repeated once every quarter
note. The period can be set according to note values (with the up/down
arrows) or ticks (with the mini-fader).
- Density – controls the density of the MIDI controller events which are
used to describe the modulation effect produced by Autopan. Here,
higher values mean a smoother curve. However, it is recommended that
you do not set the density too high since producing a large number of
Controller events can cause MIDI transmission problems.
- AmpMod – controls the overall length of the periodical envelopes
(selected using the seventh and eighth waveform selector buttons as
described above). Here, a setting of 4 results in a periodical envelope
which is repeated every 4 beats.
- Controller – allocates the target MIDI Controller to which the modulation

effect is to be applied. Pan (Controller 10), Sound Variation (Controller 70), timbre / harmonic (Controller 71) and brightness (Controller 74) are possible targets but the suitability of each controller depends upon the MIDI implementation in the target device.

• Min and Max – determine the lower and upper limits of the waveform thereby regulating the scale and range of the modulation effect.

User guide

AutoPan is an ingenious MIDI plug-in which can be used for all kinds of auto-mated modulation effects. Unfortunately, MIDI devices often suffer from 'zip-per' noise when the Pan Controller is modified in real-time so using Autopan for one of its prime purposes may not always be successful. However, with other MIDI controller targets AutoPan performs extremely well. For example, to set up an automated modulation of the cut-off parameter of the supplied Monologue VSTi, proceed as follows:

• Select a MIDI track and allocate the output port to the supplied Monologue VST Instrument. Select the 'BandFifths' preset.
• Record a simple test sequence of notes over a length of 4 bars or use an existing 4 bar MIDI recording. Here, the 4 bar length is important since it is the length of time over which the cut-off parameter is to be modulated.
• Activate the AutoPan MIDI plug-in as an Insert effect on the chosen MIDI track.
• In the Autopan interface, click on the sine waveform button, select a Period of '7680' (double click in the Period field to enter the value), select a Density of 12 and set the Controller field to Brightness (Controller 74). Set a minimum value of 5 and a maximum of 90. With a Period of '7680' the modulation cycle has a duration of 4 bars (since by default there are 7680 ticks in 4 bars).
• Commence playback and listen to the effect of the modulation in the Monologue VSTi. To see the action of the modulation open the Monologue interface by clicking on the VSTi edit ('e') button and observe the cut-off dial. If everything is functioning correctly you should see the dial move slowly back and forth throughout the 4 bar sequence.
• Try changing the speed by setting the AutoPan Period value to 1280 or 1920.
• Check out the effect of setting the Period to 8th, AmpMod to 8 and selecting the 7th or 8th Waveform Selector buttons.

Micro Tuner

Micro Tuner is a micro tuning plug-in for VST Instruments and those external MIDI devices which support micro-tuning. This allows you to set up the tuning of the target device to an alternative tuning system to the standard equal temperament tuning (also known as equal tempered tuning). Equal temperament tuning divides the octave into twelve equal intervals and this is the standard tuning system used in the West. However, other classical and experimental tunings are possible and these can add variety and interest to

Figure 15.10
Micro Tuner

musical arrangements. Micro Tuner is supplied with a number of tuning system presets including Harmonic, Pure Major, Pure minor, Mean Semitones, Pythagorean and so on. The interface features 12 value fields arranged as the keys of one octave on a musical keyboard. Tunings are adjusted in cents (one hundredth of a semitone) by dragging in the value fields. A Convert parameter adjusts the plug-in for use with VST Instruments (default) or with external MIDI devices (in real-time or non real-time modes).

User guide

In its standard role, Micro Tuner would be used as an Insert effect to change the tuning of the target MIDI device. However, it might also be used as a MIDI Send device routed to a second instance of the same instrument / sound. This allows you to use the micro tunings for thickening and chorus effects. This is particularly good for, strings, choirs and pads and for really big sounds you can assign several instances of Micro Tuner, each tuned slightly differently.

In addition to the supplied presets try the following:

0, –10, 23, –25, –14, –2, 10, 2, –8, 6, –4, –12 (Raga Bhairava)
0, 12, 4, –6, 8, –2, 10, 2, 14, 6, 18, 10 (Raga Kafi)
0, –6, –4, –2, –8, 2, –8, –2, –4, –6, 0, –10 (Valotti and Young)

MidiEcho

MidiEcho produces delay, chorus and pitch-shift effects. The parameters of MidiEcho function as follows:

- Quantize – determines the speed of the echoes relative to the current tempo. This value can be regulated in terms of ticks using the mini slider (480 ticks = a quarter note) or in terms of note values using the up/down arrow keys (Range: between 1/32T and 1/2 notes).
- Length – sets the length of the echoed note events. Regulated in terms of ticks using the mini slider (480 ticks = a quarter note) or in terms of note values using the up/down arrow keys. Using the slider you can set the length to 'Source' which means that the echoes have the same length as the MIDI input notes.
- Repeat – determines the number of echo repeats for each incoming MIDI note. Range: 1–12.
- Echo-Quant – sets up a quantizing grid which regulates where the echoes fall allowing you to set up rhythmically correct echoes regardless of the

other settings. A setting of '1' disables the effect of this parameter.

- Velo Decay – determines a velocity amount which is added or subtracted to/from each echo repeat, thereby simulating a crescendo or decay effect. Range –36 to +36.
- Pitch Decay – determines a pitch amount in semitones which is added or subtracted to/from each echo repeat, thereby changing the pitch of each consecutive echo, producing ascending and descending pitch sequences. Range –36 to +36.
- Echo Decay – adds or subtracts a number of ticks to each successive echo repeat to produce accelerated or decelerated echo effects. A setting of 100 produces no change. A setting or less than 100 produces echoes which speed up. A setting or more than 100 produces echoes which slow down.
- Length Decay – determines an amount by which the length of each echo repeat note is reduced to produce echo note lengths which are progressively shortened. A setting of 100 produces no reduction of the length and values under 100 produce progressively more reduction.

User guide

For the initial testing of MidiEcho, try using a simple piano MIDI part so you can hear the results clearly. MidiEcho does not respond well to live MIDI input and works best with pre-recorded MIDI parts. Assign MidiEcho as an Insert effect, set the parameters to the same values as those shown in Figure 15.11 (above) and play the chosen part in cycle playback mode. Experiment with the Quantize, Repeat and Velo Decay parameters to produce different echo effects. At first, try setting the Length to 'Source'. This ensures that you will at least hear the source MIDI notes. Bear in mind that the processing relies upon adding to existing MIDI note data and could, in certain circumstances, produce undesirable delays in the data flow of the rest of the music. This depends upon the density of the events in the arrangement.

Figure 15.11
MidiEcho

Try the following settings as starting points for your own experiments (Table 15.1):

Table 15.1 MidiEcho plug-in starting points

Quantize	Length	Repeat	Echo-Quant	Velo-Decay	Pitch Decay	Echo Decay	Length Decay
16th	32nd	10	1	–12	0	100	100
16T	32nd	4	1	–20	0	108	100
4th	Source	7	9	–20	0	118	100
16T	47	10	1	–12	0	98	100
4th	63	5	3	–12	0	99	100
32T	47	3	1	–12	12	99	100

Step Designer

Step Designer is a monophonic MIDI step sequencer. MIDI note data is generated by drawing events in the upper half of the grid which displays time on the horizontal axis and pitch on the vertical axis (1 octave at a time). Velocity values, gate times and two MIDI controllers may be controlled for each note by dragging the corresponding value sliders in the lower half of the display. The time display is divided into 32 steps, each of which represents a note division of the bar between 1/128th and 1/2 notes. The overall length of the pattern is variable between 1 and 32 steps.

Figure 15.12
Step Designer

Step Designer features a control panel above and to the left of the main display which includes the following parameters:

- Pattern – determines the current pattern number. Each instance of Step Designer holds up to 100 different patterns.
- Copy and Paste buttons – these are used to copy and paste the data from one pattern to another. This is excellent for creating variations of the same pattern.
- Reset and Random buttons – the Reset button resets Step Designer to its default startup settings (an empty pattern). The Random button generates a random sequence of notes in the currently displayed pattern (replaces any existing notes in the current pattern).
- Length – determines the overall length of the pattern between 1 and 32 steps.
- Quantize – determines the length of each of the 32 steps in the sequence in terms of a note value between 1/128th and 1/2 notes.
- Swing – imposes a swing feel upon the pattern, where every second note position on the grid is pushed to the right (so that it falls slightly later). A higher percentage produces more swing.
- Presets menu – allows the storage and recall of preset patterns.

- Shift octave buttons – move the pitch display up or down by one octave at a time.
- Shift time buttons – moves the order of the notes to the left or right where notes which are pushed off the end of the pattern are re-inserted at the opposite end of the sequence. This is excellent for creating pattern variations and changing the feel.
- Reverse – reverses the note order of the pattern.
- Controllers section – provides a selection menu which determines what data is visible in the lower half of the display. The Setup button opens a dialogue where you can select which two MIDI controllers are to be targeted by Step Designer (this is globally set for the current instance of Step Designer and cannot be individually set for each pattern).

User guide

To generate your own pattern in Step Designer proceed as follows:

Assign Step Designer as an Insert effect on a MIDI track. Note that Step Designer blocks all MIDI thru activity on the track so is best suited to an empty MIDI track.

- Allocate the MIDI output port of the track to a suitable MIDI device and sound patch. For this exercise, try using the supplied Monologue VST Instrument set to the 'Acid Bass' preset.
- Select a length for the pattern in the length field. The default 16 step setting is suitable for experimentation.
- Select the quantize value for each step in the Quantize field. Once again, the default 1/16 note setting is suitable for experimentation.
- Drag the mouse left to right across the note event display. A series of note events are inserted as small graphical rectangular blocks. This is a very quick manner of entering note data. You may prefer to enter a pre-defined series of notes, in which case you should click in the appropriate pitch position for each step.
- Drag the mouse across the velocity display in the lower half of the window. All velocity values are adjusted according to the position of the mouse. This is a very quick manner of entering velocity data. You may prefer to enter more precise velocity values, in which case you should drag the velocity levels for each step individually.
- Commence playback of Cubase. The pattern entered in Step Designer plays back synchronised to the current project tempo, in a continuous loop.
- During playback, try editing the notes and velocity data.
- Click on the Controllers menu and select the Gate option. Edit the gate times of the notes in the lower part of the display. The gate times affect the lengths of the notes in the pattern.
- Select the Harmonic or Brightness controllers in the Controllers menu. Edit the Harmonic and Brightness values in the lower part of the display. This produces real-time changes of the cut-off and resonance parameters in the Monologue VSTi. Open the Monologue interface to observe the movement of the parameters.
- Click on the Setup button to assign other controllers to Step Designer. Experiment with the value settings of the chosen controllers.

Other techniques

To get more out of Step Designer try the following techniques:

- To slide the octave up or down, click and drag vertically on the note list on the left of the note display. Moving notes in the current pattern out of the display results in a note name appearing, indicating the presence of notes in other octaves. This is helpful for keeping track of the notes in multi-octave patterns.
- To tie any note to the preceding note, click on any of the tie indicators found in the strip between the upper and lower sections of the interface. Ties can be implemented on any number of successive steps in the pattern and the tied note always takes on the pitch of the note to which it is attached. Changing the pitch of tied notes moves all tied steps simultaneously.

Transformer

Transformer is almost identical to Logical Editor except that it processes the data in real-time. This allows the application of elaborate MIDI processing functions without permanently affecting the data.

Transformer's functions include deleting, transforming and inserting data based upon user-configurable filters. The filter is set up in the upper part of the window and the action which should take place upon the filtered data is defined in the lower half of the window.

Figure 15.13
Transformer

User Guide

Simple functions within Transformer may be expressed in plain English, such as 'if the incoming MIDI message type is an Aftertouch message delete it'. This translates into the Transformer window as follows:

- In the upper Filter section, set the Filter target to 'Type', set the condition to 'Equal' and Parameter 1 to 'Aftertouch'.
- Ignore the Action section.
- Choose Delete as the function mode in the upper left menu.

This results in the real-time deletion of all aftertouch messages from the incoming MIDI data.

Taking a look in the pop-up menus of the various columns reveals that more elaborate filtering and transformation functions are possible. Try loading some of the presets to see how the more complex functions are set up. You may also like to consider the following two examples.

Setting a filter to restrict the input range for a chosen instrument

For restricting the MIDI input to the playing range of a trumpet, for example, proceed as follows:

- In the upper Filter section, set the Filter target column to 'Type', the Condition column to 'Equal' and the Parameter 1 column to 'Note'.
- Click on the Add Line button. Set the Filter target column to 'Value 1' (Pitch), the Condition column to 'Outside Range' and the Parameter 1 and 2 columns to 'E2 (52)' and 'D#5 (87)'.
- Choose Delete as the function mode in the upper left menu. The result is the real-time deletion (or filtering) of any notes outside the chosen range. This kind of filter is excellent for keeping within the natural note range of an instrument, if a sense of realism is what your music needs.

Changing pitch bend into pan data

To set a transformation which changes pitch bend into pan data proceed as follows:

- In the upper Filter section, set the Filter target column to 'Type', the Condition column to 'Equal' and the Parameter 1 column to 'Pitch bend'.
- In the lower Action section, add two lines using the Add Line button. For the first line, set the Action target column to 'Type', the Operation column to 'Set to fixed value' and the Parameter 1 column to 'Controller'. For the second line, set the Action target column to 'Value 1', the Operation column to 'Set to fixed value' and the Parameter 1 column to '10' (Pan Controller number).
- Choose Transform as the function mode in the upper left menu.

The result is the real-time transformation of pitch bend messages into pan data. This is good for the real-time application of pan data using your master synth's pitch wheel.

Of course, many more configurations are possible and, by using more data lines in each section, extremely complex filters and data transformations can be designed. Any efforts made with Transformer will serve you well when you use the main Logical editor

How do I make the MIDI effects a permanent part of the data?

The data produced by the MIDI effects can be made a permanent part of the data using 'Merge MIDI in Loop' in the MIDI menu (Figure 15.14).

Figure 15.14
Merge MIDI in Loop dialogue

Merge MIDI in Loop merges all non-muted MIDI events between the left and right locators in a new MIDI part which is created on the currently selected MIDI track. If there is already MIDI data on the destination track you can choose to overwrite it or merge all the data. To use Merge MIDI in Loop proceed as follows:

- Adjust the left and right locators to encompass the MIDI passage you wish to merge.
- Mute all those MIDI tracks you do not wish to include in the merge operation or, if you are working on a single track, you could use its solo button.
- Select a destination MIDI track.
- Select 'Merge MIDI in Loop' from the MIDI menu.
- Activate the 'Include Inserts' and/or 'Include Sends' options to include the desired MIDI effects.
- Activate the 'Erase Destination' option if you wish to erase the current MIDI part on the destination track and replace it with the merged data. For example, this would be the case, if you were working on a single MIDI part and wished to make its MIDI effects a permanent part of the data. Erasing the destination avoids double notes.
- De-activate the 'Erase Destination' option if you do NOT wish to erase the current MIDI part on the destination track and wish to merge all the chosen data with it. Remember that merging the data from a single part onto the same track means that you are merging the data with itself, which results in double notes.

Automation

Mix automation is considered a standard requirement in professional recording studios. It allows the producer, sound engineer or musician more scope to produce the best possible mix and gives instant recall of a mix which was performed on a previous occasion. Automation normally includes various dynamic fader and control movements which take place throughout the course of the mix. The movements are recorded on the fly and any changes may be overdubbed as many times as necessary in order to achieve the desired result. Cubase includes similar automation features and allows automation of all fader, EQ, pan and other mixer controls, all plug-in effect controls, and all VST instrument controls.

Basic automation

Basic automation can be recorded in Cubase using two methods:

1 Activating the Write buttons and recording the movements of the controls in real-time.
2 Opening an automation subtrack in the event display and drawing an automation curve.

Basic automation using the Read and Write buttons

The Read (R) and Write (W) buttons are found on every channel strip in the Mixer. The buttons are duplicated in the track list and in the Inspector. Read and Write buttons are also found on each plug-in effect interface and each VST Instrument interface.

To start using automation, create a new project or open an existing test project. Select 'Touch Fader' automation mode in the Project window toolbar and open the Mixer. Make sure you have two or three audio tracks recorded in the project. Set up Cubase to cycle on a suitable passage. Leave one or two empty bars at the start. This can be useful for any automated Mixer settings you may wish to implement before the music actually starts. Arrange a layout in a similar manner to Figure 16.1, so that you can see both the Mixer and the Project window simultaneously.

Figure 16.1
Arrange the layout of your project like
this before recording any automation

To record automation in the Mixer proceed as follows:

- Activate the Write button on one of the Audio channels in the Mixer
  (Figure 16.2). An active Write button is illuminated in red.
- Start playback in Cycle mode and simply move the fader of the Audio
  track you Write enabled (Figure 16.3).

Figure 16.2
Activate the Write button for an Audio
channel

Figure 16.3
Move the fader while in normal playback
mode

- Stop moving the fader after the first cycle and, without stopping playback, activate the Read button for the track. An active Read button is illuminated in green. On subsequent laps of the cycle, the fader moves according to the manipulations you made on the first lap of the cycle (Figure 16.4).

Figure 16.4
Activate the Read button for the Audio channel

- Stop playback. Right click / Command click on the corresponding track in the track list in the Project window. Select 'Show Used Automation' from the pop-up menu (Figure 16.5).

Figure 16.5
Select 'Show Used Automation' from the Track list pop-up menu

- Show Used Automation opens the automation subtrack(s) for the Audio track. Alternatively, you can click on the left edge of the track in the track list. If you have manipulated the channel fader, then an automation curve representing the fader movements is now shown in the event display (Figure 16.6). Automation events are shown as small black markers (handles) and these govern the actual shape of the curve.

Figure 16.6
The automation curve in the Volume automation subtrack in the event display

Figure 16.7
Drag an automation handle in the event display to change the shape of the curve

- Grab one of the handles in the automation curve using the Pointer tool near to the current position of the Project cursor and drag it vertically up and down (Figure 16.7). This changes the shape of the curve and simultaneously changes the level shown on the channel fader. Manipulating the automation handles in the subtracks is the main automation editing technique.

Basic automation by drawing automation curves in the subtracks

It is sometimes more appropriate to draw an automation curve in the event display rather than moving controls manually. Such a case might occur if you wanted to produce a simple fade in or some kind of panning manipulation.

Let's imagine that you want to pan one of your sounds from the left to the centre position at the start of the mix. To achieve this in the event display, proceed as follows:

- Right click / Command click on the track to which you wish to apply a pan effect in the Track list. Select 'Show Automation' from the pop-up menu (Figure 16.8).

Figure 16.8 (right)
Select 'Show Automation' from the Track list pop-up menu on the chosen track

Figure 16.9 (far right)
Select the standard panner from the subtrack pop-up menu

- By default, the Volume automation subtrack appears. Click in the subtrack name field and select 'Standard Panner - Pan Left - Right' from the pop-up menu (Figure 16.9).
- Activate the Read button for the pan subtrack in the track list. Select 'Beat' in the Grid Quantize menu and select the Line tool from the Project window toolbar. Draw a line at the appropriate position in the event display to produce the pan effect of your choice (Figure 16.10). Alternatively, use the Draw tool to freely draw any curve shape.
- Activate playback to hear the result. Adjust and experiment with the curve as required.

Figure 16.10
Using the Line tool to draw a pan automation curve in the standard panner subtrack

- Try using the other tools in the toolbar and different Grid Quantize menu settings to create different shaped automation curves (Figure 16.11).

Figure 16.11
Try the other tools to create different shaped automation curves

More automation

The subtrack pop-up menus do not show all the available subtracks simultaneously. To select other subtrack types, select the 'More' option (Figure 16.12). The 'More' option opens the Add Parameter dialogue from where you can select the automation subtrack of your choice (Figure 16.13).

Figure 16.12 (left)
Select other subtrack types using the 'More' option

Figure 16.13 (right)
The Add Parameter dialogue for selecting other subtrack types

Automation modes

Cubase provides five automation modes in the toolbar of the Project window. The modes operate as follows:

- Touch Fader – automation starts to be written when you click on a control during playback and continues until you release the mouse button. This is the standard automation mode for recording movements 'on the fly'.
- Autolatch – automation starts to be written when you click on a control during playback. The last set value for the control continues to be written until you stop playback or de-activate the Write button. In this mode, the release of the mouse button does not switch off the automation. Good for writing static mixes over a looped section.

Figure 16.14
Automation modes in the Project window toolbar

- X-Over – automation starts to be written as soon as you click on a control during playback. The last set value for the control continues to be written until the new automation curve crosses a point on the existing curve (or until you stop playback or de-activate the Write button). For successful operation, both the Read and Write buttons should be activated. In this mode, the release of the mouse button does not switch off the automation. Good for writing fades up to a set level on the existing curve.
- Overwrite mode – automation starts to be written for volume faders only, at their currently set values, *as soon as you commence playback*. The last set value for the control continues to be written until you stop playback or de-activate the Write button (like Autolatch). This function should be used with caution since you can easily overwrite wanted automation, but it is good for writing static volume fader mixes over a specific section or for re-setting all faders to 0dB.
- Trim mode – automation starts to be written when you click on a control during playback and continues until you release the mouse button. When trim mode is selected, the faders of channels with their Write buttons activated are temporarily reset to the mid position. When you write the automation, the changes affect the existing curve relative to the movements of the fader above or below the mid-point. More importantly, Trim mode can be used to change the automation between the left and right locators when Cubase is in stop mode. Proceed as follows: find the automation you wish to trim in the automation subtracks in the event display, set the left and right locators around the events, select Trim mode, activate Write on the appropriate channel(s) and then move the fader(s) up or down.

Why use automation?

Before using automation you must already be familiar with basic mixing. You cannot really tackle automation until you have a clear idea of what mixing itself actually involves. Bear in mind that automated mixing is not a separate magical process, it is merely one of a number of tools (albeit a rather special tool) that you can use to get a better mix. The decision to use it or not is a function of the artistic and technical imperatives of your mix.

Experimenting with automation helps you become familiar with the possibilities. However, using automation in an actual mix reveals that there are many other considerations which govern exactly how and why you might use it. One of the things to avoid is using automation just because it happens to be available. This might produce a mix with lots of intricate automation but you may lose the focus of what kind of mix the music really needs. A better approach is to think about your mix in terms of its overall musical and artistic structure and then define what this implies technically. For example, consider the following basic questions:

- Do you wish to fade in or out any sub-sections within the arrangement?
- Do you wish to add panning effects for certain instruments in the mix?
- Do you wish to mute / unmute any channels throughout the course of the

mix?

- Do you wish to create filter sweep effects in a VSTi or MIDI synth?
- Do you wish to clean up the vocal track using the volume automation curve?

Any of these options could be candidates for automation. Why? Because they all involve dynamic mixer control changes. In addition, if you do not have an external control surface, simultaneous manipulations of multiple controls in a complex mix are actually impossible with a single mouse. In this sense, automation is a necessity in Cubase.

Automation might also involve jumping from one static mix configuration to another and not necessarily smooth, continuous changes. And, of course, your mix may not need automation at all. It may simply require the same settings throughout the entire length of the project. This is perfectly acceptable since it is not a crime to not use automation!

Automation in four steps

1 Prepare for the mix

Preparing for any kind of mixing would normally involve adjusting the Mixer, and perhaps some of the other windows, to suitable settings. You may already have a mixing layout saved as a Workspace. During the mix you are likely to concentrate on specific passages using Cubase in cycle playback mode. This is particularly true when writing automation. For this reason, it is a good idea to set up Cycle markers in the Project window Marker track to encompass the specific passages where the automation is required (see Figure 16.15). To insert a cycle marker, hold Ctrl (PC) / Command (Mac) and drag with the pointer or pencil in the Marker track.

Figure 16.15
Help manage your mix by marking the structure of the musical arrangement using cycle markers in the Marker track

Other preparative measures might include re-labelling the Mixer channels, re-arranging the track order in the Project window and hiding channels that you do not wish to see.

2 Set up a basic mix

Before starting with any specific automation you may wish to set up a basic startup mix in the Mixer which sets all your faders and relevant controls to various default settings. Set this up without any write buttons activated. At this stage you are not writing automation, you are setting up a basic mix. The settings you make are used by Cubase as the basic default values for each control before any automation is applied. Try using a passage where there is activity on all the important tracks in the mix. The controls you set might

include basic fader, pan, EQ and effects settings. Remember, it is important
to not use the Write buttons on the channels at this stage.

3 Write the automation

This is where you start to fill in the details of your mix. The automation can
take place in between other mixing tasks or you could concentrate on it as a
separate process. In any case, it forms part of the overall process of gradually building the sonic image you want to hear. The following sections outline
some common elements which may benefit from automation.

Fading sub-sections of the mix

Specific channels or groups of channels may require fading in or out during
the course of the mix. This is a prime candidate for automation. To fade in
multiple channels, proceed as follows:

- Set up the left and right locators around the section of the intended fades.
  In this case, the section is marked with a cycle marker called 'multifades'
  (Figure 16.16).

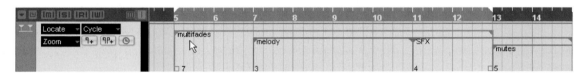

Figure 16.16
Set up the left and right locators around
the section of the intended fades

- Before proceeding, ensure that both the Read and Write buttons are de-
  activated on the relevant channels in the Mixer, since this procedure
  involves fade ins from silence. Move the relevant faders (in this case, kick
  drum, snare and hi-hat) to their lowest positions (Figure 16.17).
- Activate 'Touch Fader' automation mode on the Project window toolbar.
  Activate the Write buttons of the three tracks and activate cycle mode.
  Start playback and move the kick drum fader at the appropriate moment
  to create a kick drum fade in. Activate its Read button and verify the
  fade on the next lap of the cycle. Adjust as necessary. Proceed with the
  snare and hi-hat channels in the same manner (Figure 16.18).
- Open the automation subtracks of the relevant tracks to view the

Figure 16.17 (right)
Move the relevant faders to their
minimum values in the Mixer

Figure 16.18 (far right)
Write the automation in the Mixer using
the channel faders

automation curves (Figure 16.19). The kick drum is faded in first followed by the hi-hat and then the snare. This adds interest to the musical introduction.

Figure 16.19
The resulting volume automation curves for the kick drum, snare and hi-hat in the Project window event display

Setting up panning effects

Panning effects may also benefit from automation. The following example simultaneously pans two different synth sounds. Synth 1 is panned from left to centre and Synth 2 is panned from right to centre. For the creation of this effect proceed as follows:

- Set up the left and right locators around the section of the intended pannings. In this case, the pannings are to take place over two bars.
- Ensure that both the Read and Write buttons are de-activated for the relevant channels in the Mixer. Before writing the automation, move the pan control for the Synth 1 channel to the left and the pan control for the Synth 2 channel to the right (Figure 16.20).
- Activate 'Touch Fader' automation mode on the Project window toolbar. Activate the Write buttons of the two tracks and activate cycle mode. Start playback and move the Synth 1 pan control at the appropriate moment. Slowly drag it to the centre position over the required two bars (Figure 16.21). Activate its Read button and verify your pan on the next lap of the cycle. Adjust as necessary. Proceed with Synth 2 in a similar manner but pan it to the centre from the opposite side.
- Open the automation subtracks of the synthesizer tracks in the Project

> **Tip**
>
> To adjust the resolution of the automation data, use the Automation Reduction slider in Preferences/Editing.

Figure 16.20 (left)
Move the pan control for the synth channels to opposite sides of the stereo image

Figure 16.21 (right)
Write the panning automation

Figure 16.22
The resulting pan automation curves in
the Project window event display

Figure 16.22
The resulting pan automation curves in
the Project window event display

window to view the pan automation curves (Figure 16.22). Do not be
surprised to find that your automation curves do not look perfect. How they
look is not of primary importance. Your main concern is how they sound.

Muting tracks

It is common practice to mute certain tracks during passages when they contain no wanted audio. This silences unwanted interference which may be present on the track and helps create a cleaner mix. The easiest method of muting is to mute on the fly using the mute buttons of the relevant tracks.
Proceed as follows:

- Set up the left and right locators to encompass the bars where you
  intend to mute / unmute the chosen track. In this case, the section is
  marked with a cycle marker (Figure 16.23).

Figure 16.23
Set up the left and right locators to
encompass the section where you intend
to mute / unmute the track

- Activate the 'Touch Fader' automation mode on the Project window
  toolbar. Activate the Read and Write buttons of the relevant channel and
  activate cycle mode. Start playback and activate or de-activate the mute
  button at the appropriate points in time. Verify the mute manipulations
  on the next lap of the cycle. Adjust as necessary.
- Open the mute automation subtrack of the relevant track (Figure
  16.24). The mute curve has only two settings. When the line is in the
  upper part of the subtrack the mute button is activated. When the line is
  in the lower part of the subtrack the mute button is de-activated.

Figure 16.24
The resulting mute button automation

Creating snapshots

Automation of dynamic control movements is not the only way of using
automation. There are occasions when you need to change from one global
group of settings to another, instantaneously. Each group of settings might

be referred to as a snapshot; a non-dynamic mix which remains static for a given number of bars.

For example, a common technique involves setting up separate static mixes for the intro, verse, chorus, middle eight and solo sections. The technique outlined below is best suited to automation in Autolatch mode.

To set up a static mix for your chosen sections proceed as follows:

- Select Autolatch mode in the Project window toolbar.
- Set up the left and right locators to encompass the first passage of music where you wish to implement a static mix. Select the Cycle button on the Transport panel.
- Click on the Write button in the Mixer Common panel. This activates the Write buttons globally for all channels (Figure 16.25).
- Commence cycle playback and set up the Mixer controls for the first section (Figure 16.26). The last set value for each control continues to be written until you stop playback or de-activate the Write button. After moving any controls make sure you continue to write the data for at least one whole cycle in order to write the values over the full length of the passage.

Figure 16.25
Click on the Write button in the Common panel to globally activate all channel Write buttons

Figure 16.26
Commence cycle playback and set up the Mixer controls for the first section

- Set up the left and right locators to encompass the second passage of music where you wish to implement a static mix. Select the Cycle button on the Transport panel. Make sure the Write button is still activated on all channels.
- Commence cycle playback and set up the Mixer controls for the second section (Figure 16.27). After moving any controls make sure you continue to write the data for at least one whole cycle in order to write the values over the full length of the passage.

Figure 16.27
Commence cycle playback and set up the Mixer controls for the second section

- Continue in a similar manner to write as many static mix sections as required. When you have finished, de-activate the Write buttons. Click on the Read button in the Mixer Common panel to activate the Read buttons globally for all channels. Commence playback from the start of the music. During playback, you should see the controls change instantaneously as you pass from one static mix to the next.

4 Edit the automation

Editing techniques

Mix automation data is shown as small black markers or handles along the length of the automation curves and it is these which govern the actual shape of the curve. These are known as automation events. Automation events may be edited using the standard mouse and tool techniques of the Project window, as outlined in Chapter 4. The following are some of the most useful techniques:

- Select one or more automation events by dragging a box around the relevant area in the subtrack using the Pointer tool (Object selection tool). Alternatively, step through the events using the left / right arrows on the computer keyboard. Selected automation events are displayed in red.
- Delete one or more automation events by selecting them and pressing the backspace or delete keys on the computer keyboard. Alternatively, use the Eraser tool.
- Copy a group of automation events using Ctrl + C. Paste the copied events by moving the Project cursor to another position in the subtrack and pressing Ctrl + V. The copied events overwrite the chosen section from the Project cursor position. Alternatively, use the Range Selection tool to move (or copy by pressing Alt) the events to a new position.
- Click on any automation event and drag it to a new position to change the shape of the curve. Movements snap to the current snap resolution.
- Write a single new automation event by clicking once anywhere along the automation line.
- Write new automation events by dragging any of the draw tools (pencil, line, parabola and so on) in the automation subtrack.

Correcting irregularities

Manually writing automation in the Mixer often results in small irregularities in the automation curves. It may be appropriate to fine tune the results for a smoother effect. To smooth an automation curve, proceed as follows:

- Zoom in to the relevant subtrack so that you can see the individual automation events clearly (Figure 16.28). Set up the left and right locators and activate playback in cycle mode. In this way, you can make all edits 'on the fly' and hear the results on the next lap of the cycle.
- In this example, we delete the first group of pan automation events and move one of the handles to the left pan position at the very beginning of

Figure 16.28
Automation events before editing

bar 7 (Figure 16.29). Activate the Snap button to help place the event. The left pan position corresponds with the uppermost position in the automation curve.

Figure 16.29
Delete the first group of pan automation events and move one of the handles to the extreme left pan position at the beginning of bar 7

- Thin out the events between bars 7 and 8 and move the event located at the beginning of bar 9 to the centre pan position. Create a suitable curve between the event at bar 7 and the event at bar 9 (Figure 16.30). This gives you a smooth pan from the left to the centre pan positions over two bars.

Figure 16.30
The resulting smooth pan over two bars

You may like to tidy up other automation events in a similar manner but bear in mind that it may not be appropriate to make all automation scientifically correct. Leaving some of the rough edges may be what gives your mix its character. Above all, avoid the habit of working visually. The aim is *not* to produce a visually perfect event display but to produce a good sounding mix! Always listen very carefully as you make each change and preferably work in cycle playback mode. If the automation sounds best 'rough and ready' then leave it that way.

Moving and copying automation

Moving or copying automation events in the Project window event display are common requirements. Moving is useful for those occasions when the timing of individual events or a group of events is not quite right. Copying saves time when you have a number of repetitive sections of automation. If 'Automation Follows Events' is enabled (Edit menu), automation events are automatically attached to regular Audio and MIDI events and copied or moved with them. Here, we look at how automation events are copied and moved independently.

Three methods of independently moving groups of automation events are as follows:

Tip

Beware of correcting intentional irregularities in automation subtracks. Many irregularities may have been what you intended at the time you wrote the automation. Always listen very carefully as you make changes and preferably edit your automation while monitoring in cycle playback mode.

Tip

When moving automation handles, activate the Project window infoline. The infoline displays the start time and value of the event as you drag it. This helps place the events with greater precision. Alternatively, click directly on the value field in the infoline to activate a slider which may be used to change the value of the event.

- Select the Object selection tool and drag a selection box around the group of automation events. Press Ctrl / Command + X to cut the events. Place the cursor at the position at which you wish to paste the automation events. Press Ctrl / Command + V to paste the events.
- Select the Range selection tool and drag in the appropriate subtrack(s) (or normal tracks) to select the area of interest. Once selected, click in the shaded area (at which time a hand appears) and drag the selection to a new location.
- Select the Object selection tool and drag a selection box around the group of automation events. Click on any one of the selected events and drag the whole group horizontally backwards or forwards along the track. The horizontal movement is magnetic to the current snap resolution and you can only drag the group as far as the next event in the subtrack.

Two methods of independently copying groups of automation events are as follows:

- Select the Object selection tool and drag a selection box around the group of automation events. Press Ctrl / Command + C to copy the events. Place the cursor at the position at which you wish to paste the copied automation events. Press Ctrl / Command + V to paste the events.
- Select the Range selection tool and drag in the appropriate subtrack(s) to select the area of interest. Once selected, press Alt on the computer keyboard, click in the shaded area (at which time a hand appears) and drag a copy of the selection to a new location.

Automation follows events

If you enable 'Automation follows events' in the Edit menu, any automation data found in the same range is automatically attached to regular Audio and MIDI events when they are moved or copied. This provides one of the easiest methods of moving and repeating automation data. An example is shown in Figure 16.31.

Figure 16.31
With 'Automation follows events' enabled, copying a percussion event produces four instances of the same automated pan effect

Surround sound

Surround sound implies the use of a multiple channel sound diffusion system where there are speakers behind and to each side of the listener, as well as in front. Most surround sound configurations have their historical foundations in the film industry, which began using multichannel formats as long ago as the early 1950s. Early implementations involved a number of channels to the front of the listener and one to the rear, known as the effects channel. Early 70mm wide-screen cinemas featured five channels across the cinema screen and a surround channel which fed multiple speakers to the rear and sides of the auditorium. As wide-screen cinema fell out of fashion the need for a large number of channels across the front became obsolete. In the 1970s Dolby Laboratories encouraged the use of a surround sound system based upon three main screen channels (left, centre and right), with two low frequency bass extension channels and one surround channel to the rear. The centre channel was traditionally used for dialogue. The company also developed a 70mm format featuring a stereo surround channel. This was the forerunner of the 5.1 channel Dolby Digital Surround format.

At this point, you may well ask why Cubase should need to be equipped with surround sound when this is largely the domain of the film industry. The answer lies in the fact that, in recent times, there has been a convergence of the film sound, television sound and record industries such that they no longer work in isolation, and surround sound has become an accepted common standard among all three. In addition, surround systems are finding their way into more and more homes and the DVD-Audio disc aims to bring multichannel surround sound to the general consumer market (possibly eventually replacing standard audio CDs). Surround mixes are already a common occurrence in the audio industry. Cubase is ready to help you create your surround mix if you should need to.

Demystifying surround sound

Surround sound has been championed by two organisations: Dolby Laboratories and DTS (Digital Theatre Systems). One of the main differences between the two systems is that the audio data stream for Dolby Surround is stored on the film-strip itself (between the sprocket holes) whereas the audio data for DTS is stored on a separate laser disc. The audio encoding algorithms for both methods involve data compression techniques and both sys-

Figure 17.1
3/2 system for surround sound

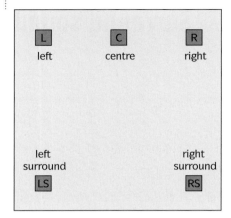

Figure 17.2
5.1 channel surround sound

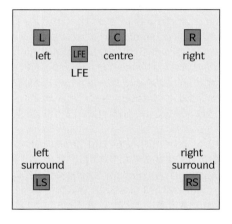

tems are already available on many DVDs and music CDs. Both use the same kind of multiple channel sound formats in order to be compatible with the current hardware installed in cinema auditoriums.

The popular 5.1 channel surround configuration is a special implementation of the standard surround setup known as 3/2. The standard 3/2 configuration forms the essential reference system for surround sound. It features a left, centre and right channel in front of the listener and left surround and right surround channels to the rear (Figure 17.1).

Figure 17.1 shows the five speakers of a basic surround setup. '3/2' simply means three channels to the front and two to the rear. The front centre channel has its origins in the film industry where it is used for dialogue. 5.1 channel surround adds an additional specialised channel to the basic 3/2 system known as the LFE channel (Low Frequency Effects channel). This is the '.1' in the '5.1' name (Figure 17.2). There are many derivations of this in other surround configurations like 3/2/1, 5/2/1, 6.1 and 7.1. In all these cases, the '1' refers to an LFE channel. The other numbers refer to the number of full-bandwidth speakers featured in the surround system and, in the first two cases, how they are distributed between the front and rear parts of the listening space.

In the film industry, the LFE channel traditionally handles sub bass frequencies between 20Hz to around 80Hz. This is used for material which will not compromise the end result if the program is reproduced on a system which cannot handle the low frequencies or does not feature an LFE channel. In may ways, the LFE channel is intended as an optional effects channel and is not considered as an essential element which must be used in order to conform to the 5.1 (or similar) standard.

Once a surround mix has been created it has to be encoded to conform to the chosen surround format. This is achieved using special software and hardware (not included in Cubase). For example, to create media suitable for playback in 5.1 channel Dolby Digital format, the multiple audio files created by a surround mix must be converted into a data stream known as AC-3. At the time of playback, the AC-3 data is decoded into the intended playback format using multi-channel audio playback hardware featuring Dolby Digital decoding. In fact, the AC-3 data stream may be decoded for mono, stereo or 5.1 channel surround playback and so represents an adaptable format.

Common surround sound formats

The common surround formats include the following:

- Dolby Stereo (Dolby Surround) – Dolby Stereo is a four channel surround format developed in the 1970s for the film industry featuring left, centre, right and monophonic surround channel (of limited bandwidth). This is sometimes referred to as LCRS. In the early days of home theatre, it was possible to decode the left, right and surround channel information using early Dolby Surround decoders.
- Dolby Pro Logic – early 'home-theatre' Dolby Surround decoders could not derive a centre channel. The introduction of the Dolby Pro Logic format allowed the decoding of the centre channel and helped create a sound quality equivalent to cinema auditoriums in the home theatre environment. Dolby Pro Logic II improved matters further since it was capable of producing five channel surround (left, centre, right, left surround, right surround) from Dolby Surround encoded material, and also enhanced surround reproduction from any other un-encoded stereo signal. The surround channels for Pro Logic II featured full bandwidth reproduction.
- 5.1 channel digital surround – a digital surround format featuring five discrete full bandwidth channels and one limited bandwidth low frequency effects (LFE) channel. These are arranged as left, centre, right, in front of the listener and left surround, right surround to the rear. Traditionally the low frequency effects channel is located between the left and centre channels in front of the listener (see Figure 17.2). 5.1 channel digital surround sound is implemented by two organisations, Dolby Laboratories and DTS (Digital Theatre Systems).
- Dolby Digital 5.1 – the Dolby implementation of 5.1 channel surround sound. This involves conversion of the six discrete audio channels into a digital data stream known as AC-3. The AC-3 data stream is later decoded using proprietary Dolby decoding equipment. Dolby Digital is the most popular surround format for DVD (Digital Versatile Disc).
- DTS – a similar 5.1 surround system to Dolby Digital. In the film industry, the DTS audio data stream is stored on a separate laser disc whereas the Dolby audio data stream is stored on the film-strip itself. When used on DVD the DTS digital data stream is recorded on the medium itself. The DTS system uses slightly less compression and some experts claim that it has a superior sound quality.
- 6.1 channel digital surround – a surround format similar to Dolby Digital 5.1 but with an additional centre surround channel to the rear. 6.1 formats include Dolby Digital EX and DTS ES.
- 7.1 channel digital surround – a surround format similar to Dolby Digital 5.1 but with additional left and right side speakers or, in the case of the proprietary SDDS 7.1 format (Sony Digital Dynamic Sound), left centre and right centre front channels to handle wide screen cinema.

Figure 17.3
The Add output bus dialogue allows you
to add an output buss in your chosen
surround format

Setting up the surround features in Cubase

General Setup

For full surround reproduction the Cubase user needs audio hardware connected to the host computer which is capable of producing the number of
audio outputs required for the chosen surround format. For example, standard 3/2 would require five audio outputs and 5.1 channel surround would
require six. Of course, the sound reproduction system would also need to
feature multiple speakers and amplifiers to match the number of channels of
the chosen format.

Creating a surround output buss

You configure the output of Cubase for surround sound by creating a surround output buss in the outputs section of the VST Connections window,
selected from the Devices menu. Proceed as follows:

- Open the VST Connections window and click on the outputs tab.
- Click on the Add button to open the Add bus dialogue. The choice of
  formats provided in the Configuration menu includes mono, stereo,
  LRCS, standard 3/2 (5.0), 5.1 surround and various other
  left/right/centre/surround/LFE permutations and quadraphonic (Quadro)
  formats (Figure 17.3). Most of these are described above. Quadro allows
  the setting up of mixes based upon the four channel quadraphonic
  format devised for vinyl records in the early 1970s.

Figure 17.4 (right)
5.1 surround buss in the VST
Connections window

Figure 17.5 (below)
5.1 surround output bus channel in the
Mixer

- Select a surround format from the Configuration menu. Since it is such a
  popular format many readers may choose the 5.1 surround format. Once
  chosen, the details of the new surround buss are displayed in the VST
  Connections window (Figure 17.4). Make sure that the channels are
  routed to the appropriate output ports of your audio hardware.
- When you create a new surround buss, a surround output channel strip is
  added in the Mixer (Figure 17.5). The meters follow the order of the
  channels as listed in the VST Connections window (from left to right).

At this point, any audio-based channels routed to the surround buss may be
mixed in surround, using the surround panner. The surround panner is available only when a surround buss is chosen in the output routing menu.

Using surround channels

Regular audio tracks are normally in mono or stereo format but when they are added to the Project they can also be assigned as surround channels in the Add track dialogue. A surround channel is appropriate for playback of multichannel interleaved files. Libraries of 5.1 surround files of this type are commonly available or you can create your own.

Surround format channels are also applicable to software samplers which include 5.1 surround support, such as Steinberg's Halion or Native Instruments' Kontakt. In the case of Kontakt, a number of its outputs may be configured in Cubase for 5.1 use. These appear in the Mixer in the normal way as VSTi channels, and may be mixed to 5.1 as desired. Kontakt is supplied with a range of surround presets in its library (see Figure 17.6).

Figure 17.6
Native Instruments Kontakt sampler configured for surround sound in Cubase

Mixing surround sound

To mix in surround sound you need to route all channels in the Mixer to the surround output bus. This is selected in the output routing pop-up menu in the upper section of the channel strip (Figure 17.7).

Alternatively, you can route a channel signal directly to any of the surround outputs using the other routing options in the menu. When a surround output is chosen for regular audio-based channels, a miniature surround panner replaces the normal pan control in the Mixer channel strip. This allows you to graphically place the sound within the surround soundfield. The cur-

Figure 17.7
Select the surround output bus in the Mixer channel output routing pop-up menu

Figure 17.8
The SurroundPan controls in the Mixer
channel strip

Figure 17.9
The surround panner interface

rent position is indicated by a blue marker. You can move the position of the marker by dragging it within the display. A slightly larger version of the surround panner is available in the extended part of the Mixer (Figure 17.8).

Using the surround panner plug-in

For more elaborate control of the surround pan position, double click on the surround panner control in the channel strip. This opens the more detailed surround panner interface (Figure 17.9).

The surround panner interface displays a representation of the speaker configuration for the chosen surround format. The level of each channel is indicated next to each virtual speaker where 0dB represents the full power of the source audio signal. The level is also indicated graphically by thick blue lines which appear at each virtual speaker. The relative levels of the channels are controlled by dragging a ball within the display, at which time the blue lines change length and the indicated levels are modified accordingly. Any of the channels can be switched off by Alt-clicking on the speaker icon. Modifier keys facilitate the moving of the ball as follows:

- Hold Ctrl / Command + Shift while dragging in the display to restrict movement to the x axis (horizontal) only.
- Hold Ctrl / Command while dragging in the display to restrict movement to the y axis (vertical) only.
- Hold Alt while dragging in the display to restrict movement to the diagonal between the top left and lower right corners.
- Hold Ctrl / Command + Alt while dragging in the display to restrict movement to the diagonal between the lower left and top right corners.

The lower part of the interface features the following:

- Mode menu – this governs the manner in which the speakers are distributed around the listening position. Standard and Position modes produce aligned front speakers as found in a cinema auditorium and Angle mode implements speakers which are equi-distant from the listening position. The default setting is Standard mode.
- Mono / stereo pop-up – determines the manner in which the single mono marker or dual stereo markers move around the display. This is particularly relevant for stereo signals where the movement of the right channel marker is mirrored on the x axis or the y axis, or both simultaneously. 'Mono Mix' is the default setting for mono channels and 'Y-Mirror' is the default for stereo channels. The left and right channels of a stereo signal routed through a surround panner set to Mono Mix are added together before entering the plug-in. A mono signal routed through a surround panner set to a stereo mode is split into two channels before entering the plug-in.
- Centre level dial – determines the percentage by which the centre channel provides the centre image where 100% results in full use of the centre channel, (in which case the left and right front channels are reduced in level when the marker is in the central vertical area), and 0%

results in zero use of the centre channel, (in which case the left and right front channels are raised in level when the marker is in the central vertical area). When the centre channel has been reduced to 0% the left / right front channels behave like a regular stereo setup where the centre sound is produced by the in-phase signals of the left and right source signals.

- LFE dial – determines the amount of the source signal which should be routed to the LFE channel. This is relevant only when the surround configuration includes an LFE channel (as in 5.1 surround).
- Divergence dials – control the differentiation of the distribution of the source signal between the different channels where levels higher than 0% result in a less exclusive distribution. i.e. the higher the percentage on the dial the less differentiation between the corresponding channels.

VST Instruments

This chapter outlines the installation and basic use of VST Instruments within Cubase and describes some of the VST Instruments supplied with the program.

What are VST Instruments?

VST is an abbreviation for 'Virtual Studio Technology' or 'Virtual Studio' and was introduced by Steinberg in 1996 for their Cubase VST MIDI+Audio sequencing software. VST Instrument is an abbreviation for 'Virtual Studio Instrument' and the term is often shortened still further to read 'VSTi'. VST-compatible audio effects and processing units come in the form of plug-ins which can be added to the host software when required. VST 2.0 technology took this concept one stage further by introducing a special kind of plug-in which allows the transmitting and receiving of MIDI data as well as audio. This encouraged the development of more sophisticated regular plug-ins but, more importantly, it inspired the development of software synthesis and sampling instruments which can operate within the convenient environment of the host software. These became known as VST Instruments.

A VST Instrument could be a software synthesizer or sampler, a software drum module or some other virtual sound-making device and, once activated inside the host software, it can be played via MIDI using an external MIDI keyboard or triggered from an existing MIDI track. In many respects, VST Instruments behave in the same way as their real-world counterparts, the only major difference being that they reside inside your computer.

System requirements and performance issues

VST Instruments require a VST 2.0 (or later) host application like Steinberg Cubase and most run on both the PC and Mac computer platforms. Cubase should already be running successfully on the computer before you install a VST Instrument. Once installed, the VST Instrument may be loaded and activated within Cubase similar to a regular plug-in effect. The sounds are triggered via MIDI, either in real-time using an external MIDI keyboard (or other controller) or from a recorded MIDI track. There are a number of computer hardware factors which affect the performance and playability of a VST Instrument. Paramount among these are CPU speed, the amount of RAM memory and audio hardware latency.

CPU speed and RAM

Software synthesis, software sampling and software effects processing are CPU-intensive activities. The number of voices available for any software instrument is, therefore, directly related to the amount of CPU power available. The drain on CPU power varies according to the number of notes being played simultaneously and according to the complexity of the tone being produced by the instrument. Many software samplers and sample-based drum modules require substantial amounts of RAM in order to run smoothly. This is particularly true for those which use disk-streaming techniques where greater use of RAM memory results in less strain on the hard disk.

Latency

Latency is the delay between the input and output of a digital audio system (expressed in samples or milliseconds). All digital audio systems take a small amount of time to respond to a user input and process the data through their hardware and software. This affects real-time performance with VST instruments since it imposes a slight delay between the moment you press a note on your MIDI keyboard and the moment you hear the sound from the instrument. If the delay is too long then it becomes impossible to play in real-time. (Real-world electronic musical instruments also suffer from a similar delay). For real-time performance, the audio hardware should preferably be capable of latency times of less than 10ms. Achieving this requires a professional-quality audio card / hardware with a special ASIO driver. (See relevant internet sites and software / hardware developer documentation for precise details of ASIO drivers and hardware system recommendations).

Installing VST Instruments

A good range of VST instruments are automatically installed when you first install Cubase. These include the Prologue, Spector, Mystic, Embracer and Monologue synthesizers, and the HalionOne sample player. There are also a wide range of VST Instruments available from third party developers (see Table 18.1 at the end of this chapter). These must be installed separately in a similar fashion to regular plug-ins, using standard software installation techniques. Follow the installation instructions supplied with the chosen VST Instrument. You can normally choose to install into the Cubase Vstplugins folder alongside the regular plug-in files, or into the shared Vstplugins folder. When you next launch Cubase, the newly installed VST Instrument is added to the list of available instruments within the software. To find out what is currently installed, select Devices / Plug-in Information.

Activating and using VST Instruments

Before you can play a VST Instrument it must first be activated in one of the slots of the VST Instruments panel. This is opened by selecting 'VST Instruments' in the Devices menu or by pressing F11 on the computer keyboard (Figure 18.1).

To load a VST Instrument into one of the panel's slots, click on a blank

Figure 18.1 (left)
VST Instruments panel

Figure 18.2 (right)
Click on a VST Instrument slot to open
the pop-up selection menu

name field. This opens a pop-up menu containing the VST Instruments which are available within your system (Figure 18.2).

Selecting a VST Instrument from the menu loads it into the slot and its name appears in the name field. The instrument is activated / de-activated by clicking on the slot's power button. By default, a single stereo output is activated for the instrument but, for those instruments with multiple outputs, you can activate any combination of outputs in the output routing menu. When first activated you may be asked if you wish to create a MIDI track assigned to the instrument, depending upon the setting in Preferences / VST / Plug-ins. Similar to regular audio channels, VSTi channels are used to regulate the volume, pan position, EQ and routing of the audio output signal from the instrument.

Figure 18.3 (left)
Click on the Edit button to open the
interface for the VSTi

To open the GUI for the VST Instrument click on the edit button (lower case 'e') in the VST Instrument slot (Figure 18.3).

In order to trigger the VST Instrument, assign the output port of a MIDI track to the instrument (if not already assigned at the time you activated the VST instrument). The output port menu for a MIDI track is found in the basic settings section of the Inspector. This features the names of any currently active VST Instruments alongside the other output ports (Figure 18.4). With the record enable button or the monitor button activated, you can now trigger the VST Instrument from a MIDI keyboard. If desired, you can make a recording onto the chosen track. You can also trigger the VST Instrument using an existing pre-recorded MIDI track if you set the track's output port to the VST Instrument.

Figure 18.4 (below)
Assign a MIDI track to a VST Instrument
in the output routing menu

VST Instrument automation in Cubase

Automation of VST Instrument parameters is achieved by activating the Write button in the GUI window of the instrument and recording the movements of the controls in real-time (Figure 18.5). The automation is written in normal playback mode; activating the record button on the Transport panel is *not*

Figure 18.5
To record the movements of the controls, activate the Write button in the GUI window of the VST Instrument

necessary. To play back the automation, activate the Read button in the GUI window of the VST Instrument.

Alternatively, automation may be created in the VST Instrument automation sub-tracks in the Project window. When you first activate a VST instrument, one or more VSTi audio tracks and a VSTi device track appear in the Project window. The VSTi audio tracks and associated sub-tracks handle regular automation like volume, pan, EQ and so on, while the VSTi device track and associated sub-tracks handle automation specific to the VST instrument. The sub-tracks may be used to edit any automation already recorded or to create automation data from scratch using the draw tools (Figure 18.6).

Figure 18.6
Create or edit VST Instrument automation in the VST Instrument Automation sub-tracks in the Project window

VSTi automation is excellent for producing filter sweeps and special effects and can add an extra dimension to synthesizer parts. For example, try using the draw tools in the VST Instrument automation sub-tracks in the Project window to create shapes which modulate the values of the filter cut-off, resonance and drive controls of the supplied Monologue synthesizer (Figure 18.7). Make sure the Read button is activated in the VSTi interface window.

Figure 18.7
Modulating the cut-off, resonance and drive controls of the supplied Monologue synth using automation curves in the VST Instrument automation sub-tracks

Converting VSTi tracks into regular audio tracks

MIDI tracks which trigger VST Instruments can be directly converted into audio files for use on regular audio tracks using Export / Audio Mixdown (File menu).

This exports all non-muted audio tracks, VST instrument tracks and MIDI tracks which trigger VST instruments between the left and right locators to an audio file. This is helpful when your computer is running out of system resources since regular audio tracks use less CPU and less RAM than VSTi tracks.

Instrument Freeze

An alternative to the above technique is to use the Instrument Freeze function. This allows you to freeze the performance of a VST instrument so that it is played back from a 'ghost' audio track rather than being calculated in real-time. Instrument Freeze takes into account all non-muted MIDI parts which are triggering the chosen VST instrument. To freeze an instrument, proceed as follows:

- Make sure that the VST instrument performance plays back exactly as required, including activating the appropriate Read buttons if you have recorded any automation.
- Open the VST Instruments panel from the Devices menu (or press F11 on the computer keyboard).
- Locate the VSTi slot for the instrument you wish to freeze and click on its 'Instrument Freeze' button to the left of the slot (Figure 18.8).
- In the 'Freeze instrument options' dialogue which appears, you can choose to freeze the instrument only, in which case any pre-fader insert effects on the VSTi channel(s) are not frozen with the instrument, or you can choose to freeze both the instrument and any pre-fader insert effects on the VSTi channel(s). 'Tail size' allows you to set a tail time for any echo or reverberation effects. A further option 'Unload instrument when frozen' helps free up still more computer resources by unloading the VSTi after the freeze operation. This is welcome for RAM-hungry software samplers.

Figure 18.8
Freezing the Monologue VSTi

The resulting 'ghost' audio file is stored in a new Freeze folder, located in the Project folder. All MIDI tracks, events and VSTi device tracks relevant to the frozen instrument are now greyed out and cannot be edited. However, the VSTi audio channels remain active and operate as if you are still triggering the VST instrument in the normal way. Frozen VST instruments can at any time be un-frozen by clicking on the Instrument Freeze button a second time.

Exploring the supplied VST Instruments

There now follow descriptions of a selection of the VST Instruments supplied with the program.

Prologue

Prologue (Figure 18.9) is a virtual analogue synthesizer featuring three oscillators, eight filter types, four ADSR envelope generators, LFO modulation, frequency modulation, ring modulation and built-in effects.

To start tweaking the parameters of Prologue, you might like to begin with a suitable basic preset. Try selecting 'Brett Bass'. This uses all three oscillators, each with sawtooth selected as the source waveform. Movement is provided by detuning oscillators 2 and 3 and character is injected by using moderate amounts of drive, soft distortion and chorus effects. This preset includes classic filter settings with the cutoff at around 8k and a small amount of resonance. The cutoff frequency is modulated by the LFO set to a slow 0.346. This produces the slow sweeping effect you can hear during the sustain part of the sound.

You can use the 'Brett Bass' preset to discover some of the other possibilities with Prologue. For example, try reducing all oscillator levels to zero and set the ring modulator control to its maximum level. This is the classic setting for ring modulation. Set the waveform of oscillator 2 to one of the vocal vowel sources (A, E, I, O or U). Audition the sound to hear how the tone acquires the voice-like characteristics of the chosen oscillator 2 waveform. Ring modulation multiplies the frequencies of oscillators 1 and 2 to produce their sum and difference frequencies. Ring modulation is commonly used to produce metallic and bell-like tones.

Now reset Prologue to the original 'Brett Bass' preset. In the oscillator 2 section, select the sine waveform, activate frequency modulation, set fine tune to +50 and ratio to 11. Reduce the filter cut-off frequency to around 5k. Audition the sound to hear how it has been transformed into an organ-like tone.

Figure 18.9
The Prologue synthesizer

As you continue to tweak the controls, do not forget to try the pitchbend range and maximum number of voices parameters in the upper left and right corners, and the portamento and legato controls to the left. Prologue also features a very comprehensive range of source waveforms including standard sawtooth, parabolic, square, triangle and sine waves along with over fifty variations in formant, vocal, partial, resonant pulse, slope and negative slope categories. The four envelope generators, two LFOs, external modulation, velocity, aftertouch and key pitch tracking may be assigned to a large number of destinations. All this, together with the the the distortion, delay and modulation effects, adds up to an analogue-style synthesizer of great flexibility and potential.

Prologue is supplied with over 200 presets which are well stocked with synth bass, lead and pad sounds.

Monologue

Monologue (Figure 18.10) is a monophonic virtual analogue synthesizer featuring two oscillators, a filter with six filter types, modulation and amplitude ADSR envelopes, LFO and effects.

Among the best techniques for getting to know a synthesizer is to program your own sounds. For this task it is best to start with something simple. Try the following:

- Select square waves for oscillators 1 and 2 and set all their controls to zero and their mix levels to 0dB. Set the noise control to off. Set the modulation sources of oscillators 1 and 2 to LFO and mod wheel respectively.
- In the filter section, select LP12 mode and set the cutoff to 74 and resonance to 31. Set the high pass and key track controls to zero. Set the left modulation source to 'mod env' and set the depth to -60%.
- In the LFO section, set the source wave to triangle, the rate to 10.98Hz,

Figure 18.10
Try setting Monologue to these simple settings as a starting point for programming your own sounds

the depth to 100% and the modulation source to mod wheel.
- In the FX section, set the overdrive and effects mix controls to zero.
- Set the mod envelope ADSR to 48, 53, 0, 0 and the amp envelope ADSR to 0, 46, 0, 0.
- Finally, set pitch bend to 2 and random pitch to 6.3. Your patch should now look the same as Figure 18.10

Auditioning this patch reveals a short, simple sound. We have stripped down the sonic possibilities to the bare essentials. We can now clearly hear the effect of any further manipulations. In all of the following experiments, audition the sound while manipulating the controls. Start by increasing the PWM control of oscillator 2. Try also increasing the modulation depth and experimenting with the effect using the modulation wheel of your keyboard. The sound is immediately richer and more interesting. Next, try changing the left filter modulation depth control. This transforms the sound between resonant and bright characteristics. Now try adding some overdrive, chorus or delay to inject more life into the sound. When you have found something which sounds promising, try adjusting the filter cutoff and resonance simultaneously by moving the handle in the x-y controller. Carefully tune the mod envelope attack to give more bite to the start of the sound and increase the decay and release of the amp envelope to give more body and duration. Finally, try increasing the oscillator 1 modulation depth to hear the effect of the LFO as you move the modulation wheel of your keyboard. If you discover an inspiring patch, don't forget to save it.

Monologue is designed specifically for creating monophonic bass, lead and sequenced synth tones. Take a look in the supplied presets for further examples and ideas.

Embracer
Embracer (Figure 18.11) is a virtual analogue synthesizer specialised in the creation of pad sounds and operating in stereo or surround modes.

Embracer features two oscillators, each with a choice of twelve waveforms. Each oscillator features a dual action tone control. This is a low-pass filter

Figure 18.11
Embracer synthesizer

when set below the centre position and a high-pass filter when set above. A width control governs the amount of spread across the stereo or surround soundfield. The tone and width controls may be simultaneously modified by dragging the circular controls in the central 'eye' display. Oscillator 2 may be de-tuned in relation to oscillator 1. Attack and velocity controls are provided for each oscillator and an overall release parameter is included. Stereo or surround mode selection and width modulation control complete the picture.

The choice of oscillator and the tone and width controls form the sound shaping heart of the unit. Dragging the handles in the central 'eye' display is among the easiest techniques for quickly creating rich synth pads. To add movement and interest, try setting contrasting width and tone values for each oscillator. For example, the settings shown in Figure 18.11 feature oscillator 1 set to a soft waveform ('soft wave') with a narrow width and fast attack, combined with oscillator 2 set to a sharper waveform ('split strynx') with a wide width and slow attack. This results in a sound with a soft and slightly distant attack beginning in the centre of the stereo image, followed by a more resonant and bright swell which fills the stereo width during the sustain part of the sound. Alternatively, to create sounds which take up less space in the mix try switching off one of the oscillators using the 'OFF' option in the oscillator pop-up menu. Experimenting with the attack velocity and level velocity controls and the coarse and fine tuning of oscillator 2 may also yield fruitful results.

HalionOne

HalionOne (Figure 18.12) is a sample player specialised in the playback of the supplied HSB (Halion Sound Bank) format samples.

HalionOne features a comparatively simple GUI showing the name of the currently loaded preset and eight control parameter dials known as 'quick controls' for modifying the sound. The quick controls vary according to the type of preset selected and, for most sounds, include cut-off, resonance, DCF filter, DCA envelope; and reverb, delay, chorus or flange parameters. Alternative controls are included where appropriate, such as the glide control in the 'Touch of Teebee' preset or the talkbox control in the 'Talking Lead' preset. An efficiency mini-fader allows you to lessen the CPU load of processor-hungry presets. This might be required for a preset like 'Atmosphere', which quickly drains your computer's resources by allocating six voices to each note played. If desired, you can bypass all effects by clicking on the effects LED.

Figure 18.12
HalionOne sample player

The strength of HalionOne lies in the range and quality of its presets. Over 600 HalionOne presets are supplied with Cubase and these include good selections in all the usual categories of bass, brass, drums and percussion, plucked, organ, piano, sound effects, strings, synth leads and pads.

Combining Cubase with applications from other developers

You can significantly increase the creative potential of Cubase by combining it with some of the more elaborate applications and VST Instruments supplied by other developers, especially those featuring modular synthesis environments and sampling. This is particularly relevant for those using Cubase for electronic music composition, orchestral composition and arranging, and sound effects creation. Favourites include Propellerhead Reason software synthesis studio (not actually a VSTi), Native Instruments Reaktor sound studio, Native Instruments Kontakt software sampler and Applied Acoustics Systems Tassman physical modelling synthesizer. Reason is not available as a VSTi but is easily integrated into Cubase using the Rewire protocol, while the others may be integrated as standard VST Instruments. These applications provide much more than ordinary VSTi software synthesizers and musical instruments. They are often complete studio, synthesis, sampling, sequencing and sound processing environments in their own right.

Figure 18.13
Kontakt. Among the best software sampler choices for Cubase users

Figure 18.14
Reaktor's Space Drone synthesizer in
action in Cubase

Reason provides analogue synthesizers, samplers, drum machines and effects together with sequencing, mixing and patching features, all within an intuitive virtual rack environment. Kontakt (Figure 18.13) is a powerful software sampler in an elegant and easy-to-use virtual rack, supplied complete with its own on-board convolution reverb and an outstanding library, the cornerstone of which is a special version of the Vienna Symphonic Orchestra sample collection. Tassman provides a modular environment where you can build your own musical instruments based upon physical modelling. This allows the creation of truly authentic re-creations of acoustic instruments and unusual hybrid instruments. Reaktor is probably the ultimate modular sound studio, allowing you to build your own instruments and effects and providing a vast library of synthesizers, samplers, effects, drum machines and sequencers (Figure 18.14). All these applications integrate well into the Cubase software environment.

Summary and VST Instruments list

VST Instruments provide a convenient means of accessing high quality sound sources within the software environment of Cubase. All that is required to trigger the sounds is one external keyboard connected to your computer via MIDI and a low latency audio card. This arrangement helps avoid elaborate external MIDI networks with complex MIDI cabling issues, and saves physical space in your recording studio. In addition, VST Instruments do not develop electronic faults and are not subject to the usual wear and tear suffered by real-world instruments. Unlike MIDI tracks which trigger external MIDI devices, MIDI tracks which trigger VST Instruments can be converted directly into audio data.

The only drawback is that running VST Instruments alongside audio tracks and effects plug-ins requires a rather powerful processor. However, if the CPU load becomes a problem you can always use Instrument Freeze or convert your VST Instrument tracks into audio tracks. These options put less strain on the computer's resources.

There is an extremely wide range of VST Instruments available, representing a vast array of different instrument types and synthesis techniques. Table 18.1 lists some of the main developers and their products.

Table 18.1 VST Instruments list

Developer	VST Instrument	Description
Antares	Kantos	Audio controlled software synthesizer
Applied Acoustics	Tassman	Modular synthesizer based on physical modelling
Applied Acoustics	Lounge Lizard	Electric piano
Arturia	Moog Modular V	Virtual emulation of a real-world Moog Modular
Arturia	Prophet V	Hybrid combination of the Prophet 5 and Prophet VS
Big Tick	Rhino	Subtractive, additive and FM synthesizer
Big Tick	Cheeze Machine	String ensemble synthesizer (Free)
Bitheadz	Unity AS-1	Virtual analogue synthesizer
Bitheadz	Unity DS-1	Sampler
iZotope	pHATmatic Pro	Loop player and sample slicer
Bojo	Impulse	Virtual analogue synthesizer
Bojo	Organ One	Organ
FXpansion	BFD	Acoustic drum module
FXpansion	DR-008	Modular drum synthesizer and sample player
GForce	impOSCar	OSCar synthesizer emulation
GForce	MTron	Mellotron emulation
Green Oak	Crystal	Semi-modular synthesizer (Free)
IK Multimedia	Sample Tank	Sample player
Image Line	Toxic III	FM synthesizer
Image Line	Wasp	Virtual analogue synthesizer
Kong Audio	ChineeKong	Chinese percussion instrument
Kong Audio	ChineeWinds	Chinese bamboo flute instrument
Korg	Legacy collection	Korg M1 and Wavestation emulation
Lin Plug	Alpha	Virtual analogue synthesizer
Lin Plug	Delta III	Semi-modular virtual analogue synthesizer
LoftSoft	FM Heaven	FM synthesizer
mda	DX10	FM synthesizer (Free)
mda	ePiano	Electric piano (Free)
mda	JX10	Virtual analogue synth (Free)
mda	Piano	Piano (Free)
MHC	Space Synthesizer	Ambient texture synthesizer
MHC	Pianos	Ambient pianos plug-in
Muon Software	Atom Pro	Simple but powerful virtual analogue synthesizer
Muon Software	Tau Pro	TB303-style acid bass synth emulation
Native Instruments	Absynth	Semi-modular synthesizer
Native Instruments	Battery	Sample-based drum and percussion module
Native Instruments	B4	Hammond B3 tonewheel organ emulation
Native Instruments	FM7/FM8	FM synthesizer

Table 18.1 VST Instruments list (cont)

Developer	VST Instrument	Description
Native Instruments	Kontakt	Sampler
Native Instruments	Massive	Hybrid synthesizer
Native Instruments	Pro-53	Prophet 5 analogue synthesizer emulation
Native Instruments	Reaktor	Modular synthesizer/rhythm processor/software sampler
reFX	Nexus	Hybrid ROM synthesizer
reFX	QuadraSID	C-64 SID chip emulation synthesizer
rgcAudio	Pentagon I	Virtual analogue synthesizer (4 oscillators)
rgcAudio	Square I	Virtual analogue synthesizer (3 oscillators)
rgcAudio	Triangle II	Virtual analogue synthesizer (Free)
Rob Papen	Albino	Semi-modular virtual analogue synthesizer
Spectrasonics	Atmosphere	Dream pad sound module based on sampling
Spectrasonics	Stylus	Vinyl remix groove and sample manipulation module
Spectrasonics	Trilogy	Electric, acoustic and synth bass module
SpeedSoft	VSampler	Software sampler
SpeedSoft	VX 7	FM synthesizer
Steinberg	HALion	Sampler
Steinberg	Hypersonic	Virtual music workstation
Steinberg	The Grand	Grand piano
Steinberg	Virtual Guitarist	Rhythm guitar module
Steinberg	Xphrase	Phrase synthesizer
Synapse Audio	Junglist	Virtual analogue synthesizer
Synapse Audio	Plucked String	Guitar synthesizer based on physical modelling
Tobybear	Deconstructor	Sample manipulator
Virsyn	Cantor	Vocal synthesis instrument
Virsyn	Cube	Additive synthesizer
Virsyn	Tera	Modular synthesizer
Waldorf	Attack	Drum and percussion synthesizer
Waldorf	PPG Wave 2.V	PPG Wave 2.2 wavetable synthesizer emulation

The Tempo Track

In Cubase, tempo is managed in two modes: Fixed tempo mode and Tempo track mode. These operate as follows:

- Fixed tempo mode – is when the tempo button in the Transport panel is de-activated. In this mode, the tempo of Cubase follows the single fixed tempo shown in the Transport panel.
- Tempo track mode – is when the tempo button in the Transport panel is activated. In this mode, tempo-based audio and MIDI tracks (those set to musical time base) follow the tempo changes of the Tempo Track.

The Tempo Track editor is for creating and editing tempo and time signature changes (Figure 19.1). It is opened by selecting Tempo Track from the Project menu, or by pressing Ctrl / Command + T on the computer keyboard. All time signature settings are active both in fixed and tempo track modes.

The Tempo Track editor is dominated by the tempo display area which shows tempo in beats-per-minute (bpm) on the vertical axis and time in the chosen time format on the horizontal axis. Tempo events are shown as small square handles along the length of the tempo curve. The shape of the curve is changed by dragging the existing handles to new locations or drawing a new curve. The shape of the curve is also governed by the curve type selection where 'jump' mode produces instantaneous tempo changes at each tempo event position, and 'ramp' mode produces smooth, graduated curves between events. Time signature events are shown in the time signature strip below the ruler.

Figure 19.1
The Tempo Track editor

The Tempo Track editor toolbar

Figure 19.2
The Tempo Track editor toolbar

The Tempo Track editor toolbar features the following:

- Object Selection, Eraser, Zoom and Draw tools – the Object Selection (Pointer) tool is for selecting events by clicking on individual events or dragging a selection box around a group of events. Selected events are shown in red. Once selected the event(s) can be dragged to a new position or edited in the tempo or time signature fields. The Eraser is used to delete unwanted events. The Zoom tool governs the zoom factor of the display and allows you to zoom in to the tempo curve for detailed editing. The Draw tool is used to draw a new tempo curve or add a new time signature.
- Autoscroll – when activated the display follows the position of the project cursor. When de-activated the display remains static and ignores the position of the project cursor.
- Snap button and menu – govern the snap resolution when inserting or moving tempo events in the display. When the snap button is activated and bars and beats is chosen in the ruler, events are placed according to the resolution chosen in the snap menu. When the ruler shows other time formats events are placed according to the visible vertical grid lines. When Snap is de-activated, events may be freely inserted or moved with no regard for bar or time positions.
- Tempo field – shows the tempo of the currently selected tempo event. The tempo value can be changed by clicking on the small up/down arrows or by double clicking on the value field and entering a tempo directly using the computer keyboard.
- Curve field - governs the curve type of the currently selected tempo events.
- Insert Curve field - governs the curve type when inserting tempo events using the Draw tool.
- Signature - shows the values of the currently selected time signature event. The time signature can be changed by clicking on the small up/down arrows or by double clicking on the value field and entering a time signature directly using the computer keyboard.
- Tempo recording slider – allows the recording of tempo events in playback mode. This is useful for creating natural-sounding tempo manipulations while listening to the music (works best with MIDI and sliced audio arrangements).
- Process tempo button - opens the Process tempo dialogue where you can define a new duration or end time for the tempo events between the left and right locators. This is good for sound to picture projects where you may wish to match bar ranges or bar positions to specific time ranges and time code addresses.
- Process bars button - opens the Process bars dialogue where you can insert, delete or replace time between the left and right locators. This provides an alternative to the insert and delete time functions in the Edit / Range sub-menu and takes time signatures into consideration.

Exploring the Tempo Track editor

Creating a tempo curve

To create a test tempo curve proceed as follows:

- Activate tempo track mode in the Transport panel and open the Tempo Track editor.
- Activate the Snap button and select 'Ramp' in the Insert Curve field.
- Select the Draw tool and click and drag in the tempo display to create your own test curve (Figure 19.3).

Figure 19.3
Create a test tempo curve in the Tempo Track editor

When inserting or moving tempo events, the precision of each tempo value depends upon the vertical zoom setting, where high zoom factors allow the insertion of tempo events whose values include fractional changes in tempo (such as 120.42, 121.62, 122.78bpm or similar). With lower vertical zoom factors the tempo values are always whole integer numbers (such as 120, 121, 122bpm).

Editing the tempo curve

To change the curve type proceed as follows:

- Press Ctrl / Command + A to select all tempo events.
- Select 'Jump' in the Curve field. The shape of the curve is modified as shown in Figure 19.4. You can also modify the shape of specific sections since jump and ramp characteristics can exist within the same curve.

Figure 19.4
Changing the curve type to Jump mode

Figure 19.5
Moving a group of tempo events

Figure 19.6
To change the tempo of the currently selected event, click on the up/down arrows in the Tempo field

- To move one or more tempo events proceed as follows:
- Select one or more tempo events using the Object Selection tool.
- Drag the event(s) to the desired location and release the mouse. The shape of the tempo curve is changed accordingly (Figure 19.5).

To edit the value of a single event in the Tempo field proceed as follows:

- Select the event whose tempo you wish to change.
- Click on the up/down arrows in the Tempo field to change the tempo in whole integer values (Figure 19.6). For precise values click directly in the Tempo field and enter the required tempo using the computer keyboard.

Inserting and editing time signature events
To insert time signature events proceed as follows:

- Select the Draw tool and click at the appropriate time position in the time signature strip. A time signature event is created (Figure 19.7). Alternatively, double click in the time signature strip with the Object Selection tool. Time signature events are always placed on the first beat of the bar.

Figure 19.7
Click in the time signature strip with the Draw tool to insert a time signature

- To edit a time signature event proceed as follows:
- Select the time signature event. A selected time signature event is shown with a red marker box.
- Click on the left or right up/down arrows to modify the appropriate element of the time signature (Figure 19.8).

Figure 19.8
To change the currently selected time signature click on the up/down arrows in the time signature field

Time display format in the ruler

The display characteristics of the ruler can be changed between linear bars and beats and linear time using the options in the lower section of the pop-up ruler options menu. This is opened by clicking on the arrow button to the right of the ruler (Figure 19.9).

Selecting 'Bars+Beats Linear' results in a display where each bar in the ruler is represented by the same horizontal distance, regardless of any tempo changes (Figure 19.10).

Figure 19.9 (above)
Click on the arrow button to the right of the ruler to open the pop-up time display

Figure 19.10 (left
The Tempo Track display in 'Bars+Beats Linear' mode

Selecting 'Time Linear' results in a display where the distance between each bar in the ruler becomes greater as the tempo is decreased (Figure 19.11).

Info

There is always at least one tempo event and one time signature at the start of the project. These first events cannot be deleted. However, the first tempo event in tempo track mode and the fixed mode tempo may be set to different values.

Figure 19.11
The same curve in 'Time Linear' mode

Why use tempo changes?

Tempo changes are not essential for music created with Cubase. However, the fact remains that the tempo of most music created using live musicians varies either subtly or dramatically. The changes in tempo add to the liveliness and 'feel' of the performance. Almost all great musical performances involve tempo changes but there are no hard and fast rules about exactly how the changes should be applied. Musical scores often involve tempo-related instructions in addition to the notes themselves but, in the context of tempo, no two musical performances are ever exactly identical.

General guidelines for song forms include increasing the tempo on all the choruses and going back to the original tempo for the verses. More subtle manipulations might include wider tempo variations in the early stages of the music and lesser tempo variations as the song progresses, giving the impression of a group of musicians settling into the 'groove'. Hook lines might benefit from slight tempo increases to generate excitement.

Info

A helpful technique for adding tempo based interest to your music is to actually extract the tempo element from the recording of a real-world live performance. How to achieve this is explained in the next section.

Matching the tempo of Cubase to the tempo of a musical performance

There are several methods of matching the tempo of Cubase to that of an audio recording of a musical performance. The most immediate and practical technique is to use the 'Merge tempo from tapping' function. This adjusts the tempo according to a sequence of MIDI notes you have recorded in time with the music. Alternatively, you can adjust the tempo using the Time warp tool. The following is a two-stage procedure which uses a combination of both these techniques. Proceed as follows:

Stage 1

Activate Tempo track mode on the Transport panel.

- If it is not already present, import the recording of the musical performance onto an Audio track. Activate Linear time base (shown by a clock symbol) on the chosen audio track (Figure 19.12).

Figure 19.12
Activate Linear time base on the chosen Audio track

- Select or add a MIDI track. Activate Linear time base and record enable the track (Figure 19.13).

Figure 19.13
Record enable a MIDI track and set it to Linear time base

- Activate record and tap on the MIDI keyboard in time with the audio material. Try using a hi-hat or rimshot sound recorded at quarter note intervals and start on the first downbeat of the first bar (Figure 19.14).

Figure 19.14
MIDI events recorded in time with the music at quarter note intervals

- Play back the recorded MIDI events and make sure their positions correspond to the timing of the audio material. If necessary, edit the positions of the MIDI events in the Key editor (with the Snap button de-activated).

- Select the recorded MIDI part and select 'Merge tempo from tapping' in MIDI / Functions. Select the desired resolution. In this case, quarter notes are selected. Activate 'Begin at Bar Start' (Figure 19.15).
- Click on OK in the 'Merge tempo from tapping' dialogue to insert tempo events into the tempo track according to the positions of the MIDI notes. Mute the MIDI track and play back the performance with the metronome click activated. The tempo of the click now matches the musical performance. Open the Tempo Track editor if you need to view or edit the tempo events (Figure 19.16).

Figure 19.15
Choose the resolution for the tempo events in the 'Merge tempo from tapping' dialogue

If your MIDI notes were recorded with sufficient accuracy, the first stage of this process may be all you need to establish an accurate tempo map of the musical performance. However, if you need still greater accuracy try completing the second stage outlined below.

Figure 19.16
The resulting tempo events in the Tempo track editor. In this case, the tempo fluctuates around 100bpm

Stage 2

- Add the Marker track in the Project window and set it to linear time base.
- Double-click on the audio event to open the Sample editor.
- Open the Hitpoint section of the Sample editor Inspector and adjust the sensitivity slider to calculate hitpoints for the audio material (Figure 19.17).

Figure 19.17
Adjust the sensitivity slider in the Hitpoint section of the Sample editor Inspector to create hitpoints

- Adjust the sensitivity slider so that hitpoints appear on the main hits in the material. Verify the audio segments by clicking between each pair of hitpoints with the Edit hitpoints button activated. The objective is to avoid the creation of too many hitpoints, especially those placed closely together, whilst also attempting to finish up with one hitpoint at each quarter note position. You may need to edit the hitpoints manually. The result when aiming for hitpoints at quarter note intervals resembles Figure 19.18. Do not be too concerned if there are not hitpoints at absolutely all quarter note positions since you are seeking a good guide and not absolute perfection.

Figure 19.18
Hitpoints created in the Sample editor for the main hits in the musical performance

Figure 19.19
Markers in the Marker track (created from the Hitpoints)

• Select 'Create markers from hitpoints' in the Audio / Hitpoints sub-menu. This creates markers in the Marker track at the positions of the hitpoints. Go back to the Project window to view the markers in the Marker track (Figure 19.19).

Figure 19.20
With the Time warp tool selected, the existing tempo events appear in the ruler

• Select the Time warp tool (in the default Warp grid mode). At this time the tempo events produced in stage 1, (above), appear in the ruler (Figure 19.20).

• In the Project window toolbar, activate the Snap button. Set the Snap type menu to events and the Grid type menu to Beat. With the snap type set to events, the marker events become 'magnetic'.

- A short vertical line appears whenever you place the Time warp tool in the event display at the same position as an existing tempo event (those visible in the ruler). Click and drag from this position to snap the corresponding tempo event to the nearest 'magnetic' marker, (Figure 19.21). If there is no marker at the position, you may need to drag the tempo event manually with the Snap button de-activated. In this case, line up the tempo event visually to just before the peak in the waveform which corresponds to the 'hit' of the beat.

Figure 19.21
Drag the tempo events to the nearest markers in the event display

- Work through the tempo events in a similar fashion, lining them up with the nearest marker events. If the tempo events appear to be dragged too far off the tempo, the marker concerned may be inaccurate. Seek out the best position for each event while auditioning the material. Many tempo events are likely to already be in the correct position.

The techniques outlined in this second stage help you refine the data created in stage 1 to produce an extremely accurate tempo map. Creating hitpoints and converting them to markers in the event display effectively provides you with rhythmic 'anchor points' upon which you can 'hang' your tempo events.

Synchronisation

Synchronisation refers to the technique of running two or more devices in perfect time with each other. This is required in Cubase systems which include external devices such as video tape recorders, tape machines, hard disk recorders, sequencers and drum machines. The devices must be connected together in some way so that they are all 'aware' of their time positions relative to the other units in the system. This is achieved using a time encoded signal (time code). Digital systems may also require the use of word clock or some other clock reference signal. One of the units in the system is chosen as the master device and the others are chosen as slaves. The master device generates the reference code for the system and the other units synchronise themselves to this. Precisely how this is achieved depends upon the application. Positional synchronisation techniques may be divided into two main categories: bar-based synchronisation and time-based synchronisation.

Info

The synchronisation of digital audio or video devices usually requires two signals: 1) time code and 2) clock. Time code is a positional reference which tells the system 'where' it should be. Clock is a frequency rate reference which tells the system at 'what speed' it should be going.

Bar-based synchronisation

This involves sending MIDI Clock between units which keeps them synchronised in terms of bar position and tempo. This is an older, entirely MIDI based technique which is recommended only when there is no other solution. A typical use includes the synchronisation of external sequencers and drum machines which do not feature MTC (MIDI Time Code).

MIDI Clock includes a clock message transmitted 24 times per quarter note and Start, Stop and Continue messages. Song Position Pointer (SPP) messages are invariably also included in the transmitted data. The receiving device responds according to the Start, Stop and Continue messages and calculates the tempo at which it should be running by measuring the time between each MIDI Clock message. The additional Song Position Pointer messages are used for calculating the current position within the song. This allows fast forward and rewind operations and the possibility of starting at any point within the music. (Before Song Position Pointers, synchronisation could only be achieved by commencing playback from the start of the song).

Time-based synchronisation

This involves the use of 'time-stamped' code which provides an absolute time-based reference for synchronisation purposes. This comes in the form of SMPTE or EBU time code and MIDI time code (MTC). Time-based synchronisation using SMPTE, EBU or MIDI time code is preferable to bar-referenced synchronisation since it is more accurate and is tempo-independent.

Time code has its origins in the film industry where the time stamped information was measured in terms of a number representing hours, minutes, seconds and frames. The resolution of the code was determined by its frame rate (e.g. 24 frames-per-second) and this was originally how many film frames passed through the camera per second. This kind of time code has been adopted for audio purposes and is now widely used in various forms throughout the audio industry.

SMPTE is an abbreviation for the Society of Motion Picture and Television Engineers and time code is often referred to by this name, (pronounced 'simptee'), since this organisation was the first to establish a time code standard. However, strictly speaking SMPTE time code is only one standard, as used in the USA. The other is EBU Time Code as used in Europe (established by the European Broadcasting Union).

The different types of time code can be identified by the manner in which they are stored and transmitted and by their frame rates. Time code is transmitted as Longitudinal Time Code (LTC), Vertical Interval Time Code (VITC) or MIDI Time Code (MTC) and these are defined as follows:

- Longitudinal Time Code (LTC) – the code is recorded as a stream of audio pulses on an audio track. LTC is commonly used for audio work and video productions.
- Vertical Interval Time Code (VITC) – this code is embedded within the video picture and is popular for video editing.
- MIDI Time Code (MTC) – this is a special kind of time code with a slightly lower resolution than LTC which is transmitted via MIDI.

Time code varies in the number of frames per second for the encoded signal. This is known as the frame rate and could be one of the following:

> 24 fps – traditional 35mm film rate.
> 25 fps – European standard for audio and PAL video (EBU).
> 30 fps – USA standard for audio work (30 Non-Drop, SMPTE time code).
> 30 dfps – NTSC broadcast format.
> 29.97 fps – NTSC colour television and video non-drop frame format (29.97 Non-Drop).
> 29.97 dfps – NTSC colour television and video drop frame format (29.97 Drop).

The basic format for all time code is hours : minutes : seconds : frames. When greater accuracy is required, the frame is divided into 80 sub-frames. For audio work, it is normal practice to use 25 fps in Europe and 30 fps in the USA. LTC and MTC time code at the latter frame rates are the types of time code with which you are most likely to come into contact in audio work.

Synchronisation in digital systems

The problems

Under normal circumstances, when Cubase is not slaved to an external device, both the MIDI and audio data are locked to the same clock (the digital audio hardware's internal clock). However, when Cubase is slaved to an external device using time code alone (MTC), the positional reference of the program is governed by the incoming time code, while the clock reference for the audio data is still locked to the internal audio clock. Due to variations in tape speed and/or audio clock speeds, this can result in timing drift between the audio recorded in Cubase and the audio recorded in the external unit and/or the MIDI data. The problem may manifest itself as a loss of clarity or as phasiness in the sound quality.

The solutions

Word Clock

A popular solution to the problem outlined above is the use of word clock. One unit is chosen as the single master time code and word clock source (sometimes also the unit where A/D conversion takes place), and all other units are slaved to this device. Word clock keeps the sample rates of digital audio hardware in synchronisation by using a clock which is referenced to the transferred data bits, normally at the same rate as the sample rate chosen for the digital audio system. Using word clock requires audio hardware equipped with word clock connectors. Many digital audio signals, such as S/PDIF, AES3 and ADAT, are self-clocking since the clock reference is embedded within the signal. With these interfaces, lock can therefore be achieved without the use of word clock. However, locking to word clock is likely to provide better jitter-free performance.

ASIO Positioning Protocol (APP)

APP is designed to ensure sample accurate positioning between suitably equipped devices. It requires audio hardware with an ASIO 2.0 driver which includes APP functionality, and the ability to read positional information in the external device (see the electronic documentation and the Steinberg website for more details about APP).

Synchronising without Word Clock

It is worth bearing in mind that some of the synchronisation problems outlined above are relevant to those systems where Cubase is slaved to an external device. You may encounter less problems if you are running a system where Cubase is always the master device. Equally, if you are synchronising Cubase to devices whose timing clocks are very stable, such as another computer or a hard disk recorder, then you may encounter minimal problems if you synchronise using time code without a reference clock. However, the fact remains that a system synchronising digital devices without a reference clock (such as word clock) cannot guarantee accurate long-term synchronisation. The longer the audio recording, the more apparent becomes the timing drift.

If you intend to set up your system without Word Clock, it may help if you use time code which was generated from your audio hardware. For this and other purposes, Cubase is supplied with a SMPTE generator plug-in (outlined in the next section).

The SMPTE Generator plug-in

Cubase is supplied with a SMPTE Generator plug-in (Figure 20.1). This can be used as an insert effect on any audio track. The audio track is routed to the appropriate output of your audio hardware and recorded onto the intended time code track of the external device. The generation of the time code may be linked to the project ruler by activating the link button. In this case, time code generation begins from the location of the project cursor when you activate playback. The frame rate matches the frame rate set in the Project Setup window (Project menu). Otherwise, deactivate the Link button and press the Generate button. This generates time code at the chosen frame rate beginning from the specified start time.

Figure 20.1
The SMPTE Generator plug-in

As well as providing a convenient time code source, the SMPTE Generator is also helpful for becoming familiar with the various different types of time code. However, be careful when routing the time code through your audio system. Reduce the volume level before pressing the generate button to avoid damage to your speakers or to your ears!!

Setting up synchronisation in Cubase

Info

VST System Link allows the sending of audio, MIDI, transport and synchronisation data between two or more computers with sample-accurate resolution. This involves connecting machines together via digital cables between ASIO audio cards, creating a system which combines the processing power of two or more computers.

It is important to have a basic understanding of the different types of time code, as outlined in the above sections, since you may come into contact with them in the peripheral equipment which you connect to your audio system. However, internally, Cubase recognises only MIDI Time Code (MTC), ASIO Positioning Protocol (APP) or VST System Link as time code sources. The practical synchronisation of Cubase to external audio hardware, like tape recorders or hard disk recorders, often implies the use of a hardware synchronisation device (synchroniser) which converts LTC time code into MTC. For professional applications, the synchroniser would also provide word clock for the system. A typical synchronisation setup of this type is shown in Figure 20.2.

Synchronisation in Cubase is managed in the Synchronisation Setup dialogue opened from the Transport menu (Figure 20.3). This is used to select

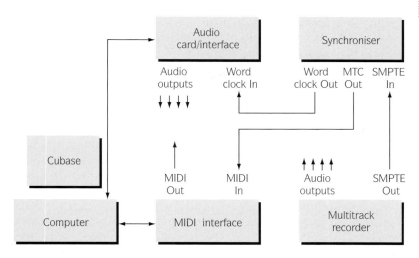

Figure 20.2
Cubase slaved to a multitrack tape or hard disk recorder featuring synchronisation via time code and word clock

the time code source, the MIDI Machine Control status, the drop out and lock behaviour, and the MIDI input and output ports for MIDI Machine Control in/out, MTC in/out and MIDI Clock out.

Figure 20.3
The Synchronisation Setup dialogue

When Cubase behaves as the slave to an external device using MTC, you need to set the appropriate MIDI Input for the time code, a start time which Cubase uses as the beginning of the project (in the Project Setup dialogue Start field), and activate the Sync button on the Transport panel (press 'T' on the computer keyboard). In this configuration, Cubase commences playback in synchronisation with the external device when it receives time code with the same or a greater value than the set start time.

Practical synchronisation in Cubase

Cubase as the master device using MIDI clock

Cubase cannot be slaved to an external device using MIDI Clock since it does not recognise incoming MIDI Clock messages. Due to the technical limitations of MIDI Clock, it is not considered a suitable format for providing master timing control of Cubase. However, Cubase can generate MIDI Clock and therefore behave as the master device for external devices which recognise the data. MIDI Clock is suitable for the synchronisation of external sequencers and drum machines. To set up synchronisation using MIDI Clock, proceed as follows:

- Connect a MIDI cable between the appropriate physical MIDI output port of your MIDI interface and the MIDI input of the drum machine or external sequencer.
- Enable the reception of MIDI Clock data in the external MIDI device.
- Open the Synchronisation Setup dialogue in Cubase by selecting 'Sync Setup' in the Transport menu (Figure 20.4).
- In the Synchronisation setup dialogue, activate the appropriate MIDI port in the 'MIDI clock destinations' section (Figure 20.5).

Figure 20.4 (left)
Select Sync Setup in the Transport menu

Figure 20.5 (right)
Activate the appropriate MIDI port in the Sync Setup 'MIDI clock destinations' section

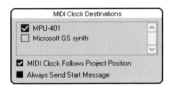

- Click on OK to leave the dialogue. Press play in Cubase to send the MIDI Clock messages. The receiving device runs synchronised to Cubase.

MIDI Clock may also be the solution if you are recording the MIDI data from a non-MTC equipped drum machine or sequencer into Cubase. In this case, configure Cubase in the same manner as above, but also connect a second MIDI cable from the MIDI out of the external device to a MIDI input port of your MIDI interface. In this setup, MIDI Clocks are transmitted via the MIDI output of Cubase to the slaved device and the MIDI note data from the external unit is sent back to Cubase via the second MIDI cable. Activating record in Cubase records the incoming data onto a record enabled MIDI track.

Cubase as the master device using MIDI time code

Using Cubase as the master device is a popular solution when synchronising external multitrack machines and video recorders and, in many circumstances, is a better solution than using it as the slave. Proceed as follows:

- Connect a MIDI cable between the appropriate MIDI output port of your MIDI interface and the MIDI input of the external device.
- Enable the reception of MTC in the external device.
- Set Cubase and the external device to the same frame rate. In Cubase, set the frame rate in the Project setup window (Project menu). For most

situations you would choose 25fps or 30fps.
- Set the start time for Cubase in the Project setup window (Project menu). Also set an appropriate start time in the external unit.
- In the Sync Setup dialogue, activate the appropriate MIDI port in the 'MIDI time code destinations' section (Figure 20.6).
- Click on OK to leave the Sync Setup dialogue. Press play in Cubase to send MTC. The receiving device plays back synchronised to Cubase.

Figure 20.6
Select the appropriate MIDI output port for the MTC in the 'MIDI time code destinations' section

Cubase as the slave device using MIDI time code

As outlined above, MTC is a particular kind of time code which can be transmitted through an ordinary MIDI cable. MTC supports 24, 25, 30 and 30 drop frame formats. The device which sends the MTC to Cubase could be a synchroniser which converts SMPTE time code into MTC or, perhaps, another sequencer. A synchroniser is often used to provide an interface between a multitrack tape or hard disk recorder and a computer based sequencer, like Cubase, and this forms the main subject matter of this section.

Before synchronisation can occur with the multitrack recorder, one of the tracks must be striped with time code (although some devices produce their own time code signal without using a track). After striping, this code is routed to the time code input of the synchroniser which drives the rest of the system. In this example, the synchroniser converts the SMPTE time code into MTC, which is routed to the computer and Cubase via a MIDI cable connected to the MIDI interface.

To set up Cubase with a multitrack recorder and a synchroniser which converts SMPTE time code to MIDI time code, proceed as follows:

- If required, stripe a track of the multitrack recorder with time code. For this task you could use Cubase's SMPTE Generator plug-in (as described above).
- Ensure that your synchroniser is correctly connected to the multitrack recorder (normally time code output of the multitrack recorder connected to the time code input of the synchroniser) and that the MTC out from the synchroniser is connected to the MIDI In of your MIDI interface.
- If you are using word clock, ensure that the word clock output from the synchroniser is connected to the word clock input of the audio card / audio hardware device.
- In the Synchronisation Setup dialogue, set time code Source to MIDI time code. Select the MIDI port for the incoming MTC in the 'MIDI time code source' input pop-up menu (Figure 20.7).

Figure 20.7
Set the time code source to MIDI time code and select the MIDI port for the incoming MTC in the Synchronisation Setup dialogue

Figure 20.8
Select the start time, frame rate and display offset in the Project Setup dialogue

- Select the appropriate start time, frame rate and display offset (if required) in the Project Setup dialogue (Figure 20.8).
- Click on the Sync button in the Transport panel to activate synchronisation (or press T on the computer keyboard).
- Cubase is now ready to slave to any incoming MTC. Rewind the multitrack recorder to before the start time of the project and commence playback. When Cubase receives time code on or after the project start time, Cubase begins playback, in synchronisation with the multitrack recorder.

Cubase automatically chases and locks to each new position selected on the external device. In the Synchronisation Setup dialogue, the Drop Out and Lock Time options dictate the speed with which Cubase reacts to the incoming code, as follows:

- Lock Time specifies the number of correct frames of time code required before Cubase locks to it.
- Drop Out Time specifies the number of incorrect frames (or drop outs) which are tolerated before Cubase abandons synchronisation.

Synchronising Cubase with a tape recorder using MIDI Machine Control (MMC)

MIDI Machine Code (MMC) is a special part of the MIDI protocol which specifies MIDI messages for the control of such things as tape transports. The implementation of MMC in Cubase allows you to set up remote control of the transport functions of external devices using the Transport panel.

The use of MMC is a two-way process involving both MMC messages and MTC. It requires both the MIDI input and MIDI output of the tape recorder to be connected to Cubase. MMC messages are transmitted from the MIDI output of Cubase to the MIDI input of the tape recorder, which controls the transport and other functions. The tape recorder transmits MTC to the MIDI input of Cubase and this locks the two machines in synchronisation. The process requires the recording of time code onto one track of the tape recorder which is converted into MTC during playback.

To set up your system and the Synchronisation Setup dialogue for use with a tape machine which supports MMC, proceed as follows:

- Ensure that the MIDI in and out cables are correctly connected between the tape recorder and Cubase and that time code has been recorded onto one track of the tape. Set up the tape recorder for MMC operation.
- In the Synchronisation Setup dialogue, set the time code source to MIDI time code. Select the MIDI port for the incoming MTC in the MIDI time code source 'MTC Input' pop-up.
- Activate 'MMC Active' in the MIDI Machine Control section. Select the MMC input and output ports and the number of audio tracks on the external device (Figure 20.9).

Figure 20.9
Typical synchronisation setup settings for MMC operation

- Select the appropriate start time, frame rate and display offset (if required) in the Project Setup dialogue (Project menu).
- Activate the Sync button on the Transport panel.
- Press the play button on the tape recorder and play the tape for a short section to allow Cubase to lock to the current time code position.
- Stop the tape and activate playback in Cubase. If all is well, the tape rolls back to just before the current time position in Cubase and commences playback. After a second or two Cubase commences playback in sync with the tape recorder. Thereafter, all Cubase transport buttons, including play, stop, fast forward and rewind, control the transport of the tape recorder.

Production tips and power tools

This chapter outlines a number of tips, techniques, high-power macro commands and workspaces which help you on your way to becoming a Cubase power user. The emphasis here is on speed and efficiency, so if improving your productivity and workflow is a priority then this chapter is essential reading. The topics covered explore some of the lesser known aspects of Cubase as well as finding new ways of using common functions.

100 speed tips

The following is a comprehensive list of tips for enhancing speed and getting the best out of Cubase. The text is divided into a number of logical categories to help you find the tip you need.

Saving and file handling

1   Select Ctrl / Command + Alt + S to save the project with an incremental number automatically appended to the file name. This function is valuable for making regular saves of the latest version of your work as the project progresses. If things go wrong in the current version you can always revert to an earlier version.
2   Always re-name your audio tracks before starting to record. Cubase uses the track name for the name of the audio file which is written to the hard disk and by using meaningful names, rather than the default 'Audio 1', 'Audio 2' and so on, the files are easier to recognise if you need to find them individually at a later stage. A take number is chronologically appended to the file name for each new recording on the same track.
3   To avoid missing file problems and confusion store each Cubase project in its own separate folder. The program is designed with the idea of storing each project file and all its associated audio, edit and image files within a single overall folder. You can have several versions of the same project within the same folder but storing completely different projects within the same folder is to be avoided.

Navigation and zooming

4   To navigate quickly between different sections of your music without dropping out of playback, activate play and hold the numeric keypad '+' key to fast forward, or the '-' key to rewind. Release the key to

instantly go back into normal playback mode. Hold Shift to increase the wind speed. This functionality depends upon the setting of File / Preferences / Transport / Stop playback while winding.

5   To use drag zooming in the ruler without affecting playback or the cursor position, hold the Shift key while dragging.

6   To quickly modify the left / right locator positions, click in the ruler while pressing Ctrl to set the left locator and while pressing Alt to set the right locator.

7   To lock the view on the start of a range selection when editing at high magnification in the Sample editor, proceed as follows: stop playback, activate autoscroll, and press L to locate the start of the selection. Finally, de-activate autoscroll before re-commencing playback. The view now remains locked to the start point.

8   The Zoom tool is often the best choice for basic zooming tasks. Click once to zoom in and double click to zoom out.

9   To achieve a full horizontal and vertical view of all events in the project, hold Shift and click once with the zoom tool in the event display.

10 To zoom in to a specific range, make a range selection using the Range selection tool followed by 'Zoom to selection'. Use 'Undo zoom' to go back to the previous zoom setting. Assign key commands to 'Zoom to selection' and 'Undo zoom' (try 'Z' and 'Alt + Z').

Event editing

11 Click in empty space in the Project window with the right mouse button to open the context sensitive Quick menu. Hold down a modifier key (Ctrl, Command, Shift or Alt) to open a pop-up toolbox instead. To reverse the Quick menu / pop-up toolbox functionality, select 'Pop-up toolbox on right click' in Preferences / Editing / Tools.

12 To repeat a number of consecutive events in the Project window select Repeat in the Edit menu (Ctrl / Command + K) and enter the number of repeats required in the pop-up dialogue. Alternatively, select the object selection tool and point at the lower right corner of the event while pressing Alt (until the pencil symbol appears). Drag to the right to repeat the events. The number of repeats is shown in a pop-up box.

13 To create a crossfade between two audio events, drag one audio event so that it slightly overlaps another. Press the 'X' key on the computer keyboard. A default crossfade is created. Double click on the crossfade area to modify the crossfade curve characteristics.

14 To cut and paste range selections within events with automatic splits and re-alignment of following events, use the range selection tool with delete time, cut time and paste time (Edit menu / Range). Delete time deletes the range selection and moves all following events leftwards to close the gap. Cut time is similar but also copies the deleted range to the clipboard. Paste time copies the clipboard at the start point of the range selection and moves all following events rightwards to make room for the pasted data.

15 To select all events on the currently selected track, use 'select all events' from the track list Quick menu.

16   To rename all events on a track to the same name, hold down any
      modifier key while renaming the track. Alternatively, select several
      events and change the name on the infoline.

17   Before opening the main editors, press 'P' followed by the numeric
      keypad divide key to set the left and right locators and cycle playback
      to the current selection. This helps keep the cursor visible within the
      edit window. The MIDI editors' horizontal zoom may need adjustment.

18   To split all selected events at the same point, select a number of events
      in the Project window and click on any one with the split tool.
      Alternatively, use the 'split at cursor' and 'split loop' commands in the
      edit menu.

19   As an alternative to the split tool for splitting events, press Alt and click
      with the object selection tool.

20   To delete all events on a track which come after the horizontal position
      at which you click, select the erase tool and click in the display while
      pressing Alt.

21   To create empty audio or MIDI parts in the Project window, press Alt
      and drag with the object selection tool. Alternatively, drag with the
      draw tool or double click between the left and right locators.

22   To nudge a selected event back or forward in time in the event display,
      use Ctrl + left arrow and Ctrl + right arrow (default key commands).
      The nudge resolution is determined by the current ruler setting and the
      grid settings in the Project window toolbar.

23   To automatically close gaps between adjacent events when modifying
      their lengths, activate the snap button and select Shuffle mode in the
      snap type menu.

24   To find the length of any range, or group of events, activate the snap
      button and choose Events in the snap type menu. Select the range tool
      and drag across the required range (the range snaps to the start or end
      of events). The length of the selection is shown in the length field of the
      infoline in the same time format as that chosen in the ruler.

Markers

25 To add standard markers, click on the add marker button found in the
     track list section of the Marker track or press the insert key on the com-
     puter keyboard. Standard markers are placed at the current location of
     the project cursor. Alternatively, add markers freely anywhere in the
     Marker track using the draw tool or during playback using the insert key.

26 To add cycle markers, press Alt + C on the computer keyboard. This adds
     a cycle marker over the current range of the left and right locators.

27 For instant cycle playback, select a cycle marker and press Shift + G. This
     places the left and right locators at the start and end of the cycle mark-
     er and automatically commences playback in cycle mode.

28 Double-click in a cycle marker in the Marker track with the range selection
     tool to globally select the cycle marker range for all tracks in the project.

29 When you have created hitpoints in the Sample editor you can generate
     markers at the hitpoint positions by selecting Create Markers from Hitpoints
     in the Audio / Advanced sub-menu. This is helpful when lining up tempo

events to audio hits using the time warp tool in the Project window.

30 In order to clarify the Marker track display in the Inspector, you may find it preferable to see the description column next to the marker ID number. To achieve this, change the position of the description column by dragging the column header to the left in the Inspector.

Key commands

31 Key commands do not exist for workspaces numbered above 9. If you prefer to avoid the mouse for activating higher numbered workspaces, use Alt + Pad 0 to open the 'Organise workspace' dialogue. Once open, use the up / down arrows to navigate the list of workspaces. Press return to activate the currently selected workspace. Press Alt / + F4 to close the dialogue.

32 Assign key commands to Calculate hitpoints and Remove hitpoints in the Key commands dialogue. Try 'K' and 'Shift + K'. These are useful for instant hitpoint creation and removal in the Sample editor.

33 Try reversing the default key commands for 'Zoom to Selection' (Alt + S) and 'Project Setup' (Shift + S). This helps navigate within the Sample editor, where you can now use Shift + F to zoom to the whole clip, Shift + E to zoom to the event, Shift + S to zoom to the current selection, and Shift + G to loop around the current selection. In other words, all the common zoom and loop key commands now use the Shift modifier key. This is easier to remember and easier to use.

34 Assign a key command to 'Transport – StartStop Preview' (try Alt + spacebar) and use this to start and stop local playback within the Sample editor or Pool. This is useful for playback of the whole clip or for playback of a range selection.

35 If you frequently need to manually activate / de-activate the monitor button for channels / tracks, assign a key command to the monitor command in the Key Commands dialogue. Try 'Ctrl + Shift + M'.

MIDI

36 When activating MIDI effects in the Inspector, the parameters of certain devices open within the Inspector itself. If this is not convenient, you can force the effect to open in a separate window by pressing Alt while making the selection.

37 To quickly select all notes of the same pitch in the Key editor, hold down Ctrl / Command and click on the relevant key in the virtual keyboard to the left of the main display.

38 The presets menu for VSTi and external MIDI devices is good for auditioning sounds on the fly. Step through the sounds in the list using the up / down arrow keys on the computer keyboard. Also try filtering presets by category or name to help find the desired sound.

39 Use the 'Edit VST instrument' button on the toolbar of the MIDI editors to quickly open the user interface for a VST instrument while working in the editor. If the Edit VST instrument button is not visible on the toolbar, select it from the toolbar pop-up menu which appears when you click on the toolbar with the right mouse button.

40 If you want to export a MIDI sequence as a Standard MIDI File and the

track concerned uses a drum map, use 'O-Note Conversion' (MIDI menu) to transpose the notes before exporting. This ensures that the correct sounds are triggered.

41 To 'humanise' the effect of Over quantize, try adding a few ticks in the Random Quantize setting of the Quantize Setup dialogue.

42 If you find yourself involved in MIDI editing tasks which seem laboriously repetitive and time-consuming, remember the Logical editor. This editor often provides one-step solutions for mouse click intensive editing and may even help avoid repetitive strain injury!!

43 To reveal the note names inside each event on the grid in the Key editor, increase the vertical zoom resolution.

44 To insert a series of notes at the same pitch in the Key editor, select the paint tool and drag it across the grid while pressing Ctrl / Command. To control the insert resolution, activate the snap button and select the desired quantize value in the Quantize type menu. Set the Length Q menu to 'Quantize Link'. Alternatively, press Alt and move the object selection tool (pointer) near to the end of an existing note and then drag across the grid. The chosen note is repeated over the range you drag.

45 Use the Controller lane presets menu in the lower left corner of the MIDI editors to organise instant recall of multiple controller lanes.

46 Click on the Edit In-Place button above the track list to toggle on and off the Edit In-Place editor for the currently selected MIDI tracks. Alternatively, use the default key command: Ctrl / Command + Shift + I.

Audio editing

47 To remove fades and crossfades, select the events containing the fades using the Object selection tool or select the range containing the fades using the range selection tool, and then select 'Remove Fades' in the Audio menu.

48 The Snap point of an audio event in the Project window is visible as a vertical blue line (when it is not in its default position at the start of the event). In the Project window, the Snap point may be modified using 'Snap point to cursor' (Audio menu). The Snap point is also adjustable in the Sample editor.

49 Try opening multiple Sample editors when you are working on several clips at the same time. This is useful for copying, pasting and merging audio between different clips.

50 To merge the current contents of the clipboard with the existing audio in the Sample editor use the Merge Clipboard function in the Process menu.

51 To avoid clicks when splitting events, try activating the 'Snap to Zero crossing' button in the Project window toolbar. You may wish to de-activate the button after editing is complete, to avoid unwanted side-effects in other editing operations.

52 When using the Process functions for editing in fine detail in the Sample editor, always work with the editor's own Snap to zero crossing button activated. This avoids clicks and glitches between the processed and unprocessed parts of the audio clip.

53 To make the tempo of Cubase fit the length of an audio event containing a drum loop, you need to know its length in beats. Select the

drum loop event, enter the beat length into the Beat Calculator (Project menu) and click on 'At Tempo Track Start'. This changes the tempo of Cubase to that of the loop. This assumes that the length of the loop has already been edited to match a precise number of bars and beats.

54 In the Audio Part editor, use the Play tool (loudspeaker icon) with the 'Edit active part only' button de-activated, to quickly switch between and audition the contents of each event, track or lane.

55 To avoid clicks between audio slices after increasing the tempo, set up auto fades in the Auto fades dialogue for the track. Tick 'auto crossfades' and de-select 'use project settings'. Try between 15ms and 30ms for the crossfade. Alternatively, try activating the fade in and fade out options with a 5ms to 10ms fade time.

56 To merge the attack of one drum sound with the decay of another proceed as follows: open the Sample editor, select a drum sound using the range selection tool and copy the sound to the clipboard. Select a second drum sound with which you wish to merge the copied sound and define the appropriate range in the Sample editor. Open the Merge Clipboard dialogue (Audio / Process menu). Set the percentage slider to '100% copy' and adjust the pre-crossfade to between 50 and 100ms. Activate the pre-crossfade tick box. Fine tune the settings while in Preview mode. When satisfied click on the Process button.

57 To mix and match sound slices between different drum loops, open a number of synchronised sliced loops or Rex files simultaneously in the Audio Part editor. Use the mute and other tools on the different events to create new rhythms and arrangements.

58 To drag and drop a range selection directly from the Sample editor into the Project window, hold Ctrl on the computer keyboard, click in the highlighted selection and drag into the event display.

59 To remove unwanted noise in between words or phrases in vocal takes or speech, try using a combination of 'Split at cursor' (Alt+X) and the Crossfade function (X). Adjust the settings in the Crossfade dialogue to resemble a bowl-shaped envelope. Use 'Split at cursor' to split the audio event whenever you hear unwanted noise and interference. When you have worked through enough audio, select all the newly split events and select Crossfade (X) to implement crossfades at all the split points. Fine tune the crossfade settings where necessary.

60 To tile two or more Sample editors on the screen, select the audio events to be edited and select Window / Minimize All, followed by Return, followed by Window / Tile horizontally. When you are finished editing, close the editor windows and select Window / Restore All.

Mixer

61 When using the Mixer to create a mix it is not convenient if channels are always automatically record enabled when selected. To disable automatic record enabling, open Preferences / Editing / Project & Mixer and disable 'Enable Record on Selected Track'.

62 To open the user interface for a VST Instrument directly from the Mixer, click on the 'Edit VST instrument' button in the VST Instrument channel strip.

63 To change a fader level for a single channel in a group of linked channels in the Mixer, hold Alt on the computer keyboard while making the change.

64 When dragging a handle in the built-in EQ curve display, press Ctrl to change the gain only, press Alt to change the frequency only, and press Shift to change the Q only.

65 To make A / B comparisons between the equalised and unequalised signal, click on the channel's EQs state button (green = EQ enabled, yellow = EQ disabled).

66 Try activating File / Preferences / Editing / Sync project and mixer selection. In this mode, the contents of an open Channel Settings window automatically follows your track or mixer channel selection. This is useful for keeping track of all the channel settings when switching between tracks / channels.

67 Any combination of channels in the Mixer can be temporarily hidden by activating the 'Can Hide' option found in each channel's pop-up menu. Show or hide the chosen channels using the 'Hide channels set to Can Hide' icon in the left panel.

68 Right click on an active Inserts state or Sends state button of any audio-based channel to open a pop-up menu of the assigned effects. Make a selection from the menu to open the GUI for each effect.

69 To copy the settings of one channel to another in the Mixer proceed as follows: 1) select the source channel and press Ctrl / Command + C to copy the channel settings to the clipboard. 2) select the target channel and press Ctrl / Command + V to paste the contents of the clipboard to the chosen channel. Alternatively, use the copy / paste icons in the Common panel.

70 Creative effects can be achieved by using more than one effect in the insert slots. Try the following: compressor followed by fuzz, fuzz followed by chorus, echo followed by flange, chorus followed by flange, tremolo followed by autopan, reverb followed by phasing, filtering followed by delay.

71 To make fine adjustments in the Mixer, hold Shift while moving a channel fader or pan control.

72 Assign a key command to 'Mixer - Section: Extended'. Try F5 or F9. This gives you instant toggling of the the extended Mixer without using the arrows in the Mixer common panel.

73 To regulate the overall level of an audio based channel after automation has been applied, use the channel's trim control or, for two or more automated channels, change the output routings to a Group and apply overall level changes using the Group channel fader.

74 To apply master buss reverb or delay which continues after the master fader has been fully attenuated, (for example, on fade outs when mixing or mastering), insert the reverb or delay effect in insert slots 7 or 8 of the master buss (i.e. post fader).

75 To set a number of tracks in the Project window or channels in the Mixer to the same input or output buss, select the chosen tracks / channels and change the input or output menu selection of any one while holding Alt.

Automation

76 To change the recording resolution for automation data, adjust the Automation Reduction slider in Preferences / Editing.

77 When moving automation handles, activate the Project window infoline. The infoline displays the start time and value of the event as you drag it. This helps place the events with greater precision. Alternatively, click directly on the value field in the infoline to change the value of the event.

78 A good way of viewing the behaviour of the different automation modes is to write the automation while viewing the corresponding sub-track in the Project window event display. Each time you click on a control when the Write button is active, the corresponding track header in the track list turns red to indicate that automation is being recorded.

79 To clarify the display of automation data in the Project window, activate 'Show Track colours' at the top of the track list and use the pop-up track colour selector for each automation sub-track to choose an appropriate colour.

Import / Export

80 Easy import – you can import multiple audio files in the file selection dialogue which appears when you select the Import medium function (Pool menu). You may also drag and drop audio and standard MIDI files directly from the desktop into the event display.

81 Easy export – before mixing down using Export / Audio Mixdown, check that all track monitor buttons are de-activated. Audio-based tracks with their monitor buttons active are NOT included in the audio mixdown. This can easily occur when using 'Tapemachine Style' or 'While Record Enabled' monitor modes since selected tracks automatically activate their monitor buttons when in stop mode or when record enabled.

82 When using Export / Audio Mixdown, make sure that any reverberation tail which occurs after the audio tracks is preserved by adding two or more bars of safety margin to the right locator position.

83 To copy tracks between projects, use Export / Selected Tracks, and Import / Track archive (File menu).

Pool

84 To find the current maximum peak amplitude and the average loudness of an audio clip, select the clip in the Pool and then select Statistics from the Audio menu. The resulting Statistics window shows the maximum peak amplitude (Peak Amplitude), which means the single highest peak found in the selection, and the average RMS power (Average), which means the average loudness of the signal.

85 Before exporting the Pool, create a special folder using Create Folder (Pool menu) and drag all the clips into it. When you later import the Pool into another Cubase or Nuendo project all the clips are neatly packaged in their own folder and are, thus, easier to find among any clips already in the current Pool.

86 To view more details about Broadcast Wave files in the Pool, click in the Info column for the file to reveal a pop-up info box.

87 To find out the total size taken up by the audio files in a project, activate the Show info button in the Pool (see the Total Size field).

88 To sort the audio files used in a project alphabetically or by type, date or path, click on the relevant column header in the Pool.

Miscellaneous

89 Try setting Preferences / Editing / Controls / Value Box to 'Increment / Decrement on Left Click and Drag'. This means that by clicking on a value field and dragging the mouse position vertically you can instantly change values in a fast, fuss-free way. The technique works well when adjusting the start, end, volume, fade in, fade out or transpose values for a selected event in the Project window Infoline. It is also good for adjusting length, pitch, velocity and channel data in the Key and Drum editor Infolines, and for changing the tempo (in fixed mode).

90 To quickly change the tempo of your project, press Shift + T on the computer keyboard followed by the up or down arrows.

91 While in the Project window, you can select tracks using the up / down arrow keys. While in the Mixer, you can select tracks using the left / right arrow keys. Several tracks / channels can be selected simultaneously by holding the Shift key while pressing the arrow keys. By default, selecting also record enables the tracks and the Shift + arrow combinations therefore provide a quick method of record enabling multiple tracks.

92 Ctrl / Command click on the click, tempo and sync buttons to open the Metronome, Tempo and Sync Setup windows respectively.

93 To name all parts dragged onto a track according to the track's name, activate 'Parts get track names' in Preferences / Editing. This is useful for copying parts between instruments in MIDI orchestral projects, where you might use a template with the tracks already named according to the instruments in the orchestra.

94 To implement tempo changes over a specific range without affecting the rest of the tempo in the project, proceed as follows: 1) As a guide, set up the left and right locators around the desired range in the ruler. 2) Select the Time warp tool in normal mode. 3) Hold Shift and click at the left and right locator positions to enter tempo events at the start and end of the selected range. Tempo changes may now be freely added within the selected range without affecting the rest of the tempo structure of the project.

95 For instant loop playback of the currently selected event in the event display, press Shift + G (Transport menu / Loop selection).

96 To set up a loop within an event, activate the Independent Track Loop button available in the Audio Part editor and MIDI editors. During playback, the chosen range loops throughout the length of the event. This is helpful for finding new loop-based arrangements. Closing the editor cancels the looping effect.

97 It is best to activate 'Copy Files to Working Directory' in Preferences / Editing / Audio / On Import Audio Files as your default setting. This means that all imported audio is always copied to the working directory

and the original source audio files are not used. This avoids missing files and accidental modification of audio files used in other projects.

98 To save different Project startup settings as templates, select 'Save as template' in the File menu and choose a suitable name in the 'Save as template' dialogue. The template is now available in the templates list whenever you select 'New project' in the File menu. Templates are useful for creating startup projects optimised for 24 track audio, 16 track MIDI, 2 track mastering and so on, or for pre-configuring the system for use with advanced software samplers and synthesizers like Kontakt and Reaktor.

99 Experts recommend using two hard disk drives with Cubase; one for the system and program files and the other for the project and audio files. This maximises performance and makes it easier to maintain the audio disk. For large capacity hard disks it is preferable to create several smaller-sized partitions since this allows easier defragmentation and management of data.

100 Back up your data. Although hard disk failure is not a common occurrence, backing up your data is essential if you wish to avoid the potentially disastrous situation of losing all your files. Popular back-up media include: spare internal hard drives, hard drives in removable caddies, external firewire drives, zip or jaz discs, CD and DVD.

Macro magic

The macro section of many Cubase setups often remains empty because, while users are aware that macros can be enormously powerful, few have the time or the patience to create their own. This section shows you how and also provides you with a time-saving startup library of powerful ready-made macros.

What are macros?

Macros are user-configurable 'super functions' made up of a number of basic functions strung together in a logical sequence. They are very powerful since a large number of moves can be reduced to a single key command. Functions that you use one after the other repetitively can now be selected at lightning fast speed via a macro command, resulting in dramatically increased efficiency and productivity. Macros are managed in the Key commands window.

Key commands window

The Key commands window is opened by selecting File / Key commands. The macro section is toggled on and off in the lower half of the display by clicking on the Show / Hide macros button (Figure 21.1). If you are new to macros there may be no macros in the list when you first go there. New empty macros are created by clicking on the New macro button. A command is added to the new macro by selecting a function from the upper half of the window and clicking on the Add command button. You can keep on adding functions to the macro to create an elaborate sequence of commands. Once created, a key command may be assigned to the macro in the macro section

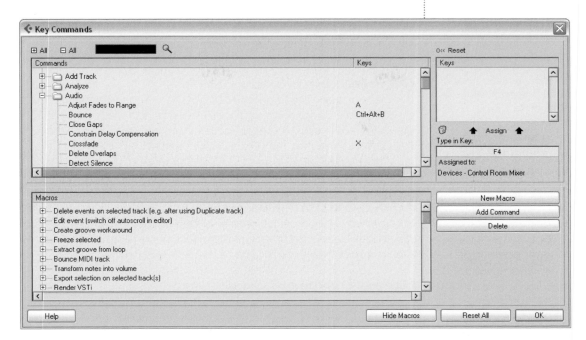

Figure 21.1
Key commands window featuring the macros section in the lower half of the display

in the upper half of the window. This means that the macro can now be activated with a single keystroke.

Macro library

The following is a list of both simple and advanced macros designed to enhance your use of Cubase and to teach you how to create your own macros by example. Each entry features the macro name, the suggested key command, the list of functions which make up the macro, and a brief description of what the macro does and how it can be used.

1 Bounce audio track [Key command – Shift+F1]

Designed to select all events on the currently selected audio track and bounce them all into one single audio event which overwrites all the original events in the event display. (This creates a new file on the hard disk and a new clip in the Pool, regardless of what you choose in the Replace dialogue which appears).

Macro 1

Edit – Select All on Tracks
Audio – Bounce

2 Bounce all audio tracks [Key command – Shift+F2]

This macro bounces all audio tracks into events of the same length, based upon the range of the overall project. This is particularly useful when you need to export multitrack audio material into another audio application which does not recognise regular global file exchange formats. You can maintain the relative positions of the audio events simply by starting all files at the same time position.

Macro 2

Tool – Range tool
Edit – Select all
Audio – Bounce
Tool – Select tool
Navigate – Up
Navigate – Down

3 Merge MIDI track [Key command – Shift+F3]

This macro merges all MIDI parts on the currently selected MIDI track and

Macro 3

Edit – Solo
Edit – Select All on Tracks
Transport – Locators to Selection
MIDI – Merge MIDI in Loop
Edit – Solo

Macro 4

Edit – Select All
Transport – Locators to Selection
Add Track – MIDI
MIDI – Merge MIDI in Loop

Macro 5

Edit – Lock
Edit – Select All on Tracks
Edit – Delete
Edit – Select All on Tracks
Edit – Unlock

Macro 6

Transport – Locate Selection
Edit – Duplicate
Transport – Locators to Selection
Transport – Set Left Locator
Edit – Left selection side to cursor
Zoom – Zoom Full

Macro 7

Transport – Locate Selection
Edit – Duplicate
Edit – Duplicate
Edit – Duplicate
Transport – Locators to Selection
Transport – Set Left Locator
Edit – Left selection side to cursor
Zoom – Zoom Full

bounces them all into one single MIDI part. Overwriting the original parts in the event display depends upon your choice in the 'Erase destination' option in the MIDI Merge options dialogue which appears.

4 Merge all MIDI tracks [Key command – Shift+F4]

This macro merges all non-muted MIDI parts in the event display into a single MIDI part on a new MIDI track. Useful for creating type 0 standard MIDI files or for mixing down a number of MIDI drum parts into a single composite part. It assumes that the pointer tool is selected.

5 Crop selection [Key command – typewriter '=']

This macro uses the lock command to shield the current selection from the delete command and its action is similar to an image crop function as found in image editing software. All you do is select one or more events on the currently selected track and execute this macro to delete all other non-selected events on the track. It is intended for operation on the currently selected track only.

6 Dupli zoom x 2 [Key command – Ctrl+F2]

Doubles the number of instances of the current range selection, automatically zooms in to the currently used area of the event display and reselects the duplicated section. It is designed to be used after having made a selection with the range selection tool (double-click on an event, for example) and may be repeated as required (by pressing the assigned key command a number of times). Repeating the macro results in useful musical numbers. For example, selecting an event with the range selection tool and pressing Ctrl / Command+F2 (the suggested key command) gives two duplicates, pressing it twice in succession gives four duplicates, pressing it three times gives eight duplicates, pressing it four times gives sixteen duplicates... and so on. The number of duplicates for each selection of the macro is always doubled. This is particularly useful when working with drum loops. If required, the zoom command may be left out of the macro. Note that all the events between the left and right locators are reselected. This allows you to use the macro for 'multiplication' rather than 'addition'. For a meaningful result, always use the range selection tool with this macro.

7 Dupli zoom x 4 [Key command – Ctrl+F4]

Quadruples the number of instances of the current range selection, automatically zooms in to the currently used area of the event display and re-selects the duplicated section. It is designed to be used after having made a selection with the range selection tool (double-click on an event, for example) and may be repeated as required (by pressing the assigned key command a number of times). Repeating the macro results in useful musical numbers. For example, selecting an event with the range selection tool and pressing Ctrl / Command + F4 (the suggested key command) gives four duplicates, pressing it twice in succession gives sixteen duplicates, pressing it three times in succession gives sixty four duplicates... and so on. The number of duplicates for each selection of the macro is always quadrupled. This is useful when working with drum loops and you can build up a large number of duplicates very quickly. If required, the zoom command may be left out of the macro. Note that all the events between the left and right locators are reselected. This allows you to use the macro for 'multiplication' rather than 'addition'. For a meaningful result, always use the range selection tool with this macro.

8 Dupli zoom + 3 [Key command – Ctrl+F3]

A simpler macro than the 'dupli zoom' multiplication macros outlined above. This simply 'adds' three duplicates to the current selection and zooms in to the used area of the display. It may be used repetitively but it always adds three duplicates and so does not always produce a musically meaningful number of events. It provides an alternative to the standard repeat command selected by pressing Ctrl / Command + K. Other similar macros could be designed for other musically useful numbers of repeats. If required, the zoom command may be left out of the macro.

Macro 8
Transport – Locate Selection
Edit – Duplicate
Edit – Duplicate
Edit – Duplicate
Transport – Locators to Selection
Transport – Set Left Locator
Zoom – Zoom Full

9 Open focused editor [Key command – W]

Sets the left and right locators to the currently selected event, opens the relevant editor, zooms in and selects the range of the event. This macro automatically organises your event selection ready for editing purposes and functions well with all event types. For a more stable view, switch off autoscroll.

Macro 9
Transport - Locators to Selection
Edit - Open
Zoom - Zoom to Locators
Edit - Select in Loop
Zoom - Zoom to Selection
Edit - Select None
Zoom - Zoom to Locators

10 Events to audio part and edit [Key command – Ctrl+Alt+E]

Puts the currently selected audio events into an audio part and opens the Audio Part editor. Simple but very useful. Ideal for editing multiple audio takes which have been recorded in cycle recording mode.

Macro 10
Audio – Events to Part
Transport – Locators to Selection
Edit – Open
Zoom – Zoom Full

11 Make loop from range selection [Key command – Alt+A]

Before using this macro you are strongly advised to make a backup of the audio clip in question. The macro is designed to make an audio event from a range selection in the Sample editor. Before activating the macro, double click on the chosen audio event to open the Sample editor and select the required range using the range selection tool. Here, it is assumed that you wish to 'extract' a rhythmic loop from the rest of the audio in the event. Upon activation, the macro sets the tempo definition loop to your chosen range selection and then adjusts the length of the audio event in the event display. Next, the Sample editor is closed and then re-opened with the focus on the newly sized audio event. From here, you might like to adjust the audio tempo definition manually before creating hitpoints and slicing the audio, or before activating musical mode, for example.

Macro 11
Tool – Audio Tempo Definition
Transport – Locators to Selection
Audio – Set Audio Event from Loop
Edit – Open/Close Editor
Edit – Open/Close Editor

12 Punch range setup [Key command – Ctrl+#]

This macro prepares Cubase for the 'Punch range record' macro outlined below (Macro 13). It assumes that no punch buttons have already been activated on the Transport panel and requires the preparation of suitable workspace and zoom presets. The zoom presets menu is found to the left of the horizontal zoom slider in the lower right corner of the Project window. The workspace presets menu is found as a sub-menu in the Window menu. The action of the macro runs as follows: 1) The Transport panel punch out button is activated. 2) A workspace, containing settings for a suitably sized Project window with a visible Transport panel, is selected. 3) A zoom preset set for a 10-15 second horizontal view (or

Macro 12
Transport – AutoPunch Out
Workspaces – Workspace 2
Zoom – Zoom Preset 2
Zoom – Zoom Tracks 4 Rows
Tool – Range Tool

some other suitable zoom setting) is selected. 4) A second zoom preset set to a four row vertical track size is selected. 5) The range tool is selected ready to make a selection for the punch in.

Macro 13

Transport – AutoPunch In
Transport – Locators to Selection
Transport – To Left Locator
Transport – Step Back Bar
Transport – Step Back Bar
Transport – Start

13 Punch range record [Key command – #]

Designed to make punch-in recording easier, this macro gives a two bar pre roll before your chosen range selection and automatically punches in and out of record mode at the start and end points. Although it is not essential, the procedure works better if you have already prepared the way using the 'Punch range setup' macro, outlined above. In any case, before starting to punch record using this macro, ensure that the cycle, punch in and pre-roll buttons are de-activated on the Transport panel and that the punch out button is activated. Select any section of your music using the range selection tool. You are now ready to start punch recording. This macro works even when a range over several tracks is selected, at which time simultaneous recording on all tracks takes place. You are also free to record on both audio and MIDI tracks at the same time. You would most often use the range selection tool to govern where recording takes place but the macro also works when you select events with the object selection tool. Overall, this macro is excellent for all kinds of detailed punch in work and, if necessary, makes it easy to punch in over the same section a large number of times. If you need a post-roll after the recorded section, activate the post-roll button and enter a post roll value in the Transport panel. This macro works best with 'Enable record on selected track' active (Preferences / Editing / Project & Mixer) and with 'Tapemachine style' selected (Preferences / VST).

Macro 14

Transport – Set Marker 9
Transport – To Left Locator
Transport – Step Back Bar
Transport – Step Back Bar
Transport – Play until Next Marker

14 Punch range playback [Key command – ']

This macro makes it easy to audition what you have just recorded with the above punch range record macro (Macro 13). It sets marker 9 at the current position of the cursor (which would normally be found placed just after the recording), rewinds to the start of the recorded section, steps back two bars and then plays back the passage up to marker 9. The macro may be used repetitively but for successful operation you should allow playback to reach marker 9 before recommencing.

Macro 15

Transport – Locators to Selection
Navigate – Right
Transport – To Right Locator
Edit – Cut
Edit – Paste

15 Reshuffle [Key command – Alt+R]

Shuffles the next event back to the end point of the current event selection. This macro always works on the next event to the right of the current selection and may be used repetitively. For a successful result, you must also select the track concerned. The outcome is the closing of all the gaps between events so that they appear consecutively on the track. Good for pulling events back together after editing which changes their lengths.

16 Retake [Key command – Ctrl+pad *]

This macro is designed primarily to be used just after recording a bad take and allows an instant re-take over the same range with a single key command. It operates on the currently selected track and functions by deleting the previously recorded event and then re-recording over the same range. It also operates by selecting any audio event over which you wish to re-record. It functions best when not in cycle mode and with pre-roll, post-roll and punch out activated. It has no effect if no event is selected.

Macro 16

Transport - Stop
Transport - Locators to selection
Transport - Locate selection
Edit - Cut
Transport - Record

Workspaces

What are workspaces?

Workspaces are complete window layouts which may be stored or recalled at any time, allowing you to quickly adapt your working environment to the task at hand. They come in two varieties:

1 Workspaces

'Workspaces' contain the layout and contents of the windows stored at various moments within the active project. They may be recalled within the active project only and are not globally available to other projects. A workspace includes window sizes, window positions, track sizes, horizontal zoom resolutions, horizontal and vertical scroll positions, ruler time settings, tool selection, mixer configuration, Transport panel configuration and so on. Essentially, most of what you can see on the screen at any given moment may be saved as a workspace (similar to taking a snapshot).

2 Workspace presets

Once created, regular workspaces may also be stored as presets known as 'Workspace presets'. These are globally available to all projects. Workspace presets store the main windows only and do not include all the details within each window. However, they have the advantage of being globally available to all projects and are useful for setting up generic window layouts for primary tasks such as recording, editing and mixing.

Organize workspaces dialogue

Workspaces are managed using the 'Organize Workspaces' dialogue which is opened by selecting Window / Workspaces / Organize, or pressing Alt + Pad 0 (Figure 21.2). This displays the list of available workspaces in the current project to the left, and the list of globally available workspace presets to the right.

Figure 21.2
Organize workspaces dialogue

There is always at least one active workspace which is indicated by a grey selection bar in the list, even if you have not yet created any workspaces in the current project. In the latter case, the default active workspace appears named as 'Main' in the list. New workspaces may be created at any time by clicking on the 'new' button. The stored data is based upon the positions and contents of the currently open windows in the project. When you create a new workspace you are obliged to name it in the list.

You can activate any existing workspace by double-clicking in its number column (#) or by selecting it and clicking on the activate button. A workspace may be locked by clicking in its box in the locked column, which keeps the selected workspace in its original form regardless of how you change the windows in the project. This means that you always go back to the original stored workspace each time you select it. To store a workspace as a preset which is available globally to all projects, move it from the left column into the right column using the arrow buttons between the two lists. If required, workspace presets on the right may be moved back to the left workspace list in a similar manner. Activating 'Auto instantiate presets' automatically copies global workspace presets into the list on the left, if there are not already workspaces created for the current project. This is useful when creating new projects. Activating 'Use IDs' allows you to re-number the workspaces in the ID column regardless of their position in the list. This is helpful when recalling specific workspaces using key commands (Alt + Pad 1-9) since the keypad numbers now refer to the ID numbers and not the list numbers.

Handling workspaces and workspace key commands

Handling workspaces requires a little practice. The first rule to keep in mind is that you are always working within the active workspace. Secondly, this active workspace can either be locked or unlocked. If it is locked, you are not actually changing what is stored in the workspace if you adjust the current window layout. However, if it is unlocked, the contents are immediately changed if you make any adjustments. A very good and easy tip for keeping an eye on your workspace status is to observe the number in brackets next to the Window menu. The number within the brackets specifies the currently active workspace, and the presence or non-presence of a full-stop next to the number denotes its lock status. For example, '(1)' means that the active workspace is number 1 and it is unlocked, whereas (1.) means that the active workspace is number 1 and it is locked.

The Organize workspaces dialogue is helpful for the overall management of workspaces but the default key commands are often better when creating and using workspaces during the heat of a recording session. The relevant key commands can be found next to the menu items in the workspaces sub-menu (Figure 21.3).

The basic sequence of events to create a workspace using the key commands runs as follows:

Figure 21.3
Workspaces sub-menu showing the default key commands

1 Set up the windows in the project as desired.
2 Press Alt + Pad / to create a new workspace. Enter a name into the pop-up dialogue.

3 Press Alt + Pad . to lock the workspace.
4 Press Alt + Pad 1-9 to recall the workspaces you create.
5 Press Alt + Pad . a second time to unlock the workspace if you need to update it.

Workspaces for workflow

Like macros, workspaces help improve your workflow. This section explains exactly how this comes about by describing the creation of three commonly required workspaces. As you no doubt already know, the primary functions of Cubase include recording, editing and mixing; so why not set up personalised workspaces with these functions in mind, each with the specific tools and window layouts needed to make each task easier? The following sections describe how to do this. Each workspace is suitable for saving as a workspace preset, thus becoming available to all projects. However, since some of the details within the windows are not stored in workspace presets, you may also wish to save the setups as regular workspaces within your default startup project.

A workspace for recording

Of course, configuring the screen environment for recording varies greatly depending on the specific recording task at hand. Audio recording might need different on-screen elements to MIDI recording and each project would undoubtedly feature variations in the number of tracks being used. However, there are a number of common factors involved. For most projects you would at least need to see the Project window and the Transport panel. The recording workspace outlined here also features the Mixer and the Pool (see Figure 21.4). It is assumed that the project already contains a number of audio and MIDI tracks added to the track list and that the overall system and VST connections are fully tested and operational.

At first sight, the screen layout shown in Figure 21.4 looks a simple affair but the secrets of this workspace are in the details inside each window. Overall, the workspace includes a reduced Project window with the Mixer open below and the Transport panel open above. Space has been allocated next to the Mixer for a small-sized Pool window. To grasp the logic of this workspace we need to consider the audio recording process itself (MIDI recording considerations are similar). Here, it is assumed that you need to record an external source, such as a live musical performance via a microphone. Like all recordings of this type, the first thing you need to verify in Cubase is the level of the input signal. Hence, this workspace features the Mixer with the input busses visible. You are therefore always ready to monitor or adjust the input level and can keep an eye on input levels throughout the recording session. Next, you would probably decide which channel you are going to record on and set its input buss accordingly. You may also need to adjust the output buss assignation. To accommodate this, the workspace features the input / output menus visible on all channels. The main output busses are also already visible so you can monitor and adjust the overall output level. The Transport panel includes the performance meter, record mode, locators, main transport, and master and sync sections. You therefore have instant access to the punch-in, punch-out, pre-roll, post-roll, click and tempo

Figure 21.4

A workspace for recording. Here, the first take of the recording session is under way.

parameters, as well as the obvious record modes and main transport buttons. In the Project window itself, the tracks are set to a vertical size of 2 rows allowing you a view of the record and monitor buttons and of the events in the event display as they get recorded (1 row may also be appropriate if you need to see more tracks simultaneously). The Inspector, Infoline and Overview switches are de-activated but you may prefer to open the Inspector for certain detailed recording operations. The open Pool window in the corner helps you keep an eye on the audio clips as they get recorded. With this window size, the clips are displayed as a simple list.

A workspace for event editing

Designing a workspace for event editing is potentially much simpler than the recording example above, since all you probably need is the Project window maximised to show the greatest amount of event display possible (see Figure 21.5). A suitable track row size is chosen to get a good view of the events (try four rows), the Infoline is activated to display information about each event as it is selected, and the active Overview helps you navigate and zoom within the whole project. An open Inspector might be helpful if you are selecting presets or changing MIDI channel parameters, or when you need to quickly open the interface for a VST Instrument. The Transport panel is also shown and features the Marker section to help with navigation, the jog wheel for detailed lining up of the cursor position, and the master level control to adjust the overall level while editing.

A workspace for mixing

Any workspace designed for mixing would, of course, include the Mixer. The workspace shown in Figure 21.6 is dominated by the extended Mixer with a Project window reduced to its minimum vertical height. The screen width shown here allows around fifteen mixer channels to be displayed in wide mode. The input and output busses have been hidden to allow a greater number of regular channels to be displayed simultaneously. Conveniently, these Mixer details are included within each stored workspace. The Project window features an enlarged Marker track to help navigate within the project and regular tracks with their row size reduced to the minimum. When the Marker track is selected, the markers are also shown in list form in the open Inspector to the left. To help still further with navigation the Transport panel is reduced to just the locator and marker sections, providing buttons for moving the cursor to the left and right locator positions, or to the first fifteen markers. The time display helps when Cubase is linked to other machines via time code and the performance meters help you keep an eye on the CPU load.

What's so good about workspaces?

Using any one of the above workspaces in isolation might be useful but the real advantage of workspaces is being able to switch instantaneously between them at any stage during the evolution of a project. This is very liberating. Rather than approaching your workflow in standard 'do all the recording, do all the editing and then mix it' fashion, you can now effortlessly jump between

Figure 21.5
A workspace for editing where the event display is made as large as possible

Info

Large orchestral arrangements often call for working on specific groups of instruments on multiple tracks. Rather than scrolling up and down in the Project window to find the required instruments, just store a number of workspaces with the appropriate vertical scroll positions. You can now switch instantly between the different project views.

Figure 21.6
A workspace for mixing, featuring the extended Mixer dominating the screen space

different streamlined environments. Of course, the advantages do not end there. You can store a workspace at any moment throughout the development of your project and go back to that particular view at any time in the future. Furthermore, you can create workspaces suitable for all kinds of other everyday Cubase tasks, such as tiling multiple editors; opening multiple insert effect interfaces; organising reduced, extended and multiple Mixer layouts; tiling a large-scale Pool window alongside the Project Browser; and so on. The possibilities are endless.

Recommended reading

Knowledge of sound recording, microphones, mixing, MIDI, sampling, sequencing, digital audio and acoustics can help you get better results with Cubase. There are a wide range of books available on these subjects. The following list should help you get started:

Anderton, Craig 'MIDI for Musicians', (Amsco Publications, 1995), 120pp.

Borwick, John 'Microphones – Technology and Technique', (Oxford: Focal Press, 1990), 241pp.

Borwick, John ed. 'Sound Recording Practice', (Oxford: Oxford University Press, 1996), 616pp.

Buick, Peter and Lennard, Vic 'Music Technology Reference Book', (PC Publishing, 1995), 160pp.

Clackett, Dave 'Handbook of MIDI Sequencing', (PC Publishing, 1996), 244pp.

De Furia, Steve and Scacciaferro, Joe 'The Sampling Book', (Omnibus Press, 2002), 152pp.

Eargle, John 'The Microphone Book', (Focal Press, 2004), 368pp.

Everest, F. Alton 'The Master Handbook of Acoustics', (New York: TAB Books, 1994), 452pp.

Gibson, David 'The Art of Mixing', (Music Sales Limited, 1997), 127pp.

Harris, John 'Recording the Guitar', (PC Publishing, 1997), 156pp.

Howard, David M. and Angus, James 'Acoustics and Psychoacoustics', (Oxford: Focal Press, 2nd edition, 2001), 416pp.

Huber, David Miles 'The MIDI Manual', (SAMS, 1991), 268pp.

Huber and Runstein 'Modern Recording Techniques', (Oxford: Focal Press,1997), 496pp.

Katz, Bob 'Mastering Audio: The Art and the Science', (Focal Press, 2002), 319pp.

Kirk, Ross and Hunt, Andy 'Digital Sound Processing for Music and Multimedia', (Oxford: Focal Press, 1999), 352pp.

Lehrman, Paul 'Midi for the Professional', (Music Sales Corp., 1993), 239pp.

Massey, Howard 'Behind the Glass', (Backbeat UK, 2000), 224pp

Mellor, David 'Recording Techniques for Small Studios' (PC Publishing, 1993), 208pp.

Millward, Simon 'Sound Synthesis with VST Instruments', (PC Publishing, 2002), 277pp.

Moylan, William 'Understanding and Crafting the Mix: The Art of Recording', (Focal Press, 2007), 424pp.

Ortiz, Joe and Pauly 'Beat It! (MIDI drum programming)', (PC Publishing, 1997), 114pp.

Owsinski, Bobby 'The Mixing Engineer's Handbook', (Music Sales Limited, 1999), 234pp.

Poyser, Debbie, Johnson, Derek and Jones, Hollin 'Fast Guide to Propellerhead Reason', (PC Publishing, 2007), 474pp

Rona, Jeffrey and Wilkinson, Scott (Editor) 'The Midi Companion', (Hal Leonard Publishing Corp, 1994), 96pp.

Rothstein, Joseph 'MIDI – A Comprehensive Introduction', (Oxford: Oxford University Press, 1992), 226pp.

Rumsey, Francis 'The Audio Workstation Handbook', (Oxford: Focal Press, 1996), 286pp.

Russ, Martin and Rumsey, Francis (Editor) 'Sound Synthesis and Sampling', (Oxford: Focal Press, 1996), 400pp.

Stavrou, Michael 'Mixing with your Mind', (Flux Research, 2004), 300pp. (available from: www.mixingwithyourmind.com)

Waugh, Ian 'Making Music with Digital Audio (Direct to disk recording on the PC)', (PC Publishing, 1997), 250pp

White, Paul 'Creative Recording 2 – Microphones and Recording Techniques', (Music Maker Books, 1995), 99pp.

White, Paul 'Home Recording Made Easy', (Sanctuary Publishing, 1997), 205pp.

White, Paul 'MIDI for the Technophobe', (Sanctuary Publishing, 1997), 184pp.

Useful websites

The internet is a very good resource for the latest information about Cubase and related products. The following lists some websites which may be of interest:

Steinberg Cubase

Steinberg main website	www.steinberg.net
Cubase.net forum	forum.cubase.net

Plug-ins

Antares	www.antarestech.com
Audio Ease	www.audioease.com
BBE Sound	www.bbesound.com
Bias	www.bias-inc.com
dB-audioware	www.dB-audioware.com
Celemony	www.celemony.com
Chandler Ltd.	www.chandlerlimited.com
DSP FX	www.dspfx.com
FXpansion	www.fxpansion.com
IK Multimedia	www.ikmultimedia.com
Izotope	www.izotope.com
Intelligent sounds and music	www.ismism.de
Native Instruments	www.native-instruments.com
Princeton Digital	www.princetondigital.com
Prosoniq	www.prosoniq.com
PSP	www.pspaudioware.com
SIR (Impulse Response Processor)	www.knufinke.de/sir
Sonic Foundry	www.sfoundry.com
Sonnox	www.sonnoxplugins.com
Tascam	www.tascam.co.uk
URS	www.ursplugins.com
Virtos Audio	www.virtos-audio.com
Voxengo	www.voxengo.com
Wave Arts	www.wavearts.com
Waves	www.waves.com

DSP powered plug-ins

Focusrite Liquid Mix	www.focusrite.com
Solid State Logic Duende	www.solid-state-logic.com
T.C. Electronics Powercore	www.tcelectronic.com
UAD powered plug-ins	www.mackie.com/uad-1

MIDI plug-ins

Franck's MIDI plug-ins	www.midi-plugins.de
Nicolas Fournel	www.nicolasfournel.com
Ntonyx MIDI effects	www.ntonyx.com
Tencrazy	www.tencrazy.com

VST Instrument developers

Applied Acoustics Systems	www.applied-acoustics.com
Arturia	www.arturia.com
Bioroid	www.bioroid.com
Bitshift Audio	www.bitshiftaudio.com
Bojo	www.bojo.dk
Delaydots	www.delaydots.com
Edirol	www.edirol.com
Fxpansion	www.fxpansion.com
GMedia Music	www.gmediamusic.com
Green Oak	www.greenoak.com
Image Line	www.fruityloops.com
Lin Plug	www.linplug.com
LoftSoft	www.loftsoft.co.uk
Maz sound tools	www.maz-sound.de
mda	www.mda-vst.com
Muon Software	www.muon-software.com
Native Instruments	www.native-instruments.com
reFX	www.refx.net
rgcAudio	www.rgcaudio.com
Spectrasonics	www.spectrasonics.net
Steinberg	www.steinberg.net
Synapse Audio	www.synapse-audio.com
TC Works	www.tcworks.de
Tobybear	www.tobybear.de
Ultimate Sound Bank	www.plugsound.com
VirSyn	www.virsyn.de
Yellow tools	www.yellowtools.de

Audio cards / hardware

Apogee	www.apogeedigital.com
Creamware	www.creamware.com
Creative	www.creative.com
Echo	www.echoaudio.com
Edirol	www.edirol.com
E-MU	www.emu.com
ESI (Ego Systems Inc.)	www.esi-pro.com

Focusrite	www.focusrite.com
Korg	www.korg.com
Lexicon	www.lexiconpro.com
Lynx	www.lynxstudio.com
Mackie	www.mackie.com
Mark of the Unicorn (MOTU)	www.motu.com
M Audio	www.midiman.com
Metric Halo	www.mhlabs.com
RME	www.rme-audio.com
T.C. Electronics	www.tcelectronic.com
Turtle Beach	www.tbeach.com
Yamaha	www.yamaha.com

Soundbanks and samples

Convolution impulse responses	www.noisevault.com
FM sounds	www.thedx7.co.uk
Groundloops sampled loops	www.groundloops.com
KVR VSTi sound libraries	www.kvraudio.com
PrimeSounds sample library	www.primesounds.com
Reaktor (Len Sasso)	www.swiftkick.com/reaktor.html
Reaktor (Paul Swennenhuis)	www.midiworld.org/AuReality
Reaktor (Wave In Head)	www.waveinhead.de
Sample swap	www.sampleswap.org
Sonomic	www.sonomic.com
Sound ideas	www.sound-ideas.com
Tassman library	www.hvsynthdesign.com
Time and space	www.timespace.com
WizooSounds sample library	www.wizoosounds.com

Sound synthesis, synthesizers and music technology

Hammond organ	theatreorgans.com/hammond/faq
Mellotron	members.aol.com/tronpage
Mellotron	www.mellotron.com
Moog	www.moogmusic.com
Moog synthesizers	moogarchives.com
Synthesizers and synthesis	www.vintagesynth.org
Synthesizer history	www.obsolete.com/120_years
Synthesizer information and links	www.synthesizers.com
Synth zone	www.synthzone.com

General interest

Acousti Products	www.acoustiproducts.com
Acoustics	www.mhsoft.nl
Acoustics	www.ethanwiner.com/acoustics.html
Acoustic analysis	www.etfacoustic.com
Analogx utilities	www.analogx.com
audio CD A/B tests	www.theabcd.com
audio comparison CDs	www.3daudioinc.com
Audio forums	www.audioforums.com

Audio production database	www.note2.com
Auralex acoustics	www.auralex.com
Apple website	www.apple.com
Arbiter Group PLC	www.arbitergroup.com
Carillon	www.carillondirect.com
CD-Recordable FAQ website	www.cdrfaq.org
Computer Music Magazine	www.computermusic.co.uk
Computer isolation boxes	www.iso-box.com
Digital domain	www.digido.com
Electronic music publishing	www.raw42.com
Electronic music website	www.em411.com
Hard drive performance (DskBench)	www.sesa.es
Kustom PCs	www.kustompcs.co.uk
KVR Audio plug-in resources	www.kvraudio.com
Mac audio and music site	www.macmusic.org
Metal grille pop-shields	www.stedmancorp.com
MIDI Farm	www.midifarm.com
MIDI utilities	www.midiox.com
Millennium Music	www.millennium-music.biz
Musician's Tech Central	www.musicianstechcentral.com
Music XP website	www.musicxp.net
PC hardware analysis	www.cpuid.com
Plug-in Spot VSTi resources	www.pluginspot.com
Pro audio network	www.digitalprosound.com
Pro audio reference	www.rane.com/digi-dic.html
Professional recording resources	www.prorec.com
Project studio handbook	theprojectstudiohandbook.com/directory.htm
Quiet PC	www.quietpc.com
Recording Industry network	www.artistpro.com
Red Submarine	www.sub.co.uk
Rightmark audio analyser	audio.rightmark.org
Shareware Music Machine	www.hitsquad.com
Silent PC components/cases	www.antec.co.uk
Silent PC components/cases	www.paq.ltd.uk
Silent PC review	www.silentpcreview.com
Softpedia general utilities	www.softpedia.com
Sonic Spot resources	www.sonicspot.com
Sound on Sound magazine	www.soundonsound.com
Studio design	www.johnlsayers.com
Studio design (SAE)	www.saecollege.de/reference_material
Studiospares	www.studiospares.com
Studio tips	www.studiotips.com
Tom's PC hardware guide	www.tomshardware.com
University of York	www.york.ac.uk/inst/mustech
Utilitygeek general utilities	www.utilitygeek.com
Virtual Guitarist website	www.bornemark.se
VST central VSTi listings	www.vstcentral.com
Windows optimisation	www.ccleaner.com

Glossary

A/D converter Analogue-to-digital converter. A device which converts analogue data, such as an audio signal from the real world, into digital data (a sequence of numbers) which can be retained in computer memory or stored on digital media such as hard disks, CD and DVD.

ADSR Attack, Decay, Sustain, Release. A four-breakpoint envelope type used to control how the amplitude of a sound evolves over time. ADSR envelopes are also used to control the spectral evolution of a sound by modulating the cut-off frequency of a filter.

AES Audio Engineering Society. International organisation responsible for setting standards in the audio industry.

AES3 A digital signal interface standard agreed by the Audio Engineering Society and the European Broadcasting Union. Also known as AES-EBU, this uses 110 Ohm cable terminated in XLR connectors.

AES-EBU See AES3

Aftertouch The action of applying pressure to one or more keys of a musical keyboard after the onset of a note or chord. Also referred to as 'Channel Aftertouch' or 'Channel Pressure', it is transmitted via MIDI as Aftertouch messages and affects all notes present on the same MIDI channel by the same amount. It can be used to produce various real-time performance effects such as volume or brightness modulation and vibrato.

AGP Accelerated Graphics Port. Slot found on a computer's motherboard designed to accept graphics cards. Advantageous for audio since using an AGP graphics card optimises the use of the computer's resources and is unlikely to interfere with audio performance.

Algorithm A clearly defined, step-by-step set of instructions designed to achieve the completion of a specific task. Algorithms are invariably translated into computer programming languages and used as the building blocks for computer programs.

Aliasing A particular type of digital audio distortion which manifests itself as additional frequency components which do not form part of the original audio signal. This occurs when a signal has been sampled at too low a sampling rate to accurately capture the details of the high frequency components.

All-pass filter A filtering device which involves delaying frequency components by varying amounts and mixing the result with the original signal. Unlike conventional filtering, no attenuation in the amplitudes of the frequencies takes place.

AM Amplitude Modulation. A sound effect achieved by modulating the amplitude of one audio signal (the carrier) by another signal (the modulator). When the modulator is an LFO, tremolo effects are produced. When both signals are in the audible range, a more complex signal containing the carrier and the sum and difference frequencies of the carrier and modulator is produced (sometimes used for sound synthesis).

Amplifier A device which increases or decreases the amplitude of a signal which passes through it.

Amplitude A measure of the depth of the compression and rarefaction cycles of a sound signal where the peak amplitude is the point of maximum displacement from the mid-point of the signal's waveform. The amplitude contributes to the perceived loudness of the signal.

Analogue In audio, refers to a sound signal whose waveform has a value at every point in time. There are no discrete steps between each point and an analogue recording is usually that which has been made onto audio tape. Also used to describe analogue synthesis (as opposed to digital synthesis).

Arpeggiator A device for automatically repeating a group of notes in a cyclic pattern, usually by stepping through the notes of a chord which is held down on the musical keyboard.

ASIO Audio Stream Input Output. Computer protocol developed by Steinberg for handling audio recording and playback in digital audio systems.

Attack The shape and duration of the first part of a sound event where the amplitude rises from zero to its peak level (as implemented in an ADSR envelope).

Attenuation The reduction of the amplitude of a sound signal (or of a component within the signal).

Balance i) describes the relative levels of two or more sound elements (for example, when setting up a mix on a mixing console). ii) MIDI Controller 8. Used to adjust the relative levels of two components of a sound.

Band-pass filter A filter which allows a band of frequencies between two cut-off points to pass through with little change while significantly attenuating frequencies both above and below the pass band.

Band-reject filter A filter which significantly attenuates a band of frequencies between two cut-off points while allowing the rest of the signal to pass through with little change.

Bandwidth i) The range between two frequency points within the spectrum of an audio signal. ii) The overall frequency range of the spectrum of an audio signal.

Bank Select A combination of MIDI Controllers 0 and 32. A Bank Select message is usually immediately followed by a Program Change and allows switching to as many as 16384 different Banks.

BIOS Basic Input / Output System. A program residing in a ROM memory or flash BIOS chip on a computer's motherboard, responsible for the basic initialisation of the processor, memory, I/O devices and operating system.

Bit Acronym for 'binary digit'. The smallest unit of information in a binary number, represented as a 1 or a 0.

Bit depth The number of levels of measurement available in a digital audio system during A/D and D/A conversion. For example, a 16-bit system features 65536 possible discrete values which can be used to measure the amplitude of an audio signal. Greater bit depth results in greater dynamic range.

Boot A term used to describe starting a computer. This can take the form of a 'cold start', when the computer is booted from its switched off state, and a 'warm start', when the computer is restarted in its switched on state.

BPM Abbreviation for Beats Per Minute. Musical tempo expressed as the number of beats which occur in one minute. For example, at a tempo of 60BPM each beat of the bar has a duration of one second.

Breath Controller A breath operated device connected to a synthesizer used to change the volume or timbre of a sound. It is transmitted via MIDI as Controller 2.

Byte An 8-bit binary number (e.g. 0011 1010), creating the fundamental unit of measurement for computer media. A kilobyte (Kb) is 1,024 bytes, a megabyte (Mb) is 1,024 kilobytes and a gigabyte (Gb) is 1,024 megabytes.

Buffer Temporary storage area used to store data as it flows in, out and through a computer system.

Carrier In frequency modulation, amplitude modulation and ring modulation, the carrier is the audio signal to which modulation is applied. The carrier normally governs the perceived pitch of the resulting tone.

CD ROM Compact Disc Read Only Memory. A read-only CD containing data which can only be read by a computer CD drive and not an audio CD player.

Cent One hundredth of a semitone. A unit in musical instrument tuning systems used for fine adjustments of pitch.

Centre frequency The centre point of the passband or stopband in a band-pass or band-reject filter.

Chorus An effect produced by passing a signal through one or more delay lines and modulating the delay time(s) with an LFO. The result is mixed with the original signal. The modulation of the delay times produces changes in the perceived pitch and timing, creating the illusion of an ensemble of sound sources.

Comb filter A filter comprised of multiple amplitude response curves (or resonances) located at harmonic intervals relative to a chosen fundamental frequency. Passing a signal through such a filter emphasises the chosen harmonics in the source sound and can often change its perceived pitch.

Compressor An automatic level adjustment device which normally results in loud parts of the signal becoming quieter and quiet parts becoming louder. Compression converts a large dynamic range into a smaller dynamic range.

Control Change A type of MIDI message used to control various parameters other than the musical notes. Control Change messages contain information about the Controller number (0 - 127) and its value (0 - 127). Each Controller number has a specific function and the more commonly used Controllers include modulation (01), breath control

(02), main volume (07), pan (10), expression (11) and sustain pedal (64).

CPU Central Processing Unit. The main processor or chip controlling the operations of a computer, usually found on the main circuit board (motherboard).

Cross modulation The interconnection of the outputs of two oscillators to eachother's frequency inputs resulting in a complex frequency-modulated signal.

Cut-off The frequency at which the response of a filter passes from the pass band to the stop band (or vice versa), i.e. the frequency at which the filter starts to have an effect.

D/A converter Digital-to-analogue converter. A device which converts digital data into analogue data. For example, before we can hear the music on an audio CD, the digital information picked up by the read head of the CD player must first be converted into analogue form using a D/A converter.

DAT Digital Audio Tape. Digital audio recording format using 3.81mm wide tape in small cassettes. Began as a consumer format but later became widely accepted in the professional audio industry. DAT is now used less since mixing directly to hard disk and storage on other media is more convenient.

Decay i) As part of an envelope (e.g. ADSR), describes the shape and duration of a second part of a sound event where the amplitude falls from its peak level to its sustain level. ii) In general terms, describes how a sound fades away to silence.

Decibel (dB) A unit of relative measurement of sound level between audio signals on a logarithmic scale. For example, increasing the level of an input signal by 6dB results in an output which is double the amplitude of the original. Attenuating the level by 6dB results in an output which is half the amplitude.

Delay A replication of a signal which occurs at a set time after the original. Used in audio for delay, echo, chorus, flanging and other effects.

Digital Digital systems handle information as numerical data. For example, a digital waveform is measured as a succession of discrete points in time (samples), each of which is represented by a value (the maximum range of which forms the bit depth [or wordlength]). The quantity of these samples within a given time frame forms the sample rate. The audio on a CD is recorded at 16-bit / 44.1kHz, i.e. 44,100 16-bit wordlength samples per second.

Distortion A non-linear audio process which adds extra frequencies to the signal, thereby changing its waveform and harmonic structure.

Dither Audio processing technique which counteracts quantisation noise in digital audio recordings. Quantisation distortion occurs at very low levels when there are not enough bits in the system to accurately measure the signal. Noise shaped dithering involves converting the quantisation distortion into another kind of signal and re-distributing it to parts of the audio spectrum where it is less obvious to the human ear.

DMA Direct Memory Access. Describes access to RAM without passing through the main processor.

Download The process of loading a file from another system, such as from the internet or other network, into one's own computer.

Driver Software which provides the communication protocol between a hardware device and the operating system of the host computer. The hardware is usually set up and initialised via the driver software.

DSP i) Digital Signal Processing. The processing of signals using digital microprocessors. ii) Digital Signal Processor. A special computer chip which has been optimised for the high-speed numerical computations required for the processing of audio signals.

DVD Digital Versatile Disc. 5 inch diameter disc with around seven times the capacity of a regular compact disc, able to store data in computer, audio and video formats. DVD-A (DVD-Audio) is a high-quality format for stereo and multichannel audio.

EBU European Broadcasting Union. An organisation responsible for setting audio and broadcasting standards in Europe.

Echo A particular kind of delay where the delayed signal is clearly distinguishable from the original, often involving repeating echos. Delay effects may be classed as echo when the delay time is increased to around 30ms or more, (i.e. when the ear begins to clearly differentiate the delayed and original signals).

EIDE Enhanced Integrated Drive Electronics. A standard for fast data transfer between the host computer and mass storage devices, such as hard drives and CD ROM drives.

Emphasis See Resonance

Envelope The shape of a sound's amplitude variations over time (usually plotted on a graph of amplitude against time with break-points for each stage in the sound's evolution). One of the most common envelope shapes is the ADSR envelope.

Envelope Generator (EG) A device which generates a time-varying control signal (envelope) used to modulate the amplitude of a sound (usually based upon a set of values entered by the user). Envelope generators are also commonly used to modulate the frequency of the cut-off point of a filter.

Equalisation (EQ) Increase/attenuation of the levels of different frequency bands (e.g. bass, mid and treble) within a signal for corrective or creative purposes.

Expression MIDI Controller 11. Used to change the volume of a note while it is sustaining.

FAT File Allocation Table. A small area of a computer's hard drive containing an index which is used to keep track of all data stored on the disk.

Feedback Circuit which allows the connection of the output signal back to the input, producing additional frequency components within the signal, (when used for overdrive and saturation effects), or for creating echo repeats, (when used for delay effects).

FFT Abbreviation for Fast Fourier Transform. An optimised version of the Fourier Transform (Joseph Fourier), a mathematical procedure for calculating the frequency components of a sound from the waveform.

Filter A device which attenuates one or more chosen frequency bands within a sound while allowing the others to pass through unchanged.

Firewire Data communication standard also referred to as IEEE-1394. Supports the serial transfer of data at 400Mbit/sec or 800Mbit/sec.

Flanging An audio effect created by mixing a delayed version of a signal with the original and modulating the delay time with an LFO while also applying an amount of feedback.

FM Frequency Modulation. A sound synthesis technique (or effect) where the frequency of one signal (the carrier) is modulated by another (the modulator). In the sound synthesis sense, FM implies that both frequencies are within the audible range and, when this is the case, multiple frequencies known as sidebands are added to the signal.

Frequency The number of times a periodic sound wave oscillates per second, measured in hertz (Hz).

Frequency domain The representation of a sound signal on a graph of amplitude versus frequency. This shows the spectrum of the signal.

Fundamental The lowest frequency component within a periodic soundwave and normally that which gives the tone its perceived pitch.

Gain A measure of the increase in relative amplitude level between the input and output of an amplifier.

Gate i) An audio device which radically attenuates the level of an input signal when it falls below a certain threshold. Used especially to filter out

unwanted background noise and interference in the inactive parts of speech or musical performance. ii) The time between the moment a note is triggered by pressing a key on a musical keyboard (key on) and when the note is ended by releasing the key (key off).

General MIDI (GM) An addition to the MIDI protocol, (not formally a part of the MIDI Specification), providing a standard set of rules for patch mapping, drum and percussion note mapping, multi-timbrality, polyphony and various other elements. Roland introduced an enhanced version of the GM standard known as GS (General Standard) and Yamaha introduced similar enhancements known as XG (Extended General MIDI).

Harmonic Component within a sound whose frequency is a whole integer multiple of the fundamental.

Headroom The difference between the current level of a recorded signal and the maximum output level of the recording medium.

Hertz (Hz) A unit for measuring frequency. It expresses the number of oscillations per second of a periodic soundwave. The greater the number of hertz, the higher the perceived pitch of the sound.

Hexadecimal A base sixteen numbering system often used by computer programmers as an alternative to decimal or binary systems. The decimal numbers 0-9 are expressed as 0-9 in hexadecimal and decimal 10-15 are expressed as the letters A-F. Hexadecimal numbers have much more in common with the way that computers actually work than decimal numbers and they are less cumbersome than binary numbers. Thus they have proved extremely efficient for the analysis and understanding of computer data.

Hold pedal Middle foot pedal featured on acoustic pianos which, when pressed down, sustains the concurrently played note(s) but allows any subsequent notes to be played normally for as long as the pedal is held down. A similar foot pedal is featured on some electronic musical keyboards to create a similar effect. In MIDI-based applications the pedal action is transmitted using MIDI controller 66, (also referred to as sostenuto).

High-pass filter A filter which significantly attenuates the frequencies below a chosen cut-off point while allowing those above to pass through with little change.

HTML Hypertext mark-up language. A language used in the creation of web pages.

Internet Global network of computers interconnected via telephone lines. The internet is now the largest information resource in the world and provides a wide range of services and entertainment.

ISP Internet Service Provider. Internet users must subscribe to one of the ISPs which provide access to the internet.

Jumper A small clip for connecting pins on a circuit board to enable hardware re-configuration. Jumpers are found on such things as computer motherboards, extension cards and hard drives.

Latency The delay between the user input and the time it takes for a real-time digital audio system to respond and process the data through its hardware and software.

Level A measure of the amplitude of an audio signal.

LFO Abbreviation for low frequency oscillator. A type of oscillator which operates below the normal hearing range, often used for modulating a second oscillator to produce vibrato, tremolo and other modulation effects.

Limiter A peak level control device used to reduce the gain of the input signal when the input level exceeds the chosen threshold. A limiter is usually characterised by a very fast attack time and gain reduction which acts upon only the loudest peaks in the signal.

Logarithmic A manner in which to manage scales involving very large numbers and helpful in music and acoustics for understanding the human perception of sound intensity and frequency. The ear's

response to these phenomena is logarithmic and not linear. For example, plotting frequency on a graph logarithmically shows equal pitch intervals (an equal distance between successive octaves) rather than a linear plot which shows equal frequency intervals (a doubling of the distance between successive octaves).

Loudness The subjective response of the ear to the amplitude and spectrum of a sound signal.

Loudness contour The shape of the amplitude of a sound as it evolves over time. The same meaning as envelope shape (see envelope, above).

Low-pass filter A filter which significantly attenuates the frequencies above a chosen cut-off point while allowing those below to pass through with little change.

Master keyboard A MIDI equipped keyboard (often with no sound generating circuitry) used to control a network of MIDI modules and devices. Sometimes referred to as a 'mother keyboard'.

MIDI Musical Instrument Digital Interface. A data communication standard, first established in 1983, for the exchange of musical information between electronic musical instruments and, subsequently, computers. This involves the serial transfer of digital information, (MIDI Messages), via 5 pin DIN connectors. MIDI Messages are governed by a pre-defined set of rules and syntax known as the MIDI Specification.

MIDI Channel A channel for the sending and receiving of MIDI messages between devices. MIDI specifies 16 separate channels and each MIDI device can be set to be receptive to messages on one of these channels or, in the case of a multi-timbral instrument, on several specified channels at the same time.

MIDI Clock A timing related MIDI Message embedded in the MIDI data stream. MIDI Timing Clocks are sent 24 times per quarter note and along with Song Position Pointer, Start, Stop and Continue messages are used to synchronize MIDI-based sequencers, drum machines and other MIDI devices. Unlike SMPTE/EBU Time Code, MIDI Timing Clock is tempo-dependent.

MIDI Controller A type of MIDI Message used to control various musical parameters other than the notes themselves, such as Modulation, Volume and Pan. Controllers are also referred to as 'Continuous Controllers' and 'Control Change messages'.

MIDI Event MIDI data once it has been recorded into a MIDI-based sequencer. This is in contrast to 'MIDI Message' which refers to the same data as it is being sent down the MIDI cable.

MIDI File A standardised file format providing a way of transferring MIDI data between different software sequencers, hardware sequencers and computer platforms. There are three types of MIDI File: Type 0 stores the data as a single stream of events, Type 1 contains multiple parallel tracks and Type 2 allows sets of independent sequences to be stored in a single file. Type 1 is the most popular format.

MIDI In 5 pin DIN socket found on all MIDI-equipped devices used to receive MIDI data.

MIDI interface A hardware interface which provides a link between a computer and external MIDI devices, normally providing at least one MIDI input and one MIDI output with more advanced units providing multiple MIDI sockets and synchronization facilities.

MIDI Machine Control (MMC) An addition to the MIDI Specification to facilitate the control of tape transports and other devices.

MIDI Message A short sequence of MIDI data which passes a discrete instruction or command to the receiving device. MIDI Messages include such things as Note On, Note Off, Polyphonic Pressure, Control Change, Program Change, Aftertouch, and System Exclusive messages.

MIDI Mode An operational mode governing how a MIDI device manages data on different MIDI Channels and whether it performs polyphonically or

monophonically. There are 4 modes including Mode 1 (Omni On/Poly); response to messages on all MIDI channels and polyphonic, Mode 2 (Omni On/Mono); response to messages on all MIDI channels and monophonic, Mode 3 (Omni Off/Poly); response to messages on chosen MIDI channel(s) and polyphonic, Mode 4 (Omni Off/Mono); response to messages on chosen MIDI channel(s) and monophonic. Most units power up in Mode 3.

MIDI Out 5 pin DIN socket found on all MIDI equipped instruments used to send MIDI data.

MIDI Thru 5 pin DIN socket found on most MIDI equipped instruments providing a copy of the MIDI data received at the MIDI In. In other words, the data passes through the unit on to a further destination.

MIDI Time Code (MTC) A type of time code which is sent via MIDI, used to synchronize MIDI-based sequencers and other MIDI devices. Similar to SMPTE/EBU time code, MTC is an absolute timing reference measured in hours, minutes, seconds and fractions of a second and so does not vary with tempo.

Modulation i) The modification of one signal by another to produce effects (e.g. vibrato and tremolo). For realtime performance, the intensity of the modulation effect is controlled by the modulation wheel found on the control panel of electronic musical keyboards. Modulation is transmitted via MIDI as MIDI Controller 1. ii) The basis for FM and AM sound synthesis techniques.

Modulator i) The control signal which applies a modulating effect to a second signal. ii) The modulating part of a carrier:modulator pair of oscillators in FM synthesis.

Multi-timbral The ability of a synthesizer or module to produce several different sounds at the same time, controlled on different MIDI Channels.

Native processing Digital audio processing involving the computer's own processor and other resources rather than external digital signal processing hardware.

Noise A sound comprised of randomly distributed and inharmonic frequency components.

Notch filter A specialised type of band-reject filter which significantly attenuates a very narrow band of frequencies between two cut-off points while allowing the rest of the signal to pass through with little change.

Note On A MIDI message produced by pressing a key on a musical keyboard (or by the onset of a pre-recorded MIDI event). A Note On message starts the sounding of a musical event. It contains information about the Pitch and the Velocity of the note.

Note Off A MIDI message produced by releasing a key on a musical keyboard (or by the termination of a prerecorded MIDI event). A Note Off message starts the release phase of a musical event. It contains information about the Pitch of the note to be switched off and the Velocity with which the key was released.

Octave An interval in pitch between two tones corresponding with a doubling (or halving) of the frequency. In Western music there are 12 notes in each octave.

Operating system An organised collection of software at the next level up from BIOS which enables the user to communicate with the computer. The operating system provides the interface between BIOS and the applications running on the computer.

Oscillator A device which produces a periodic, alternating signal. Oscillators are used for generating periodic waveforms of a given amplitude and frequency.

Overtone Spectral component in a composite sound signal located at a higher frequency than the fundamental.

Pan The panoramic position of a sound within the stereo image. Most devices with two or more audio outputs feature a pan control. Pan data is transmitted via MIDI as Controller 10.

Parametric EQ Flexible signal filtering arrangement based upon a centre frequency selector, a Q control and a gain control. The centre frequency selector allows you to tune in to the frequency band you wish to process, the Q control regulates the width (filter slope characteristics) of this band and the gain control provides the means to boost or cut the chosen frequencies.

Patch A configuration of the controls of an electronic or software synthesizer which creates a specific sound. Also referred to as program, voice, sound or preset. Each patch can usually be stored in the instrument's memory for later recall.

PCI Peripheral Component Interconnect. A PCI bus is a standard computer slot for cards and extension boards and is widely used for connecting audio cards.

PCI Express A faster version of the standrad PCI bus, suitable for connecting audio cards and other peripherals.

PCM Pulse Code Modulation. Coding scheme involving the conversion of binary numbers into electronic pulses and fundamental to the conversion of analogue signals into digital form during the sampling process.

Phase The relationship between two or more components of a waveform (or of separate signals) in terms of the relative position of the compression and rarefaction parts of their waveforms. Phase is expressed in degrees.

Phasing An audio effect created by mixing a phase shifted version of a signal with the original and modulating the phase shifting with an LFO while also applying an amount of feedback.

Pink noise A sound signal whose acoustical energy decreases (as the frequency increases) at a rate of 3dBper-octave. This results in a signal with equal acoustical energy in each octave. Pink noise is useful in acoustic measurements since it approximates the frequency spectrum of typical audio signals and produces a flat response on a constant Q spectrum analyser.

Pitch The subjective response of the ear to the frequency of a sound signal.

Pitch Bend Variation of the pitch of a sounding note (e.g. the bending of a note on a guitar). It is transmitted via MIDI as Pitch Bend data and on electronic keyboards is usually applied in real-time using a pitch wheel on the control surface of the instrument.

Plug and Play A standard developed by Microsoft and Intel to enable extension cards and peripheral hardware to be automatically recognised and installed in PC computer systems.

PMCD Pre-Master CD. A special format, originally developed by Sonic Solutions, to allow glass masters to be cut directly from CD-R. Sometimes used (wrongly) to describe any Red-Book-standard CD-R master from which a glass master can be made for mass CD duplication.

Pole An element in filter design responsible for the characteristics of the filter slope between the pass band and the stop band where a 1-pole filter results in a filter slope of 6dB per octave, a 2-pole filter gives a slope of 12dB per octave, a 4-pole filter gives a slope of 24dB per octave and so on.

Polyphonic Having the capacity to play more than one note simultaneously.

Portamento A sliding of pitch between consecutively played notes (similar to glissando).

Program Change A type of MIDI message used to remotely change the Program number or patch in a MIDI device. There are 128 available program numbers but when used in conjunction with Bank Select messages the number of possible program slots is significantly expanded.

Pulse wave A periodic sound wave containing odd numbered harmonics similar to a square wave but with certain harmonics in the series missing. Pulse waves are characterised by their pulse width which is the proportion of one complete cycle for which the waveform remains in the compression (or positive) part of its waveform. A pulse wave with a pulse width of 1/n lacks each nth harmonic.

PWM Pulse Width Modulation. The cyclic modulation of the pulse width of a pulse wave using an LFO as the modulator.

Q A measure of the selectivity and filter slope characteristics of a filter, where low Q values select a wide bandwidth and high Q values select a narrow bandwidth. Also referred to as resonance or emphasis.

Quantisation The process of transforming a continuous analogue signal into a series of discrete values during analogue-to-digital conversion.

Quantisation noise A noise produced when converting very low level audio signals, due to insufficient bit depth (lack of resolution). The noise results from the rounding up or down of some of the least significant bits used to express the signal and is heard as a 'graininess' in the sound reproduction.

Quantize A term used in hardware and software sequencers to describe the action of automatically moving recorded notes onto the nearest fraction of a bar according to a quantize value. For example, using a quantize value of 16 (meaning 1/16 notes) shifts all inaccurately played notes onto the nearest 1/16 division of the bar. More elaborate methods of quantizing material include moving notes 'towards' a quantize value according to a percentage (iterative quantize) and moving notes according to a prerecorded 'feel' template (groove quantize).

RAM Random Access Memory. Volatile memory for the temporary storage of data.

Real-time Instantaneous output (or result) from an input. Real-time digital audio processing refers to processing where there is virtually no delay between the input signal and the processed output signal. Recording music into a sequencer in real-time means that the performance is recorded instantaneously as it is played, much like recording onto a tape recorder.

Release The shape and duration of the final part of a sound event where the amplitude falls from its sustain level to zero.

Resonance The frequency or frequencies at which a device or object vibrates in sympathy with itself. Many filters are endowed with resonant behaviour normally characterised by a boost in the frequencies around the cut-off point. The shape and intensity of this boost in frequencies is regulated by a resonance control (often also referred to as Q or emphasis).

Resynthesis Analysis-synthesis technique where an existing sample is analysed and arranged into a set of parameters and values (e.g. pitch, amplitude and phase for each harmonic) which are used as the basis for synthesizing a new sound.

Reverberation Multiple series of reflections occurring after the original sound in an acoustic space. Also known as reverb, reverberation is characterised by three phases: the original sound which arrives directly from the source to the listener's ear, after a short pause the early reflections from nearby surfaces and finally a complex mass of multiple reflections which fade to silence (known as the reverb tail).

Ring modulation Amplitude modulation technique wheretwo oscillator signals are multiplied to produce the sum and difference of their frequencies in the output. The original frequency of the source signal is not present in the output.

ROM Read Only Memory. Memory with fixed contents which cannot be overwritten.

SACD Super Audio Compact Disc. A high fidelity CD format utilising DSD technology (Direct Stream Digital), developed by Sony and Philips. Rivals the DVD-A format.

Sample i) A snapshot of a digital audio signal at one moment in time. ii) A recorded segment of digital audio.

Sampler Musical instrument which allows the recording, editing, modifying and playback of segments of digitally recorded sound.

Sampling rate In digital audio recording the sampling rate is the number of times an analogue signal is measured per second during the process of analogue-to-digital conversion. For example, the audio on a CD is recorded at a sampling rate of 44.1kHz, i.e.: 44,100 samples per second.

Sample resolution See 'Bit depth'.

Sawtooth wave A periodic sound wave containing all the harmonics in the natural harmonic series with the level of each harmonic at 1/n that of the fundamental (where n = the harmonic number). A sawtooth wave has a saw shaped waveform, hence its name.

SCSI Small Computer System Interface. A communication buss system available in several standards, supporting fast data transfer speeds (up to around 240Mbit/second) and the connection of several devices on the same buss (usually hard drives).

Semitone A shift in pitch of half a tone. In mathematical terms, a change in pitch of one semitone is achieved by multiplying or dividing the frequency by 1.0595. The keys on a piano keyboard are arranged in one semitone steps.

Signal-to-noise (S/N) ratio The ratio of the signal level to the noise level in a system, usually expressed in decibels (dB's). The larger the value of the S/N ratio the lower the level of the background noise.

Sine wave A pure, periodic sound wave based upon the mathematical sine function containing a single component at the fundamental. A sine wave has a sinusoidal waveform.

SMPTE Society of Motion Picture and Television Engineers. An American organisation responsible for setting film and audio standards and recommended practices. For convenience, time code is often referred to as 'SMPTE' (pronounced 'simptee') but, in fact, this is only one type of time code.

Song Position Pointer A MIDI message often included when synchronizing MIDI devices using MIDI Timing Clocks. It allows the slaved instrument to be synchronized to the same position in the music as the master instrument after fast forward and rewind operations.

S/PDIF Sony Philips Digital InterFace. A digital signal interface standard using 75 Ohm cable terminated in RCA phono connectors.

Spectrum A representation of a sound in terms of its constituent components at one point in time or averaged over a chosen time frame. Expressed graphically in the frequency domain as vertical lines (or peaks) where each line represents a component at a different frequency and amplitude. A spectrum gives a good idea of a sound's timbral quality.

Square wave A periodic sound wave containing all the odd-numbered harmonics in the natural harmonic series with the level of each harmonic at $1/n$ that of the fundamental (where n = the harmonic number). A square wave has a square-shaped waveform, hence its name.

Steady-state The segment within the envelope of a sound event where the timbre and amplitude is relatively constant. It is within this part of the sound where a loop can be applied using sampling techniques for the artificial sustaining of a note.

Step-time A method of entering notes into a sequencer one step at a time (also referred to as Step input). The pitch, position and duration for each entry is predetermined and after input is complete the music can be played back at any tempo. Step-time provides a useful method of entering notes into a sequencer when real-time performance is either too fast or too complicated.

Sustain The part in the evolution of a sound event which determines the amplitude level which sustains for as long as the note is held.

Sustain Pedal A foot pedal on acoustic and electronic pianos used to produce a sustaining of all played notes for as long as the pedal is held down. MIDI Controller 64 (also known as the Damper pedal).

Synthesizer An electronic or software-based musical instrument specialised in the creation of a wide range of tones and sound textures beyond those encountered in conventional musical instruments. A synthesizer is normally endowed with a performance interface (a musical keyboard), a control interface (GUI or front panel controls) and a synthesis engine (sound processing circuitry).

System Exclusive A type of MIDI Message allowing non-standardised communication between MIDI devices. Used for the transfer of Manufacturer Specific System Exclusive and also Universal System Exclusive data. Manufacturer Specific System Exclusive includes a unique ID for each manufacturing company and might be used to change or control almost any parameter in the receiving device as deemed appropriate by the manufacturer. Universal System Exclusive data includes MIDI Machine Control, MIDI Show Control, Sample Dump Standard, MIDI File Dump, General MIDI On and General MIDI Off.

Timbre Tone colour, or harmonic structure which gives a sound its sonic identity.

Time Code A time encoded signal recorded onto audio or video tape for time and point location and synchronisation purposes. It is sometimes referred to as 'SMPTE' (pronounced 'simptee') but, in fact, SMPTE is only one standard, as used in the USA. The other is EBU Time Code as used in Europe. Time code is measured in hours, minutes, seconds, frames and subframes.

Time domain The representation of a sound signal on a graph of amplitude versus time. This shows the waveform of the signal.

Tremolo A periodic variation in the loudness of a tone produced by modulating its amplitude with a low frequency oscillator (LFO), usually set in the range between 1 and 10Hz.

Triangle wave A periodic sound wave containing all the odd-numbered harmonics in the natural harmonic series with the level of each harmonic at $1/n^2$ that of the fundamental (where n = the harmonic number). A triangle wave has a triangle-shaped waveform, hence its name.

Trigger A short pulse which instructs a synthesizer to start a process like the sounding of a note or the generating of an envelope.

USB Universal Serial Bus. High speed data communication standard allowing the serial transfer of data at up to 12Mbit/second for USB 1 and 480Mbit/second for USB 2.

VCA Voltage Controlled Amplifier. Type of amplifier used in analogue synthesis where the gain is regulated by a control voltage.

VCF Voltage Controlled Filter. Type of filter used in analogue synthesis where the cut-off frequency is regulated by a control voltage.

VCO Voltage Controlled Oscillator. Type of oscillator used in analogue synthesis where the frequency is regulated by a control voltage.

Velocity The speed (or force) with which a key is pressed or released on an electronic keyboard instrument. Normally, the harder a key is struck

the louder the resulting note and the higher the velocity value. Velocity might also be used to affect the brightness, vibrato, sustain or some other expressive element within the sound. It forms part of the actual MIDI note data, (the third byte of Note On and Note Off messages), and does not assume a separate MIDI data category.

Vibrato A periodic variation in the pitch of a tone produced by modulating its frequency with a low frequency oscillator (LFO), usually set in the range between 1 and 10Hz. Vibrato produces a characteristic 'warbling' effect and is usually applied during the sustain part of the sound.

Virtual analogue Simulated analogue synthesis using digital signal processing techniques in software synthesis instruments.

Volume i) Generic term for loudness, amplitude or level. ii) MIDI Controller 7. Used to regulate the volume of notes in a MIDI recording. Also referred to as Main Volume.

VSTi Abbreviation for VST Instrument (Virtual Studio Instrument).

Waveform The shape of a sound wave when represented on a graph of time versus amplitude. Typical synthesized periodic waveforms include sawtooth, square, triangle and pulse.

White noise a sound signal whose acoustical energy remains the same for any given linear bandwidth within the frequency spectrum. White noise produces a 'hissing' sound.

Appendix 1
Computer hardware

Those with at least a superficial understanding of what goes on inside their computer are likely to get more out of Cubase. However, the first thing that Cubase users should bear in mind is that computer hardware and software changes extremely quickly and it is therefore difficult to keep up with the latest developments. While it is acknowledged that the specifications of your computer are important for system performance, this book is dedicated to Cubase itself and not to in-depth computer coverage. Any information contained in this appendix should therefore be regarded as additional to the main focus of the text. For more detailed coverage of computers readers are advised to consult the relevant books, magazines and websites. For precise computer recommendations for Cubase consult the Steinberg user documentation or the Steinberg website.

There now follows coverage of the basic hardware components of a computer and how these elements are likely to affect the Cubase user.

Motherboard concerns

The motherboard is a large circuit board inside the computer to which almost all other components are connected in some way. It is the central hub of activity and includes a wide range of slots and sockets. These generally include connectors for the CPU, RAM, hard drives, CD ROM / DVD drives, and serial and parallel ports. Also included are expansion ports for peripheral devices such as PCI, PCI Express, AGP, USB and Firewire, which may be used to connect audio hardware devices, MIDI interfaces, graphic cards, SCSI cards, printers and so on. The motherboard also contains the BIOS (Basic Input Output System).

Each motherboard features what is known as a chipset. Each chipset is endowed with the characteristics required to communicate with the latest processors, RAM and hardware devices. Motherboards and their chipsets are continually updated in order to maintain compatibility with the latest developments in computer hardware.

Processor choice

The processor or CPU (Central Processing Unit) is effectively the brain of the computer where the calculations and processing of data takes place. Processor speeds are measured in GHz (gigahertz) and guaged by the number of cores used (such as single-core, dual-core, quad-core and so on). In general, the faster the speed and the greater the number of cores, the shorter the performance time for any given operation. The processor choice dictates the choice of motherboard. Due to the rapid rate of change in the computer industry, you are advised to check the latest magazines and catalogues to find out the current state of affairs in the computer processor market.

RAM matters

With ever more memory-hungry operating systems and computer applications, lots of RAM is essential to run your system smoothly. RAM is an abbreviation for Random Access Memory. This is a temporary storage area and, when computations need to be performed, the data required is first stored there and then accessed at high speed by the computer's processor. If there is insufficient RAM the hard disk is used as a virtual memory expansion area. This slows things down since access to data on the hard drive is slower than access to RAM. Any such slowing down of the computer's performance may not be so important for non musical programs but for real-time applications which use native audio processing, like Cubase, optimal access to high speed RAM is essential for smooth operation. The amount of available RAM (among other things) directly affects how many audio tracks, plug-ins and virtual instruments your system can handle. It also affects the smooth operation of software sampling instruments which use RAM as a storage area for sample data. It therefore pays to have as much RAM as possible.

The hard disk

The hard disk is where the operating system, program applications (including Cubase) and all other important data is stored permanently. When it is needed, this data is retrieved from the hard disk and processed in other parts of the system. Large and fast hard drives are essential for optimum Cubase performance. Size is important for giving you enough space to record all your data and speed affects the rapidity with which data can be retrieved from the disk (which, in turn, affects the number of simultaneous audio tracks you can run in Cubase).

Digital audio eats up hard disk space extremely quickly. Recording 16-bit audio at 44.1 kHz sampling rate (CD quality) takes up 5MB of disk space per mono minute. This means that a CD in its final stereo format would need around 600-700MB of disk space. When you record multiple tracks in Cubase your space requirements are likely to be much greater. If you intend to use high resolution 24-bit and 32-bit float audio then your disk space requirements are increased still further. However, size is not the only consideration when choosing a hard drive.

Multi-track digital audio puts heavy demands on the speed and efficiency of the drive. Large amounts of data must be transferred from the disk to the audio hardware in the fastest possible time. The data stream for each track is accessed in rotation and the data blocks on the disk may not always be found in convenient locations. For 16-track audio the read head of the drive is attempting to be in sixteen different places at the same time so that you can hear your audio with no delay and in perfect synchronisation. In reality, the data is stored in advance in a buffer which helps speed up the rate of data transfer. Add to this the fact that the hard disk may also be expected to simultaneously record during playback, then you can begin to appreciate why the hard drive needs to be particularly efficient. The main indicator of hard drive performance is the sustained data transfer rate (DTR). The DTR is the amount of data which can be read from the disk within a given time frame, measured in MB per second. Other indicators include the average access time, the average time it takes for the read head to find and retrieve a piece of data on the disk, and the rotation speed. Common rotations speeds include 5400, 7200 and 10,000rpm. 7200rpm or better is recommended for audio applications.

Although a single hard disk can produce adequate results, the use of two (or more) hard disk drives is highly recommended for audio-based computer systems. One drive is used for the system and program files, and the other is used for the project and audio files. This arrangement can significantly increase your track count and makes it easier to maintain and defragment the audio drive.

The choice of hard drive generally revolves around two types: Parallel ATA and Serial ATA. These are both from the same ATA / IDE interface standard which stands for Advanced Technology Attachment / Integrated Drive Electronics. There is also the slightly less popular SCSI standard (Small Computer Systems Interface).

ATA / IDE hard drives include controller hardware on the drive itself which manages the input and output of the data. ATA refers to the interface specification and IDE refers to the device type. Most drives are of an improved IDE type known as Enhanced IDE (EIDE) and their mode of data transfer is Ultra DMA (Ultra Direct Memory Access). Direct memory access allows data to be transferred to and from the hard drive without using the CPU. This results in a more efficient use of the system's resources since the CPU can engage in other calculations while the hard drive transfers data to and from RAM. Drives of this type are sometimes referred to as ultra ATA or ultra DMA. Traditional parallel ATA drives (PATA) are slowly being replaced by serial ATA drives (SATA). The latter use a serial interface which provides faster sustained transfer rates.

Whatever kind of hard drive you use for your Cubase setup, remember to organise a method of backing up your data. Hard drives can develop faults, and system crashes can result in damage to data on the disk. Popular back-up media include: spare internal hard drives, hard drives in removable caddies, external firewire drives, zip or jaz discs, recordable CD and DVD. Although hard disk failure is thankfully not a common occurrence, backing up your data is essential if you wish to avoid the potentially disastrous situation of losing all your files.

Audio hardware

Installing suitable audio hardware in your computer system is very important for the successful operation of Cubase. By audio hardware we mean a single audio card, a combined audio card with hardware interface or a separate audio device linked to the computer in some way (via USB or Firewire connectors, for example).

The audio hardware should be capable of recording and playing back digital audio using the hard drive to store the data. Audio hardware for computers commonly falls into the following categories:

- Budget stereo in/out devices – these normally feature digital audio recording capability, a MIDI interface, (usually on a dual joystick / MIDI port D-type socket) and MIDI synthesizer and/or sampling facilities. A card of this description is often a consumer card designed primarily for the games market.
- High-end audio cards and hardware featuring multiple inputs and outputs. These devices usually include an external rackmount unit or break-out box and have been designed with the professional recording industry in mind. Such devices are normally suitable for connection to both Mac and PC computers and they are the preferred choice for Cubase users.

For use with Cubase the audio hardware should:

- be able to record and play back stereo digital audio using the hard drive as the storage medium
- be a stereo or multiple input / output device with at least 16-bit resolution and 44.1kHz sampling rate
- be equipped with a high-performance ASIO driver (Audio Stream Input Output)

The main factors to bear in mind before choosing your audio hardware can be summarised as follows: the signal-to-noise ratio (or dynamic range), the bit resolution of the A/D and D/A converters, the THD and frequency response figures, the number of line / mic inputs and outputs, the MIDI and digital I/O, the on-board synthesizer features (if you need them), the ADAT facilities (if you need them), ASIO driver availability, expected latency figures and so on. The presence of digital in and out sockets is also important, especially if you intend to record from or mix down to external digital media. Digital I/O improves the quality of both the record and playback path.

Low latency is essential if you are hoping to monitor your recordings via Cubase or if you are intending to trigger VST Instruments live via MIDI, and it also improves the general responsiveness of the software. All professional audio hardware is supplied with dedicated ASIO drivers which help reduce the latency figures to acceptable levels. A well written ASIO driver can reduce latency to around 3-10ms and those products quoting similar figures are preferable.

No matter how fast your processor and no matter how much RAM you have, the actual sound quality is finally governed by the audio hardware. However, this is not to say that if you have first class audio hardware you are guaranteed a high quality audio result – you also need to have a high quality microphone, (if you are recording vocals or live instruments), and, if the signal is passing through a mixing console, then this too must be of the highest quality possible. In addition, you must be monitoring the results through a good amplification and speaker system optimally placed in an acoustically balanced room. In other words, all stages in the recording and playback path should be of optimum quality. Your audio hardware might be viewed as a kind of cross-roads along this audio path – it is at the critical point in the recording and playback processes.

Graphics card

Computers require a graphics card in order to produce the image we see on the monitor screen. Graphics cards contain an amount of on-board RAM. The more RAM available, the greater the number of possible colours and the greater the potential resolution of the images produced. More importantly, more RAM means that graphics operations are less likely to interfere with audio operations. For Cubase, it is sufficient to use a 16-bit display quality but higher bit depths are unlikely to detract from the audio performance. Popular screen resolutions for Cubase might be anywhere between 1024 x 768 pixels to 1600 x 1200 pixels, depending upon the screen size and monitor specifications. Dual or triple monitor setups are popular among Cubase users and for this purpose a graphics card with dual or triple output ports is required. Output ports can be of the standard VGA variety or DVI. DVI is a digital interface which helps improve image quality. It is also recommended that you use a graphics card featuring passive cooling (i.e. no fan) since this helps cut down the overall noise of the computer.

The DVD/CD drive

A DVD-ROM drive is essential to install Cubase, since the program is supplied on a DVD-ROM disc. Luckily, DVD-ROM drives are standard in most computers, and most DVD-ROM drives can read both DVD-ROM and CD-ROM discs. DVD-ROM stands for Digital Versatile Disc Read Only Memory and describes a type of read-only disc similar to standard CD-ROMs (Compact Disc Read Only Memory). DVDs can store more data than CDs.

A variation on the DVD/CD-ROM drive is the DVD/CD-RW drive (DVD/CD Recorder). This allows you to write and read data to/from DVDs or CDs using DVD and CD recordable media. DVD/CD-R discs allow you to write data only once on the DVD/CD whereas DVD/CD-RW discs allow you to write data on the same disc many times. Recordable DVDs and CDs are extremely popular among Cubase users for backup purposes and for recording audio CDs. Cubase can directly import the data from standard audio CDs using the Import Audio CD option. To burn your own Red Book audio CD requires additional software (such as Wavelab, Sound Forge or Bias Peak).

A DVD/CD drive does not have to be enormously fast for Cubase. Drives are supplied in a variety of speeds such as 32 speed, 48 speed and so on, and most are adequate for general purpose use. The speed refers to the number of times faster the data is transferred to and from the disc when compared to an ordinary audio CD drive. However, for serious CD burning it is more the overall accuracy which is important. High precision drives supplied by Plextor (or similar) are recommended for this purpose.

The monitor

Monitor choice revolves around CRT (cathode ray tube) or TFT-LCD flat-screen types. Due to price considerations some are tempted to buy the smallest monitor but, for use with Cubase, this is a false economy. Cubase needs space to spread out and the use of multiple windows and their organisation on the screen demands a lot from the monitor.

TFT-LCD flat-screen monitors are an excellent alternative to CRT type computer monitors since their use results in less eye strain and general fatigue and they take up less space in cramped studios. In addition, CRT type monitors may cause significant hum when used near instruments such as electric guitar and electric bass, whereas TFT-LCD monitors do not produce this effect.

Remember that the monitor is one of the most important points of contact you have with the program and you may spend an awful long time gazing into it. As well as size, it is important to have a monitor capable of giving a crisp, clear image with good focus, brightness and colour controls. To enhance the visual interface still further, dual-monitor setups are always worth considering.

The keyboard and mouse

Of all the peripheral devices surrounding the computer, the humble keyboard and mouse are the most familiar. They provide points of tactile contact with the machine and methods by which we can give it instructions.

For Cubase, it pays to know how to use these basic tools and what to look for in the hardware sense. Most Cubase users would argue that learning to type has nothing to do with creating music and they are probably right. But if you are the kind of user who must search for each letter and symbol before you type it then you are going to be handicapped in your use of Cubase and, for that matter, most other computer software. Naming tracks, saving songs and using keyboard shortcuts all require some level of keyboard skill. So, if you are going to use the keyboard, you may as well choose one which is comfortable and then become very familiar with it. Some of the cheaper keyboards are not very pleasant to use and for the faster typist may not be sensitive enough. The final choice is a personal matter.

As for the mouse, the most comfortable shape and size depends on the characteristics of your hand. The final choice is, once again, a personal matter but it pays to make some comparisons between different models. Some users may prefer a trackball, where the cursor position is regulated by a rolling ball in the top part of the device. A wheel mouse is useful in Cubase for scrolling within the Project and other windows. Other possibilities include the use of wireless and optical keyboards and mice. These offer considerable flexibility if you need to move from one desktop or instrument location to another, and an optical mouse can be used on a wider range of surfaces than a standard mouse.

Noise issues

Unfortunately for computer users in general and particularly for musicians and recording studios, most computers make a certain amount of noise. This can prove extremely obtrusive when you are trying to listen to your latest musical masterpiece. Most of the noise comes from the various fans inside the computer case and the CD and hard drives.

A number of specialist PC computer suppliers provide computers which have been built specifically with noise minimisation and audio work in mind. These normally feature ultra quiet power supplies and hard drives housed in special acoustic enclosures. Computers of this type are the preferred option for Cubase users.

Appendix 2
MIDI messages

MIDI messages

The following table shows some of the most common MIDI messages. All data is shown in hexadecimal notation with the decimal equivalent below.

Table A2.1 MIDI messages

Message type	Function	Status byte	Data byte	Data byte	Data byte	Comments
Channel Voice messages						
Note off	Terminates a note event	8nH 128	kkH kk	vvH vv	–	kk = key number (0-127), vv = velocity (0-127)
Note on	Starts a note event	9nH 144	kkH kk	vvH vv	–	kk = key number (0-127), vv = velocity (0-127)
Polyphonic key pressure	Polyphonic key pressure	AnH 160	kkH kk	vvH vv	–	pressure for each individual key, kk = key number, vv = pressure
Control change	Generic control function	BnH 176	ccH cc	vvH vv	–	for wheels, switches, pedals etc. cc=controller no., vv =control value
Program change	Changes receiver's program number	CnH 192	ppH pp		–	pp = program number (0-127)
Channel key pressure	Channel key pressure (Aftertouch)	DnH 208	vvH vv		–	vv = amount of pressure applied (0-127)
Pitch bend	Changes pitch of notes on same channel	EnH 224	ffH ff	ccH cc	–	ff = fine changes (0-127), cc = coarse changes in pitch (0-127)

455

Table A2.1 MIDI messages (cont)

Message type	Function	Status byte	Data byte	Data byte	Data byte	Comments
Channel Mode messages						
Control change	Reset all controllers	BnH 176	79H 123	00H 0	–	resets all controllers to their default values
Control change	Local on/off	BnH 176	7AH 122	vvH vv	–	disconnects keyboard from sound-making circuitry (0=Off, 127=On)
Control change	All notes off	BnH 176	7BH 123	00H 0	–	terminates all currently playing notes
Control change	Omni mode off (all notes off)	BnH 176	7CH 124	00H 0	–	the receiver responds only to messages sent on its MIDI channel
Control change	Omni mode on (all notes off)	BnH 176	7DH 125	00H 0	–	the receiver responds to messages on all MIDI channels
Control change	Mono mode on/poly mode off (all notes off)	BnH 176	7EH 126	vvH vv	–	the receiver responds monophonically, vv = no of channels
Control change	Poly mode on/mono mode off (all notes off)	BnH 176	7FH 127	00H 0	–	the receiver responds polyphonically
System messages (a number of examples)						
System Exclusive	Manufacturer-specific	F0H 240	iiH ii	nnH-nnH nn-nn	F7H 247	ii = Manufacturer ID (0-127), nn - nn = almost any sequence of data dependent on function of message, F7H = end of the SysEx message
Active sensing	Transmitting instrument saying 'I am still here'	FEH 254	–	–	–	message transmitted every 300ms
MIDI clock	MIDI timing clock for sychronisation	F8H 248	–	–	–	message transmitted 24 times per quarter note
System reset	Resets receiver to power-up state	FFH 255	–	–	–	initialises all parameters to their default state

Table A2.1 MIDI messages (cont)

Message type	Function	Status byte	Data byte	Data byte	Data byte	Comments
Commonly used Control Change messages						
Control change	Modulation	BnH 176	01H 1	vvH vv	–	01H (1) = modulation, vv = modulation amount (0-127)
Control change	Breath controller	BnH 176	02H 2	vvH vv	–	02H (2) = breath control, vv = breath control amount (0-127)
Control change	Foot controller	BnH 176	04H 4	vvH vv	–	04H (4) = foot pedal control, vv = control amount (0-127)
Control change	Channel volume (Main volume)	BnH 176	07H 7	vvH vv	–	07H (7) = main volume, vv = volume level (0-127)
Control change	Pan	BnH 176	0AH 10	vvH vv	–	0AH (10) = pan, vv = pan value (0-127)
Control change	Expression	BnH 176	0BH 11	vvH vv	–	0BH (11) = expression, vv = control value (0-127)
Control change	Sustain pedal	BnH 176	40H 66	vvH vv	–	40H (66) = sustain pedal, vv = control value (0-63 = Off, 64-127 = On)

Notes

All message data is shown in hexadecimal notation with the decimal equivalent below.

n in the Status byte is a value between 0 and 15 designating one of the sixteen MIDI channels.

cc, ff, ii, kk, pp, vv are values between 0 and 127.

Appendix 3
MIDI controllers

No	Controller	No	Controller	No	Controller	No	Controller
0	Bank Select MSB	32	Bank Select LSB	64	Damper pedal on/off	96	Data increment
1	Modulation wheel	33	Mod wheel LSB	65	Portamento on/off	97	Data decrement
2	Breath control	34	Breath control LSB	66	Sustain pedal on/off	98	NRPN LSB
3	Undefined	35	Undefined	67	Soft pedal on/off	99	NRPN MSB
4	Foot controller	36	Foot controller LSB	68	Legato Footswitch	100	RPN LSB
5	Portamento time	37	Portamento time LSB	69	Hold 2	101	RPN MSB
6	Data Entry	38	Data entry LSB	70	Sound Variation	102	Undefined
7	Channel Volume	39	Channel Volume LSB	71	Timbre	103	Undefined
8	Balance	40	Balance LSB	72	Release Time	104	Undefined
9	Undefined	41	Undefined	73	Attack Time	105	Undefined
10	Pan	42	Pan LSB	74	Brightness	106	Undefined
11	Expression	43	Expression LSB	75	Sound Control #6	107	Undefined
12	Effect control 1	44	Effect control 1 LSB	76	Sound Control #7	108	Undefined
13	Effect control 2	45	Effect control 2 LSB	77	Sound Control #8	109	Undefined
14	Undefined	46	Undefined	78	Sound Control #9	110	Undefined
15	Undefined	47	Undefined	79	Sound Control #10	111	Undefined
16	Gen Purpose #1	48	Gen Purpose #1 LSB	80	Gen Purpose #5	112	Undefined
17	Gen Purpose #2	49	Gen Purpose #2 LSB	81	Gen Purpose #6	113	Undefined
18	Gen Purpose #3	50	Gen Purpose #3 LSB	82	Gen Purpose #7	114	Undefined
19	Gen Purpose #4	51	Gen Purpose #4 LSB	83	Gen Purpose #8	115	Undefined
20	Undefined	52	Undefined	84	Portamento Control	116	Undefined
21	Undefined	53	Undefined	85	Undefined	117	Undefined
22	Undefined	54	Undefined	86	Undefined	118	Undefined
23	Undefined	55	Undefined	87	Undefined	119	Undefined
24	Undefined	56	Undefined	88	Undefined	120	All Sound Off
25	Undefined	57	Undefined	89	Undefined	121	Reset All Controllers
26	Undefined	58	Undefined	90	Undefined	122	Local control on/off
27	Undefined	59	Undefined	91	FX 1 Reverb Depth	123	All notes off
28	Undefined	60	Undefined	92	FX 2 Trem Depth	124	Omni mode off
29	Undefined	61	Undefined	93	FX 3 Chorus Depth	125	Omni mode on
30	Undefined	62	Undefined	94	FX 4 Celeste Depth	126	Mono on/Poly off
31	Undefined	63	Undefined	95	FX 5 Phaser Depth	127	Poly on/Mono off

Appendix 4
General MIDI

For the convenience of those using General MIDI (GM) synths and modules and in order to avoid some of the confusion which can arise on the subject, this appendix outlines the essentials of the General MIDI protocol. There are three main types of General MIDI devices:

- GM – General MIDI. The first GM standard devised by Roland.
- GS – General Standard. The same as General MIDI but with additional features devised by Roland.
- XG – Extended General MIDI. The same as General MIDI but with additional features devised by Yamaha.

The essential idea of GM/GS/XG MIDI synths and sound modules is that they all share a common language. A MIDI sequence played back using one GM module will sound much the same on any other GM module. Cubase provides the Track Control MIDI effect plug-in which allows the editing of various GS/XG parameters. In addition, to select programs using GM names, activate the GM device in the MIDI Device manager window (Device menu) and select the GM device in the 'out' field of the MIDI track. You can now select GM programs by name rather than number.

The following outlines the basic practical protocol for all GM/GS/XG devices, (note that the full GM protocol encompasses many more parameters than those described here):

- A minimum of 24-voice polyphony.
- Multi-timbrality on 16 MIDI channels where each channel can play a variable number of voices from the available polyphony.
- Drum sounds are always on MIDI channel 10, and each drum is allocated to a specific MIDI note number (as shown below in the 'Standard GM drum map' table).
- The sounds available comply with the program numbers and 128 presets of the standard bank of GM sounds, as in the following table:

Table A4.1 Standard bank of General MIDI sounds

No	Name	No	Name	No	Name	No	Name
1	Piano 1	9	Celesta	17	Organ 1	25	Nylon-str. Gt.
2	Piano 2	10	Glockenspiel	18	Organ 2	26	Steel-str. Gt.
3	Piano 3	11	Music box	19	Organ 3	27	Jazz Gt.
4	Honky-tonk P.	12	Vibraphone	20	Church organ	28	Clean Gt.
5	E. Piano 1	13	Marimba	21	Reed Organ	29	Muted Gt.
6	E. Piano 2	14	Xylophone	22	Accordion Fr	30	Overdrive Gt.
7	Harpsichord	15	Tubular bell	23	Harmonica	31	Distortion Gt.
8	Clav	16	Santur	24	Bandneon	32	Gt. harmonics
33	Acoustic Bass	41	Violin	49	Strings	57	Trumpet
34	Fingered Bass	42	Viola	50	Slow Strings	58	Trombone
35	Picked Bass	43	Cello	51	Syn. Strings 1	59	Tuba
36	Fretless Bass	44	Contrabass	52	Syn. Strings 2	60	Muted Trumpet
37	Slap Bass 1	45	Tremelo Str.	53	Choir Aahs	61	French Horn
38	Slap Bass 2	46	Pizzicato Str.	54	Voice Oohs	62	Brass 1
39	Synth Bass 1	47	Harp	55	SynVox	63	Synth Brass 1
40	Synth Bass 2	48	Timpani	56	Orchestral Hit	64	Synth Brass 2
65	Soprano Sax	73	Piccolo	81	Square Wave	89	Fantasia
66	Alto Sax	74	Flute	82	Saw Wave	90	Warm Pad
67	Tenor Sax	75	Recorder	83	Syn. Calliope	91	Polysynth
68	Baritone Sax	76	Pan Flute	84	Chiffer lead	92	Space Voice
69	Oboe	77	Bottle Blow	85	Charang	93	Bowed Glass
70	English Horn	78	Shakuhachi	86	Solo Vox	94	Metal Pad
71	Bassoon	79	Whistle	87	5th Saw Wave	95	Halo Pad
72	Clarinet	80	Ocarina	88	Bass & Lead	96	Sweep Pad
97	Ice Rain	105	Sitar	113	Tinkle Bell	121	Gt. Fret Noise
98	Soundtrack	106	Banjo	114	Agogo	122	Breath Noise
99	Crystal	107	Shamisen	115	Steel Drums	123	Seashore
100	Atmosphere	108	Koto	116	Wood Block	124	Bird
101	Brightness	109	Kalimba	117	Taiko	125	Telephone 1
102	Goblin	110	Bagpipe	118	Melo Tom 1	126	Helicopter
103	Echo Drops	111	Fiddle	119	Synth Drum	127	Applause
104	Star Theme	112	Shannai	120	Reverse Cymb.	128	Gun Shot

Table A4.2 Standard GM drum map

Note	No	Drum name	Note	No	Drum name
C1	36	Bass Drum	D3	62	Mute High Bongo
C#1	37	Side Stick	D#3	63	Open High Conga
D1	38	Acoustic Snare	E3	64	Low Conga
D#1	39	Hand Clap	F3	65	High Timbale
E1	40	Electric Snare	F#3	66	Low Timbale
F1	41	Low Floor Tom	G3	67	High Agogo
F#1	42	Closed Hi-Hat	G#3	68	Low Agogo
G1	43	High Floor Tom	A3	69	Cabasa
G#1	44	Pedal Hi-Hat	A#3	70	Maracas
A1	45	Low Tom	B3	71	Short Whistle
A#1	46	Open Hi-Hat	C4	72	Long Whistle
B1	47	Low Middle Tom	C#4	73	Short Guiro
C2	48	High Middle Tom	D4	74	Long Guiro
C#2	49	Crash Cymbal 1	D#4	75	Claves
D2	50	High Tom	E4	76	High Wood Block
D#2	51	Ride Cymbal 1	F4	77	Low Wood Block
E2	52	Chinese Cymbal	F#4	78	Mute Cuica
F2	53	Ride Bell	G4	79	Open Cuica
F#2	54	Tambourine	G#4	80	Mute Triangle
G2	55	Splash Cymbal	A4	81	Open Triangle
G#2	56	Cowbell	A#4	82	Shaker
A2	57	Crash Cymbal 2	B4	83	Castanets
A#2	58	Vibraslap	F0	29	Scratch Push
B2	59	Ride Cymbal 2	F#0	30	Scratch Pull
C3	60	High Bongo	A0	33	Metronome
C#3	61	Low Bongo	B0	35	Acoustic Bass Drum

Appendix 5
Additional software

While Cubase is undoubtedly a powerful music creation and audio editing tool, many users may wish to expand the possibilities with additional software. For music production and sounds effects creation popular choices include Native Instruments Kontakt and Reaktor, Propellerhead Reason, Applied Acoustics Systems Tassman, Tascam Gigastudio and Steinberg Halion. For audio editing, CD and DVD creation check out Steinberg Wavelab, Bias Peak or Sony Sound Forge. Wavelab (Figure A5.1) has established a very good reputation among mastering engineers. It includes leading edge audio editing, restoration and analysis tools, and for the creation of audio CDs and DVDs provides the intuitive and easy-to-use audio montage window. Other features include high quality DIRAC time stretching and pitch shifting, Crystal Resampler professional sample rate conversion, K system metering, effect morphing, batch processing and a Spectrum editor for surgical editing in both the time and frequency domains.

Figure A5.1
Steinberg Wavelab for audio editing, restoration, analysis and CD/DVD creation

Index